# COCAINE

# COCAINE

## FROM COCA FIELDS TO THE STREETS

Enrique Desmond Arias
and Thomas Grisaffi,
editors

DUKE UNIVERSITY PRESS
Durham and London 2021

© 2021 DUKE UNIVERSITY PRESS
Cover designed by Drew Sisk
Text designed by Matthew Tauch
Typeset in Alegreya and Helvetica by Westchester Publishing
Services

Library of Congress Cataloging-in-Publication Data
Names: Arias, Enrique Desmond, editor. | Grisaffi, Thomas, [date]
editor.
Title: Cocaine: from coca fields to the streets / Enrique Desmond
Arias and Thomas Grisaffi.
Description: Durham: Duke University Press, 2021. | Includes
bibliographical references and index.
Identifiers: LCCN 2021001611 (print) | LCCN 2021001612 (ebook)
ISBN 9781478013723 (hardcover)
ISBN 9781478014652 (paperback)
ISBN 9781478021957 (ebook)
Subjects: LCSH: Cocaine industry—Latin America. | Cocaine
industry—United States. | Drug traffic—Social aspects—Latin
America. | Drug traffic—Social aspects—United States. | Drug
control—Latin America. | Drug control—United States. | Coca
industry—Social aspects. | BISAC: SOCIAL SCIENCE / Anthropology /
Cultural & Social | HISTORY / Latin America / General Classification:
LCC HD9019. C632 L29 2021 (print) | LCC HD9019. C632 (ebook) |
DDC 364.1/3365—dc23
LC record available at https: //lccn.loc.gov/2021001611
LC ebook record available at https: //lccn.loc.gov/2021001612

Cover art: Illustration by Drew Sisk, based on a map of drug
trafficking routes by Tim Stallman.

# CONTENTS

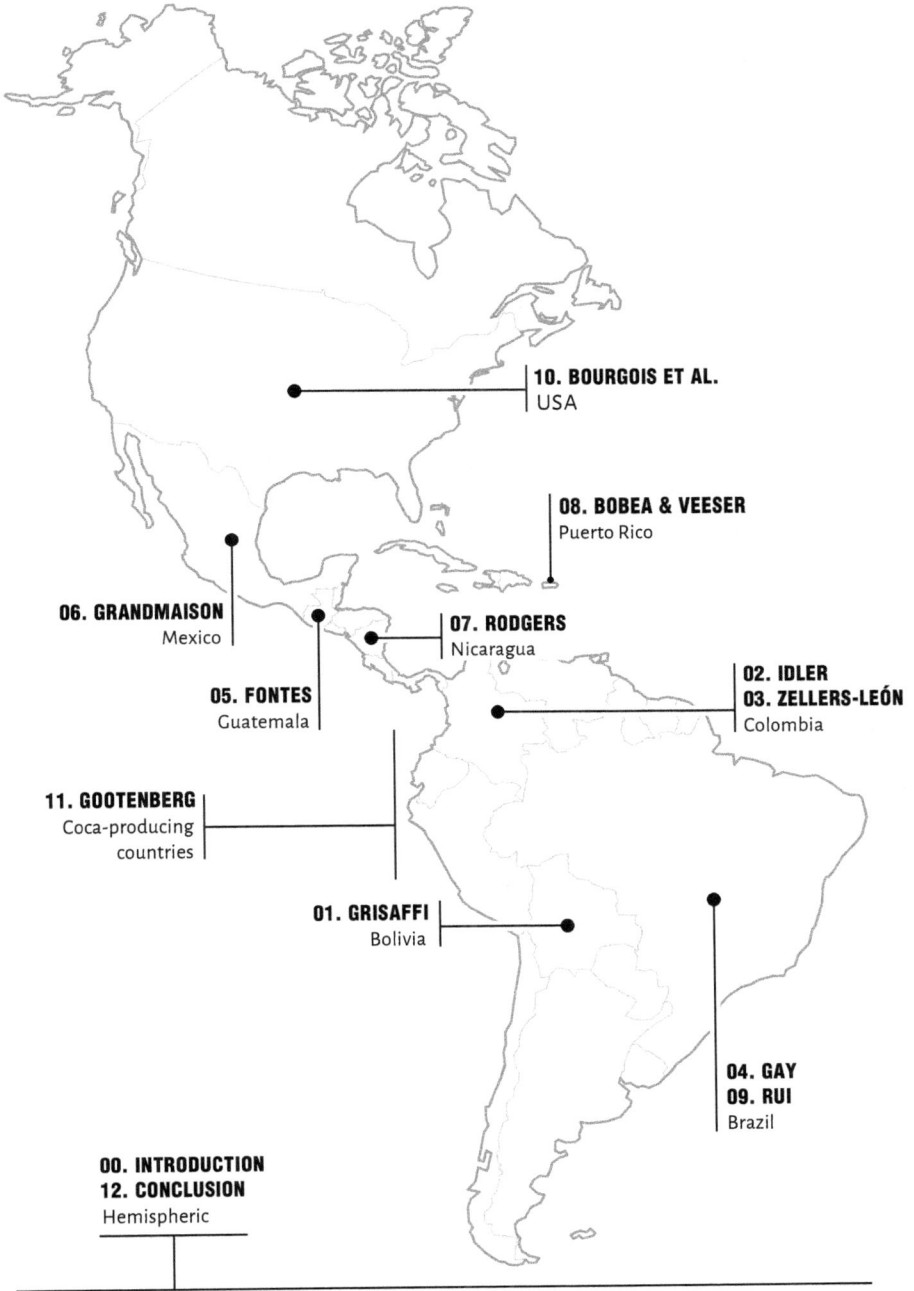

**10. BOURGOIS ET AL.**
USA

**08. BOBEA & VEESER**
Puerto Rico

**06. GRANDMAISON**
Mexico

**07. RODGERS**
Nicaragua

**05. FONTES**
Guatemala

**02. IDLER**
**03. ZELLERS-LEÓN**
Colombia

**11. GOOTENBERG**
Coca-producing
countries

**01. GRISAFFI**
Bolivia

**04. GAY**
**09. RUI**
Brazil

**00. INTRODUCTION**
**12. CONCLUSION**
Hemispheric

# ACKNOWLEDGMENTS

This book started life as a series of panels titled "Cocaine's Products" at the Latin American Studies Association's 2016 annual congress in New York. The panels counted on the participation of Javier Auyero, Robert Gay, Lilian Bobea, Paul Gootenberg, Autumn Zellers-León, Taniele Rui, Benjamin Lessing, Graham Denyer Willis, Dennis Rodgers, and Philippe Bourgois. The editors organized two further workshops, one in London and one in Arlington, Virginia. These events involved some of the original LASA participants but also others, including: Rivke Jaffe, Annette Idler, Adam Baird, Jeff Garmany, Henrik Vigh, David Skarbeck, Axel Klein, Gareth Jones, Lucia Michelluti, John Collins, Anthony Fontes, Louise Shelley, Lisa Breglia, Michael Polson, and Nicholas Barnes. We would like to extend our sincere thanks to all the participants, who provided fascinating papers and engaged in lively discussion. They all played a significant role in shaping this project.

This book owes a big debt to the Social Science Research Council/Open Society Foundations' "Drugs, Security, and Democracy" (DSD) research program on Latin America. Many of the authors in this volume were involved in the DSD network as fellows or mentors. We gratefully acknowledge the research support provided to many of our authors by the DSD. We also acknowledge the DSD's supportive network, which allowed collaborative and cross-disciplinary research projects to take form. We would particularly like to thank Cleia Noia, Ana Meg Rama, Nicole Levitt, Daniella Sarnoff, and Mary MacDonald at the SSRC for their work on behalf of and support for the DSD program. We would also like to thank David Holiday at the Open Society Foundations and Marcus Gottsbacher during his time at the International Development Research Centre for their support of the program.

At George Mason University we would like to thank Des Dinan and the Center for Global Studies, which provided financial support to our meeting. We would also like to thank the Transnational Crime and Corruption Center and its director Louise Shelley for logistical and intellectual support for the conference. Marco Alcocer, now at the University of California at San Diego, provided invaluable assistance in organizing the meeting at George Mason.

The Institute of the Americas and the Institute for Advanced Study at University College London (UCL) provided support for this project. The editors would particularly like to thank Paulo Drinot and Oscar Martinez.

We also thank Elizabeth Detmeister at Baruch College for her invaluable editorial assistance.

This volume would not have been possible without the skilled support we received from Duke University Press. In particular, we would like to thank Gisela Fosado for her engagement with and support of the project. Thanks are also due to Alejandra Mejía and Susan Albury for facilitating production, Tim Stallmann for creating the maps, and Nancy Zibman for compiling the index. We also greatly appreciated constructive criticism by the two anonymous reviewers. Their critiques have greatly strengthened this volume.

Arias extends his thanks to the Schar School of Policy and Government and the Marxe School of Public and International Affairs, which provided supportive working environments while developing this project. The Baruch College Fund provided important financial support in the final stages of manuscript preparation. He would also like to thank Julia, Cameron, and Sebastian for their support, company, and affection.

Grisaffi gratefully acknowledges the Global Challenges Research Fund and the European Research Council (Anthropologies of Extortion, ERC-2019-ADG 884839/EXTORT) for funding his research. He is grateful for the support of Elisavet Kitou, Colin Bulpitt, and colleagues in the Geography Department at the University of Reading. He would like to thank his family in Britain, France, and Germany, and his close collaborators Insa Lee Koch and Haku Lee Grisaffi Koch for feedback and guidance on this project and others.

ENRIQUE DESMOND ARIAS
AND THOMAS GRISAFFI

## INTRODUCTION

# THE MORAL ECONOMY OF THE COCAINE TRADE

Peru's Apurímac, Ene, and Mantaro River Valley (VRAEM) is a center for coca cultivation and drug production. Small planes fly in to pick up cocaine paste, stopping in Bolivia where the drug is refined into cocaine hydrochloride, and then dispatched to Brazil for onward sale to Europe, but also to feed the growing local market in cities like Rio de Janeiro and São Paulo. A single plane can carry 300 kg (660 lb) of cocaine paste, worth some $350,000. Orlando Mejia, a retired Bolivian pilot who worked flying drugs shipments for over twenty years, explained that this is dangerous work. Not only do the pilots face possible arrest, they also land their planes on extremely short dirt strips, and by his reckoning there are hundreds of fatalities each year. But the chance to earn up to $15,000 per flight makes it worthwhile. "Most [pilots] are inexperienced, they are young—they just want to earn a bit of cash and they risk it all," he said.

The small planes are unable to pass over the Andes as they cannot fly high enough—so all flights are channeled to the far north of Bolivia, which is low-lying. Orlando said that when he was a pilot there had been a long-standing agreement with the authorities that they would turn a blind eye at certain hours to allow fleets of aircraft to pass at the same time. He described how on the Bolivian side there are landing strips—some no longer than two soccer pitches, where the planes can refuel and the pilots can pick up some food, operating as a kind of service center for the drug industry.

The pilots not only carry drugs, but shuttle people back and forth as well. Peruvian suppliers and Bolivian buyers have to broker deals worth tens if not hundreds of thousands of dollars. But with no state to guarantee the contract, this is a risky business. To ensure trust, the family clans, which dominate the trade in this region, exchange family members, normally a nephew or son, in lieu of payment. If the drugs or cash do not reach their final destination, then the family member does not return home.

Sebastián, a young Bolivian man, spent three years traveling back and forth to the VRAEM as a human guarantee for drug deals brokered by his uncle. When asked if this was dangerous work, he confided that he was more afraid of flying in the small planes than any threat to his person on the part of drug traffickers. In Sebastián's telling, this was a predictable, stable, and safe occupation. "Peruvians are just like us . . . it's relaxed— we look after each other," he said. Sebastián explained that while in the VRAEM he was paid $1,000 a month to hang out with people he considered to be friends. He played football, drank beer, and had a good time. After three years he retired so that he could care for his young daughter. He used the money he had earned to buy a small house in an impoverished suburb of Cochabamba and a car that he ran as a taxi.

......................

We open with this short vignette because it captures one of the key issues of our volume—namely the internal governance processes of the illicit cocaine trade, which rely on debt, trust, and negotiation with state authorities. Further, it highlights how, for people like Sebastián and Orlando, engagement in the cocaine trade is not something that is considered to be morally reprehensible. There are good reasons why Sebastián took up work in the drug trade—he would earn no more than fifteen dollars a day driving a taxi in Cochabamba—but through his involvement in the illicit business he was able to build a modest yet secure life for his young family. The drug trade, then, can be a source of stability, a path to social mobility, and a driver of economic growth, enabling relegated spaces to be incorporated into global markets.

Recent years have seen an explosion in writing about drug-related gangs and violence in Latin America. This emerging body of research provides scholars and the policy community with a resonant picture of the experience of life and politics in different places affected by the drug trade. The story as it is currently told, however, is a narrative of the experience of particular neighborhoods, cities, and countries affected, usually in negative ways, by this commerce. While these researchers acknowledge the effect of global drug markets on the places they examine, there has been little scholarly scrutiny of the broader drug commodity chain as it moves from production to consumption. Lost in the story are the specific ways the narcotics trade plays out in the region and how it has developed a complex process of self-regulation in the shadow of a state power that formally seeks to destroy it.

Building on this idea of self-regulation, we have titled this introduction "the moral economy of the cocaine trade" for two reasons. First, we seek to capture the idea that the illicit cocaine trade is often viewed in highly moralistic terms. Second, the title highlights how this illicit trade is governed by its own internal logic that connects to—but also diverges from—dominant economic models and is often deeply implicated in local, normatively regulated exchanges, like the kind of arrangements described in the opening of this chapter. The moral economy represents the ways that economies produce and are produced by social norms and expectations. While this occurs in legal markets, as is evidenced in the work of others (Thompson 1971; Scott 1977), in markets operating at the margins of the law, norms of exchange are essential not just to the operation of those markets but also to the ways those markets engage with and shape the communities around them. Social relations along a robust international illicit supply chain affect and are affected by the norms the economic activity in the supply chain generates.

Here we bring together scholars to examine the nature of the interconnection between sites along cocaine's global supply chain and the implications of those interconnections for social, political, and economic experiences in places affected by the trade and, conversely, how those interconnections affect the cocaine trade. Our contributors work on different phases of the drug trade to examine how formal government agents, acting both within and outside the law, and criminal actors seek to manage the flow of illicit drugs to maintain order and earn profits. We asked contributors to consider how the drug trade is embedded in specific places, but also to interrogate what impact the movement of drugs has on (re)ordering social relationships, shifting political processes, and generating secondary markets. In so doing, the volume outlines the ways that different iterations of the cocaine commodity chain produce and are produced by processes of self-regulation and how these forms of governance are rooted in alternative "moral economies."

Over the past decade, Latin American governments have pushed back against United States–funded and designed "supply-side enforcement" to tackle the drug problem. Regional leaders have argued for more effective and humane alternatives to supply disruption and repression, including the creation of regulated markets for narcotic substances, amnesties, transitional justice, and greater investment in harm-reduction practices (LSE IDEAS 2014). Concurrently, some Latin American countries have unilaterally made changes to domestic drug policy, provoking an unprecedented crisis for the international drug control regime (Klein and Stothard 2018). In this context, understanding the illicit governance processes of the supply chain is a pressing issue that points to how, on the one hand, executing drug dealers will add to the burden of violence but, on the other, state and social actors can develop more constructive strategies to address the manifold needs of the populations affected by drugs.

This introduction sets out the volume's argument in seven steps. The first section considers the broader literature on commodity chains to highlight how the flow of commodities affects lifeworlds. The second and third sections outline our understanding of the moral economy framework. Parts four and five bring the discussion back to cocaine, with a consideration of the dynamics of illicit production and governance, and their implications for the lived experience of communities affected by the trade. The penultimate section lays out a framework to examine the cocaine commodity chain in a more systematic fashion. The chapter ends with an outline of the contributions to follow.

## COMMODITY CHAINS

Global cocaine manufacturing in 2017 reached its highest level ever: an estimated 1,976 tons of pure cocaine, more than double the level recorded in 2013 (UNODC 2019: 13). The total retail value of the illicit cocaine trade equaled between $94 and $143 billion in 2014, the most recent year for which figures are available (May 2017).[1] The largest retail markets are in North America, which accounts for around 47 percent of the global market, followed by the markets of Western and Central Europe, with 39 percent of the market (OAS 2013: 10).[2] Cocaine use in Latin America has increased dramatically over the last decade. This is compounded by the rapid growth of the middle class, which means a growing local demand for all kinds of consumer goods, both licit and illicit. Brazil, with an estimated 3.3 million regular users, represents the second biggest national market in the world (see Gootenberg, this volume). More recently, Africa and Asia have emerged as cocaine trafficking and consumption hubs (UNODC 2018b). The cocaine trade, then, is not something marginal or insignificant; rather, it is a key part of the global economy, with a turnover similar to a global corporation like Allianz or Volkswagen (see Statista 2020), providing employment for hundreds of thousands, if not millions of people. And yet analysts know relatively little about how this complex commodity chain functions (see map I.1 for main trafficking routes).

With its conceptual roots in world systems theory, economic sociologists have used the notion of commodity chains, and more recently global value chains, to offer critical perspectives on state- and firm-focused analyses of global economies (Friedberg 2003; Bair and Werner 2011; Hough 2011). One of the most influential accounts in this genre is Sidney Mintz's (1986) history of the sugar trade, which traces that commodity over a 350-year span. In telling this story, Mintz links sugar with the historic emergence of capitalism, European conquest, African slavery, and the emergence and reproduction of an exploited working class in the United Kingdom.

The strength of Mintz's study, and the work that has followed, is that it offers an interconnected and process-oriented analysis of the emergence, development, and change of transnational production structures (Hopkins and Wallerstein 1986). Rather than seeing production and consumption as market processes regulated by sovereign actors, these scholars focus attention on how transnational production and consumption generate particular social and economic interactions among peoples and places across the globe (Gereffi 1994; Bair 2009). This perspective also exposes how various legal businesses, state officials, criminal groups, ordinary citizens, transnational corporations, and NGOs are linked into a web of exchanges, often with one site being unaware of the other (Scheper-Hughes 2000; Nordstrom 2007).

Sugar is particularly relevant to this study as it has several parallels to cocaine. It starts life as a plant and ends up as a white powder that is popular all over the world (see figure I.1). Where governments subsidize sugar, these same institutions heavily regulate cocaine. Sugar is seen as a source of pleasure, and in Mintz's narrative it even functions as a kind of drug—at one point he even refers to sugar as an "opiate" (Mintz 1986: 174). Building from Mintz, we know that commodity production and distribution transforms lifeworlds, but the creation of an illegal commodity, such as cocaine, transforms the lived experience, economies, environments, and society in particular ways that are not only unforeseen, but deliberately hidden from the eyes of researchers and public authorities. While it is possible to unpack one space in which an illicit product transmutes elements of social life, disambiguating these changes across the locales sitting along an entire chain of production is particularly difficult. It requires examining a cross

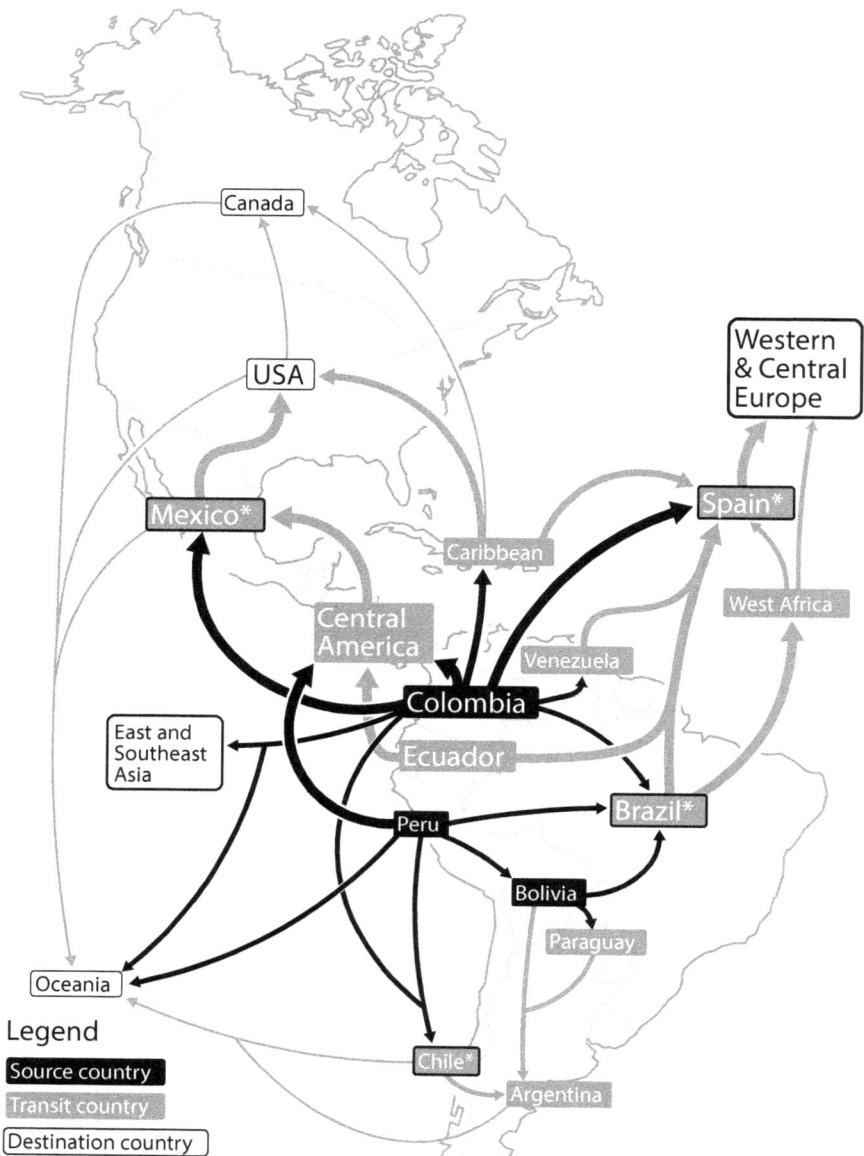

Canada

USA

Western
& Central
Europe

Mexico*

Caribbean

Spain*

Central
America

West Africa

Venezuela

East and
Southeast
Asia

Colombia

Ecuador

Brazil*

Peru

Bolivia

Paraguay

Oceania

Chile*

Argentina

Legend

Source country

Transit country

Destination country

*Transit and destination country

Larger arrows and country names indicate
higher volume of flows. Flows to Southern and East Africa, Middle East, and South Asia
are not shown.

MAP I.1  Map of trafficking routes.

FIGURE I.1  Coca plant in the VRAEM, Peru.

section of relationships that maintain themselves formally isolated from one another and whose participants publicly seek to deny their connection.

Some scholars, working from macro and historical perspectives, have applied the logic of commodity chains to cocaine, pointing out the critical ways that consumption and law enforcement in the Global North disrupt life and create violence in drug-producing and transshipping countries (Wilson and Zambrano 1994; Stares 1996). Paul Gootenberg (2008), for one, has developed a systematic analysis of how the cocaine trade in the early twentieth century emerged out of particular market structures in North America, Europe, and Asia. The particularities of how firms in Germany, Japan, and the United States managed production generated particular life experiences and political consequences in locales as diverse as Peru and Indonesia. This work has made visible the association of different sites in the cocaine production chain. However, these writers, often working at a historical remove, have done less work on the complex and often clandestine governance processes associated with how illicit narcotics production chains actually operate on the ground today.

It is critical to note here that cocaine is entangled with other licit and illicit supply chains. As Gootenberg (2008) explains, cocaine's very illegality today is tied to the politics of the global production of cocaine and other competing anesthetics in the early and middle twentieth century. While the cocaine trade, with its marked volume and value, plays a substantial role in the social life of many communities in the Americas, it is also impossible to completely divorce it from other illicit supply chains. Mexican cocaine trafficking organizations emerged as groups of growers and suppliers of opium and marijuana, and those commodities continue to play a role in their activities, alongside newer drugs like fentanyl. Cocaine dealers in the United States do not always limit themselves to just dealing cocaine, and drug consumers are not necessarily tied to one specific licit or illicit narcotic.

## MORAL ECONOMIES

Why do farmers in Bolivia not sell their coca leaves to the highest bidder? How come drug traffickers in Colombia require "brokers" to buy up cocaine paste? And what purpose does it serve for drug gangs to fund childcare services in Rio's favelas? These questions are not easily answered, because the functioning of the illicit trade defies the logic of mainstream economic theory, which assumes that all action is self-interested, oriented toward maximizing perceived personal gain. We argue that the cocaine value chain produces and is, in part, produced by social expectations or moral economies at various sites along that chain. To understand these moral economies, their effects on the cocaine trade, and their implications for how the cocaine trade affects social relations in different places, scholars should think more broadly about the interrelationship of social relationships, political hierarchy, and capital.

E. P. Thompson (1971) coined the term *moral economy* in his seminal work on food riots in eighteenth-century Britain. Thompson asked: When do grievances result in collective action? The source of unrest in Thompson's case lay in the tension between two models of the economy. The peasants, on the one hand, had a moral economy that valued guaranteed subsistence and fair play. The encroaching capitalist forces and, to a certain extent, feudal landowners, on the other hand, valued profit maximization and wealth accumulation, often at the expense of rural subsistence. In the face of rising grain prices, peasants rioted to demand fair prices as opposed to market prices.

Thompson uses the notion of the "moral economy" to critique W. W. Rostow's mid-1940s analysis of poverty as a source of food riots.

Thompson argued that poverty and hunger are necessary, though insufficient, factors to explain these riots. Rather, hunger and the failure of those in possession of food to adequately respond to that hunger can, under some circumstances, initiate a response among the hungry that leads to collective action. For Thompson, the perception of social relations, exchanges, and the norms that govern those relationships are essential for understanding when collective violence occurs. In this way, Thompson illustrates the existence of a noncapitalist way of understanding exchange, or, in Polanyi's (1957) terms, how the economy is "embedded" in deeper social processes.

Thompson's essay informed James Scott's *The Moral Economy of the Peasant* (1977), which sought to understand the conditions under which peasants in Southeast Asia would rebel, as well as a litany of other works (Goodman 2004; Edelman 2005; Fassin 2005). Yet, as Edelman (2012: 63) has pointed out, the proliferation of the concept of "moral economies" has also resulted in it losing its analytical purchase: more recent uses of the concept have employed it to refer to purely "moralizing" or social aspects of life, as opposed to the relationship between customary understandings of justice and the underlying political and economic conditions that Thompson had in mind (see also Fassin 2009; Palomera and Vetta 2016). In this vein, and extending these criticisms further, Alexander, Brunn, and Koch (2018) have recently advocated for a use of "moral economies" that places at its heart questions about the state and governance. They ask, at a time when different legal and political frameworks govern interactions and relationships between public assets, goods, and citizens, what are the different moral economies that are at stake? Who gets to decide which moral economies are legitimate and should take precedence over others? And whose relationships, understandings of justice, and expectations of the common good are silenced in this process?

Building on these more recent uses of the term *moral economy*, we understand moral economic activity as being rooted in the mutual obligations that arise when people exchange with each other over the course of time, in turn building up debt and mutual dependencies (see Carrier 2018). We start from the assumption that there is no such thing as a unitary or single moral economy, but instead conflicting, overlapping, and sometimes mutually exclusive understandings at stake. Here we use the term *moral economy* to analyze a number of alternative economic and social systems that emerge outside of, in parallel with, in opposition to, or even in conjunction with mainstream capitalist market economies and governance frameworks. We want to do justice to the moral economy concept, and so we relate these alternative economies to global capitalist processes—specifically neoliberalism. We understand neoliberalism to be a radicalized form of capitalism, stemming from a utopian political project to enhance conditions for accumulation and restore power to economic elites (Harvey 2005). In the Americas, this has taken the form of free trade agreements, cuts in public expenditure, the sale (and closure) of public utilities, the privatization of publicly owned resources, and relaxed environmental and labor regulations. It is not that the state has retreated so much as it has been reconfigured with the strengthening of the state's ability to police disorder—specifically, the marginal urban masses who have been the victims of aggressive free market reforms (Wacquant 2014; Auyero and Sobering 2017). In Latin America, repression is often carried out in the name of the "war on drugs" or the "war on gangs" (Rodgers 2009; Müller 2015).

We know that economies, including capitalist economies, never operate according to a "pure" market logic of individual profit maximization—but rather always intersect with (dynamic) social, political, and cultural relations, including various conceptions of morality (Zaloom 2006; Graeber 2014). So why do we treat the drug trade as a special case? In the illegal economy, the same rules do not apply as in the legal economy. Drug trafficking organizations face the constant threat of defection, (sometimes) hostile communities, and pressure from government interdiction efforts. Illegal entrepreneurs cannot turn to the state to arbitrate a dispute, nor can they always resort to violence in order to solve problems; the costs would simply be too high. Most of the time, then, the drug trade is built on trust among myriad actors directly inside but also adjacent to the trade. Drawing inspiration from economic anthropologists going right back to the seminal work of Marcel Mauss (1990), we argue that this trust is rooted in reciprocal relationships—namely, debt and the expectation that debt will be paid back. The way these reciprocal relationships are structured—who is included and excluded, the sanctions for nonpayment, the expectations regarding time horizons and interest—are all rooted in localized conceptions of honor, pride, and what it means to be a good person (see Piot 1999: 52–75; Sanchez et al. 2017).

There is an emerging body of work that draws on the moral economy concept to understand the drug trade. Philippe Bourgois and Jeff Schonberg (2009) describe the webs of reciprocity and mutual obligation between homeless addicts, particularly in relation to the sharing of drugs as a way to buy favors, love, and loyalty on the streets of San Francisco (see also Bourgois 1998; Wakeman 2016). Meanwhile, Karandinos and colleagues

(2014) describe how, when viewed through a Maussian lens, street violence associated with the drug trade, which at first might appear to be mindless, brutish, and irrational, can be understood as part of a broader moral framework governing social life. From this perspective, violence is a resource that is used according to a deeper social logic that emphasizes loyalty and masculinity. Karandinos clearly illustrates how debts do not necessarily stick to an individual, but rather are extended to kin, friends, or even fellow gang members (see also Rodgers 2015; Koch 2017).

These writings invite us to move away from viewing the cocaine trade as simply a series of economic transactions and to consider how these exchanges are rooted in existing social relations but are also generative of new social orders. The importance of this work is that it exposes how processes of exchange tie people together into dense webs of reciprocity that extend across space and time. This is particularly important for the current study as it uncovers the basic social principles underlying the governance of the drug trade. Just like the gift exchanges analyzed by Marcel Mauss almost a hundred years ago, the ongoing exchange of drugs, coca leaf, precursor chemicals, money, and violent acts functions as a form of social contract, allowing the trade to endure in the shadow of the state. As such, we cannot measure these localized "exchanges" according to the standard liberal yardsticks. These exchange practices have their own logic, representing an alternative "moral economy" that can only be uncovered through in-depth qualitative fieldwork. The next section examines some of the theoretical implications of this approach.

## A FRAMEWORK FOR UNDERSTANDING COCAINE'S MORAL ECONOMIES

By invoking the language of moral economies, we acknowledge the Marxist and anarchist roots of this concept. For Thompson, a Marxist historian, the moral economy explains why riots and rebellion against the encroaching capitalist order occurred in eighteenth-century England. His work explicitly critiqued what he saw as Rostow's overly deterministic and economic understanding of the connections between poverty and rebellion (Thompson 1971: 76–78). For James Scott, a political scientist with a complex relationship to both Marxism and anarchism, the moral economy of Southeast Asian peasants explains as much why rebellions occur as why they do not and, more precisely, why peasant rebellions are unlikely to transform easily into social revolutions. In both cases, economic exchanges are productive of self-regulating social relations. Wealthier peasants, landlords, bakers, and millers were expected to abide by norms that enabled poorer peasants to survive in difficult times, in part by allowing peasants to accept relatively lower incomes in times of plenty in exchange for support in times of need. The growth of the global capitalist market in England and, 150 years later, in Southeast Asia generated pressures on these arrangements that led to riots, uprisings, and revolts.

Much of the policy discussion of the drug trade today begins from neo-Weberian state-centric premises that seek to explain drug violence in the institutional context of failing states or poor state policy (see O'Donnell 1993; Snyder and Durán-Martínez 2009; Ungar 2011; Arias 2017; Durán-Martínez 2018). These works provide important insights that explain the outbreak and persistence of violence in some locales. But they miss the broader set of exchanges and relationships that underlie the drug trade, which not only help to explain the occurrence of violence and peace but offer a nuanced account of why the drug trade becomes embedded in some communities and not others, what effects the trade has on relationships within those communities, and how those communities change the drug trade.

In short, just as hunger only offers a partial explanation for why bread riots occur, state failure and institutional crises only offer a partial explanation of the drug trade, its local exchanges, and the violence, or lack thereof, associated with it. To understand the drug trade, we need to go beyond states and organizational conflict to perceive how the trade is tied to preexisting social relationships, exchanges, and norms, and how it transforms and is transformed by those relationships, exchanges, and norms in specific places on the value chain. This has four implications, two of which are derivative of the Marxist roots of this concept, another one from its anarchist ascendency, and a fourth that has implications for the direction of the Weberian frameworks that have dominated this debate.

First, consistent with the Marxist concept of historical materialism, commodity chains are economic phenomena that transform locales in their material form and social relations. The presence of the drug trade engages with and changes underlying social relations. Sitting on the margins of state protection, the drug trade has to operate in the context of social norms in order to derive protection from the state, but it also has the effect of transforming norms, relationships, and spaces through its contact with them (see Grisaffi, this volume; Rui, this volume).

Second, the drug trade is a site of social conflict through which individuals resolve differences over the norms of conduct within their community, the place of particular communities in licit and illicit international markets, and who benefits from the profits derived from those markets. While we do not see this violence as revolutionary, we believe it is critical to acknowledge Kalyvas's (2015) insight that criminal violence often is a substitute for social conflict in highly urban societies. We also take heed of Goldstein's (2004) argument that violence is, at least in part, related to how the poor position themselves as citizens and subjects in contemporary Latin American political systems (see Zellers-León, this volume).

Third, acknowledging the anarchist origins of this idea, as much as the drug trade is discussed in terms of violence and its pernicious effects on society and politics, much of the trade occurs peacefully under mechanisms of self-government at the margins of state power (Biondi 2014; Hirata and Grillo 2019). The dynamics of these governing norms and modes at different points of the commodity chain are essential to understanding the trade. Key in this are exchanges that take place largely outside of government oversight and the ways that those exchanges sustain the life of the poor and the illicit trade in contemporary Latin America (see Fontes, this volume). At the same time, it is important to recognize that these localized forms of governance in a transnational trade also articulate with the state at various points, generating layered forms of governance of social and criminal norms that govern relationships in the context of imperfect state power (see Denyer Willis 2015; Le Cour Grandmaison, this volume)

Fourth, these dynamics have implications for Weberian approaches to drug violence. While drug policy debates are often driven by state-centric neo-Weberian analyses, much of the emerging scholarly discussion on the drug trade adopts a post-Weberian perspective at least partially rooted in Kalyvas's (2006) writing on the micro-dynamics of civil conflicts. From this perspective, the drug trade and its attendant violence is seen as emerging from interactions between the state and multiple criminal organizations. The particular postures adopted by the state and these organizations as they contend with one another for control of the illicit trade generates the violent dynamics (Snyder and Durán-Martínez 2009; Lessing 2017; Durán-Martínez 2018; Lessing and Willis 2019).

The moral economy points to normative drivers of behavior around illicit markets and institutional decision making by both state operatives and criminal leaders (see, for example, Arias and Rodrigues 2006). Gang leaders make their decisions within a future-oriented framework, in which they plan to have relations with state officials, with other criminal organizations, or with the communities that they operate in, and these expectations shape and regulate their behavior. Knowledge of these frameworks is critical to understanding interactions among criminal groups, state, and society and the movement of goods through the illicit value chain (see Idler, this volume). Finally, expectations among various parties in different instantiations of the value chain also affect the governance dynamics, as criminals, state actors, and society draw on these shared assumptions to exercise governance amid cocaine's economies.

These insights open up new ways to understand the cocaine trade and respond to its more pernicious effects. Tackling the violence associated with the drug trade necessarily involves more than putting down an uprising or even just addressing demand for drugs and addiction. It means focusing on the imperfections of the insertion of many Latin Americans into the global capitalist economy, their reliance on informal social networks for survival, how the drug trade and other forms of crime in part survive on and emerge from those very same networks, and the failure of the contemporary political and economic systems to deliver on their promise of inclusion. These broader imperfections in the economy at large point to the limitations of drug legalization in addressing the greatest challenges Latin Americans face, and the ways in which the key drivers of crime may have little to do with the juridical status of narcotics per se (see Bergman 2018). The next section takes up these issues empirically by examining how cocaine affects local social dynamics in areas that intersect with its supply chain.

## COMMODITY PRODUCTION AND THE FORMATION OF SOCIAL ORDERS

For years, the logic of global prohibition has dominated the debate on drug policy. In this narrative, illicit narcotics are a source of disorder that contributes directly to violence, organized crime, urban blight, poor health outcomes, and a shorter life. In the context of the Global South, the power of drug trafficking organizations is used to highlight the putative weakness of the state. The solution to these problems is often more repression and, of course, transfers of largely military and police aid from the Global North to drug-producing and transshipping countries in Latin America and the Caribbean. In the end, narcotics become a consumable artifact that moves among largely disconnected and autonomous locales where they cause

FIGURE I.2 The urban margins of Medellín, Colombia.

physical harm and enrich only a few. This narrative, of course, misses central issues in the nature of how the drug trade operates and interacts across different societies. Most critically, narcotics are deeply embedded in particular local social interactions and, just like the sugar supply chain, their movement is at once rooted in the existing social order, but also generative of new social orders, economic opportunities, and political structures.

At its source in the foothills of the Andes, poor farmers rely on this illegal harvest in order to survive. Those who do well invest the proceeds into small businesses but also social relations, for instance by becoming sponsors of community fiestas, school football teams, or the local church (Grisaffi, this volume). Meanwhile the trafficking of illicit goods provides important economic opportunities for the poor and working classes in urban peripheries in Latin America (see Feltran 2019; Fontes, Rodgers, this volume) (see figure I.2) and the United States (Bourgois et al., this volume) and has made an important contribution to the creation of wider cultural life (Sneed 2008; Oosterbaan 2009; Jaffe 2012). Underpaid and poorly professionalized state actors often seek to capture rents within the drug trade to supplement relatively meager salaries (Arias 2006). Finally, social and political elites seeking their own enrichment become involved in these economic exchanges (Gillies 2018; Bobea and Veeser, this volume). As a result of these complex interactions, relationships, and (economic) dependencies, local drug trades are remarkably resilient and government agents may have little interest in effectively combating illicit trade even though its agents might publicly call for such action.

Academic research points to the importance of illicit processes in the construction of broader licit and illicit lifeworlds (Gambetta 1996; Varese 2001; Holston 2008; Koster and Smart 2019). The illicit lifeworld is not necessarily violent, nor is it simply something outside the law. Rather, illicit activity generates a host of formally unregulated interactions that often interface with otherwise legal relationships, generating at times sustainable social dynamics that governments may find difficult to repress (see Roitman 2006; Muehlmann 2013). Indeed, many operating in and around the drug trade are not themselves illegal entrepreneurs. For example, owners of a bar where cocaine users stop for a drink before or after buying drugs have a connection to the illicit economy. And many involved directly in illegal activity may not think of themselves primarily as criminals when, for example, they transport precursor chemicals to friends and relatives who they know process cocaine. Still, all of these people are affected by and bear witness to the economies and dangers of the drug trade they live amid.

None of this should be taken to mean that crime weakens the state. Rather, crime can be productive of state power just as it can be productive of a host of other social relationships (Jaffe 2013; Sanchez 2016; Michelutti et al. 2018). Research has described how in Latin America's poor neighborhoods, municipalities, and regions, where the state has an uneven presence, drug gangs operate neighborhood-level administrative regimes, oftentimes in collaboration with state actors (see Arias 2017; Le Cour Grandmaison, this volume). To give but one example, during the coronavirus pandemic, drug traffickers in Rio de Janeiro's favelas imposed curfews and limited social gatherings to a maximum of two people (Barretto and Phillips 2020).

Sophisticated policy discussions of the drug trade can only occur in the context of a nuanced understanding of drug commodity chains and what they achieve. Narcotics are not merely legal artifacts or poisons that destroy communities and political entities. Rather, they are commodities that emerge from human labor and are moved across vast regional and global supply chains. This process includes agricultural production, various stages of manufacture, financing and insurance, transportation and its attendant support operations, transshipment and storage, cross-border smuggling, distribution and wholesaling, packaging, retail sale, and final consumption. At each of these stages, complex social, economic, and political relations emerge that sustain but also depend on the trade. These activities result in systems of order, forms of economic sustenance, capital accumulation, secondary investment, and of course violence.

If we view the cocaine trade as generative of social and economic orders, then we can also understand that any alteration in the commodity chain will have widespread impacts. It will affect not just the drug gangs, but also the police and politicians who take bribes, the family members of dealers who depend on the trade for their income, or store owners and taxi drivers in towns where coca is grown. This has implications for the drug policy debate. Different repressive policies may remove particular actors from the drug trade but leave in place a local economic ecology that favors the emergence of new criminal actors to take their place in local economic exchanges and in the wider commodity chain. Alternatively, major shifts toward legalization might encounter real barriers among parties interested in perpetuating the illicit trade for either political or monetary gain. More critically, a move toward legalization could result in a cascade of destabilizing effects across a broad swath of communities in the Western Hemisphere whose populations face a variety of urgent social and economic challenges.

## ADVANCING A SYSTEMATIC UNDERSTANDING OF COCAINE COMMODITY CHAINS

Laid out on the maps contained in the UNODC's *World Drugs Report*, the cocaine commodity chain appears like a smooth set of arrows flowing from production to consumption sites (see map I.1). The reality, of course, is far more complex. As drugs move from crop-producing regions to consumption sites, it passes through various transit corridors, often with stopovers at transshipment sites, to wholesalers and retail distributors before they arrive in the hands of consumers. Thus, to understand the implications of an illicit commodity chain across different sites, it is critical to be specific about the nature of different locales of commodity chain activities, the way they link together, and the particular issues experienced in each locale. This section lays out components of this analytical lens.

The value of cocaine changes dramatically as it moves from the places where it is produced to the market, increasing in value by as much as 1,000 percent. This shifting value chain reflects a great deal of unevenness, with rewards usually flowing to the individuals and organizations that control the movement of the product through the riskiest sections of the supply chain. Thus, as in many other types of business, the distributor, not the manufacturer, is the one who achieves the highest margins. Understanding the basic framework of the cocaine commodity chain involves perceiving not just the type of activity that occurs in a particular place, but also the relative and absolute value of that work.

Cocaine starts life as coca leaf, a shrub that is cultivated in the foothills of the Andes. In coca-growing regions of Bolivia, Peru, and Colombia, cocaine is relatively cheap; a kilo of unrefined cocaine paste can cost as little as US$900 in Peru's VRAEM coca grower region, and production is labor intensive. Thus, the coca/cocaine economy involves a large swath of the population, is widely tolerated, and is only minimally hidden from view. This is very different from the cocaine economy in the US, where the stakes are higher, fewer people are involved, and its activities are clandestine. A critical analysis of the commodity chain, thus, has to focus on the sites of value shift and how those inflection points, which are sites of intense and valuable labor, generate an array of different local outcomes.

Communication and control also affect the commodity chain. The nature of how these spaces are connected together by physical movement and organizations affects how the commodity chain alters a place. In some cases, large portions of the resources are siphoned away from particular places by powerful organizations based elsewhere. In other cases, local groups control a particular portion of the supply chain. Here we could look at coca production in Bolivia. In the early 1980s, Colombian cartels bought up Bolivian coca leaf and transported it to Colombia, where it was processed into cocaine paste. It was only later that Bolivian peasants learned how to process drugs and were then able to keep more of the profits. This was good business for the Colombian cartels because it reduced their transport costs and Bolivian labor was comparatively very cheap. Building on these observations, we argue that in order to understand how the commodity chain produces a lifeworld in a particular locale, we need to take into consideration several factors:

1   *The nature of the illicit market:* The number of market actors and how those market actors tend to do business has an impact on the nature of competition in those spaces and the interrelationship between different participants in the illicit marketplace (Arias 2017). The nature of the illicit market points to important issues such as how many people earn their living in the market, what ability illicit laborers have to demand high wages, and the extent to which local organizations work among themselves and with

other actors to regulate the nature of illicit commerce. This in turn has effects on a host of other activities. In places that require a high degree of skill or risk tolerance, there will often be a smaller pool of available laborers and capitalists relative to the population. As the pool of available workers becomes relatively more concentrated, this will affect the nature of the local market and its relationship to the wider population. In some cases, there may be a broad popular involvement in the market, whereas in other places the actual market operators may be limited and highly specialized. Each of these dynamics will express itself in the local life-world in different ways in terms of how an array of goods are demanded and exchanged in those spaces.

2 *The degree of illicit capital accumulation:* The extent to which illicit capital accrues in a particular place is critical to the way that the illicit commodity chain affects that place. As illicit entrepreneurs accumulate resources, they can then spend those funds on a host of activities. Some of this might involve further developing their business, but their activities will likely also cross over into legal activities as they seek to launder money and diversify. Some of these resources support political, social, and artistic activities. The nature and level of this type of capital accumulation are essential for understanding how particular places are affected by the commodity chain.

3 *The relative weight of the illicit market in the broader local economy:* In places where the illicit economy plays a relatively larger role, it will have greater collateral effects on everyday life and shape the broader local economy. The problem of Dutch disease, in which the influx of foreign currency from the cocaine trade overvalues the local currency and atrophies other economic activities, offers an excellent example of this type of effect (on Dutch disease, see Thoumi 2003).

4 *The interaction between the illicit commodity chain and licit authority:* Multiple systems of legitimate authority operate in a specific locale and may have varying relationships to the illicit market. In some cases, powerful religious figures or effective and respected government officials may find ways of limiting the impacts of the trade in a particular place. In other locales, political, civic, and cultural leaders may become implicated in the trade, which may deepen and shape their influence in particular ways. Some portions of the trade may occur in spaces relatively distant from state power. Depending on other factors, these legitimate authority structures may have relatively more or less authority over the illicit trade. In some cases, these actors may be direct market participants and in others they may work for market leaders.

We can use variations across these four categories of activity to understand the nature of the moral economies of the cocaine trade in different places along the commodity chain. What follows is a general description of commodity chain conditions where different operations take place, how this intersects with licit and illicit governance, and the implications of this for the moral economy of exchanges in locales where these conditions predominate and within the commodity chain as a whole.

For the sake of parsimony, this section will take up three key operations in the commodity chain: growing and processing, transshipment and smuggling, and distribution and consumption. This classification, however, should not be read as inherently discrete or deterministic of moral economies. Different operations in the cocaine trade do not always take place in isolation. Indeed, they often occur in the same space, even while one activity predominates. For example, Putumayo, Colombia, may be a center for coca cultivation, but there are also consumers in the region, and drugs are stored and shipped out. Similarly, the effects are not deterministic but rather are socially embedded and probabilistic. Suppliers, dealers, and consumers often buy, sell, and transport other licit and illicit drugs. Perhaps most importantly, the ways these types of conditions come together in particular locales and their particular mixture shape local moral economies in interactions with various other social, political, and economic factors that operate in those locales. Thus, cocaine production, like other types of economic activity, contributes to multiple complex local dynamics, helping to shape moral economies in varied ways, but is not singularly determinative of them.

## Coca Growing and Processing Areas

There are two main activities at the agro-industrial stage of the cocaine trade: coca growing and processing leaves into cocaine paste. Coca leaf production is labor intensive, requiring many workers and vast expanses of land;[3] hence, these activities remain in peasant hands. In Peru, Colombia, and Bolivia (the three main coca-growing countries), coca cultivation is typically concentrated in marginal areas, characterized by limited state presence, inadequate infrastructure, and high rates of poverty. In this context, coca complements subsistence farming and, in the absence of other income-generating activities, is one of the few pursuits that provide farmers with access to cash income (Grisaffi and Ledebur 2016: 9).

The first stage of cocaine production is a relatively simple process that takes place in small workshops located close to the coca fields or in urban peripheries. Drug workers labor in rudimentary operations to soak shredded coca leaf in solvents to extract the cocaine alkaloid. Processing cocaine paste can be mastered without formal training. The *químico* (chemist), a mid-level technician usually drawn from among local farmers, oversees this procedure. Cocaine paste production supports a broad range of jobs. These include smuggling precursor chemicals, processing leaves, and transporting cocaine base paste to secondary processing locations for producing purified cocaine hydrochloride. The drug workers also require lookouts, cooks, and coca leaf suppliers.

The second stage, refining of paste into pure cocaine, takes place in laboratories that are more capital intensive—in Bolivia it can cost from $150,000 to $300,000 depending on the size of the operation. This stage of processing requires industrial chemicals that are difficult to acquire,[4] a workforce of up to thirty people, and the refineries that are often protected by armed guards. The process is more complex, requiring a higher level of training; as such the chemists are in demand and might travel internationally for work opportunities. For instance, many of the chemists in charge of refining cocaine in Bolivia come from Colombia.

Coca growing and cocaine production produce dynamics that can shape local moral economies in particular ways. The industry supports a large number of people who occupy relatively low-skilled positions in the drug trade. The trade has a modest though substantial effect on the economies of these countries,[5] but the large number of workers at this stage of the process means that there is often relatively little capital accumulation (see figure 1.3). These diffuse earnings do little to generate sizable new industries and businesses since most of the income from coca sits at other places in the commodity chain.[6] Still, the infusion of funds can help to stabilize families' livelihoods, keep a greater portion of the population in rural areas, and can support some existing small businesses, such as the moto-taxis that Zellers-León discusses in her chapter (this volume).

While production generates particular economic dynamics, these become inserted into particular national and local contexts, yielding different and varied moral economies. In Colombia, for example, coca production occurs in a highly repressive and violent environment. These conditions contribute to substantial collective action problems, where agricultural workers use personal networks to carefully and, often at great cost, support collective endeavors in difficult circumstances (see Ramirez 2011; Idler, this

FIGURE I.3 A village in the VRAEM coca-growing region of Peru.

volume). The moral economy under these circumstances is characterized by insularity among a tightly knit population that could be subject to violence by various armed actors, often based elsewhere, that use force to accumulate some of the capital that accrues at this stage of production (see Durand Guevara 2007; Kernaghan 2009; Ramirez 2011). Lacking substantial capital accumulation, these areas are often characterized by survival-based exchanges among family members and close friends (Vellinga 2007). The story, however, is quite different in Bolivia, where, since 2006, strong agricultural unions allied to the state control the coca trade and have pressured the government to legalize coca cultivation in specific areas (Grisaffi 2019). While the local drug trade is firmly rooted in kinship networks, there is more space for collective action and greater capital accumulation among agricultural workers (see Grisaffi, this volume). Thus, the conditions in the supply chain generate dynamics that have varied effects in localities that have different social, political, and economic conditions.

### Transshipment Areas

The principal activities of cocaine transshipment areas involve storing and smuggling goods. These activities require the most complex skills of any of the activities in the cocaine commodity chain. Getting drugs across borders leads to schemes that involve secreting goods in shipping containers and altering electronic records, building kilometer-long transit tunnels (Graham 2011), using submarines to cross maritime frontiers (Woody 2016), and skillful low-altitude airplane flying (Marosi 2011), to say nothing of administering large fleets of airplanes and networks of airfields (Woody 2016). Moreover, the substantial skills required for this labor mean that at least a portion of those involved make substantial profits, although major dealers may also develop low-skilled enforcement networks (see, for example, Gay, this volume, and Fontes, this volume).

The expertise required to bring drugs across international borders enables powerful traffickers to accumulate a large portion of the wealth associated with the trade (Vellinga 2007). This can lead to competition between trafficking organizations. State officials may be complicit but may have less tolerance for elevated violence. As a result, they may seek to resolve drug conflicts, leading to markets characterized by a few participants. But this is not always the case. Clawson and Lee (1996) describe how in the 1980s Colombia's Medellín Cartel advanced financing and provided insurance against cargo loss to smaller-scale traffickers to ensure wider participation in that city's cocaine market and, thus, to deflect some attention from their own activities.

Transshipment markets tend to have a few large market participants who then employ a modest number of workers at different skill levels. While a great deal of attention falls on drug gang members, these workers make up a fairly small though highly visible portion of the population of cities like Kingston, Cali, or Tijuana. Since the trafficking endeavor at this stage requires resources and expertise, these actors are employed by major criminal enterprises led by a few powerful individuals. Due to the illicit nature of this stage of the commodity chain, there are relatively few legal norms that delimit practices, leading, on occasion, to atrocities (Durán-Martínez 2015). The nature of these risks contributes to efforts to establish dominance over a market either through an agreement among a few powerful market participants or through outright dominance by a single participant.

The substantial earnings coupled with the relatively small number of market participants leads to significant capital accumulation that can enable illicit entrepreneurs to start or take over licit businesses (see McSweeney et al. 2018; Le Cour Grandmaison, this volume). These actors may take control of large portions of the licit economy and even, as a result of Dutch disease and insecurity, limit the growth of the economy as a whole. Due to the necessity of a transportation network, much of the transshipment tends to occur in places where there is some state presence, and state officials are often involved in the trade (Morrison 1997; Ellis 2009: 183). As a result, law enforcement operates at least sporadically, and public services are available to the population due to the networked nature of the places where many of these activities take place.

The significant capital accumulation opportunities associated with this phase of the cocaine trade contribute to very different conditions as they interact with particular local dynamics. The activities of the Medellín and Cali cartels in the 1980s and 1990s reflect how particular criminal structures using their accumulated capital generate very different local conditions, with the Medellín group confronting the state (Lessing 2017) in a bloody terror campaign, whereas the Cali organization sought to accommodate the state and quietly maintain order in their areas of operation. In Mexico, considerable amounts of the resources associated with the drug trade historically flowed to politicians associated with the Partido Revolucionario Institucional (PRI), who maintained their own protection rackets, yielding relative calm in Mexico for many years. The transition to competitive elections in Mexico contributed to the breakdown of these structures, and traffickers, taking advantage of the capital available to them, have over the past two decades engaged in a long-term conflict over that country's drug trafficking plazas (Dell 2015; Rios 2015; Trejo and Ley 2018). The Caribbean, another key transshipment hub, tells a third story. Here gangs have typically shipped drugs abroad in small parcels, often on airplanes or fast boats. Gang leaders have greatly enriched themselves generating patronage networks and also have sought the protection of political figures. Lacking the immense profits associated with controlling trafficking networks, as was the case in Mexico and Colombia, Caribbean traffickers have more limited capital, political power, and patronage structures.

### Distribution and Consumption Sites

Markets focused on distribution and retail sales are broad, diverse, and, in general, characterized by low skills and intense competition. Once drugs have crossed the principal international frontier into a major consumption market in North America, Europe, some major Latin American cities, or Asia, internal distribution and sales are relatively straightforward. A worker can move drugs around in the trunk of a car rather than hidden in a submarine or airplane. Successful retail sales can, of course, involve some skill, but not necessarily more so than any other type of retail work. Certainly, working in this environment requires less formal training than many similar jobs in the licit economy (see Bobea and Veeser, this volume; Bourgois et al., this volume). The relatively low skill levels also mean that there are substantial opportunities for market competition. In a broad and vibrant retail market it is difficult for individual firms, mafias, or gangs to gain control of large sectors of the market; barriers to entering the market are low, and thus the ability to consolidate power in the market is attenuated. In a wealthy economy, cocaine also has to compete with numerous other drugs for market share. As a result, there is a great deal of competition that has the effect of controlling prices even as law enforcement buoys them. Thus, while market participants can make substantial profits, those profits end up diffused across many market participants. The result is, often, a low level of capital accumulation and some dealers risking their lives and freedom but living in impoverished conditions (Levitt and Venkatesh 2000).

For all the income generated by the drug trade in consuming countries, amid the size of the economy of London, Paris, New York, or Buenos Aires, the trade has only a limited impact on the broader economy of the city or country. Given this and the limited capital accumulation of those involved in the trade, the cocaine commodity chain has relatively limited impacts on the wider economy and society in these places. That said, within certain circumscribed neighborhoods and communities, drug-related income is often an important tool for survival (see Bourgois et al., this volume, Bobea and Veeser, this volume).

In the vast majority of cases, major consumer markets operate in spaces where there exists a high degree of state presence. Elevated cocaine consumption is driven by a broad and deep consumer culture that depends on an active state presence that provides policing, social regulation, good schools to promote human capital formation, and investment in infrastructure for businesses to support economic growth. Substantial levels of state enforcement and broader economic opportunities have the concomitant effect of keeping the market divided.

In these cases, highly divided and poorly resourced criminal groups have little expression outside of the often impoverished neighborhoods where they operate. In these spaces, drug dealing can fit into family survival strategies and exchanges among broader kin and friendship networks. At the same time, they have little wider impact outside of these networks, and there are few expectations of gang leaders in comparison with those who operate in other spaces in the drug commodity chain. The experience of

Philippe Bourgois's (1995) drug dealers in East Harlem in the 1980s reflects this condition. The strong presence of the state and the highly divided nature of illicit trades cause the trade's impacts on governance to be highly localized and limited, even as it may have robust effects in particular communities.

The moral economies of drug consumption sites are fragmented. On the one hand, it builds on survival exchanges within the poor communities that often warehouse drugs and provides a site for the more organized criminal activities needed to administer the trade. Here some limited patronage relations may operate, but, at the same time, lacking significant capital accumulation, there is little expectation that the drug trade will support broader development of the economy or culture. Individuals operating around the drug trade in these sites are often expected to provide a modicum of security and limited norm enforcement in exchange for silence from neighborhood residents facing police questioning. Lacking capital accumulation and operating amid larger licit economies, people living and working in consumption sites often do not have the relative resources necessary to overcome barriers to collective action, preventing the establishment of robust social norms. Consumers may also develop their own moral economy based on reciprocity and knowledge sharing, though these effects are quite limited, since resources flow up the supply chain from this group and, as consumers rather than laborers, most spend their time largely outside the drug supply chain. Table 1.1 comparatively outlines these categories.

As with different other phases of the cocaine trade, the fragmented dynamics of consumption sites only manifest themselves in the context of local social, economic, and political dynamics. In São Paulo, as Taniele Rui's chapter in this volume shows, the Primeiro Comando da Capital, a powerful criminal organization in that city that emerged out of violence in the state prison system, manages the varied drug-consumption markets across the city, supporting local norms of behavior among drug consumers and forcing disruptive addicts to consume drugs in central areas of town away from residential neighborhoods. In the northeastern United States, on the other hand, the consumption marketplace is much more fragmented, dominated by competing gangs and small-scale criminal networks. Bourgois and colleagues (this volume) show how the complex normative exchanges in consumption sites are negotiated among gangs, often through the mediation of respected older illicit market participants. Thus, consumption markets have complex norms of exchange and patronage

TABLE I.1  Comparing Sites in the Cocaine Value Chain

| | ACTIVITY | MARKET STRUCTURE | CAPITAL ACCUMULATION | ILLICIT PORTION OF ECONOMY | POLITICAL CLIMATE | GOVERNANCE AND MORAL EXCHANGE |
|---|---|---|---|---|---|---|
| **Production** | Mid-level skill: farming/processing cocaine paste | High levels of participation | Low | Large | Limited state presence | Significant exchanges among narrow, geographically isolated population facing significant collective action problems |
| **Transshipment** | Smuggling of various types usually requires substantial skill; high-skill labor | Usually oligopolistic or monopolistic | Often high | Wide variation | Mixed state presence, at times with high levels of corruption | Widespread patronage exchanges from wealthy drug traffickers to connected portions of the population |
| **Consumption** | Minimal end shipment, marketing, retailing; low skill | Competitive | Moderate capital presence but low accumulation | Small | Significant state presence, mixed levels of corruption | Limited survival exchanges within impoverished urban communities; little ability to overcome collective action problems |

that support retail sales and drug use, but those dynamics are driven by local conditions specific to particular cities.

## OVERVIEW OF THE BOOK

Building on this integrated notion of the international drug trade, combined with firsthand insights, the chapters presented here examine the nature of both licit and illicit processes of governance at different places along the drug production chain. We asked contributors to discuss their particular cases across a specific set of issues that define governance of the illicit trade; these include: understanding criminal market dynamics; analyzing illicit market dispute resolution strategies; discussing product and quality regulations; understanding illicit capital accumulation and its impacts on the commodity chain; and, finally, analyzing contacts between the illicit market and legitimate state and social sectors. Methodologically, all of our chapters are based on extended qualitative or archival research. The authors of these chapters have conducted extended locally embedded research based on nuanced and in-depth interviews or, in one case, archival analysis. Here we provide a brief overview of each chapter.

Thomas Grisaffi's chapter analyzes the moral economy of coca cultivation and drug processing in Bolivia. Grisaffi explains that the coca leaf has myriad traditional uses in indigenous Andean culture, but the bulk of the local crop ends up in the maceration pit to be transformed into cocaine. This chapter illustrates how cocaine paste production is organized around closed kinship networks that help to regulate the trade and that build the trust to advance this industry. The market for coca leaf generates high levels of employment in production and smuggling, and the cocaine dollars trickle down to support a large informal sector, strengthening these family ties and contributing to local economic development and consumption. Grisaffi argues that, as a result of the presence of the strong agricultural unions that have had close connections to the state that protected coca grower interests, since 2006 the Chapare has not experienced the kind of chaos, violence, and disorder witnessed at other sites along cocaine's commodity chain.

Annette Idler's chapter considers how Colombian coca farmers are articulated into the larger cocaine commodity chain. Idler analyzes the "moral borderland economy" that emerges in regions where illicit cross-border flows and the logics of armed conflict converge. These are dangerous spaces where, despite high levels of mistrust, different actors, including peasant coca farmers, non-state armed groups from rebels to paramilitaries, and entrepreneurs, have to work together to turn a profit. In this context, brokers are important figures who facilitate exchanges and in so doing link up the nodes of the commodity chain. This chapter emphasizes the essential role of self-regulation in these markets. But, as Idler points out, not all brokers are to be trusted, presenting danger and confusion for those at the lowest rungs of the trade. These spaces also become centers of counter-state organizing by guerrilla groups that seek to profit from and administer the trade. These organizations are empowered by the economics of the drug trade and also seek to govern elements of the trade. Thus, the economies of the drug trade produce organizations that both compete with the state and govern elements of the trade. Idler argues that it is essential for policy makers to understand how these exchanges of drugs, coca, and precursor chemicals function if they are to develop successful strategies to minimize danger for those in harm's way.

Autumn Zellers-León's account draws out the clash of two opposing economic worlds—one premised on subsistence crops, tradition, and mutual dependence on the one hand, and the perceived corrupting and individualizing impacts of coca cultivation on the other. This chapter focuses on how the coca supply chain, as it operates in Cauca, Colombia, generates resources that allow young people to acquire consumer goods, including motorcycles, which transform their communities and social and economic opportunities. These motorcycles and the coca economy more generally, however, also produce intense moral debate within the Nasa indigenous community regarding the "cultural" loss some local leaders believe the coca market generates. Amid these debates, social relations change, with motorcycle owners being viewed as local "big shots" and growing in standing in the community. For others, though, involvement in drug crop production is seen as a source of shame and potential danger, made visible through the proliferation of undocumented, and hence illegal, motorbikes. According to Zellers-León, the moralizing language surrounding coca cultivation is disempowering as it distracts attention from real material issues, namely the dire need for land reform and state investment in long-neglected rural areas. Finally, Zellers-León shows the importance of close-knit networks in evading state repression and how these operate in coca growing zones.

Robert Gay's chapter bridges smuggling and local retail and consumption of drugs in Brazil. He narrates the story of Bruno, an ex-corporal in the Brazilian navy who, while stationed on the border with Bolivia, became a large-scale drug trafficker. Bruno's involvement in the illicit trade deepens once he is sent to prison in Rio, where he becomes involved in the Comando Vermelho, one of Rio's most powerful drug gangs. Now in retirement, the drug trade continues to haunt Bruno, as debts accrued through a lifetime of illicit activity catch up with him. Gay's chapter illuminates how the drug trade, with its infusion of cash, changes Brazil's frontier, its prisons, and its shantytowns. The chapter also reflects on how norms play out in the Brazilian drug trade, examining how customs of behavior can contribute to success or failure in the drug market and expectations of conduct in prison life. Finally, Gay's chapter highlights how organized prison gangs influence the Brazilian drug trade and control populations. The chapter makes clear the ways that gang affiliation, concepts of honor, and the expectations of reciprocity structure the illicit trade.

Anthony Fontes then takes us to Guatemala, following cocaine as it travels north from the border with Honduras to an inner-city neighborhood in Guatemala City and finally to prison. Our guides for this journey are Trompas and Juanga, young men from poor neighborhoods who had few options but to engage in the illicit trade. The chapter shows how, as the cocaine snakes its away across the country, it articulates with and (re)orders local social worlds for good and bad. The chapter makes clear how infusions of cash from the drug trade support small towns in Guatemala, though much of the capital is accumulated by powerful individuals and gangs that control the trade. Ultimately the winners are those at the top, the big fish, the politicians and generals, but even for those caught at the lowest rungs, the trade still provides employment and an opportunity to earn, at the very least, a dignified living in a space of restricted opportunity. The moral economy emerges throughout the text as reciprocal exchanges—of jobs, support, and cash—tie people together into dense networks of debt and dependency.

Further north, we arrive in Mexico, where Romain Le Cour Grandmaison focuses on the role of the Caballeros Templarios (Knights Templar), a drug trafficking organization, and the hegemonic power they exerted in the state of Michoacán. Le Cour Grandmaison argues that strong men or "caciques" have long held sway in Mexico's rural hinterland, distributing state resources in exchange for loyalty, votes, and obedience. However, with the arrival of cocaine in the mid-1990s, these established relationships of patronage broke down, as criminal actors now had sufficient economic resources to work autonomously from the state. Those who control drugs, like the Knights Templar, are able to redefine local political authority to the extent that they position themselves above the state, making them the de facto regional authorities—controlling the local economy, government, and population. Le Cour Grandmaison intersects with the moral economy debate by arguing that drugs are disruptive in that they can force a break in reciprocity, in this case between the state and society. In so doing, they restructure sociopolitical relationships. This chapter further reveals the deep entanglement between drug trafficking organizations and the state as these groups seek to oversee municipal budgets.

Informed by Bourdieu's writings on cultural capital, Dennis Rodgers's chapter focuses on the tangible and intangible capital developed through engagement in the drug trade. Rodgers recounts the life stories of Bismarck and Milton, both former drug dealers who live in a poor neighborhood in Managua, the capital city of Nicaragua. He explains how these entrepreneurial individuals used capital accumulated in the drug trade to invest in a range of legal business ventures—including kiosks, real estate, and a tortilla business—using those resources to, at least for a time, change how other sectors of the economy operate. It is not just the economic capital that transfers to the licit realm, but embodied knowledge too. This includes a "just-in-time" tortilla delivery service modeled on a previous drug supply system and the use of violence and intimidation to ensure prompt rental payments. More broadly, Rodgers's account highlights the challenge of turning drug profits into long-term sustainable and sometimes legal business ventures.

Like Brazil, Puerto Rico is both a drug transshipment point and a site of consumption. Lillian Bobea and Cyrus Veeser's chapter examines the informal governance of the illicit cocaine trade, and how it structures everyday life in San Juan's poorest neighborhoods, the principal sites of retail drug dealing and consumption in that city. Bobea and Veeser show how the drug gangs build alliances with local communities, investing in amenities and administering justice, making inhabitants less dependent on the police. But this "protection" comes at a cost. Here communities must side with the gangs and purposefully exclude the state. The trade has economic multiplier effects, infusing the local economy of poor neighborhoods with resources that would not otherwise be available, promoting exchanges that establish and reinforce local norms associated with the drug trade. Some of these resources line the pockets of police and politicians, helping to implicate the state in the trade and changing the institutional implementation of social norms in particular communities and on the island more generally. But, in an age of economic crisis and political uncertainty, this established order and relative stability is starting to break down. Increasing numbers of people, mostly young men, are seeking out opportunities in the illicit trade, which concomitantly raises the competition, violence, and breakdown in the prior moral economy.

With cocaine's "shift south," drug use has expanded dramatically in Brazil. Taniele Rui analyzes the emerging "crack epidemic" in Rio de Janeiro and São Paulo. Based on long-term participant observation and interviews, Rui demonstrates how drug gangs govern marginal spaces and the impact that this has on the distribution of drug users and the development of the so-called cracklands, drug consumer hot spots. The influx of markets reconfigures urban space, setting up new sets of norms and expectations of how people will behave in different urban spaces. In São Paulo, drug use is highly visible, taking place openly on the street; meanwhile, in Rio de Janeiro, problematic crack consumption is mostly restricted to the favelas. Rui traces this spatial configuration to the specific criminal histories of each city and their respective moral economies, which impact on the way these organizations have managed the drug trade. The criminal gangs that operate in each city, as they interact with state and society, seek to maintain certain norms to avoid state repression and popular rejection. She suggests that the state's repressive policing tends to displace drug users rather than dealing with the drug consumption. Moreover, locking up users might actually worsen the drug problem by providing the criminal organizations with thousands of new recruits.

We now arrive at the mainland United States, to examine the moral economy of street dealing in Philadelphia. Philippe Bourgois, Laurie Kain Hart, George Karandinos, and Fernando Montero draw on six years of ethnographic fieldwork to tell the story of brothers Tito and Leo, Puerto Rican youth who are chasing their "American dream" to become "bichotes" (big shots), which ends with both in prison. Bourgois and colleagues lay out the structure of the local drug trade, including the attributes of a successful worker, upward mobility within the illicit business, the territorial control of the "corner," and the frequent deployment of lethal violence. The authors are careful to stress that the high levels of interpersonal violence observed on the street are shaped by the structural or everyday violence of poverty, racism, police repression, and "chronic incarceration," something that the drug dealers themselves are acutely aware of. This chapter intersects with the moral economy debate by showing how the drug trade is structured around kinship relations and survival strategies, and is framed by concepts of hypermasculinity. The chapter in particular shows how relationships evolve between dealers and the communities where they operate amid the dynamics of entrenched poverty driven by neoliberal policies that privilege accumulation by the wealthy and corporations and the repressive policing and mass incarceration policies pursued in the United States and some other countries to maintain order amid rising inequality. Cocaine dealing, in this context, is not just an important survival strategy for some households, but is a commodity around which some young people seek to build their social standing in a world where there are few social or professional options open to them that can help them advance and achieve even modest prominence by legitimate means.

The final substantive chapter is by Paul Gootenberg, a historian who traces out future changes in the cocaine commodity chain. Gootenberg explains the cocaine commodity chain's "shift south" away from the US market, which is fast becoming a "pot nation," not to mention the growing legal opiate crisis, toward emerging markets and transshipment poles like Brazil. Not only have consumer markets moved in a southerly direction, but production sites have too. Gootenberg highlights how Peru has emerged as an epicenter of illicit cocaine production and Bolivia is now a transshipment country as cheaper Peruvian cocaine paste flows east toward established and emerging markets in Europe and Asia. The pivot south in the larger drug commodity chain has implications for drug politics. As US influence has waned in the region, and cocaine has become an increasingly obsolete target for US policy makers, Andean states have taken up the reins, putting forth a diversity of governing responses. This ranges from Colombia's triumphant "state-building quest" for "post–drug war" control and Bolivia's "nationalist indigenous" drug control strategy, to Peru's "cocaine denial." More broadly, this chapter highlights how commodity chains are never stable, and when they shift a cascade of opportunities, dangers, and policy responses reveal themselves. In so doing, Gootenberg provides us with a framework for anticipating how the localized moral economies will change in coca-growing and drug-processing regions all the way from Putumayo in Colombia to the Chapare in Bolivia.

Taken together, these chapters provide a vivid and compelling account of the cocaine commodity chain from source to market. The volume outlines the ways that different iterations of the cocaine commodity chain engage in processes of self-regulation and how these exchange relations are rooted in deeper social logics that are specific to particular locales and social milieus, but also how the movement of drugs reorients local social, political, and economic dynamics. Building on this more nuanced understanding of cocaine's moral economies, Enrique Desmond Arias concludes by proposing an outline for a more progressive drug policy, one that acknowledges the important and productive role drugs play in the lives of those who survive at the urban and rural margins.

**NOTES**

1 The global market for all drugs has been calculated at between $426 billion and $652 billion (May 2017). Consumers in the United States spent around $150 billion on cocaine, heroin, marijuana, and methamphetamine in 2016 (Midgette et al. 2019: xi). Expenditure on cocaine in the United States declined from about $58 billion in 2006 to $24 billion in 2016 (Midgette et al. 2019: 26).

2 All drug revenue estimates—and particularly those for total global illicit drug revenues—should be interpreted as broad approximations and not as precise knowledge.

3 There are currently an estimated 245,000 hectares of land under coca cultivation (UNODC 2019: 13) and around 237,000 families dependent on coca cultivation in the Andes (Grisaffi, Farthing, and Ledebur 2017: 132).

4 The chemicals used to refine pure cocaine are most often diverted from legal supplies in the chemical industry, but some cocaine manufacturers, especially in Colombia, aim to achieve self-sufficiency by producing these substances themselves (UNODC 2020: 21).

5 In 2017 the market for dried coca leaf in Bolivia was worth up to $374 million, representing 8.7 percent of Bolivia's GDP in the agricultural sector (UNODC 2018a). In Colombia in 2016, this figure was over $560 million, but given Colombia's larger economy this only represented 3 percent of agricultural GDP (UNODC 2017).

6 A UN study from 2005 estimated that only about 1 percent of the final retail value of cocaine finds its way back to the Andean coca farmers (UNODC 2005).

**REFERENCES**

Alexander, Catherine, Maja Bruun, and Insa Koch. 2018. "Political Economy Comes Home: On the Moral Economies of Housing." *Critique of Anthropology* 38, no. 2: 121–39.

Arias, Enrique Desmond. 2006. "The Dynamics of Criminal Governance: Networks and Social Order in Rio de Janeiro." *Journal of Latin American Studies* 38, no. 2: 293–25.

Arias, Enrique Desmond. 2017. *Criminal Enterprises and Governance in Latin America and the Caribbean*. Cambridge: Cambridge University Press.

Arias, Enrique Desmond, and Corinne Rodrigues. 2006. "The Myth of Personal Security: Criminal Gangs, Dispute Resolution, and Identity in Rio De Janeiro's Favelas." *Latin American Politics and Society* 48, no. 4: 53–81.

Auyero, Javier, and Katherine Sobering. 2017. "Violence, the State, and the Poor: A View from the South." *Sociological Forum* 32: 1018–31.

Bair, Jennifer. 2009. *Frontiers of Commodity Chain Research*. Stanford, CA: Stanford University Press.

Bair, Jennifer, and Marion Werner. 2011. "The Place of Disarticulations: Global Commodity Production in La Laguna, Mexico." *Environment and Planning A* 43: 998–1015.

Barretto, Caio, and Tom Phillips. 2020. "Brazil Gangs Impose Strict Curfews to Slow Coronavirus Spread." *Guardian*, March 25.

Bergman, Marcello. 2018. *More Money, More Crime: Prosperity and Rising Crime in Latin America*. New York: Oxford University Press.

Biondi, Karina. 2014. "Etnografia no Moviemento: Território, Hierarquia, e Lei no PCC." Doctoral dissertation, Universidade Federal de São Carlos.

Bourgois, Philippe. 1995. *In Search of Respect: Selling Crack in El Barrio*. Cambridge: Cambridge University Press.

Bourgois, Philippe. 1998. "The Moral Economies of Homeless Heroin Addicts: Confronting Ethnography, HIV Risk, and Everyday Violence in San Francisco Shooting Encampments." *Substance Use and Misuse* 33, no. 1: 2323–51.

Bourgois, Philippe, and Jeffrey Schonberg. 2009. *Righteous Dopefiend*. Berkeley: University of California Press.

Carrier, James. 2018. "Moral Economy: What's in a Name." *Anthropological Theory* 18, no. 1: 18–35.

Clawson, Patrick, and Rensselaer Lee. 1996. *The Andean Cocaine Industry*. New York: Palgrave Macmillan.

Dell, Melissa. 2015. "Trafficking Networks and the Mexican Drug War." *American Economic Review* 105, no. 6: 1738–79.

Denyer Willis, Graham. 2015. *The Killing Consensus: Police, Organized Crime, and the Regulation of Life and Death in Urban Brazil*. Berkeley: University of California Press.

Durán-Martínez, Angélica. 2015. "To Kill and Tell? State Power, Criminal Competition, and Drug Violence." *Journal of Conflict Resolution* 59, no. 8: 1377–402.

Durán-Martínez, Angélica. 2018. *The Politics of Drug Violence: Criminals, Cops and Politicians in Colombia*. New York: Oxford University Press.

Durand Guevara, Anahí. 2007. "El movimiento cocalero y su difícil construcción en el Perú: Itinerario de desencuentros en el río Apurímac." In *Hablan los diablos: Amazonía, coca y narcotráfico en el Perú, escritos urgentes*, edited by Hugo Cabieses, Baldomero Caceres, Roger Rumrrill, and Ricardo Soberón. Quito: Abya-Yala and TNI.

Edelman, Marc. 2005. "Bringing the Moral Economy Back in . . . to the Study of 21st-Century Transnational Peasant Movements." *American Anthropologist* 107, no. 3: 331–45.

Edelman, Marc. 2012. "E. P. Thompson and Moral Economies." In *A Companion to Moral Anthropology*, edited by Didier Fassin. Oxford: Wiley Blackwell.

Ellis, Stephen. 2009. "West Africa's International Drug Trade." *African Affairs* 108, no. 431: 171–96.

Fassin, Didier. 2005. "Compassion and Repression: The Moral Economy of Immigration Policies in France." *Cultural Anthropology* 20, no. 3: 362–87.

Fassin, Didier. 2009. "Moral Economies Revisited." *Annales: Histoire, Sciences Sociales* 64, no. 6: 1237–66.

Feltran, Gabriel. 2019. "(Il)licit Economies in Brazil: An Ethnographic Perspective." *Journal of Illicit Economies and Development* 1, no. 2: 145–54.

Friedberg, Susanne. 2003. "French Beans for the Masses: A Modern Historical Geography of Food in Burkina Faso." *Journal of Historical Geography* 29, no. 3: 445–63.

Gambetta, Diego. 1996. *The Sicilian Mafia: The Business of Private Protection*. Cambridge, MA: Harvard University Press.

Gereffi, Gary. 1994. "The Organization of Buyer-Driven Global Commodity Chains: How U.S. Retailers Shape Overseas Production Networks." In *Commodity Chains and Global Capitalism*, edited by Gary Gereffi and Miguel Korzeniewicz, 95–122. Westport, CT: Praeger.

Gillies, Allan. 2018. "Theorising State–Narco Relations in Bolivia's Nascent Democracy (1982–1993): Governance, Order and Political Transition." *Third World Quarterly* 39, no. 4: 727–46.

Goldstein, Daniel. 2004. *Spectacular City: Violence and Performance in Urban Bolivia*. Durham, NC: Duke University Press.

Goodman, Michael. 2004. "Reading Fair Trade: Political Ecological Imaginary and the Moral Economy of Fair Trade Foods." *Political Geography* 23, no. 7: 891–915.

Gootenberg, Paul. 2008. *Andean Cocaine: The Making of a Global Drug*. Chapel Hill: University of North Carolina Press.

Graeber, David. 2014. *Debt: The First 5,000 Years*. Brooklyn, NY: Melville House.

Graham, Marty. 2011. "As the Drug War Goes Underground, Feds Call in the Robot." *Wired*, December 19. Accessed December 19, 2018. https://www.wired.com/2011/12/robot-tunnels/.

Grisaffi, Thomas. 2019. *Coca Yes, Cocaine No: How Bolivia's Coca Growers Re-Shaped Democracy*. Durham, NC: Duke University Press.

Grisaffi, Thomas, Linda Farthing, and Kathryn Ledebur. 2017. "Integrated Development with Coca in the Plurinational State of Bolivia: Shifting the Focus from Eradication to Poverty Alleviation." *Bulletin on Narcotics* 41: 131–57.

Grisaffi, Thomas, and Kathryn Ledebur. 2016. "Citizenship or Repression? Coca, Eradication and Development in the Andes." *Stability: International Journal*

*of Security and Development* 5, no. 1. https://www.stabilityjournal.org/articles
/10.5334/sta.440/.

Harvey, David. 2005. *A Brief History of Neoliberalism*. Oxford: Oxford University
Press.

Hirata, Daniel, and Carolina Grillo. 2019. "Movement and Death: Illicit Drug
Markets in the Cities of São Paulo and Rio de Janeiro." *Journal of Illicit Economies and Development* 1, no. 2: 122–33.

Holston, James. 2008. *Insurgent Citizenship: Disjunctions of Democracy and Modernity in Brazil*. Princeton, NJ: Princeton University Press.

Hopkins, Terence, and Immanuel Wallerstein. 1986. "Commodity Chains in the
World-Economy Prior to 1800." *Review (Fernand Braudel Center)* 10, no. 1: 157–70.

Hough, Phillip. 2011. "Disarticulations and Commodity Chains: Cattle, Coca, and
Capital Accumulation along Colombia's Agricultural Frontier." *Environment
and Planning A* 43: 1016–34.

Jaffe, Rivke. 2012. "The Popular Culture of Illegality: Crime and the Politics of
Aesthetics in Urban Jamaica." *Anthropological Quarterly* 85, no. 1: 79–102.

Jaffe, Rivke. 2013. "The Hybrid State: Crime and Citizenship in Urban Jamaica."
*American Ethnologist* 40, no. 4: 734–48.

Kalyvas, Stathis. 2006. *The Logic of Violence in Civil War*. Cambridge: Cambridge
University Press.

Kalyvas, Stathis. 2015. "How Civil Wars Help Explain Organized Crime—And
How They Do Not." *Journal of Conflict Resolution* 59, no. 8: 1517–40.

Karandinos, George, Laurie Hart, Fernando Montero Castrillo, and Philippe
Bourgois. 2014. "The Moral Economy of Violence in the US Inner City." *Current Anthropology* 55, no. 1: 1–22.

Kernaghan, Richard. 2009. *Coca's Gone: Of Might and Right in the Huallaga Post-
Boom*. Stanford, CA: Stanford University Press.

Klein, Axel, and Blaine Stothard, eds. 2018. *Collapse of the Global Order on Drugs:
From UNGASS 2016 to Review 2019*: Bingley, UK: Emerald.

Koch, Insa. 2017. "Moving beyond Punitivism: Punishment, State Failure and
Democracy at the Margins." *Punishment and Society* 19, no. 2: 203–20.

Koster, Martijn, and Alan Smart. 2019. "Performing In/Formality beyond the
Dichotomy." *Anthropologica* 61: 20–24.

Lessing, Benjamin. 2017. *Making Peace in Drug Wars: Crackdowns and Cartels in
Latin America*. Cambridge: Cambridge University Press.

Lessing, Benjamin, and Graham Denyer Willis. 2019. "Legitimacy in Criminal
Governance: Managing a Drug Empire from Behind Bars." *American Political
Science Review* 113, no. 2: 584–606.

Levitt, Steven, and Sudhir Venkatesh. 2000. "An Economic Analysis of a Drug-
Selling Gang's Finances." *Quarterly Journal of Economics* 115: 755–56.

LSE IDEAS. 2014. "Ending the Drug Wars." In *Report of the LSE Expert Group on the
Economics of Drug Policy*, edited by John Collins. London: London School of
Economics.

Marosi, Richard. 2011. "Ultralight Aircraft Now Ferrying Drugs across US-Mexico Border." *Los Angeles Times*, May 19. https://www.latimes.com/archives/la-xpm -2011-may-19-la-me-border-ultralight-20110520-story.html.

Mauss, Marcel. 1990. *The Gift: Forms and Functions of Exchange in Archaic Societies.* London: Routledge.

May, Channing. 2017. *Transnational Crime and the Developing World.* Washington, DC: Global Financial Integrity.

McSweeney, Kendra, David Wrathall, Erik Nielsen, and Zoe Pearson. 2018. "Grounding Traffic: The Cocaine Commodity Chain and Land Grabbing in Eastern Honduras." *Geoforum* 95: 122–32.

Michelutti, Lucia, Ashraf Hoque, Nicolas Martin, David Picherit, Paul Rollier, Arild Ruud, and Clarinda Still, eds. 2018. *Mafia Raj: The Rule of Bosses in South Asia.* Stanford, CA: Stanford University Press.

Midgette, Gregory, Steven Davenport, Jonathan Caulkins, and Beau Kilmer. 2019. *What America's Users Spend on Illegal Drugs, 2006–2016.* Santa Monica, CA: RAND Corporation.

Mintz, Sidney. 1986. *Sweetness and Power: The Place of Sugar in Modern History.* Harmondsworth, UK: Penguin.

Morrison, Shona. 1997. "The Dynamics of Illicit Drugs Production: Future Sources and Threats." *Crime, Law and Social Change* 27, no. 2: 121–38.

Muehlmann, Shaylih. 2013. *When I Wear My Alligator Boots.* Berkeley: University of California Press.

Müller, Markus-Michael. 2015. "Punitive Entanglements: The 'War on Gangs' and the Making of a Transnational Penal Apparatus in the Americas." *Geopolitics* 20, no. 3: 696–727.

Nordstrom, Carolyn. 2007. *Global Outlaws: Crime, Money, and Power in the Contemporary World.* Berkeley: University of California Press.

OAS. 2013. "The Economics of Drug Trafficking." In *The Drug Problem in the Americas: Studies.* Washington, DC: Organization of American States.

O'Donnell, Guillermo. 1993. "On the State, Democratization, and Some Conceptual Problems: A Latin American View with Glances at Some Postcommunist Countries." *World Development* 21: 1355–69.

Oosterbaan, Martijn. 2009. "Sonic Supremacy: Sound, Space and Charisma in a Favela in Rio de Janeiro." *Critique of Anthropology* 29: 81–104.

Palomera, Jaime, and Theodora Vetta. 2016. "Moral Economy: Rethinking a Radical Concept." *Anthropological Theory* 16, no. 4: 413–32.

Piot, Charles. 1999. *Remotely Global: Village Modernity in West Africa.* Chicago: University of Chicago Press.

Polanyi, Karl. 1957. *The Great Transformation: The Political and Economic Origin of Our Time.* Boston: Beacon.

Ramirez, Maria Clemencia. 2011. *Between the Guerrillas and the State: The Cocalero Movement, Citizenship and Identity in the Colombian Amazon.* Durham, NC: Duke University Press.

Rios, Viridiana. 2015. "How Government Coordination Controlled Organized Crime: The Case of Mexico's Cocaine Markets." *Journal of Conflict Resolution* 59, no. 8: 1–22.

Rodgers, Dennis. 2009. "Slum Wars of the 21st Century: Gangs, Mano Dura and the New Urban Geography of Conflict in Central America." *Development and Change* 40, no. 5: 949–76.

Rodgers, Dennis. 2015. "The Moral Economy of Murder." In *Violence at the Urban Margins*, edited by Javier Auyero, Philippe Bourgois, and Nancy Scheper-Hughes. Oxford: Oxford University Press.

Roitman, Janet. 2006. "The Ethics of Illegality in the Chad Basin." In *Law and Disorder in the Postcolony*, edited by Jean Comaroff and John Comaroff, 247–72. Chicago: Chicago University Press.

Sanchez, Andrew. 2016. *Criminal Capital: Violence, Corruption and Class in Industrial India*. London: Routledge.

Sanchez, Andrew, James Carrier, Christopher Gregory, James Laidlaw, Marilyn Strathern, Yunxiang Yan, and Jonathan Parry. 2017. "The Indian Gift: A Critical Debate." *History and Anthropology* 28, no. 5: 553–83.

Scheper-Hughes, Nancy. 2000. "The Global Traffic in Human Organs." *Current Anthropology* 41, no. 2: 191–224.

Scott, James C. 1977. *The Moral Economy of the Peasant: Rebellion and Subsistence in Southeast Asia*. New Haven, CT: Yale University Press.

Sneed, Paul. 2008. "Favela Utopias: The Bailes Funk in Rio's Crisis of Social Exclusion and Violence." *Latin American Research Review* 43, no. 2: 57–79.

Snyder, Richard, and Angélica Durán-Martínez. 2009. "Does Illegality Breed Violence? Drug Trafficking and State Sponsored Protection Rackets." *Crime, Law and Social Change* 52: 253–273.

Stares, Paul. 1996. *Global Habit*. Washington, DC: Brookings Institution.

Statista. 2020. "The 100 Largest Companies in the World Ranked by Revenue in 2019." Accessed July 11, 2020. https://www.statista.com/statistics/263265 /top-companies-in-the-world-by-revenue/.

Thompson, Edward P. 1971. "The Moral Economy of the English Crowd in the Eighteenth Century." *Past and Present* 50: 76–136.

Thoumi, Francisco. 2003. *Illegal Drugs, Economy, and Society in the Andes*. Washington, DC: Woodrow Willson Center.

Trejo, Guillermo, and Sandra Ley. 2018. "Why Did Drug Cartels Go to War in Mexico? Subnational Party Alternation, the Breakdown of Criminal Protection, and the Onset of Large-Scale Violence." *Comparative Political Studies* 51, no. 7: 900–937.

Ungar, Mark. 2011. *Policing Democracy: Overcoming Obstacles to Citizen Security in Latin America*. Baltimore: Johns Hopkins University Press.

UNODC. 2005. *Alternative Development: A Global Thematic Evaluation*. New York: United Nations Office on Drugs and Crime.

UNODC. 2017. *Colombia: Monitoreo de territorios afectados por cultivos ilícitos 2016*. Bogotá: United Nations Office on Drugs and Crime.

UNODC. 2018a. *Estado Plurinacional de Bolivia: Monitoreo de Cultivos de Coca: 2017*. La Paz: Oficina de las Naciones Unidas Contra la Droga y el Delito.

UNODC. 2018b. *World Drug Report 2018: Analysis of Drug Markets*. Vienna: United Nations Office on Drugs and Crime.

UNODC. 2019. *World Drug Report 2019: Book 4, Stimulants*. Vienna: United Nations Office on Drugs and Crime.

UNODC. 2020. "Drug Supply: Book 3." In *World Drug Report 2020*. Vienna: United Nations Office on Drugs and Crime.

Varese, Federico. 2001. *The Russian Mafia: Private Protection in a New Market Economy*. Oxford: Oxford University Press.

Vellinga, Menno. 2007. "The Illegal Drug Industry in Latin America: The Coca-Cocaine Value Chain." *Iberoamericana: Nordic Journal of Latin American and Caribbean Studies* 37, no. 2: 89–105.

Wacquant, Loïc. 2014. "The Global Firestorm of Law and Order: On Punishment and Neoliberalism." *Thesis Eleven* 122, no. 1: 72–88.

Wakeman, Stephen. 2016. "The Moral Economy of Heroin in 'Austerity Britain.'" *Critical Criminology* 24, no. 3: 363–77.

Wilson, Suzanne, and Marta Zambrano. 1994. "Cocaine, Commodity Chains, and Drug Policings: A Transnational Approach." In *Commodity Chains and Global Capitalism*, edited by Gary Gereffi and Miguel Korzeniewicz, 297–316. Westport, CT: Greenwood.

Woody, Christopher. 2016. "'El Chapo' Guzmán Had More Airplanes Than the Biggest Airline in Mexico." *Business Insider*, May 4. https://www.businessinsider.com/el-chapo-guzman-mexico-drug-trafficking-airplanes-2016-5.

Zaloom, Caitlin. 2006. *Out of the Pits: Traders and Technology from Chicago to London*. Chicago: Chicago University Press.

# 01 THE WHITE FACTORY

COCA, COCAINE, AND INFORMAL GOVERNANCE
IN THE CHAPARE, BOLIVIA

The best time to plant coca is in the rainy season when the ground is wet and soft. My friend Milton walked in front of me, digging out holes in the damp soil with a stick, and I followed behind, placing a small coca plant into each one and closing the earth around it. After an hour or so, my back was hurting, and I was sweating in the tropical heat. Milton finally called a break. We sat in the shade of a tree and shared a bag of coca leaves. Milton, like many peasant farmers in Bolivia, consumes coca most days. He packed a wad of leaves into the side of his cheek and added a small amount of bicarbonate of soda to release the leaf's active property, cocaine alkaloid. The level of cocaine is very low, but it has a positive impact, energizing the chewer.

I was wearing a T-shirt that I had bought in a tourist market in the city of Cochabamba. Across the back it read "coca is not cocaine" in Spanish. It made Milton laugh; he joked, "Well sometimes it is . . . actually coca usually is cocaine." I was unsure how to react; during fieldwork people would often challenge me about my views on coca; it was generally assumed that as I was a foreigner I would think that coca was a truly awful thing. And so, wary not to offend Milton and be perceived as an imperialist "gringo," I stuffed a bunch of leaves into my mouth and insisted that I thought it was a perfectly fine shrub. Milton laughed at me: "Come on, Tomás, where do you think all the coca really goes? You think people can chew all this coca? If there was no cocaine, then there would be no coca trade. It all goes to the 'white factory.'"

I was surprised by Milton's candid admission about cocaine production—the so-called white factory. I had visited the region many times since 2005, but until that point nobody had wanted to talk openly about drugs. Most people either avoided my questions or flat-out denied it went on. I had tried in every possible way to make clear to people that I was not judgmental; going out in the heat to plant coca and chewing the leaf to stress solidarity was one way to do this. Finally, Milton and others rewarded me for my perseverance and opened up about this controversial issue.

...........................

Indigenous communities throughout the Andean region have used the coca leaf for spiritual and medicinal purposes for thousands of years, but the coca leaf is also the raw material used to produce cocaine. Bolivia is caught at the very lowest rungs of the international drug trade; it is the world's third largest producer of coca leaf after Colombia and Peru, and produces an estimated 275 metric tons of cocaine annually ("Peru and Bolivia Are Unlikely Allies" 2018). According to some economists, the coca-cocaine circuit is the third largest source of revenue for Bolivia, after hydrocarbons and mining (Schipani 2010). In contrast to other nations where cocaine production and trafficking are widespread, illegal drugs are not associated with high levels of violence in Bolivia (UNODC 2020: 53).

Drawing on long-term ethnographic fieldwork carried out between 2005 and 2019, I present a case study from the Cochabamba Tropics (also known as the Chapare), one of Bolivia's two principal coca-growing zones, to analyze the motivations, consequences, and functioning of cocaine paste production, a first step toward making refined cocaine. We will see that the majority of the population are involved in the illicit trade, through engaging in growing, drying, and commercializing coca leaf, processing cocaine paste, or smuggling precursor chemicals. Most farmers do not consider participation in the drug trade to be a moral question; cocaine paste processing is simply a way to make a living in a geographic space where few other economic opportunities exist. In telling this story, this chapter stands in stark contrast to Zellers-León's account in this volume.

I advance two main arguments. First, I argue that we cannot understand how the local drug economy functions unless we comprehend how it is rooted in deeper social processes, namely "reciprocity" as a guiding principle of everyday sociality. I illustrate how the illicit trade, which involves a complex local supply chain, builds on existing social relationships, but is also generative of new relations, and as such, draws people together into dense networks of debt and dependency while simultaneously excluding outsiders. Drug workers are called on to reinvest some of their profits into social relationships through the sponsorship of community-oriented activities. The community works together as a corporate unit to ensure the steady production of coca and cocaine paste, for the benefit of all.

Second, while the agricultural unions that operate in the Chapare cannot and should not be thought of as criminal organizations, they nevertheless unwittingly facilitate the illegal trade. This is because they exclude the state and keep international drug trafficking organizations at bay, allowing drug processors to go about their work with minimal disruption. In addition, the unions act as a parallel form of governance in the region, thereby providing a framework for the enforcement of illicit contracts and the peaceful resolution of disputes. Taken together, these factors mean that, far from generating chaos, disorder, and inequality, the illegal drug trade contributes to the region's economic prosperity and social and political stability.

This chapter begins with an overview of coca, outlining its traditional uses and the legislation controlling its production and sale. It then traces the history of migration to the Chapare, drawing attention to the way colonization was intimately bound to the growth of the illicit drug industry. The final section examines cocaine paste production in the Chapare today, with an emphasis on the way the movement of cocaine ties people together into dense social networks and the role the unions play in governing the region. The conclusion reflects on the Chapare's place in the drug commodity chain and the potential future impacts of any change to drug policy at the international level.

### COCA LEAF: SACRED AND PROFANE

Coca (*Erythroxylum coca*) is a perennial shrub native to the Andean region, where it has been grown and used for medicinal and nutritional purposes for up to eight thousand years (Dillehay et al. 2010). Coca is most often chewed, but it can also be consumed as a tea. Users value its properties as a mild stimulant, suppressing feelings of hunger, thirst, and fatigue. Unlike Peru and Colombia, where coca use is restricted, in Bolivia coca use "... is accepted across most sectors, regions, and ethnicities" (Gootenberg 2017: 5). An EU-funded study published in 2013 concluded that about 3 million Bolivians, around 30 percent of the population, chew coca on a regular basis, and the majority consume coca as a tea or in the form of other legal coca-based products (CONALTID 2013). Alongside its nutritional value, coca serves important social and cultural functions. It is a central element of rituals from birth to death, and many consider the leaf to be sacred (Carter and Mamani 1986). The widespread use of coca in Bolivia has contributed to what Paul Gootenberg (2017: 5) has referred to as "coca nationalism" (see also Ehrinpreis 2018).

The reason Andeans have long held coca in such high esteem is precisely because it contains cocaine alkaloid, the chemical that makes coca powerful, but also dangerous in the eyes of lawmakers. In 1961 the UN listed the coca leaf as a "schedule one drug" alongside the most dangerous and restricted substances, including heroin and cocaine on the UN Single Convention on Narcotics. Bolivia's military government ratified the Convention in 1976. The UN Convention calls on signatory governments to eradicate all coca bushes, even those that grow wild, and to abolish the traditional practice of coca leaf chewing, within twenty-five years of ratification. The 1961 Convention thus provided the justification and legal framework for subsequent US-backed forced coca eradication policies in the Andes, including Bolivia's draconian anti-drug Law 1008 that outlawed cultivation in the Chapare (Farthing 1997).

The US drug warriors' focus in the Andean region has been the aggressive eradication of coca crops. Eradication is most often done manually: military conscripts, accompanied by heavily armed members of the police, enter small farmsteads to uproot coca plantations. Forced eradication has proven to be both ineffective and damaging: eradicating crops destroys local economies, criminalizes some of the poorest and most vulnerable sectors of society, and legitimizes repressive policing. In the Andean region, eradication teams have killed, abused, and seriously wounded scores of coca farmers, torched homesteads, and incarcerated thousands of people (Youngers and Rosin 2005). Not only has crop eradication sown violence; it has manifestly failed to achieve its goal of reducing coca acreage. All it does is displace coca cultivation to new areas, contributing to deforestation (Reyes 2014).

The election of President Evo Morales (2006–19) and his Movimiento al Socialismo (MAS) party marked a sea change for drug policy in Bolivia. Morales, an indigenous Aymara and former coca grower, argued that coca in its natural state is not a drug and that it could benefit humanity. In 2009 Morales chewed coca leaf at the UN in Vienna, stating: "We're for the coca leaf but against cocaine." He went on to argue that the ban of the crop amounted to a ban of a culture, and was a "major historical mistake" (Grim 2009). In 2013 Bolivia scored an important victory when it won the right to permit legal coca leaf chewing on Bolivian territory. However, the international export of coca-based products, such as coca tea, soap, or candies, remains a proscribed activity (Jelsma 2016).

Early in his first term, Morales moved to fulfill his campaign promise to break with the US-backed anti-drug strategy, which focused on the forced eradication of coca crops and the criminalization of growers. The new policy, known as "coca yes—cocaine no," draws on the coca growers' own distinction between coca leaf and cocaine: building on a 2004 agreement between coca growers and the Carlos Mesa administration (2003–5), it legalized the cultivation of a small amount of coca leaf in specific zones (known as a *cato*), encouraged the coca unions to self-police to ensure growers do not exceed this limit, and envisioned the industrialization and export of (legal) coca-based products. Scholars have hailed Bolivia's approach as a less repressive and more effective way to control coca production (Grisaffi and Ledebur 2016; Pearson 2016). And yet there is a contradiction here, because while Morales talked about coca as a legitimate crop with myriad legal uses, as Milton remarked in the introduction to this chapter, "coca usually is cocaine."

## COCA, COCAINE, AND COLONIZATION

The Cochabamba Tropics, or the Chapare as it is more commonly known is, along with the Yungas near La Paz, one of Bolivia's two major coca-growing zones. It's a vast region equivalent in size to New Hampshire, stretching over three provinces, Chapare, Tiraque, and Carrasco. The population of this tropical agricultural zone stands at just shy of 200,000 people; the majority are migrants from the Cochabamba valleys and mining centers in the highlands, many of whom were previously engaged in militant miners' trade unions (INE 2014). Over 80 percent of the local population self-identify as Quechua, and most people are bilingual, speaking both Quechua and Spanish (PNUD 2005: 302).

Farmers from the highlands and valleys first settled this frontier jungle region in the 1950s and 1960s. The "colonizers," or "pioneers" as they call themselves, formed into self-governing units known as *sindicatos* (syndicates or agricultural unions) and set out into the jungle to claim land. Among the first things the colonizers did were clearing an area for a football pitch and constructing a building for their monthly union meeting (see figure 1.1). When they were first established, the unions were mainly responsible for controlling land, but their remit soon extended far beyond that. Given the almost total absence of the state, the unions became the de facto regional authorities responsible for managing and taxing the coca

FIGURE 1.1 A coca union meeting.

trade, administering justice, and investing in and building small-scale public works such as roads, schools, health clinics, and river defenses—an example of what Idler (this volume) describes as "shadow citizenship." "Back then there was nothing; we had to organize and do it ourselves like little states. If we wanted roads, we made them, if we wanted a school-house, we built it," said one farmer. To this day the unions play an important role in self-governance, but they have to constantly negotiate their autonomy with an encroaching state (Grisaffi 2019: 84–108).

The settlers established small farms on plots measuring between five and ten hectares, and planted a range of crops including maize, rice, citrus fruits, and bananas. From the early days of colonization, coca was a crop that the farmers grew primarily to sell on the market (mostly to the miners in Potosí), and it accounted for the bulk of their cash income (Laserna 2000). Life was tough for the settlers. People recall that it took them a long time to get used to the weather, which is far hotter and more humid than their communities of origin in the highlands and valleys, and they despised the "clouds of mosquitoes." The settlers had a lot to learn; none had experience with warm-weather tropical farming, and some ex-miners, who migrated to the region in the mid 1980s, had no agricultural experience whatsoever. The poor roads meant that it could take several days to get to Cochabamba, the nearest city.

Initially the pace of migration to the Chapare was low, most people lived there for only part of the year, and there were high rates of abandonment (Clawson and Lee 1996: 134). However, this all changed in the late 1970s when increasing demand for cocaine in the United States and to a lesser extent Europe, made cocaine paste the nation's most profitable export commodity. The drug trade got a kick-start when Colombian criminal organizations came searching for cheap raw materials—initially coca leaf, but eventually cocaine paste too—which they transported to Colombia to refine into crystallized cocaine (cocaine hydrochloride), and from there exported to the United States and Europe (Gootenberg 2008: 274).

The Chapare's population exploded as tens of thousands of unemployed workers and hard-pressed farmers flocked to the region to seek work in the illicit industry, hitting a high of 400,000 in the mid-1980s— double what it is today (Dunkerley 1990: 45). Most migrants were involved in growing, drying, or marketing coca leaves. Others found work processing cocaine paste in primitive workshops located close to the coca fields, where they earned relatively high wages in comparison with other forms of unskilled labor (Rivera 1990). The local cocaine trade also generated indirect employment, including jobs for bartenders, traders, taxi drivers, and restaurateurs. In addition, a large number of people who transported the inputs necessary to process cocaine such as gasoline, chalk, and bicarbonate of soda also participated in the industry. To give but one example, James Painter (1994: 57) describes how in the mid-1980s at least two thousand people were involved in transporting and selling toilet paper in the Chapare, which processors also used for filtering and drying cocaine paste.

A local shopkeeper described the Chapare at that time as being in the midst of a "gold rush." He said he could shift bicycles, crates of rum, and radios with ease. Inflation was rampant, and the Chapare became one of the most expensive places in the country to live, with a single bread roll costing more than a dollar. And yet, while there was money in the tropics, the conditions were hard. The drug workers—known locally as *pichicateros*—lived on a diet of tinned sardines and noodles, and they took shelter in makeshift houses constructed from rough-cut planks, thatched roofs, and beaten mud floors. The combination of the precariousness of cocaine production, the emerging threat of the US-backed "war on drugs," and the fact that for many the Chapare was simply not a nice place to live ruled out permanent investment in the region. The migrants, who were overwhelmingly men, invested their cash in the city of Cochabamba, where the streets teemed with new cars and there was a construction boom; the Chapare meanwhile remained a pocket of rural poverty.

The "coca boom" (1979–85) could not have come at a better time. The Bolivian economy was battered by the combination of a severe drought, hyperinflation, and a draconian government-engineered deflation that pushed unemployment to over 20 percent (Dunkerley 1990). Bolivia's economic safety net through this tumultuous time was the coca and cocaine trade, which generated between $600 million and $1 billion annually, matching (if not exceeding) total revenue from all legal exports (De Franco and Godoy 1992: 387). The cocaine dollars trickled down to support a large informal economy and absorbed labor from the rapidly declining mining and industrial sectors (Blanes 1989; Mansilla 1992). James Painter (1994: 54) has argued that in so doing, coca and cocaine provided "critical support" for the success of the National Revolutionary Movement government's austerity program (referred to as "economic stabilization").

The coca growers and cocaine paste processors were not the major beneficiaries of this industry, however. They are best thought of as the "proletariat" of the cocaine trade (Aguilo 1986). The real winners were the large-scale landowners in the states of Beni and Santa Cruz, who managed the refinement and transport of cocaine paste outside the country. They were ideally placed for this trade as they had large holdings of land in remote parts of the country, airplanes, and landing strips (Dunkerley 1984: 318–19). Most importantly, these landowners were well connected to military and political elites, who in some cases became directly involved in the illicit trade (Gillies 2018).

## COCA UNION MOBILIZATION

In July 1986, when the coca trade was booming, the Reagan administration, in collaboration with the Bolivian government, sent 160 US soldiers to Bolivia to initiate efforts to destroy drug laboratories and to set up and train La Unidad Móvil de Patrullaje Rural (the Rural Mobile Patrol Unit), more popularly known by its acronym UMOPAR, the special anti-drug police force. "Operation Blast Furnace," as it was known, marked the start of US involvement in Bolivian drug control, an issue that would henceforth define

US-Bolivian relations (Grandin 2006: 215–18). The repression of the drug trade fell disproportionately on the peasant farmers, who gain the least from the trade, while the "big fish" were seldom arrested (Dunkerley 1990: 45).

In 1988, Bolivia passed anti-drug Law 1008 (in force until 2017) under heavy US pressure. Law 1008 permitted 12,000 hectares of coca cultivation in the Yungas of La Paz to supply the domestic legal market; all other coca, including that in the Chapare, was outlawed and slated for eradication. Initially, the Bolivian government paid Chapare farmers two thousand dollars per hectare to eradicate their crops, but this policy failed. For every coca plant destroyed, the farmers planted new coca seedlings elsewhere, and total acreage kept creeping up (Clawson and Lee 1996: 221). One farmer explained that they would take the eradication payment and reinvest it in new crops, while the military did the hard work of uprooting old and unproductive plantations. "We're not stupid," he said. Given the poor results, in 1997 the Hugo Banzer administration (1997–2001), followed by his vice president Jorge Quiroga (2001–2), implemented a no-holds-barred forced eradication program.

The militarized approach dramatically reduced coca cultivation in the region, but the security forces were repeatedly denounced for their gross violation of human rights (Ledebur 2005; Salazar Ortuño 2008: 137–238). The carrot was an ill-thought-out USAID-led scheme to encourage farmers to grow legal crops, but these projects repeatedly failed to implement viable programs to benefit coca growers and their families. As a result, forced eradication caused economic hardship and fueled discontent (Marconi 1998; Farthing and Kohl 2005).

In the face of ongoing military and police repression, the Chapare coca growers' unions organized their 45,000 members to resist the state's anti-coca policies by blocking roads, leading marches, and staging national-level protests. The union also set up its own party in 1995, which eventually became the MAS (Anria 2018: 62–69).[1] The unions argued that they were small-scale farmers producing a crop for which there was no substitute that could yield even remotely comparable earnings. Further, they drew attention to the sacred status of coca leaf for Andean indigenous peoples, arguing that the US-backed attack on coca was an attack on the very idea of Bolivian sovereignty. In the context of a growing global indigenous rights movement, the union's emphasis on coca's cultural and symbolic significance gained domestic and international support, propelling coca union leader Evo Morales to the presidency (Grisaffi 2010; Vargas 2014).

As I sat drinking a soda in a shabby roadside bar with Mauricio, a coca farmer in his late thirties, a beat-up Toyota Corolla sped by with the police in hot pursuit. Mauricio explained that whoever was in the car must have been caught with drugs at the police checkpoint, which was only ten miles down the road. Mauricio was unhappy about the dangerous driving: "There are kids about, they could have killed someone!" he said. But when I asked him what he thought about the fact that they were drug traffickers, his response was muted: "Look, a person has to make a living from something." Mauricio's words summed up the view of most coca farmers, who see participation in the drug trade as a commonsense response to a difficult economic situation. He went on to explain that "everyone is involved in the white factory . . . somehow."

Mauricio grew up in the Chapare but spent several years living in the city of Cochabamba, where he worked as an administrator in local government. He moved back to the region in 2008 to be closer to his parents and to help them out on their farm. Five years later, in 2013, he decided to set up a cocaine paste workshop. This was not an unusual career choice, but rather a logical step along a well-trodden path, one that, in an overwhelmingly male-dominated trade, his brothers and uncles had taken before him. Mauricio was enthusiastic about the opportunity to make some cash from this new venture. He told me, "Look, I worked in public administration but the wage is really low. Here [in the Chapare] I can make money from coca. The life is better, there is no obligation to go the office every day." He explained that with coca cultivation and his "other occupation," drug processing (known locally as *pichicata*), he could make well over US$1,000 a month, a substantial income in a country where the monthly minimum wage is less than $300. He was obviously doing well; when I last saw him in August 2019, he was driving an almost new pickup truck, and he informed me that his daughters were studying at a private school in the city of Cochabamba.

The first step in processing cocaine is relatively simple.[2] The drug workers soak shredded coca leaves in a mixture of gasoline, sulfuric acid, and caustic soda to extract the cocaine alkaloid. These days most drug workers use leaf shredders, adapted cement mixers, and large tanks of up to a thousand liters to turn over the mulch. But these are recent developments. When I began fieldwork in 2005, everything was done by hand. Most workshops relied on young men, known as *pisa-cocas*, to stomp on the coca leaf for several hours to mix up the solution. This is a particularly noxious task that turns the coca stomper's toenails green. The costs associated with entering the cocaine paste trade are low. The equipment is cheap to buy, the skills required are easy to learn, and processors can purchase the chemicals at a hardware store or gas station. Even so, not just anyone can set up a cocaine paste workshop. Only local people who are embedded in their community have access to the necessary inputs. To understand why this is the case, we have to examine more closely Andean notions of reciprocity and how those ideas operate in the context of the cocaine trade.

Anthropologists have long argued that reciprocity is a core organizing principle of Andean indigenous communities (Harris 2000; Bolton 2002). In the Chapare this is no different; from the perspective of most Chapare farmers, a "good person" is not a self-reliant individual, but rather someone who demonstrates loyalty and care toward people and place (see Grisaffi 2019: 96–100). Farmers in the Chapare use the Quechua term *ayni* (mutual aid) to refer to the constant exchanges that characterize daily life (see Allen 1981: 165). Ayni can be practiced in a number of ways. People might gift one another food, work in a neighbor's fields for no pay, or even lend unused portions of their land to others so that they might farm it. The point is, each person has to be entangled in the lives of others, offering support when called on, but also asking for assistance in turn. These daily exchanges tie people into dense relationships of debt and dependency and become a central way of drawing boundaries between insiders and outsiders (Albó 2002: 10). Only those who live up to these social expectations are considered to be true members of the community and deserving of its protection. They are the ones who are able to engage in the region's main economic activity—namely drug production. Let us now consider each step of the drug trade to elaborate on this point.

To make one kilo of cocaine paste, the owner of a workshop requires at least six sacks of coca (although often they use more), each weighing fifty pounds.[3] They buy this coca from accredited merchants, who are mostly local women and landowners in their own right (see figure 1.2). In theory the merchants are supposed to take all of the coca they buy from local farmers to the official state-sanctioned coca market in Sacaba, on the outskirts of the city of Cochabamba, to be sold for traditional uses such as chewing or the celebration of rituals like the Q'owa, but hardly any of the Chapare crop ends up there.[4] Rather, the merchants divert the coca so that it might feed the illicit local and national cocaine trade. They do this because the drug processors pay around twenty cents per pound over the going price at state-sanctioned markets.[5]

FIGURE 1.2  Coca merchants wait outside the market to buy coca.

The sale of coca in the Chapare is not a free market. At the very bottom of the chain are the farmers. They grow coca leaf, which they dry and pack into fifty-pound sacks (see figure 1.3). Depending on the quality of the land, they might produce anywhere between four and eight sacks per cato (a plot measuring 40 × 40 meters) every three to four months. Like any agricultural product, the price of coca fluctuates significantly. Over the period I conducted fieldwork (2005–19) the price has been as low as nine Bolivianos ($1.30) to over fifty Bolivianos ($7.30) per pound. The farmers sell their coca to a local merchant who, more often than not, is a member of their extended kin group, a sister, cousin, or affine, or someone who they are tied to through fictive kinship, known as *compadrazgo* (godparenthood). In turn, the merchants look after the farmers' interests, including providing them with cash advances for a portion of the harvest or helping out the farmer's children economically—including acting as godparents to them.[6]

When it comes to selling the coca, Merchants also operate within restricted networks. The amount of coca available on a particular day is finite, and the coca merchants will only sell to established contacts; this often means their kin relations and members of their base-level union—in other words, their neighbors. The merchants will simply not sell coca in large

FIGURE 1.3 Drying coca in the Chapare.

quantities to people they do not know—first, because they are suspicious of outsiders as a result of decades of US Drug Enforcement Administration (DEA) spying,[7] and second because if they sold the coca to an unknown party, they would be letting down their regular clients, who might shun them on a future occasion.

Gasoline is another important input. To process each kilo of cocaine paste, the drug workers require at least one hundred liters (about twenty-six gallons) of gasoline, along with a range of other chemicals. However, there are tight controls on the movement of these precursors. Local gas stations only allow people to buy one tank per day, and they add pink dye to it, which makes it less attractive for cocaine paste production. There are also regular checkpoints along the roads where the police search vehicles, impounding suspicious chemicals and arresting smugglers. As a result, the essential ingredients are in short supply. Given the difficulty of buying gasoline locally, taxi drivers who ply the route from the Chapare to Cochabamba, a four-hour ride, smuggle fuel, doubling the price in and around the coca-growing region to about ten bolivianos per liter.[8] Like coca, this is not a free market. Smugglers will only ever sell chemicals to their regular clients, who they are often tied to through kinship or compadrazgo.

Finally, there is the issue of where the cocaine workshop should be located. A drug processing site does not take up much space, but generally people do not want one located on their property since, if a coca union–led commission or the police discover it, the farmer will lose his or her land and potentially face a jail sentence. Drug workers, then, have two options. They can either set up a workshop on their own land, with all the risk that this entails, or they can set it up on someone else's land and pay a "ground rent," transferring the risk to someone else. For Mauricio (introduced above), the latter option was more appealing. His parents' land was located along a main road and as such it was easily accessible to the militarized police (UMOPAR), raising the likelihood that he would be caught. But also because of its location in the main colonization area, the land had high value, and it made no sense to risk losing it. Mauricio therefore decided to establish his workshop in a remote jungle area and pay the landowner, who was the godson of Mauricio's parents, a fee for doing so.

In 2013 Mauricio was a new entrant in the illicit trade. He was able to establish his workshop because, while he had lived away from the Chapare for some years, he was by no means an outsider. Mauricio was a member of an established and respected Chapare family. As such he had the contacts necessary to rent land for his workshop and acquire the necessary inputs. He secured a steady supply of coca from an aunt and gasoline from his godfather. His siblings, meanwhile, helped him cover the US$4,000 start-up costs. Mauricio pledged to repay the money with interest once he had sold his first batch of cocaine paste. He spoke of his siblings as "partners" or "investors." Mauricio hired three of his male cousins, aged between sixteen and eighteen years, to do the hard work. These laborers, known as *peons*, were responsible for carrying the heavy bags of coca, moving barrels of chemicals, and operating the machinery, for which they were paid around thirty dollars per *entrada* (session). Mauricio had worked as a pisa-coca stomper in his youth and, as a result, he was familiar with the process and able to oversee operations and act as a "cook" or "chemist."

From the very beginning Mauricio knew he would sell the cocaine paste to Don Jenaro, a local man who was also Mauricio's godfather and who had paid for his wedding celebrations. Jenaro had a plot of land where he grew coca and oranges, but he also had a side business as an *acopiador* (collector). This involved buying up bricks of cocaine paste—valued at between $1,600 and $1,800 dollars in 2019—and arranging for them to be delivered to buyers in the city. When the paste was ready, Jenaro would visit Mauricio at his home to check the product and pay for it. This was normally a convivial

FIGURE 1.4  Travel by canoe in the Chapare.

moment; Jenaro would bring along a bottle of Singani, a type of brandy produced in Bolivia, so that they could share a few drinks together. Along with Mauricio, Jenaro had many other "godchildren," and all of them were duty-bound to sell the paste they produced to him. He was, after all, their godfather and, in the words of Mauricio, "you cannot deny your *padrino*."

Don Jenaro then hired third parties, normally teenagers, taxi drivers, or members of the large itinerant work force of landless peasants who are always on the lookout for work, to smuggle the drugs out of the region. Packages of cocaine would be taped onto the chests of young children, stowed in car door panels, or loaded into lorries under thousands of oranges. Some carry the product by foot to the city of Cochabamba, a five-day trek with the risk of robbery. People also go on canoe trips along the winding rivers all the way to the department of Beni and farther toward the frontier with Brazil (see figure 1.4, and Robert Gay, this volume). In December 2019, Don Grego, a taxi driver, told me that he would shift fuel to the Chapare and cocaine paste to the city. He moved between thirty and forty kilos each time—he said it was not worth the risk to move less—for which he earned a hundred dollars per kilo. Don Grego said that it was relatively easy to bribe the anti-drug police to get illicit goods through the checkpoints. For every petrol canister he would have to pay the officials around seven dollars, but he said things got a bit more complicated (and expensive) if they discovered cocaine paste.

In Andean indigenous communities there is a strong pressure for resources to be redistributed between community members. In the highlands there are explicit leveling mechanisms in place, which revolve around the sponsorship of saint's day festivals. The sponsors are responsible for paying for lavish feasts, bands, sound systems, decorations, and dance troupes, which can put them into debt for many years (see Abercrombie 1998). In the Chapare, similar leveling mechanisms are at work. Mauricio and others who are involved in drug production have more disposable income than their peers who are not directly involved in these activities, and as such they are strongly pressured by the community to sponsor community-oriented activities such as paying for the school graduation trip, organizing a band for a fiesta, or buying matching uniforms for the local football team. Drug workers might also be asked to act as a padrino or madrina (godfather or godmother) for individuals, for example, to pay for marriage celebrations, first confirmation, or quinceañera celebrations.[9]

Mauricio received many such requests, and he honored each one. In turn he had a great many godchildren and was held in high esteem in the village, feted as a generous and kind person who was worthy of the community's protection. This in turn benefited Mauricio as local people supported his activities, for instance by ensuring he had access to a steady supply of coca leaf and precursor chemicals and that the local agricultural union would not interfere with his business. On the contrary, anyone who the community perceived to have surplus cash, gained through licit or illicit means, but who did not invest in their social relations in this way was said to be immoral and would lose rights within the community. For example, if they worked as a drug processor, the union would close down their workshop and expel them from the community.

## IN THE SHADOW OF THE STATE

The Bolivian state has always had a fragmented presence across Bolivia's territory, leading one UN development project report to classify it as a "state with holes" (PNUD 2007: 99). It is not that these holes represent a vacuum, however; rather, these "non-state spaces" (Scott 2010) have been filled by regional elites, indigenous organizations, social movements, and trade unions, and they exert governing functions. Nowhere is this more true than in the Chapare, where the coca unions constitute "the region's primary civil authority, practicing a de-facto autonomy" (Gutierrez Aguilar 2014: 80).

The agricultural unions of the Chapare are not directly involved in the cocaine trade. On the contrary, the unions oppose illicit cocaine production in their official proclamations, and when Morales was in power (2006–19) the unions collaborated with the state crop-monitoring agency to restrict coca cultivation (Grisaffi 2016; Grisaffi, Farthing, and Ledebur 2017). They have also organized ad hoc commissions to check that no member is producing cocaine paste on union-controlled land. This has had the effect of pushing drug production deeper into the jungle and away from the main colonization areas (Grisaffi 2014).[10] And yet, while the union has made efforts to counter the drug trade, the hegemony it exercises in the region has unwittingly provided a framework that enables the drug trade to function. This is because the union effectively excludes the police, provides alternative dispute resolution mechanisms, and suppresses the activity of criminal organizations. I will now look at each of these in turn.

### The Union Purposely Excludes the Police

It was July 2, 2006, the night of the election for members of an assembly that would rewrite Bolivia's constitution. High-level union leaders and local municipal councillors had gathered on the terrace of the union-owned and -operated radio station to drink beer and listen to the results as they rolled in. The mayor, who was himself a coca grower and union member, had invited the local police commander and his driver to join the party. As the night progressed, people paid less attention to the results and more attention to drinking and dancing. A female union leader asked the male police commander for a dance, he agreed, and this provoked a huge amount of laughter. My friend, Diego, expressed his surprise at the spectacle: "only one year ago you would never have seen this . . . an officer and a *cholita* [female coca grower who wears traditional clothes][11] . . . dancing!"

The dancing police officer was jarring to Diego because until the December 2005 MAS victory, the coca growers had viewed the state as an enemy, one that was set on destroying their livelihoods. The unions purposely excluded the state and would not even permit agents of ostensibly benign arms of the state, such as development workers or those involved in land titling, to enter their communities. The only way the state entered then was through law enforcement activities in the form of militarized interventions conducted by UMOPAR. For Diego, the dance was a sign that with Morales and the MAS in power, this relationship had started to thaw.

But even so, most people continued to be suspicious of the police, who many describe as "more criminal than the criminals."

A police official explained that the regular police (i.e., not the militarized anti-drug police) tend to stay in the main towns and do not venture into the rural hinterland. He said that there are many areas where his officers simply cannot go, or first have to ask permission from the union leadership before they enter. "Here the police, well, we have the law on our side, but they [the coca growers] have more power. They don't just control the unions, but the communities too . . . they decide who comes and who goes . . . we just stay at the margins." For exactly this reason, the police refer to the Chapare as *la tierra de nadie*, a no man's land. Even the militarized special anti-drug police find that their movements are curtailed. There have been reports of coca farmers facing down government troops and even holding members of the UMOPAR hostage when they entered coca union territory without prior consultation ("Cocaleros del Chapare" 2014; Paco 2019).

The state's limited reach has obvious implications for the illicit trade. In the more remote areas of the Chapare, such as the colonization area of Isiboro Secure (Polígono Siete), where state presence is minimal, drug workers can operate safe in the knowledge that police are unlikely to detect and arrest them. Coca farmers described how in these areas the drug trade occurred more or less "in the open." During a December 2019 trip to the Chapare, coca farmers told me that the trafficking of precursor chemicals and drugs was booming. Don Grego, the taxi driver introduced above, explained: "There are no controls, no one is controlling it!" We might consider this hands-off approach to be a positive development given that it is the very policing of the drug trade that in many places has provoked violence and disorder (Lessing 2017).

Coca growers would, on occasion, denounce the illicit activities of their neighbors to the police by, for instance, tipping them off about when a shipment of drugs would pass through the UMOPAR checkpoint or informing on the location of a drug workshop. This was not driven by a desire to see the local trade wiped out, nor to attack a competitor, however. Rather, the involvement of the UMOPAR police was generally a way to punish someone for a personal grievance, which might have nothing to do with the drug industry per se, but might include a perceived lack of respect, a dispute over land boundaries, or marital infidelity, among a range of other factors. Drawing inspiration from Insa Koch (2018), I argue that in these instances the police are used as an ally to pursue personal vendettas rather than to seek an abstract idea of justice or to reduce the illicit drug trade.

Following the November 2019 toppling of Morales, which has been described as a "coup" (Cusicanqui 2019; Levitsky and Murillo 2020), the Chapare population once again has come to view the police as "the enemy." On November 15, 2019, the police suppressed a coca grower–organized march to demand new elections, leaving eleven people dead, 120 injured, and over 180 detained. In response, coca farmers damaged local police installations, forcing the police to abandon the region for several months (Vargas 2019). The farmers hung mannequins dressed as policemen from lampposts along the main road that bore placards reading *"policia pillado, policia linchado"* (police caught, police lynched).[12]

### The Union Has a Role as a Regional Authority

Within the Chapare, the unions function like a parallel state working to address common problems, from administrating land to setting transport fares and maintaining local roads (see Grisaffi 2019: 105–7). One of the most important roles of the local union is to regulate, often in a coercive way, daily coexistence and interaction between members. Ongoing disputes within the community, including robbery, disagreements over land boundaries, or outstanding debts, are dealt with at the monthly union meeting, where the issue is debated and resolved with the participation of the entire community. The union has the power and authority to make sure that people respect communally determined resolutions. As one union member told me, "When we say something, we make people respect it. We are very strict." The union's authority derives from the fact that it controls access to land. If any member contravenes a union mandate, the leadership can order the sale of land at a price they determine and expel the person from the community. This is said to be the most severe punishment because, in the words of one farmer, "If you are expelled from the union, you lose your land, your family, your neighbors—it is like you are an orphan."

In the previous section we saw how coca growers are embedded in complex networks of exchange involving labor, coca, precursor chemicals, and cocaine paste. But of course, the debts that people incur are not always repaid in a timely fashion, and people can and do come into conflict. Disputes between people who work in the drug industry mean disputes between neighbors or even members of the same family, and they tend to be resolved in a pragmatic rather than a violent manner. If people cannot solve a problem on their own, they can turn to the union and have their case heard at the monthly meeting. If a debt is linked to the cocaine trade, such as a failure to pay a worker for processing cocaine paste, the reason will not be publicly acknowledged, however. It will simply be spoken of as an outstanding debt. During fieldwork I witnessed many occasions where debts were settled in a peaceful and calm manner at union meetings. Even if one of the parties was not happy with the final verdict, they nevertheless knew they would have to follow the union's command, because if they did not they risked losing their land.

## The Union Suppresses Organized Criminal Activity

Illegal armed actors operate in coca-growing regions of Colombia (Idler, this volume) and Peru (Grisaffi et al. 2020: 23); they intimidate farmers, dictate prices, and in some cases force people off the land. There have long been media reports that transnational organized crime networks control the drug trade in the Chapare (see, for example, Cuiza 2018), but this seems unlikely. The union is a powerful organization, which is able to mobilize thousands of its members to face down state forces, including setting up armed militias to fight against militarized eradication units. It is inconceivable, then, that a handful of Colombians, Mexicans, or Brazilians would be able to take control of this vast region, a task that even the Bolivian state has been unable to achieve.

The unions take an active role in policing their own communities and providing security. For example, when youth gangs reared their head in the village where I lived, the local union stamped them out immediately. The local *corregidor* (who is responsible for maintaining order and administering justice), a union-appointed position, called on parents to bring their gang-affiliated sons to the main plaza, where he whipped them and forced them to confess their crimes. Outsiders (known locally as *Phistakus*) are treated with the most suspicion, and anyone who is thought to be involved in an activity that goes against the community's interest faces the very real possibility that they will suffer the violence of "community justice." Punishment includes stripping the suspect naked and then tying him or her to the *palo santo*, a tree that is home to thousands of poisonous biting ants, tying up the culprit and dousing them in petrol (this is mostly only ever a threat, but several people have been burned alive), hanging by the neck, or burying them in sand with only their head sticking out. While this behavior might sound brutal, most coca growers support the idea of violent punishment. People say that violent acts send a strong message that will deter people from committing crimes in their area. I was told that "the criminals are afraid to come here" and "they don't dare commit crime here." Vigilantism of this kind is by no means unique to the Chapare, but can be witnessed right across the Andes (Starn 1999; Goldstein 2012; Wemyss 2019).

Finally, while the unions exclude criminal actors, it is also the case that criminal organizations would have no real interest in controlling the Chapare coca or cocaine paste trade, as there would be very little to gain. The union manages the local coca markets and protects the coca plantations from eradication. Thus, there is a guaranteed flow of high-quality coca leaf that is sold to drug processors and traffickers. In addition, while the price of Bolivian coca leaf is higher than either Peruvian or Colombian coca leaf, it is nevertheless the lowest point in the value chain and is labor-intensive to produce. From the perspective of a transnational organized crime group, then, directly governing the coca and cocaine paste trade in the Chapare would not make economic sense. There are more profitable niches that they can dominate.

In 2019, a retired senior official of the special anti-narcotics police force (FELC-N), confirmed that cartels do not operate in Bolivia, but the emissaries of international drug trafficking organizations—who are mostly Colombian—do. They stay in upmarket hotels in the city of Santa Cruz and would not dream of setting foot in the Chapare. They have their local contacts who commission the production, purchase, and transport of the drugs. The official said that the emissaries like doing business in Bolivia precisely because of the low levels of violence. He went on to explain that for the emissaries "Bolivia represents an acceptable level of risk"; they pay for police protection and bribes to the local judiciary: "They know that they are very unlikely to be arrested, and if they are they will spend one year in prison—maximum."

## CONCLUSION

The Bolivian drug trade is entrepreneurial in spirit. Drug workers raise capital, invest in equipment, and hire laborers to manufacture a product, which they sell at a profit. And yet it cannot be understood exclusively through a rational economic lens; local drug workers simply do not act as self-maximizing individuals. Rather, we have seen that the illicit trade has its own logic that prioritizes reciprocity, kinship, and community over self-interested behavior. Drug workers, like Mauricio, utilize preexisting social networks, often built on kinship relations, to secure access to the coca and precursor chemicals they need and to sell the final product. This might mean forgoing profit to honor long-standing commitments to suppliers or buyers. Mauricio reinvests some of his profits into events or goods that benefit everyone. Such gifts oblige others, who in turn look out for his interests. Conversely, people who are not part of these ongoing exchange networks are locked out of participation in the local drug trade. They cannot buy coca leaf or gasoline, hire workers, or work in peace, free from the intrusion of union leaders. In sum, the local cocaine trade is deeply embedded in the community; people work together to produce and traffic cocaine paste in accordance with strongly held ideals of what it means to be a "good person" and to advance their local community.

One of the reasons why the illicit trade is an accepted and tolerated aspect of everyday life is that it continues apace in relative peace. The stability of the trade can be traced to the influence of the unions. In a place where the state's presence is patchy, the unions, which are hegemonic in the region, act as de facto authorities, regulating relations between union members and even nonmembers who reside in the region. Everyone has to abide by the union's orders, and if they do not, they face a range of sanctions, which, as we have seen, can be severe. Thus, when business agreements are not fulfilled, such as when debts go unpaid, the parties in conflict have nonviolent ways to resolve the dispute. In addition, the union excludes the state and keeps criminal organizations at bay. Combined, these factors mean that the drug trade can function in relative peace and contribute to the economic prosperity of the region. This local moral order prioritizes reciprocity, equality among kin and neighbors, and well-being.

I want to conclude by making a broader point regarding drug policy. People took up growing coca and processing cocaine in the first place because of the devastation caused by neoliberal structural adjustment, which left them without jobs or agricultural livelihoods. At its very lowest rungs, the cocaine trade generates high levels of employment, including providing jobs for men and women, and younger and older people, and contributing to (local) economic stability. Indeed, it could be argued that coca cultivation and cocaine paste production are drivers of development, offering farmers an unparalleled avenue for social mobility (see also Pellegrini 2016). Coca cultivation is far more lucrative than "fair trade" coffee or cacao, for instance. Given the important role coca and cocaine paste production play in the regional economy, any change to the cocaine commodity chain will be strongly felt in this region (see also Gutierrez 2020).

The coca unions have never been able to openly and honestly represent the interests of their membership, because to do so would be to acknowledge their dependence on an illicit commodity chain. Instead, the coca growers' unions have always argued that "coca is not cocaine" and promoted the decriminalization of coca leaf, which they say could be used to produce a range of legal products, such as coca tea, diet pills, or liquor. However, this policy might well go against the farmers' interests. If coca were legal, anyone would be able to farm it, and history tells us that when coca plantations are extensive the price drops (see Painter 1994). A more frank conversation is needed about the future of drug policy, one that acknowledges the importance of drug dollars to the poor people who survive at the lowest rung of the international cocaine trade.

## ACKNOWLEDGMENTS

Grisaffi gratefully acknowledges the Global Challenges Research Fund (Drug Crops and Development in the Andes), the European Research Council (Anthropologies of Extortion, ERC-2019-ADG 884839/EXTORT), the Leverhulme Trust and the SSRC/OSF Drugs Security and Democracy Fellowship for funding his research.

### NOTES

1 Leonidas Oikonomakis provides a vivid account of the internal debates that underlined the decision to form the MAS, placing emphasis on the role of organic intellectuals in steering the movement away from armed rebellion (Oikonomakis 2019: 169–94).

2 The cocaine paste still needs to be refined into pure cocaine (known locally as *la fina*), a higher-value product costing around US$5,000 per kilo in Bolivia in 2019. This is a more complex process, requiring high levels of skill, equipment, and expensive chemicals, such as acetone and potassium permanganate, that can only be acquired via the legal chemical industry. The production site might cost up to $300,000 to set up, and count on a workforce of up to thirty people; these are very different from the artisanal cocaine paste workshops found in the Chapare. Within Bolivia, the refining of cocaine mostly takes place in the Beni department, although in 2019 a former anti-narcotics police official explained that over recent years crystallization labs had also been found in the Cochabamba Tropics. Because Peruvian cocaine paste is so much cheaper than its Bolivian equivalent (around $800 per kilo as opposed to $1,800), traffickers buy it to supply the Bolivian-based refineries, with the finished product being shipped to the market in Brazil. As such, Bolivia is at once a production and transshipment site (Paredes 2017).

3 The amount of coca required depends on the processing method, the quality of the precursor chemicals, and the alkaloid content of the leaf. Chapare

coca growers—and in some interviews the police too—take pride in the fact that Chapare coca has a high alkaloid content. Drug workers who employ the mechanized approach and have a good supply of gasoline (meaning they do not have to recycle it) might require only six sacks of coca. In the past, those who relied on the older "coca stomping" method required up to fourteen sacks.

4  A UN study estimated that only 6 percent of Chapare coca ends up in the legal coca market (UNODC 2018).

5  In 2006, when the agricultural union attempted to enforce a rule that merchants must take all their coca to the legal market, the local merchants rebelled against the union leadership.

6  As coca merchants are often wealthier than their coca farmer peers, they are named as godparents to their clients' children, and might pay for school materials, trips, or special celebrations such as a school graduation trip or church confirmation.

7  Morales expelled the DEA from Bolivia in 2008 for allegedly conspiring against his government.

8  According to one gasoline smuggler—or *cistenero* as they are known locally—the expansion of petrol stations in the heart of drug production areas in recent years means that there is less demand for fuel smuggled from Cochabamba.

9  *Quinceañera* refers to the celebration of a girl turning fifteen.

10  Drug processors told me that they have been forced to alter their behavior, setting up production sites in ever more remote areas and never maintaining a production site in one place for more than two weeks. Often, absentee landowners are unaware production ever occurred on their property.

11  In the Chapare, *cholita* is a word used to describe women who wear traditional Andean clothing—including a layered, gathered skirt. While in some contexts this phrase is used as a slur, within the Chapare, women who wear such clothes might refer to themselves or their friends who dress this way using this term.

12  In March 2020, the state built up the number of troops and police in the region and targeted leaders for arrest on false claims of terrorism (Miranda 2020).

**REFERENCES**

Abercrombie, Thomas. 1998. *Pathways of Memory and Power: Ethnography and History among an Andean People*. Madison: University of Wisconsin Press.

Aguilo, Federico. 1986. "Los Peones de la Cocaína." *Cuarto Intermedio* 1: 44–57.

Albó, Xavier. 2002. *Identidad Etnica y Politica*. La Paz: CIPCA Cuaderno de Investigación.

Allen, Catherine. 1981. "To Be Quechua: The Symbolism of Coca Chewing in Highland Peru." *American Ethnologist* 8, no. 1: 157–71.

Anria, Santiago. 2018. *When Movements Become Parties: The Bolivian MAS in Comparative Perspective*. Cambridge: Cambridge University Press.

Blanes, Jose. 1989. "Cocaine, Informality, and the Urban Economy in La Paz, Bolivia." In *The Informal Economy: Studies in Advanced and Less Developed Countries*, edited by Alejandro Portes, M. Castells, and L. Benton. Baltimore: Johns Hopkins University Press.

Bolton, Margaret. 2002. "Doing Waki in San Pablo de Lípez: Reciprocity between the Living and the Dead." *Anthropos* 97, no. 2: 379–96.

Carter, William, and Mauricio Mamani. 1986. *Coca en Bolivia*. La Paz: Editorial Juventud.

Clawson, Patrick, and Rensselaer Lee. 1996. *The Andean Cocaine Industry*. New York: Palgrave Macmillan.

"Cocaleros del Chapare mantienen de rehenes a 16 policías antidroga." 2014. *Los Tiempos*, October 1.

CONALTID. 2013. *Gobierno presenta resultados del Estudio Integral de la Hoja de Coca*. La Paz: Secretaria de Coordinacion Consejo Nacional de Lucha Contra el Trafico Ilicito de Drogas, Ministerio de Gobierno.

Cuiza, Paulo. 2018. "Gobierno conmina a O Globo demostrar 'con pruebas' presencia de supuesto jefe del PPC en Bolivia." *La Razón*, April 17.

Cusicanqui, Silvia Rivera. 2019. "Genealogía de un 'golpe'? 12 de Noviembre del 2019." *YouTube*, n.d. Accessed November 13, 2019. https://www.youtube.com/watch?v=Ls7i_iG8yn4&feature=youtu.be&fbclid=IwAR3vxlelLGgerwcAETOqhNe775aqUQoX-MoizhvT7hNIoyBMzyCgSFJtCJQ.

De Franco, Mario, and Ricardo Godoy. 1992. "The Economic Consequences of Cocaine Production in Bolivia: Historical, Local, and Macroeconomic Perspectives." *Journal of Latin American Studies* 24, no. 2: 375–406.

Dillehay, Tom, Jack Rossen, Donald Ugent, Anathasios Karathanasis, Víctor Vásquez, and Patricia J. Netherly. 2010. "Early Holocene Coca Chewing in Northern Peru." *Antiquity* 84: 939–53.

Dunkerley, James. 1984. *Rebellion in the Veins: Political Struggle in Bolivia, 1952–82*. London: Verso.

Dunkerley, James. 1990. *Political Transition and Economic Stabilisation: Bolivia, 1982–1989*. London: Institute of Latin American Studies.

Ehrinpreis, Andrew. 2018. "Coca Nation: Labor, Indigeneity, and the Politics of the Coca Leaf in Bolivia, 1900–1962." PhD diss., State University of New York at Stony Brook.

Farthing, Linda. 1997. "Social Impacts Associated with Anti-Drug Law 1008." In *Coca, Cocaine, and the Bolivian Reality*, edited by Madeline Barbara Léons and Harry Sanabria. Albany: State University of New York Press.

Farthing, Linda, and Benjamin Kohl. 2005. "Conflicting Agendas: The Politics of Development Aid in Drug-Producing Areas." *Development Policy Review* 23, no. 2: 183–98.

Gillies, Allan. 2018. "Theorising State-Narco Relations in Bolivia's Nascent Democracy (1982–1993): Governance, Order and Political Transition." *Third World Quarterly* 39, no. 4: 727–46.

Goldstein, Daniel. 2012. *Outlawed: Between Security and Rights in a Bolivian City*. Durham, NC: Duke University Press.

Gootenberg, Paul. 2008. *Andean Cocaine: The Making of a Global Drug*. Chapel Hill: University of North Carolina Press.

Gootenberg, Paul. 2017. "Cocaine Histories and Diverging Drug War Politics in Bolivia, Colombia, and Peru." *Contracorriente* 15, no. 1: 1–35.

Grandin, Greg. 2006. *Empire's Workshop: Latin America, the United States and the Rise of the New Imperialism*. New York: Metropolitan.

Grim, Ryan. 2009. "Bolivian President Chews Coca during Speech at UN." *Huffington Post*, April 11. Accessed August 13, 2018. https://www.huffingtonpost.co.uk/entry/bolivian-president-chews_n_174075.

Grisaffi, Thomas. 2010. "We Are Originarios . . . 'We Just Aren't from Here': Coca Leaf and Identity Politics in the Chapare, Bolivia." *Bulletin of Latin American Research* 29, no. 4: 425–39.

Grisaffi, Thomas. 2014. "Can You Get Rich from the Bolivian Cocaine Trade? Cocaine Paste Production in the Chapare." Andean Information Network, March 10. http://ain-bolivia.org/2014/03/can-you-get-rich-from-the-bolivian-cocaine-trade-cocaine-paste-production-in-the-chapare/.

Grisaffi, Thomas. 2016. "Social Control in Bolivia: A Humane Alternative to the Forced Eradication of Coca Crops." In *Drug Policies and the Politics of Drugs in the Americas*, edited by Bia Labate, Clancy Cavnar, and Thiago Rodrigues. Cham, Switzerland: Springer.

Grisaffi, Thomas. 2019. *Coca Yes, Cocaine No: How Bolivia's Coca Growers Reshaped Democracy*. Durham, NC: Duke University Press.

Grisaffi, Thomas, Linda Farthing, and Kathryn Ledebur. 2017. "Integrated Development with Coca in the Plurinational State of Bolivia: Shifting the Focus from Eradication to Poverty Alleviation." *Bulletin on Narcotics* 61: 131–57.

Grisaffi, Thomas, Linda Farthing, Kathryn Ledebur, Maritza Paredes, and Alvaro Pastor. 2020. "Turning Over a New Leaf: Regional Applicability of Innovative Drug Crop Control Policy in the Andes." Lima: Pontificia Universidad Católica del Perú. Accessed July 8, 2020. http://departamento.pucp.edu.pe/ciencias-sociales/files/2016/01/Turning-Over-a-New-Leaf.pdf.

Grisaffi, Thomas, and Kathryn Ledebur. 2016. "Citizenship or Repression? Coca, Eradication and Development in the Andes." *Stability: International Journal of Security and Development* 5, no. 1. https://www.stabilityjournal.org/articles/10.5334/sta.440/.

Gutierrez, Eric Dante. 2020. "The Paradox of Illicit Economies: Survival, Resilience, and the Limits of Development and Drug Policy Orthodoxy." *Globalizations* 17, no. 6: 1008–26.

Gutierrez Aguilar, Raquel. 2014. *Rhythms of Pachakuti: Indigenous Uprising and State Power in Bolivia*. Durham, NC: Duke University Press.

Harris, Olivia. 2000. *To Make the Earth Bear Fruit: Essays on Fertility, Work and Gender in Highland Bolivia*. London: Institute of Latin American Studies.

INE. 2014. "Instituto Nacional de Estadistica: Nota de Prensa." La Paz: Instituto Nacional de Estadistica. Accessed September 3, 2015. http://www.ine.gob .bo/pdf/boletin/np_2014_4.pdf.

Jelsma, Martin. 2016. "UNGASS 2016: Prospects for Treaty Reform and UN System-Wide Coherence on Drug Policy." In *Center for 21st Century Security and Intelligence Latin America Initiative*. Washington, DC: Brookings Institution.

Koch, Insa. 2018. *Personalizing the State: An Anthropology of Law, Welfare and Politics in Austerity Britain*. Oxford: Oxford University Press.

Laserna, Roberto. 2000. "Desarrollo alternativo en Bolivia: Análisis preliminar de una experiencia inconclusa." Seminario Internacional, Bogotá, Colombia, Pontificia Universidad Javeriana, August 12.

Ledebur, Kathryn. 2005. "Bolivia: Clear Consequences." In *Drugs and Democracy in Latin America: The Impact of U.S. Policy*, edited by Coletta Youngers and Eileen Rosin, 143–84. Boulder, CO: Lynne Rienner.

Lessing, Benjamin. 2017. *Making Peace in Drug Wars: Crackdowns and Cartels in Latin America*. Cambridge: Cambridge University Press.

Levitsky, Steven, and María Victoria Murillo. 2020. "La Tentación Militar en América Latina." *Nueva Sociedad* 285: 4–11.

Mansilla, H. 1992. "Economía informal e ilegitimidad estatal en Bolivia." *Nueva Sociedad* 119 (May–June): 36–44.

Marconi, Reinaldo. 1998. *El drama de Chapare: La frustración del desarrollo alternativo*. La Paz: Centro de Estudios para el Desarrollo Laboral y Agrario.

Miranda, Boris. 2020. "Crisis en Bolivia: La 'guerra declarada' que se vive en el Chapare, el bastión de Evo Morales al que el gobierno acusa de 'terrorismo' (y cómo lo defiende el expresidente)." BBC, June 19. Accessed July 2, 2020. https://www.bbc.com/mundo/noticias-america-latina-53112041.

Oikonomakis, Leonidas. 2019. *Political Strategies and Social Movements in Latin America: The Zapatistas and Bolivian Cocaleros*. Cham, Switzerland: Palgrave Macmillan.

Paco, Alanoca. 2019. "Romero: 'No hay mano blanda para unos ni mano dura para otros.'" *El Deber*, March 6. Accessed August 2, 2020. https://eldeber .com.bo/bolivia/romero-no-hay-mano-blanda-para-unos-ni-mano-dura -para-otros_35604.

Painter, James. 1994. *Bolivia and Coca: A Study in Dependency*. Boulder, CO: Lynne Rienner.

Paredes, Iván. 2017. "Beni, en Bolivia, es el centro de 'recarga' y transporte de narcos Peruanos." *El Deber*, November 5.

Pearson, Zoe. 2016. "Coca Sí, Cocaína No? The Intimate Politics of International Drug Control Policy and Reform in Bolivia." PhD diss., Ohio State University.

Pellegrini, Alessandra. 2016. *Beyond Indigeneity: Coca Growing and the Emergence of a New Middle Class in Bolivia*. Tucson: University of Arizona Press.

"Peru and Bolivia Are Unlikely Allies in the War on Drugs." 2018. *Economist*, August 18. Accessed January 31, 2020. https://www.economist.com/the-americas /2018/08/18/peru-and-bolivia-are-unlikely-allies-in-the-war-on-drugs.

PNUD. 2005. *Bolivia: Atlas Estadístico de Municipios*. La Paz: Programa de las Naciones Unidas para el Desarrollo, Instituto Nacional de Estadística.

PNUD. 2007. *El Estado del Estado en Bolivia: Informe nacional sobre Desarrollo Humano*. La Paz: Programa de las Naciones Unidas para el Desarrollo, Instituto Nacional de Estadística.

Reyes, Luis Carlos. 2014. "Estimating the Causal Effect of Forced Eradication on Coca Cultivation in Colombian Municipalities." *World Development* 61: 70–84.

Rivera, Alberto. 1990. "El Chapare Actual." In *Debate Regional: El Chapare actual; sindicatos y ONG's en la Region*, edited by Carlos Toranzo Roca. Cochabamba: CERES.

Salazar Ortuño, Fernando. 2008. *De la coca al poder: Políticas públicas de sustitución de la economía de la coca y pobreza en Bolivia, 1975–2004*. Buenos Aires: Consejo Latinoamericano de Ciencias Sociales.

Schipani, Andres. 2010. "Cocaine Production Rise Spells Trouble for Bolivia." BBC, June 16. http://www.bbc.co.uk/news/10231343.

Scott, James. 2010. *The Art of Not Being Governed: An Anarchist History of Upland Southeast Asia*. Singapore: NUS.

Starn, Orin. 1999. *Nightwatch: The Politics of Protest in the Andes*. Durham, NC: Duke University Press.

UNODC. 2018. "El 94% de la Coca de Chapare No Pasa por el Mercado Legal." La Paz: United Nations Office on Drugs and Crime. http://www.unodc.org /bolivia/es/press/entrevista_erbol.html.

UNODC. 2020. "Book 6: Other Drug Policy Issues." In *World Drug Report 2020*. Vienna: United Nations Office on Drugs and Crime.

Vargas, Gonzalo. 2014. "Identidad en el Chapare: De cocaleros a indígenas originarios campesinos." *Nueva Crónica y Buen Gobierno*, April 16.

Vargas, Ollie. 2019. "Bolivia's Free Territory of Chapare Ousted Coup Regime, Braces for Bloody Re-Invasion." *Struggle for Socialism*, December 28. Accessed July 8, 2020. https://www.struggle-la-lucha.org/2019/12/28/bolivian -free-territory-of-chapare-ousted-coup-regime-braces-for-bloody-re -invasion/.

Wemyss, Martyn. 2019. "Lynching as a Cultural System in Highland Bolivia." *Political and Legal Anthropology Review*.

Youngers, Coletta, and Eileen Rosin, eds. 2005. *Drugs and Democracy in Latin America: The Impact of U.S. Policy*. Boulder, CO: Lynne Rienner.

# <u>02</u> TRACING COCAINE SUPPLY CHAINS FROM WITHIN

ILLICIT FLOWS, ARMED CONFLICT, AND THE MORAL
ECONOMY OF ANDEAN BORDERLANDS

Illicit trade has affected economies and societies for centuries. As Manuel Castells put it, it is as old as humankind: "In the biblical account of our origins, our plight began with the illegal traffic of apples" (Castells 2010: 172). Drug trafficking and other forms of transnational organized crime have shaped the evolution of states and the interactions of groups and individuals across borders (Andreas 2014). They have fueled wars between states, and they constitute an important income source for rebels, paramilitaries, and other armed actors to sustain their fighting against or with governments in armed conflict and other violent contexts across the globe. The international cocaine trade in particular has caused considerable human suffering and undermined livelihoods, including of the communities that reside in territories which host cocaine production (Idler and Garzón Vergara 2021).

I argue that we need to focus on the internal workings of the cocaine trade to better understand, and ultimately mitigate, its repercussions on the communities in which it is embedded. I thus challenge prevailing approaches in both academia and policy that assume an outsider's view on the cocaine business and analyze, or respond to, supply chain steps—namely, cultivation, processing, domestic transport, international trafficking, and market distribution—in isolation. Numerous studies have contributed to a better understanding of production and consumption and the ways in which trafficking routes can be mapped (see, for example, Thoumi 1995; Buxton 2006). Scholars such as Paul Gootenberg have traced the evolution of drugs over time and space (Gootenberg 2021; see also Gootenberg, this volume). Others such as Mats Berdal and Monica Serrano have discussed trafficking across borders (Berdal and Serrano 2002). Yet while these individual steps in the supply chain have been studied, we know much less about the interconnected processes and relationships that hold these steps together and how these in turn affect local communities in which they take place.

Policy makers likewise focus on individual supply chain steps, but such approaches have not had much success at stemming the flows of cocaine (Idler and Garzón Vergara 2021). US-led counter-drug strategies in the Andean region, for example, concentrate on eradicating coca plants, destroying laboratories, or detaining small-scale traffickers. However, targeting those on the lowest rungs of the cocaine trade has failed to reduce the cocaine business in any significant way. To be sure, fumigation, manual eradication, and alternative development programs diminished the area of coca cultivation in Colombia—the world's main cocaine producer—between 2007 and 2013 by 51 percent (UNODC 2014a: 16). However, innovations in processing methods and transportation have maintained relatively stable levels of cocaine production over the last two decades; every year, tens of tons of cocaine are seized (UNODC 2012). The large number of farmers, the abundance of territories available for new cultivation, the ease of replacing destroyed laboratories, and the ready supply of new small-scale smugglers make it easy to continue cultivation and to fill the places of those who are captured or killed. Similarly, targeting the violent non-state groups (including rebels, paramilitaries, and criminals) involved in the drug trade in an isolated way has only hardened the trend of the drug business's constant adaptation and reconfiguration. In 2012, for example, the three top leaders of the "Rastrojos," a Colombian criminal group heavily involved in drug trafficking, were arrested or surrendered (InSight Crime n.d.). Nevertheless, the voids were filled almost instantly by other groups and individuals, leaving the cocaine supply chain without any major interruptions. Violent non-state groups ranging from insurgents to criminal organizations continue to draw on the cocaine trade as a lucrative income source to increase their economic, political, or military power. Likewise, violence originating in the drug trade and in related forms of organized crime persists, as the soaring homicide rates in Latin America attest (UNODC 2014b: 21–23). Even the 2016 peace deal between the Revolutionary Armed Forces of Colombia (FARC) rebels and the government of Colombia, which was supposed to "solve the drug problem," did not help mitigate the issue. In fact, coca cultivation rose again in Colombia in the post-accord years (UNODC 2016, 2018).

Against the backdrop of these futile responses to the illicit cocaine business, this chapter proposes to change the way we think about the cocaine trade in the context of armed conflict by tracing cocaine supply chains from within rather than from an outsider's perspective, the conventional approach to the "conflict-crime nexus," especially in the field of political science (see, for example, Eilstrup-Sangiovanni and Jones 2008; De Boer and Bosetti 2017). It asks how transactional cocaine supply chain relationships at the production steps and the processes involved in these impact the social, political, and economic experiences of communities embedded in them, especially in conflict situations in which illicit economies fuel violence. Specifically, drawing on data from multiyear fieldwork in marginalized spaces at the Colombia-Ecuador and Colombia-Venezuela border, this chapter analyzes the moral economy that emerges in peripheral regions where illicit cross-border flows and the logics of armed conflict converge. I argue that, in contexts where the cocaine economy overlaps with armed conflict or other forms of organized violence, the processes and relationships that drive cocaine supply chain networks contribute to an environment of mistrust and violence, to uncertainty among the local population, and to the alienation of communities from the central state. At the same time, armed actors gain in perceived legitimacy and social recognition, since their ability to provide economic opportunities widens people's tolerance margin for abusive means to achieve their goals. The processes and relationships that constitute cocaine supply chain networks and keep them stable in contexts of organized violence are interconnected. The implications of this interconnected nature go beyond experiences in the places affected by the trade. Exploring cocaine supply chains from within, rather than adopting an outsider's view that scrutinizes cocaine supply chain steps in isolation, reveals the rift between excluded communities striving to sustain their livelihoods, and power centers whose very power projection widens this rift. This reflects state–society relationships in the era of globalization driven by market forces in a more general manner.

The remainder of this chapter is organized in the following way. First, I discuss what I consider to be the moral economy of borderlands where cocaine economies and armed conflict coincide. I then conceptualize cocaine supply chain networks and illustrate how they play out at the first steps of production and trafficking in contexts of organized violence. This serves to highlight three repercussions on the environments in which these economies are embedded: mistrust and violence, uncertainty, and the deepening of the alienation of local communities from central governments. Finally, I reflect on the repercussions on state–society relationships and conclude by pointing to implications for policy interventions in times of conflict as well as during transitions from war to peace.

## THE MORAL ECONOMY OF BORDERLANDS AMID CONFLICT AND CRIME

"Colombia has more territory than state," an interviewee said to me when I visited a war-torn Colombian border region during one of my many field trips. In the border areas that Colombia shares with Ecuador and Venezuela, this observation is perhaps more accurate than in any other part of the country. These transnational spaces are distant from political and economic power centers. Their inhabitants are not just at the geographical margins of the state; they have also been marginalized socially, through the absence of infrastructure, state services, and deficient integration into the national economy (Idler 2019). Illicit economies prosper in such contexts where state capacities are weak and no (legal) alternative livelihoods are available (Felbab-Brown 2010: 178). Likewise, the existence of illicit cross-border flows and the logics of armed conflict in border areas are presupposed by state neglect. These dynamics shape people's everyday lives not just locally, but also have wider implications for the state. They deepen the disconnect between central governments and citizens at the margins, and perpetuate the state's unequal treatment of parts of the citizenry (Ramírez 2011). Decentering the state and shifting our attention to the borderlanders' marginalized voices reveal experiences and practices that remain hidden otherwise and reduces ideological biases in our analysis (see Horkheimer 1969; Nugent and Asiwaju 1996; Krause and Williams 1997). Thus, contrary to state-centric approaches, this chapter adopts a transnational borderland perspective to study the moral economy of borderlands.

Building on E. P. Thompson's (1971) seminal work on food riots two centuries ago, in the introduction to this volume, Arias and Grisaffi discuss the moral economy of the cocaine trade. The term *moral economy* refers to an alternative way of understanding exchange that is not (only) shaped by capitalist market logics but also informed by deeper societal and cultural processes (Polanyi 2001). In the context of the Andean border regions that concentrate the first steps of the cocaine supply chain (cultivation, processing, transport, and starting points of international trafficking), the social processes in which the cocaine economy is embedded are intrinsically intertwined with two factors: illicit cross-border flows and the logics of the Colombian armed conflict. As I argue, this context gives rise to an "extreme case" of the moral economy of the cocaine trade, namely the moral economy of borderlands at the convergence of conflict and crime.

Grasping this moral economy requires tracing these first steps of the cocaine supply chain and shedding light on the entanglement of the illicit economy built around it with the local social order. This means exploring how communities experience the processes through which it takes shape, and how these experiences clash with state-centric views from outside that put the illegality of the cocaine business at the center of attention. It demonstrates that the moral economy of borderlands at the convergence of conflict and crime is characterized by three elements that shape people's social, political, and economic experiences in these sites embedded in wider cocaine economies: mistrust and violence, uncertainty, and the alienation from the central government. In the remainder of this chapter, I outline the logics of crime and conflict in the Andean borderlands, specifically the Colombian-Ecuadorian and Colombian-Venezuelan borderlands. This serves to highlight the processes of the cocaine supply chain networks that shape this extreme case of the moral economy of the cocaine trade.

## THE LOGICS OF ILLICIT CROSS-BORDER FLOWS

In the 1970s, Colombia emerged as the world's largest cocaine producer. During this period, coca was primarily cultivated in Bolivia and Peru, while Colombia was in charge of processing and trafficking after its market share in cannabis had shrunk (UNODC 2010: 81). With the emergence of two major drug cartels in Medellín and Cali in the 1980s, Colombia's role became more monopolistic. When the Cali and Medellín cartels were destroyed in the early 1990s and the cocaine market became more disorganized, the paramilitaries and the FARC, two major actors in Colombia's decades-old armed internal conflict, intensified their involvement in the drug business, which constituted an important income source for them. While the paramilitaries became the protagonists in international cocaine trafficking, the insurgents expanded their activities to directly control production and distribution (Sanderson 2004: 51; Bonilla and Moreano 2009). From 2003 to 2006, the paramilitary umbrella organization Autodefensas Unidas de Colombia (AUC; United Self-Defense Forces of Colombia), founded in 1997, demobilized. This process accelerated the proliferation of a variety of paramilitary splinter groups and other criminal and drug-trafficking right-wing groups, subsumed by the Colombian government under the term BACRIM (bandas criminales emergentes; emerging criminal bands). These groups now engage in the illegal drug business as well, and enter relationships with other violent non-state groups to enhance economic benefits (ICG 2010: 9).

The cocaine trade affects not only Colombia, but the entire Andean region, and it is interconnected with multiple other forms of transnational organized crime. Though the acreage has shrunk, coca cultivation is still widespread in Peru and Bolivia. Coca has been detected in the border zones of Ecuador, Brazil, Panama, and Venezuela. The Andean border zones are also sites of processing cocaine paste (an impure form of cocaine) into cocaine. Finally, all Andean states are starting points for international drug trafficking routes that embed local cocaine economies into wider global illicit markets. One route, for instance, starts in Colombia and continues via Ecuador, the Galápagos Islands, and Central America to the final destination, the United States. Another route begins in Bolivia, Peru, or Colombia, from where cocaine is trafficked to Venezuela or Brazil and from there, via West Africa, to Europe (UNODC 2010: 85–105).

The Andean borderlands in particular are geostrategic corridors of the global cocaine business. They feature the region's largest areas of coca cultivation, cocaine laboratories, and are the starting points of major international trafficking routes. The border regions are the areas that have seen the greatest increase in coca cultivation since the peace agreement between the FARC and the government, signed in 2016. Combined with the illicit flows of gasoline, precursors, arms, and people, and connected services such as money laundering, these features yield unique cross-border dynamics. Due to its dollarization, Ecuador, for instance, is a focal point for money laundering and the country of origin of chemical precursors that are required to process the coca leaves (Bonilla and Moreano 2009). Venezuela is important for the provision of cheap gasoline, essential for the production of cocaine paste (see figures 2.1 and 2.2). A Colombian ex-combatant described it to me the following way: "The border offers many advantages. It is a place where commerce, arms trafficking, and drug trafficking thrive. Even money laundering is thriving. [Border areas] are places that lend themselves to these exchanges and activities. You can carry them out at night, during the day, at any time. And there are always people who are willing to support you in it. That is, not only to take a share of it themselves—because often [they do]—but also to receive [the illicit goods]."[1] The prevalence of illicit cross-border activities in marginalized

FIGURE 2.1 Pimpinero stand in Cúcuta to sell smuggled gasoline, 2012. Photo credit: Annette Idler.

FIGURE 2.2 Cars queuing in Venezuela to fill their tanks with gasoline, typically smuggled to Colombia, 2012. Photo credit: Annette Idler.

regions influences people's perceptions of what is legitimate and illegitimate behavior, thereby shaping the social processes in which the cocaine economy is embedded. From a borderland perspective, non-state forms of governance produce their own logic of order in which pursuing illicit activities across the border unites a transnational community. This is different from, if not opposed to, a state-centric perspective, according to which borderlands in vulnerable regions are unruly zones where the border as a marker of territorial sovereignty is the feature most deserving of attention. Conflict studies, for example, consider the relevance of borderlands for national security issues, for example, as sanctuaries for rebels (Salehyan 2007). Against this, anthropological studies ask how boundaries are constructed through social discourse, how power relations between the two sides of the border are defined (Morehouse, Pavlakovich-Kochi, and Wastl-Walter 2004: 28), and where the state's margins are (Asad 2004). Bringing such studies into dialogue reveals the divergence of local perceptions in borderlands and views from the center, and of the moral economy of borderlands where cross-border activities may be illegal, yet are perceived as legitimate.

## THE LOGICS OF THE ARMED CONFLICT

While coca and cocaine production shape social and political processes in many regions of the Andes, including in Bolivia and Peru (see, for example, Grisaffi, this volume), in the borderlands that Colombia shares with its neighbors, the logics of the Colombian armed conflict constitute additional factors relevant to the local moral economy. These logics influence social processes intertwined with the cocaine economy through the ways in which the role of the state is perceived to be primarily exercised through (often illegitimate) violence. In regions where civilian state institutions are absent, the only experience people have of the state is one of abusive military personnel, corrupt police officers, and self-interested border officials.

Closely linked to the country's security strategies, Colombia's recent drug policies date back to 2000, when Plan Colombia, a counter-drug and counterinsurgency strategy backed by the United States, was implemented (Tate 2015). Initiated as a counter-narcotics program that sought to reduce coca cultivation via aerial crop fumigation, after 9/11 it focused more on the counterterrorism. In late 2003, Plan Colombia's second phase, Plan Patriota, launched an intense military offensive in southern Colombia, where coca cultivation was expanding. This plan was followed by Plan Consolidation, designed to target areas where weak institutional state presence, high rates of violence, terrorist threats, illicit crop cultivation, and drug trafficking converged. The plan aimed to consolidate state presence—first with a military and then a civilian focus—and to substitute coca crops with alternative economic development projects. However, it never really moved from the military to the civilian components (Poe and Isacson 2011). And even at this writing (2021), alternative economic development projects that were announced in the context of the peace deal implementation prevail on paper, but less so in practice (see also Grisaffi and Ledebur 2016: 13–14).

The confrontational character of the relationship between people involved in the cocaine economy on the one hand and the state on the other can be observed across all steps of the cocaine supply chain. It shapes people's everyday lives across Colombia's border areas. At the cultivation steps in southern Colombia, scholars such as María Clemencia Ramírez (2011) have shown how coca farmers were exposed to state action that took away their livelihoods. Similarly, in 2012, coca farmers in the Catatumbo region of the department of Norte de Santander, on the border with Venezuela, told me that the announcement of coca fumigation the following week had spread fear and a presentiment of danger.[2] People knew they had to harvest as much as possible within the little time they had left or else they would not be able to sustain their families. And beyond that, people knew that they would have to expect violent clashes between the state forces and the guerrillas who would retaliate for the destruction of their income source—and the communities' livelihoods. The logics of the conflict also concern the processing steps. In the same region, those involved in the cocaine business constructed mobile cocaine laboratories so that they could easily move them should military forces arrive.

These dynamics make it easy for guerrillas to find individuals who sympathize with their anti-state discourse. In a community meeting I attended in southern Colombia in 2012, for example, a FARC *miliciano* (a FARC member in civilian clothes) who denounced the government's operations to destroy coca cultivation without providing any alternative options was applauded by the community, including a teacher, who stated: "We are in a war against the state. The state has abandoned us."[3] Of course, the FARC miliciano did not mention that the presence of armed groups itself impedes licit economic opportunities because it deters companies from investing in such regions. Even if they do, as in Putumayo, where the oil industry did attract investors, local community members were often branded as collaborators of the guerrillas, reducing their chances of being hired.[4] Since the FARC demobilized in 2017, little has changed for local coca farmers. During a research visit to the same region in 2017, coca farmers asked me what they should do when the eradicators arrive, knowing that there still were not any alternative livelihood options in place. When debating whether or not they should resist, they asked: "Shall we fight against them?"[5]

## TRACING COCAINE SUPPLY CHAINS FROM WITHIN

Having contextualized the moral economy of the Andean borderlands with the logics of illicit cross-border flows and of the Colombian armed conflict, I now zoom in on these spaces to trace the cocaine supply chain and related economic activities from the bottom up. This facilitates understanding the social, political, and economic experiences of local communities that participate in, or are exposed to, the cocaine trade. It reveals three major outcomes of the moral economy in these spaces: mistrust and violence, uncertainty, and the alienation of these communities from the state.

## CONCEPTUALIZING COCAINE SUPPLY CHAIN NETWORKS

The cocaine business can be conceptualized as overlapping supply chain networks.[6] Various actors who engage in relationships along and across them maintain these supply chains (Idler and Forest 2015). Given the illicit nature of the cocaine trade, they operate outside the law and enforce compliance with violence. In contexts where supply chain networks are embedded in settings of organized violence, these actors are typically violent non-state groups, including, on the one hand, conflict actors such as rebels and paramilitaries, and on the other hand, criminal organizations such as drug cartels.

In transactional cocaine supply chain relationships at the first steps of production, violent non-state groups are at "arm's length." They are independent and on an equal footing with each other. They typically respect territorial limits of influence within which each violent non-state group exerts economic, social, and/or political control (Idler 2019).[7] This territorial segmentation arises from the division of labor in the supply chain of an (illegal) product or service in which each of these groups assumes one or several functions (Deville 2013: 65). Specialization maximizes profits from the different steps. Although it usually leads to only limited commitment between the armed actors, they remain indirectly connected through financial or material transactions (Idler 2020). The relative stability of such supply chain relationships suggests that the parties involved accept a certain degree of interdependence. Being affected by the other party's actions and knowing that one's own actions have implications for the other facilitates the institutionalization of the relationship, which allows its continuity, even if modifications are necessary or certain groups are substituted by other ones. The "basics" of the arrangements—for example, regarding who controls the territory where these arrangements take place—remain the same; the rules of the game do not have to be constantly renegotiated.

Such forms of cooperation that are of mutual benefit to the parties involved normally presuppose that these parties reduce distrust between each other. In the introduction to this volume, Arias and Grisaffi argue that, given the illicit nature of the cocaine economy, transactions are based on trust relationships rather than enforceable contracts (see Gambetta 1990, 2009: 28). While this is the case in contexts where illicit actors operate in opposition to the state only, in contexts of armed conflict, hostility among conflict actors prevents them from establishing such trust relationships. Instead of assuming trust relationships, I therefore conceptualize these supply chain relationships as embedded in a context of mistrust and consider how these groups manage to reduce distrust sufficiently in order to engage in such relationships (Idler 2019).

In the absence of trust, supply chain transactions require some form of regulation and enforcement (Gambetta 1993: 17; Felbab-Brown 2010: 179). Groups that perceive each other as enemies in particular, for example, due to their diametrically opposed ideologies, do not reduce distrust directly. Instead, they draw on a third party, a broker, to reduce distrust and to facilitate the institutionalization of supply chain relationships at the first stages of production: "Cooperation with the broker is 'stabilized' through [a] duty of fidelity on both sides: he or she builds up a reputation of trustworthiness, or at least of being as good as his or her word, when it comes to these illicit business deals. The groups value the broker as a reliable and credible business partner and in return honor their side of the deal" (Idler 2019: 45–46). While the broker bridges the "trust-gap" between the various violent non-state groups that engage along and across cocaine supply chain networks, general intergroup distrust persists. This is also the case in business transactions across various forms of transnational organized crime. The convergence of the economic interests of two groups that engage in spot sales or barter agreements, for example, arms-for-drugs deals, may be sufficient for them to reduce distrust in a specific business deal, but they still mistrust each other outside this arrangement, especially in their wider interactions that include violent disputes (Idler 2019). Figure 2.3 illustrates the networked nature of cocaine supply chains (Idler 2020: 341).

In the context of the Andean region, a human rights defender in 2011 described the processes and mechanisms that link the various supply chain steps in the following way:

> People cultivate coca. There is nothing else to do. Why do they cultivate coca? Some because they think it's more lucrative or because the financiers oblige them, or well, they don't oblige them, but they tell them to cultivate. In any case, people cultivate coca. They process it in an artisanal way and convert it into coca base. Up until here this process involves the farmer and the small intermediary. The cocaine base paste currently costs 1,200,000

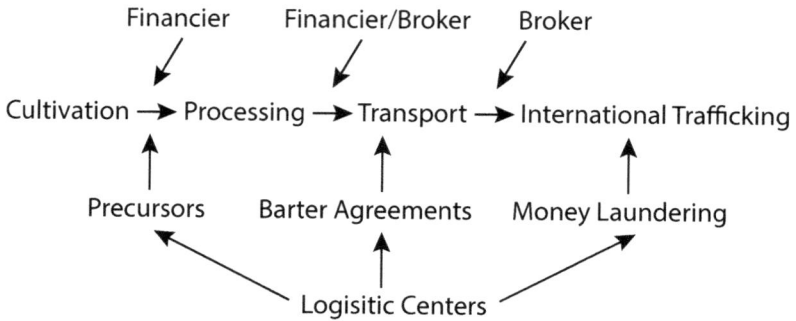

FIGURE 2.3 The networked nature of cocaine supply chains.

pesos [around US$423 or €460 in 2011]. Then they sell it to the Rastrojos or the FARC. They in turn negotiate with drug traffickers via an intermediary. The FARC charge a tax to those who cultivate coca, a tax to who possesses cocaine base, and that's it, but in some cases, they also negotiate with traffickers for arms or money with which they buy arms. The intermediary can sell the cocaine base to others or process it in laboratories into [pure] cocaine and this is how the cocaine leaves the country. It is exported in motorboats. They have large boats and cover the white wake with blue plastic. These are boats with two 200 [horsepower] motors that go to Central America. They are very quick, but they still have to be very conscious of the navy.[8]

These brokers are often small local groups that know the region very well. As he explained further:

These groups of drug traffickers are not the Rastrojos themselves. If you stopped the coca cultivation in Nariño, the cocaine business would not stop in this zone. The merchandise leaves the country from here [Pasto] to the region of Tumaco and the entire Pacific coast toward Costa Rica and Mexico. The Mexican cartels, especially the Sinaloa Cartel, have their people here in Tumaco. They are in charge of negotiating with the FARC or the Rastrojos or the Águilas Negras and, to do so, there are small groups of intermediaries in the entire Pacific coast, in Ipiales, Pasto, and Tumaco in charge of negotiating with them. . . . [The intermediaries talk to the Rastrojos or the cartels] in order to arrange the exchange, to buy the cocaine. They are local narcos. It's people who come from Norte del Valle, from Pasto, from this region. They are small groups who work with the Rastrojos now, but who continue to be intermediaries. . . . In some cases [they also negotiate with the FARC].[9]

As this brief discussion of cocaine supply chain networks shows, persistent mistrust among various violent non-state actors, the varying role of brokers, and the participation of local communities in the cultivation of coca and the processing of coca leaves are among the major characteristics of the illicit business. Continuing to adopt an analytical lens from within, in what follows, I demonstrate how these features translate into a moral economy shaped by mistrust and violence, uncertainty, and the deepening of the communities' alienation from the state.

## MISTRUST AND VIOLENCE

The first repercussion of cocaine supply chain networks on the social, political, and economic processes in which local communities are embedded is the environment of mistrust that emerges in such contexts, where various violent non-state groups, especially ideologically opposed ones, engage in cocaine supply chain relationships. Even if brokers and other mechanisms help reduce intergroup distrust sufficiently for the supply chain to function relatively uninterruptedly, the groups that participate in transactions along the chain still mistrust one another. The intergroup distrust translates into the violent non-state groups' mistrust toward the local population—after all, they might be informants for the enemy. This may not be evident at the core of the territories where these groups operate, because here it is unlikely that others would meddle in the dominant group's affairs. For example, in regions where the FARC had full territorial control of coca-growing areas, they engaged in a mutually reinforcing relationship with local communities in which the guerrillas provided public goods and services, and the community members in turn obeyed their rules and recognized their authority (see Grisaffi, this volume, for similar dynamics related to Bolivian unions and coca). I call this social order "shadow citizenship" (see, for example, Idler 2014; Idler, Mouly, and Garrido 2018). However, at the fringes of these territories mistrust creeps in. This is where various groups engage in economic exchange, and where compliance is harder to enforce.

The following is an extract of an interview I conducted with a couple who were both former FARC guerrillas. It illustrates how rebel actors imagine the civilian population as potential betrayers and how this suspicion can translate into violence. In 2006, the man, when he was a member of the FARC, had been the supervisor of a cocaine production site for the first processing steps, which locals call *cocinas* (kitchens). Located in Nariño, a border department in southern Colombia, the site was controlled by the FARC:

AUTHOR: Who was in charge [of the kitchen]?

EX-GUERRILLA HUSBAND: The guerrillas, but inside there were civilian workers. I was with them for two years as a supervisor. . . . We were there to support them. Sometimes people came; therefore we protected them with arms. . . . The laboratories are practically theirs [the FARC's], because they use them to finance themselves. . . .

AUTHOR: What did they do with the cocaine afterward?

EX-GUERRILLA WIFE: They pass it on to other countries. There were people in charge of this. . . . This was in 2006, our kid was two and a half years old.

EX-GUERRILLA HUSBAND: We were working in a *cocina*. . . . There were infiltrators [among the civilians who worked in the *cocina*]. Infiltrators always tried to join. We noticed that there were two guys—

EX-GUERRILLA WIFE: [interrupts] They had only spent two months there, no more!

EX-GUERRILLA HUSBAND: They belonged to the paramilitaries and later they [FARC] realized it and they killed them.

AUTHOR: So they were . . .

EX-GUERRILLA HUSBAND: Civilian workers! Around one month later, they burnt the laboratories, they burnt everything.

AUTHOR: The paramilitaries?

EX-GUERRILLA WIFE: The army.

EX-GUERRILLA HUSBAND: Through them [the paramilitaries].[10] They arrived straight away. It was a hidden place that no one could find, but they came straight there. After that I decided to leave. Through my brother, because the truth is . . . if you kill someone, they kill you. . . . Therefore, we left. In the *cocina* there were also civilians. There were around six civilians at the entrance and six of the organization and three with radios inside.[11]

The second implication is the general environment of uncertainty that arises from the mechanisms that link various steps of the supply chain. Most of the literature focuses on how the guerrillas sustained a flourishing cocaine economy that ensured a steady income source to sustain their fighting through taxing this economy and in return protecting coca cultivation. Against this, and in line with the conceptualization of the supply chain relationships among violent non-state groups that I outlined above, I focus here on the third parties, or brokers, who mediate between various groups and thus serve as mechanisms to link the various steps. At the supply chain step of cultivation, these intermediaries are *financieros*, as my interviewees called them, that is, individuals who buy the farmers' coca leaves or cocaine paste and sell them to other violent non-state groups who further process or traffic the product.

These financieros, or financiers, are businesspeople who typically work in the service of violent non-state groups, such as rebels, drug cartels, or right-wing groups. In the case of the cocaine business, financiers ensure that the first steps of the cocaine supply chain stay connected in at least three ways. First, the financiers buy the cocaine paste from the farmers in order to sell the product to other groups in charge of processing the paste into refined cocaine.[12] In places where there are no roads on which the farmers would be able to take licit products such as bananas or coffee to the markets, the financiers arrive at the farms to buy the cocaine paste. As interviewees from three different coca cultivation regions (Norte de Santander, Nariño, and Putumayo) in Colombia confirmed to me, coca farmers cannot choose their clients; they have to sell their product to certain financiers. "They only sell to them, to no one else. If you sell to another person, they will punish you, punish you, punish you!" explained one of the interviewees.[13] Whether they cultivate coca at all is arguably the farmers' choice. "The communities are not forced [to cultivate], but they are told: 'Okay, if you cultivate you have to sell to me, I'm your only client and whoever wants to, can sell to this client.'"[14] Second, if any of their clients are no longer able to sell coca due to state-backed fumigation or manual eradication, they look for other farmers to ensure the supply for the laboratories. Third, if farmers attempt to substitute coca with other crops, the *financieros* may increase the prices of the coca to make the deal more lucrative (Idler 2019). They therefore require detailed knowledge of the coca production sites and the local farmers involved, and have to be well-connected with violent non-state groups that are willing to buy the initial product, that is, coca leaves or cocaine paste.

Financiers are crucial to maintain the labor-intensive first production steps, yet they also contribute to uncertainty. Generally speaking, "uncertainty refers to the state of an organism that lacks information about whether, where, when, how, or why an event has occurred or will occur" (Knight 1921). Uncertainty thus constitutes a negatively perceived state of affairs. In violent settings pervaded by mistrust, uncertainty can become lethal, and it contributes to fear. As Koonings and Krujit (1999: 15) note, "fear is the institutional, cultural and psychological repercussion of violence. Fear is a response to institutional destabilization, social exclusion, individual ambiguity and uncertainty."

The existence of financiers, individuals who work in an informal capacity, increases the communities' uncertainty as to how to behave, and their exposure to abuse. Since communities interact with the financiers rather than with those in whose service they work, community members tend to be ignorant about the identity of those who administer the laboratories, and about those who control the other supply chain steps, including the armed groups that are present in the territory. It is unclear who operates in the name of whom, or who decides to impose a new price. In hostile environments such as ongoing armed conflict, financiers can change frequently as a result of captures or killings, since they do not count on the same kind of protection as brokers at the higher-end supply chain steps. This fueled fear of persecution and death among community members for at least three reasons. First, when financiers were caught, the farmers who sold coca to them were accused by the authorities of being collaborators. Second, new financiers tended to implement new rules, sometimes without informing the coca farmers about these new rules, about the product's price, or about when and where they should sell it. Third, confusion about the financiers' identity caused harm. In some cases, people came to a village pretending to be financiers sent by one of the violent non-state groups. Farmers sold them the paste and once the "real" financier arrived, they were punished for selling it to others.[15]

## ALIENATION FROM THE STATE

The third implication of cocaine supply chain networks for the moral economy of borderlands at the convergence of conflict and crime concerns the interaction between cocaine supply chain networks and licit authority.

People's experiences of cocaine supply chain networks in marginalized regions such as the Colombia-Ecuador and Colombia-Venezuela borderlands unhinge the foundations of perceived state legitimacy. These experiences reinforce the disconnect of these already alienated communities from the state. In other contexts, authority—both of the state and of violent non-state actors—rests on the capacity of the "governor" to provide basic services and public goods, including security and justice. The authority's provision of economic opportunities is just one of many ways that encourage people to consent to this authority. In regions at the fringes of transactional supply chain relationships, the violent non-state groups' mistrust toward the local communities makes such (illicit) authority, or shadow citizenship, hard to attain. The communities' fear of punishment for noncompliance with the groups' rules hampers it, especially when punishment is perceived to be based on suspicion only and hence arbitrary. And yet violent non-state groups can counterbalance this trend by providing (illegal) economic opportunities where state-provided legal opportunities are absent. Such opportunities in an environment where people have difficulty sustaining their families' livelihoods foster the communities' loyalty toward the groups, rather than toward the state. This is favored by the "tendency toward transgression" that results from the empirical legitimacy of illicit economic activities, activities that alienate people from the state while drawing them closer to the illegal groups (Korf and Raeymaekers 2013: 5).

As a result, the state—embodied in customs officials, police, and military officials—may turn into a greater threat to people's livelihoods than the armed actors (Vorrath 2010: 85–87). After all, as Andreas (2009: 22) notes, "smuggling is defined by and depends on the state's exercising its metapolitical authority to criminalize without the full capacity or willingness to enforce its laws." The following account from 2011 of a farmer from southern Colombia who was involved in producing cocaine paste, illustrates how the state is perceived as a threat rather than a protector, while money from Cali (drug cartels) promised income:

> You sell [the cocaine paste], you go to the village, and the buyers come to the village. . . . Every weekend they come. For example, for one week everyone harvested. . . . On Sunday, everyone went to the village and there were the people, and the money from Cali arrived . . . big burlap bags . . . they found the ways to get the money to the village. . . . Every Sunday we took [cocaine paste] to the village. The women, not the men, took out cocaine paste from the farms because the police were there. When they showed up,

they searched the men, but not the women, and we stuck the paste here onto our body and kept it here until the village. Then we took it out and sold it in the village. One gram of merchandise costs 1,000 pesos [around US$0.52 or €0.38 in 2011] . . . it was a thousand grams, one kilo is a thousand grams, right? This is a lot of money. . . . Of course . . . , we helped, but the men did the work; it was very hard work. The women, we sowed the coca, and we took the cocaine paste off from the farm, because there were always checkpoints with soldiers and policemen, and they always searched the men.[16]

The chances of making money through smuggling cocaine paste outweighed the risks in a context where alternative livelihood options were scarce, calling into question the "default solution" of bringing in the state to improve people's well-being.

In other cases, people perceived state officials to be a threat to livelihoods not just because they merely carried out their functions, but because they actively acted in opposition to the communities, fueling grievances among them. The continuation of the farmer's account reflects people's discontent:

To be honest, the government can say what it likes, but what brings money is coca. . . . Look, the cacao is currently very cheap. . . . One pound is worth forty cents. This will never happen to coca. . . . Here, there isn't much coca, but further down there is a lot and people harvest 1,000 or 2,000 *arrobas*.[17] The thing is that it is not convenient for the government to eliminate the coca. They live off it. Their work depends on it, they come to eradicate it. But they never eradicate everything, why should they? They leave some seeds so that in four or five years it grows again. They don't want to finish it off because [it]'s their own business. . . . Even soldiers, the military: if there wasn't so much coca in Colombia, what would they need such large armed forces for? . . . It wouldn't be convenient for them because they would lose their jobs. If there was no problem anymore, they would need neither the army nor the police force. . . . It's also the government's fault because . . . they gave us some poor seeds of corn and some fish. . . . They thought we would live on this and that's it. But the seeds didn't even grow. . . . If they give you something, even if it is cacao, if they gave us a credit at low interest rates, so that people would stop growing coca, but if they don't do this there is nothing we can do. . . . Imagine, this is not a town, this is all countryside. You don't have money; you don't have anything. They come and give you some poor corn seeds that won't grow. This is going to help us? It will never help anyone, it doesn't help![18]

The armed actor's capacity to provide opportunities in the cocaine and related economies not only deepens the disconnect of the communities from the state, it also draws them closer to those actors. It increases the citizens' "tolerance margin" vis-à-vis illicit rules of behavior, and vis-à-vis the risks the armed actors expose them to. Even if people disagree with taking these risks, they are left in limbo. On the one hand, people benefit from the gap between the state's laws and the lack of enforcement of these laws, what Caldeira and Holston (1999: 692) might refer to as "disjunction." On the other hand, they also suffer from this gap. As these communities are not able to demand protection from the state, since they are involved in illicit activities themselves, armed actors can abuse people without fearing consequences. This limbo effectively silences calls for justice. At the Colombia-Venezuela border shared by Norte de Santander in Colombia and southern Zulia state in Venezuela, for example, people have been pressured to smuggle cocaine hidden in tires, children's toys, dogs' stomachs, women's breast implants, and inside the bodies of dead babies passed off as being asleep.[19] Both the gratitude for the "job opportunity" and the fear of the consequences when speaking out against those behind the business prevent people from reporting such "working conditions" to the state or from taking action against them on their own.

## CONCLUSION

This chapter has shown that tracing cocaine supply chains from within facilitates a nuanced understanding of the convergence of armed conflict and organized crime and its repercussions on local communities, an approach that is neglected by the conventional literature on the conflict–crime nexus and related phenomena. In particular, a focus first on local perceptions rather than outsider views, and second on interconnected processes and relationships between supply chain steps, rather than on individual sites in isolation, has provided valuable insights that point to several key factors essential to understanding the cocaine trade, its impacts of varied locales, and possible policy responses.

First, (re)gaining the state's perceived legitimacy and credibility among communities involved in cocaine economies should be a priority for governments. Contrary to outsiders' perceptions, the state is not necessarily perceived to be the solution, and the armed actors are not necessarily perceived to be "the bad guys." Without perceived legitimacy, the state's presence is futile.[20] Inhabitants may only perceive states as a valid alternative to illicit authority if they demonstrate efficiency, efficacy, and credibility. During a fieldwork trip to Putumayo in 2017, some farmers explained to me that they would go to the demobilization camp to discuss how to solve issues such as disputes between neighbors and a FARC commander, rather than turning to the local police.[21] This demonstrates that the farmers considered the FARC more efficient and more closely connected with the community than the local state authorities. Lund (2006: 693) notes that "what is legitimate varies between and within cultures and over time, and is continuously (re)established through conflict and negotiation." In historically neglected regions, governments need to negotiate their legitimacy by demonstrating credible commitment to taking care of the coca farmers, its citizens.

Providing feasible legal economic opportunities, not just through alternative development projects, but also the necessary road and communication infrastructure to sustain them, constitutes the most obvious entry point to regain state legitimacy. Fostering legal markets for coca is another, albeit more contested one. It would reduce the vulnerability of rural communities vis-à-vis the various armed groups and other illegal actors in their territory. It could thwart the power of criminal organizations involved in the illicit drug trade and enhance the security of rural communities (Idler 2021). Operating within the legal economy, communities might be more able to resort to the protection of the state in the face of threats posed by groups that operate illegally and who may want to divert the coca into the illicit cocaine market. Being able to assert their right to security and physical integrity would curb the authority and perceived legitimacy of the illegal actors and thus deprive them of political and economic power. It would also foster a sense of belonging to the state, rather than perpetuating the marginalization of inhabitants living on the national periphery. This way, it could transform shadow citizenship, characterized by a mutually reinforcing relationship between local citizens and violent non-state groups, into citizenship among the farmers—one that does not exist just in legal frameworks, but one that is actually recognized by the state.[22]

Second, tracing relations rather than analyzing fixed categories of actors shifts attention to the mechanisms that connect different steps in the cocaine supply chain. It reveals the agency of those who otherwise remain in the background, an important insight for designing interventions to enhance security along the cocaine supply chain. Financiers render the cocaine supply chain more stable while fueling uncertainty among the local population. Regulating the coca market would change this condition of vulnerability: the function of financiers could be taken over by licensed negotiators with transparency regarding their identity and their employer to make them accountable for their actions. Bolivia's approach to coca control, which includes accredited merchants in charge of the coca trade, could provide useful insights to establish a Colombian model (see, for example, Grisaffi, Farthing, and Ledebur 2017). Armed groups would have less social control over communities, as the mechanism of financiers silencing the farmers' voices would become void. Focusing on processes and relationships matters for strategies and policies to promote transitions from war to peace such as those in post–FARC peace deal Colombia. In regions where people do not have alternative livelihoods, transforming the illicit market into a licit one should take priority over other forms of bringing state institutions in to regain the perceived legitimacy as outlined above. As one of my interviewees put it, "We can't eat human rights."[23] Focusing on these processes and relationships should also be a priority to bring about peace. With a view to enhancing our understanding of how to work toward positive peace, Diehl (2016: 8) called for studying processes that lead to positive peace as opposed to "examining factors immediately preceding and following armed conflict." The processes linked to the cocaine economy persist throughout periods of armed conflict and "post-conflict." In fact, they prolong the lived experience of conflict in sites affected by it because the logic of mistrust and violence as outlined above persists, regardless of the formal end of the armed conflict. In Colombia's peripheries, transforming the illicit economy into legal economic opportunities therefore constitutes a critical step toward peace on the ground, not just on paper.

**NOTES**

Part of this research was assisted by the Drugs, Security and Democracy Fellowship Programme administered by the Social Science Research Council and the Universidad de los Andes in cooperation with and funds provided by the Open Society Foundations and the International Development Research Centre, Ottawa, Canada.

1  Author interview with ex-combatant, Colombia, 2012.
2  Author interviews with various coca farmers, Catatumbo, Colombia, 2012.
3  Participant observation by the author during a community meeting in Putumayo, Colombia, 2011.
4  Various author interviews in Sucumbíos, Ecuador, 2012.
5  Author interviews with farmers, Putumayo, 2017.

6 For a detailed conceptualization of illicit supply chain networks, see Idler 2020.

7 The operational territories of violent non-state groups typically coincide with an urban–rural divide (Laverde and Tapia 2009; Tickner, García, and Arrezea 2011).

8 Author interview with human rights defender, Pasto, Colombia, 2011.

9 Author interview with human rights defender, Pasto, Colombia, 2011.

10 It was common practice for the Colombian army and the paramilitaries to share intelligence with each other or indeed collaborate in order to fight the FARC.

11 Author interview with ex-combatants couple, Colombia, 2011.

12 Various interviews with coca farmers and civil society representatives in the Colombian departments of Nariño, Putumayo, Norte de Santander, and Cesar, Colombia, 2011–12.

13 Author interview with farmer, Putumayo, Colombia, 2011.

14 Author interview with international agency staff, Putumayo, Colombia, 2011.

15 Author interview with civil society representative, Putumayo, Colombia, 2011.

16 Author interview with farmer, Putumayo, Colombia, 2011.

17 One *arroba* equals 11.3 kilograms.

18 Author interview with farmer, Putumayo, Colombia, 2011.

19 Author interview with high-ranking police commander, Maracaibo, Venezuela, 2012.

20 For a discussion of perceived legitimacy in the context of Colombian marginalized communities, see Idler, Mouly, and Garrido (2018).

21 Author interviews with various farmers, Putumayo, Colombia, 2017.

22 Certainly, as Ramírez shows with her analysis of *cocalero* movements, there are cases where communities have demanded citizenship rights, which in itself is a manifestation of citizenship—but not necessarily one that is recognized by the state (Ramírez 2011).

23 Author interview with local farmer, Colombia, Colombia, 2017.

**REFERENCES**

Andreas, Peter. 2009. *Border Games: Policing the U.S.-Mexico Divide*, 2nd ed. Ithaca, NY: Cornell University Press.

Andreas, Peter. 2014. *Smuggler Nation: How Illicit Trade Made America*. New York: Oxford University Press.

Asad, Talal. 2004. "Where Are the Margins of the State?" In *Anthropology in the Margins of the State*, edited by Veena Das and Deborah Poole, 279–88. Santa Fe, NM: SAR Press.

Berdal, Mats R., and Monica Serrano. 2002. *Transnational Organized Crime and International Security: Business as Usual?* Boulder, CO: Lynne Rienner.

Bonilla, Adrián, and Hernán Moreano. 2009. "Narcotráfico en El Ecuador: 1989–2009." In *La Guerra Contra las Drogas en el Mundo Andino: Hacia un Cambio de Paradigma*, edited by Juan Gabriel Tokatlian, 125–64. Buenos Aires: Libros del Zorzal.

Buxton, Julia. 2006. *The Political Economy of Narcotics: Production, Consumption and Global Markets*. London: Zed.

Caldeira, Teresa P. R., and James Holston. 1999. "Democracy and Violence in Brazil." *Comparative Studies in Society and History* 41, no. 4: 691–729.

Castells, Manuel. 2010. *End of Millennium*, 2nd ed. Oxford: Wiley-Blackwell.

De Boer, John, and Louise Bosetti. 2017. "The Crime-Conflict Nexus. Assessing the Threat and Developing Solutions." New York: United Nations University Centre for Policy Research.

Deville, Duncan. 2013. "The Illicit Supply Chain." In *Convergence: Illicit Networks and National Security in the Age of Globalization*, edited by Michael Miklaucic and Jacqueline Brewer, 63–74. Washington, DC: National Defense University.

Diehl, Paul F. 2016. "Exploring Peace: Looking beyond War and Negative Peace." *International Studies Quarterly* 60, no. 1: 1–10. https://doi.org/10.1093/isq /sqw005.

Eilstrup-Sangiovanni, Mette, and Calvert Jones. 2008. "Assessing the Dangers of Illicit Networks: Why al-Qaida May Be Less Threatening Than Many Think." *International Security* 33, no. 2: 7–44. https://doi.org/10.1162/isec.2008.33.2.7.

Felbab-Brown, Vanda. 2010. "Rules and Regulations in Ungoverned Spaces: Illicit Economies, Criminals, and Belligerents." In *Ungoverned Spaces: Alternatives to State Authority in an Era of Softened Sovereignty*, edited by Anne L. Clunan and Harold A. Trinkunas, 175–92. Stanford, CA: Stanford University Press.

Gambetta, Diego. 1990. *Trust: Making and Breaking Cooperative Relations*. Cambridge, MA: Blackwell.

Gambetta, Diego. 1993. *The Sicilian Mafia: The Business of Private Protection*. Cambridge, MA: Harvard University Press.

Gambetta, Diego. 2009. *Codes of the Underworld: How Criminals Communicate*. Princeton, NJ: Princeton University Press.

Gootenberg, Paul. 2021. "Building the Global Drug Regime: Origins and Impact, 1909–1990s." In *Transforming the War on Drugs: Victims, Warriors, and Vulnerable Regions*, edited by Annette Idler and Juan Carlos Garzón Vergara, 49–78. New York: Oxford University Press.

Grisaffi, Thomas, and Kathryn Ledebur. 2016. "Citizenship or Repression? Coca, Eradication and Development in the Andes." *Stability: International Journal of Security and Development* 5, no. 1. https://doi.org/10.5334/sta.440.

Grisaffi, Thomas, Linda Farthing, and Kathryn Ledebur. 2017. "Integrated Development with Coca in the Plurinational State of Bolivia: Shifting the Focus from Eradication to Poverty Alleviation." *Bulletin on Narcotics* 51: 131–57.

Horkheimer, Max. 1969. *Dialektik der Aufklärung; Philosophische Fragmente*. Frankfurt am Main: Fischer Taschenbuch Verlag.

ICG. 2010. "Improving Security Policy in Colombia." Bogotá: International Crisis Group.

Idler, Annette. 2014. "Espacios Invisibilizados: Actores Violentos No-Estatales y 'Ciudadanía de Sombra' en las Zonas Fronterizas de Colombia." *Estudios Indiana*: 213–34.

Idler, Annette. 2019. *Borderland Battles: Violence, Crime, and Governance at the Edges of Colombia's War*. New York: Oxford University Press.

Idler, Annette. 2020. "The Logic of Illicit Flows in Armed Conflict: Explaining Variation in Violent Nonstate Group Interactions in Colombia." *World Politics* 72, no. 3: 335–76. doi:10.1017/S0043887120000040.

Idler, Annette. 2021. "Warriors, Victims, and Vulnerable Regions: A Critical Perspective on the War on Drugs." In *Transforming the War on Drugs: Victims, Warriors, and Vulnerable Regions*, edited by Annette Idler and Juan Carlos Garzón Vergara, 19–49. New York: Oxford University Press.

Idler, Annette, and James J. F. Forest. 2015. "Behavioral Patterns among (Violent) Non-State Actors: A Study of Complementary Governance." *Stability: International Journal of Security and Development* 4, no. 1. https://www.stabilityjournal.org/articles/10.5334/sta.er/.

Idler, Annette, Cécile Mouly, and María Belén Garrido. 2018. "Between Shadow Citizenship and Civil Resistance: Shifting Local Orders in a Colombian War-Torn Community." In *Local Peacebuilding and Legitimacy: Interactions between National and Local Levels*, edited by Landon E. Hancock and Christopher Mitchell, 43–62. London: Routledge. https://www.routledge.com/Local-Peacebuilding-and-Legitimacy-Interactions-between-National-and-Local/Hancock-Mitchell/p/book/9781138224148.

Idler, Annette, and Juan Carlos Garzón Vergara. 2021. "Fifty Years of the War on Drugs: A Moment of Uncertainty." In *Transforming the War on Drugs: Victims, Warriors, and Vulnerable Regions*, edited by Annette Idler and Juan Carlos Garzón Vergara, 1–18. New York: Oxford University Press.

InSight Crime. n.d. "Rastrojos." InSight Crime: Organized Crime in the Americas (blog). http://www.insightcrime.org/groups-colombia/rastrojos.

Knight, Frank H. 1921. *Risk, Uncertainty and Profit*. Boston: Houghton Mifflin.

Koonings, Kees, and Dirk Krujit. 1999. *Societies of Fear: The Legacy of Civil War, Violence and Terror in Latin America*. London: Zed.

Korf, Benedikt, and Timothy Raeymaekers. 2013. *Violence on the Margins: States, Conflict, and Borderlands*. New York: Palgrave Macmillan.

Krause, Keith, and Michael C. Williams. 1997. *Critical Security Studies: Concepts and Cases*. London: UCL Press.

Laverde, Zully, and Edwin Tapia. 2009. *Tensión en las Fronteras*. Bogotá: CODHES.

Lund, Christian. 2006. "Twilight Institutions: Public Authority and Local Politics in Africa." *Development and Change* 37, no. 4: 685–705.

Morehouse, Barbara J., Vera Pavlakovich-Kochi, and Doris Wastl-Walter. 2004. "Introduction: Perspectives on Borderlands." In *Challenged Borderlands: Tran-*

*scending Political and Cultural Boundaries*, edited by Barbara J. Morehouse, Vera Pavlakovich-Kochi, and Doris Wastl-Walter, 3–11. Aldershot, UK: Ashgate.

Nugent, Paul, and Anthony Ijaola Asiwaju. 2020. *African Boundaries: Barriers, Conduits, and Opportunities*. London: Pinter.

Poe, Abigail, and Adam Isacson. 2011. "Stabilization and Development: Lessons of Colombia's 'Consolidation' Model." Washington, DC: Center for International Policy.

Polanyi, Karl. 2001. *The Great Transformation: The Political and Economic Origins of Our Time*. Boston: Beacon.

Ramírez, María Clemencia. 2011. *Between the Guerrillas and the State: The Cocalero Movement, Citizenship, and Identity in the Colombian Amazon*. Durham, NC: Duke University Press.

Salehyan, I. 2007. "Transnational Rebels: Neighboring States as Sanctuary for Rebel Groups." *World Politics* 59: 217–42.

Sanderson, Thomas M. 2004. "Transnational Terror and Organized Crime: Blurring the Lines." *SAIS Review* 24, no. 1: 49–61.

Tate, Winifred. 2015. *Drugs, Thugs, and Diplomats: U.S. Policymaking in Colombia*. Stanford, CA: Stanford University Press.

Thompson, E. P. 1971. "The Moral Economy of the English Crowd in the Eighteenth Century." *Past and Present* 50, no. 1: 76–136. https://doi.org/10.1093/past/50.1.76.

Thoumi, Francisco E. 1995. *Political Economy and Illegal Drugs in Colombia*. New York: United Nations University Press.

Tickner, Arlene B., Diego García, and Catalina Arrezea. 2011. "Actores Violentos No Estatales y Narcotráfico en Colombia." In *Políticas Antidroga en Colombia: Éxitos, Fracasos y Extravíos*, edited by Alejandro Gaviria Uribe, 413–45. Bogotá: Universidad de los Andes.

UNODC. 2010. *The Globalization of Crime: A Transnational Organized Crime Threat Assessment*. Vienna: United Nations Office on Drugs and Crime.

UNODC. 2012. "Colombia: Coca Cultivation Survey 2011." Bogotá: United Nations Office on Drugs and Crime.

UNODC. 2014a. "Colombia: Coca Cultivation Survey 2013." Bogotá: United Nations Office on Drugs and Crime.

UNODC. 2014b. "Global Study on Homicide 2013: Trends, Contexts, Data." Vienna: United Nations Office on Drugs and Crime.

UNODC. 2016. *World Drug Report 2016*. Vienna: United Nations Office on Drugs and Crime.

UNODC. 2018. *World Drug Report 2018: Analysis of Drug Markets*. Vienna: United Nations Office on Drugs and Crime.

Vorrath, Judith. 2010. "On the Margin of Statehood? State-Society Relations in African Borderlands." In *Understanding Life in the Borderlands: Boundaries in Depth and in Motion*, edited by I. William Zartman, 85–104. Athens: University of Georgia Press.

# 03 DRUG CROPS, TWISTED MOTORCYCLES, AND CULTURAL LOSS IN INDIGENOUS COLOMBIA

In 2013, indigenous youth activists gathered for their yearly regional meeting in a clearing in the green mountainous terrain of Colombia's southwestern department of Cauca. They discussed their community's most urgent issue, the impact of drug crop production. During the meeting, one young man, Jonas, addressed his peers with the following reflection on changes brought on by the drug trade: "What are we eating? We are feeding our bodies and our thoughts with lots of stuff from outside. We need to think about the land before we fall in love with clothes and motorcycles. Beauty doesn't last. We want to be like the whites, but we have to be like we really are, like original peoples." For activists such as Jonas, global commodities like brand name clothes and motorcycles are some of the most visible signs of the breakdown of social cohesion that has been brought on by the drug trade. Like Jonas, many activists presented global commodities as being at odds with their identity as "original peoples" (first peoples).

The circulation of global commodities in Cauca contributes to what geographer Cindy Katz (2004) has characterized as "rural cosmopolitanism," an increasing fluidity between the city and the countryside. With the availability of motorcycles, household electronics, and smartphones, indigenous farmers are no longer only producers in the global economy—they increasingly share a consumer culture with others throughout the world.

The drug trade has been instrumental in this transition from an economy based on artisanal production, local barter, and limited cash exchange to a cash-based consumer economy.

Overall, the increased access to goods and services has meant an improved quality of life for many indigenous people. But their insertion into the global commodity chain has not been on equal terms. Many commodities were introduced to these communities via illegal means, through money earned through drug production, exacerbating the moral discourses around "modern" consumption. Indigenous people's involvement in illicit exchanges means that they are in regular contact with illegal armed groups vying for control of resources, labor, and markets. Indigenous *comuneros* (community members) have reported that drug traffickers often have cooperative relationships with the Colombian military, local elites, and state officials. Together, these powerful groups dominate the local trade in licit and illicit goods (see also Idler, this volume).

This chapter identifies a paradox: On the one hand, drug crops are a vehicle for social mobility and development. But on the other hand, the drug trade is associated with diminishing values and indigenous ways of life. Community leaders and cultural activists, such as the youth leader cited above, grapple with myriad social problems such as alcoholism, disobedient youth, increasing drug use in the community, and disrespect for indigenous authorities. Some of these problems predated the drug economy, and others were exacerbated by it.

For Cauca's indigenous people, the strengthening of cultural identity has always been an important part of indigenous political resistance. They have mobilized against elites, state, and non-state actors that have exploited their land and labor. However, as some scholars have argued, movements based on cultural identity alone limit the advancement of oppressed groups when separated from redistributive demands (Goldberg 1994; Fraser 1997; Hale 2002, 2005). In this chapter I outline how indigenous people draw on available discourses about cultural loss and youth, and argue that the ways that cultural activists talk about the drug economy reflect broader political tensions between indigenous authorities and the state.

This chapter primarily focuses on indigenous community leaders and cultural activists, set apart from indigenous authorities. Indigenous authorities, who make up *cabildos*, headed by indigenous governors, are the legitimate political representatives of the indigenous community, and are charged with enforcing governance in indigenous territories—including Colombian drug policy that prohibits drug production. Community leaders and activists have less political position at stake than cabildo members, and have more flexibility in their critiques of the drug economy, drug policy, and indigenous and state authorities. These critiques may be shaped by their own proximity to the cabildo via groups in which they participate, or their own direct experience as former cabildo members. Although I focus in this chapter on community activists, I wish to highlight that the context from which I draw—an indigenous school and youth activists—was more subject to the oversight of indigenous authorities. They did not represent groups that were openly critical of indigenous authorities, or the political structure that made and enforced drug policy.

## COCAINE AND COCA FARMING IN COLOMBIA

Most popular histories of the drug trade in Colombia mark its beginning with Pablo Escobar's notorious cocaine enterprise in the late 1970s and 1980s. Colombia became known the world over as the leading exporter of cocaine and a crucible of unspeakable violence at the hands of Escobar and other drug entrepreneurs who struck back at the state that frantically tried to rein them in. Among these vengeful acts of the drug traffickers were the assassinations of judges, journalists, and politicians who furthered the cause of extradition to the United States. It also included the organization of urban paramilitary gangs that continue to terrorize some of the country's poorest neighborhoods to this day. In some policy circles, Colombia was referred to as a "narco-democracy" for the ways in which the state was corrupted by or held hostage to the interests of drug traffickers (Youngers and Rosin 2005). Escobar's reign came to a dramatic end in 1993 when, with the assistance of US Special Forces and intelligence agencies, Colombia's military shot Escobar dead on a rooftop in Medellín.

While Colombian drug trafficking is the subject of innumerable texts, documentaries, and dramatizations, drug production is a lesser known component of the drug commodity chain outside policy circles. Within international policy circles, drug production is a regular focus due to US supply-side reduction strategies, which target "producer countries" such as Colombia and have dominated international drug policy since the 1970s, along with the increasing criminalization of demand in the US. Outside of these policy circles, drug production is less dramatic and less spectacular to the general public. Drug crop farmers as well as cocaine laboratory workers are represented as part of the social backdrop in mainstream media. They are poor farmers, often darker skinned and humble compared to the modern, urban, and savvy drug entrepreneurs. While elements of the racialization and urban/rural divide between drug traffickers and drug crop producers are true, the complexity of drug crop producers' worlds is rarely portrayed.

Needless to say, drug crop producers make up a crucial part of the drug commodity chain, but they are the most exploited. Drug crop cultivators earn about 2 percent of the overall profit (Ramírez, Stanton, and Walsh 2005; Camacho, Gaviria, and Rodriguez 2011). For example, while the US street value of a pound of marijuana is generally over a thousand dollars, a Colombian farmer in 2015 was earning about ten to fifteen dollars for that same pound. While in some cases farmers are compelled by armed groups to produce, the higher earnings from illicit crops compared to licit crops often provides enough incentive for cash-poor Colombian farmers to grow drug crops without much coercion. Small-scale entrepreneurship exists within producing communities, in which some individuals rent plots to grow coca or marijuana and sell to *compradores*, or buyers. There is a strong dividing line between production and trafficking, as compradores generally do not invest in land, and indigenous people almost never cross into the comprador class. As Sanabria (1993) pointed out in his work on Bolivia, because of the relatively small profits from production compared to trafficking and export, there is little incentive for traffickers to control production. In fact, this provides more incentive to maintain that dividing line—investing in production would drive up costs, so there would be less profit to be made.

While they might make some cash, indigenous farmers' economic mobility within illicit markets is limited. They may cultivate drug crops, or rent out their land so that others can do so. However, none have been known to act as buyers who purchase harvested marijuana to be sold, or coca leaves or paste to be processed into cocaine in a laboratory, respectively. Some engage in what is referred to as "micro-trafficking" by transporting small quantities for sale in the region, but they do not have the access to large vehicles or networks of corrupt military and police officers needed to become mid- or large-scale traffickers. One lawyer who regularly represented indigenous defendants told me that indigenous farmers are often caught trafficking small quantities of drugs, but large-scale drug traffickers are seldom arrested. He insisted that there was collusion between drug traffickers and local police.

Throughout the 1980s and early 1990s, Colombia's drug policy makers were preoccupied with the war against major drug traffickers seeking political control in the country and resisting extradition to the United States.

But after decades of failed attempts to rein them in, policy makers shifted harsh measures toward drug crop cultivators, too. In 1999, the US and Colombian governments signed Plan Colombia, which led to the criminalization of drug crop cultivators, authorized the increased use of aerial fumigation as a form of drug control, and, most significantly, associated drug crop cultivation with the guerrilla insurgent activity (Ramírez, Stanton, and Walsh 2005; Youngers and Rosin 2005). Colombia is the only nation in the world that has permitted the use of aerial fumigation to combat drug crop cultivation.

Colombia's Law 30 of 1986 made provisions that allowed indigenous communities to cultivate up to thirty coca plants for local traditional use and exchange.[1] There were provisions in drug laws that have mandated alternative development programs for indigenous and campesino drug crop growers, some of which were implemented in the 1990s, though with limited effect. Aerial fumigation programs have generally not targeted the indigenous coca-growing regions of Cauca, though the area has been a site of intense military activity as the Colombian government has long fought guerrillas in the region.

Until recently, the impact of the illicit drug economy on indigenous farming communities has rarely been examined by scholars. While some scholars have researched the drug economy in agricultural communities, some of which may have been indigenous, they have not focused on indigenous identity (for example, Sanabria 1993; Ferro 1999; Ramírez 2011). Earlier examples of ethnographic work that highlighted indigenous communities and illicit crop cultivation include Field's (1994, 1996) work in Colombia; and in geography, Steinberg, Hobbs, and Mathewson (2004). Recently, Grisaffi (2019) and Pellegrini (2016) have examined the relationship between Bolivia's coca growers and state-backed notions of indigeneity promoted by former President Evo Morales. Grisaffi's work looks more explicitly at how Bolivia's national indigenous identity is set against the illicit cocaine trade, and how coca farmers navigate both indigenous indigeneity and new policies that support legal coca production.

Colombian indigenous people's lives overlap with the drug economy in two crucial ways. The first is by their living relationship to it. By 1999, it was estimated that 41 percent of Colombia's indigenous people had been directly affected: either they had participated in the drug trade or drug traffickers had set up operations in or near their communities (Perafán 1999). The second is through the claim to a distinct historical relationship with the raw materials of drug production: plants and land. This is distinct from what is found in other sites of drug production, such as a methamphetamine laboratory in the United States, or a cocaine laboratory in a nonindigenous rural part of Colombia where producers do not assert such claims. For example, coca is widely known as a plant native to the Andes, recognized for its "traditional" use among Andean indigenous communities before the Conquest and, more importantly, before drug trafficking (Henman 1987). However, this claim extends to plants in general, as a key aspect of indigenous cosmovision is recognition of agency in all of the plant crops that they cultivate, whether illicit or not (Rappaport 1985, 1998; Yule 2004).

## COCA AND THE MORAL ECONOMY

Andeanists have upheld coca as a quintessential symbol of Andean indigenous culture (Allen 1981, 1988; Henman 1987). As with other Andean communities, in Cauca dried coca leaves are available in weekly markets, and coca has traditionally been a sacred plant used for work, rituals, and medicine by the Nasa, Misak, and other indigenous communities of Colombia's highlands. In local narratives, the cultivation of coca for drug production is seen as a threat to these cultural practices. This culturalist narrative, promoted by some Andeanist scholars and indigenous activists, holds that cocaine production defiles the sacred role of coca and other ritualistic and medicinal plants in indigenous traditional life (see, for example, Henman 1987; Pacini and Franquemont 1986; Perafán 1999). At the same time, drug crop production, which introduces market relations and cash, is said to disrupt local indigenous systems of social and economic order. This set of harmonious social relations set against a corrupt profit-seeking market economy echoes E. P. Thompson's (1971) notion of the moral economy.

For Thompson, a moral economy was the basis on which exploited groups would make demands. In peasant studies, a "moral economy" refers to a precapitalist system of exchange that maintained social cohesion and buffered inequalities among small-scale agriculturalists living under feudalism (Scott 1976). However, as Raymond Williams (1973) pointed out, scholars have often romanticized the past when they used the term *moral economy* to describe a socially harmonious "precapitalist" past that never really existed. These precapitalist social arrangements, he points out, were often just as oppressive as the capitalist ones.

Following Williams's critique, anthropologist and historian William Roseberry wrote: "As some might argue, the 'moral economy' need not have existed in the past; it may be *perceived* in the past from the perspective of a disordered present. The images of a moral economy may be a *meaningful* image even if 'what actually happened' was less idyllic" (1989: 57). Roseberry acknowledged the significance of drawing attention to the roles of pre-capitalist practices of artisans and peasants in challenging modernization theorists' dismissal of the past. Such a "meaningful image" comes into play as indigenous people discuss coca and the drug economy.

The view that indigenous economic practices in their "purest" form are isolated from the global economy has been shaped by (now outdated) anthropological notions of indigenous people in the Andes as historically discrete groups that are set apart from modernity (see debates reviewed by Starn 1994). In Colombia, anthropologists working in the first half of the twentieth century were drawn to studying indigenous people living on reservations or *resguardos* (communally held lands) because there they could document "exotic" indigenous practices supposedly untouched by outside influences (see, for example, Bernal Villa 1954). Anthropologists paid little attention to the racial, class, and colonial hierarchies in which these resguardo communities were situated. Furthermore, indigenous communities living closer to urban centers, such as those living in Cauca's northern region, were deemed to be less interesting for study, and as such were largely ignored.

Indigenous cultural-historical claims to coca and other plants used for drug production have lent themselves to binary distinctions between "traditional" and "modern" uses of sacred plants. Bolivian drug policy in recent years is an example (see Grisaffi, this volume). Under President Evo Morales, a former coca grower, Bolivia implemented a policy of "social control" in which the government regulates coca production for a legal internal market. This has been effective in Bolivia, a country with a majority indigenous population, many of whom continue to use coca on a regular basis. Under the slogan "Coca yes, cocaine no," the government has supported a campaign that depicts cocaine as a white man's drug, and its production and consumption as the continuation of colonial practices, while coca is presented as a traditional plant of indigenous people. This has provided a model that sets traditional coca against its derivative product, cocaine.

Coca is documented as biologically native to the Andes, and was historically used and distributed in the Incan empire prior to the Spanish conquest. Coca's continued distribution was advanced by Spanish colonial officials, who saw that it helped indigenous laborers get through long days working in silver mines and haciendas. The market was controlled largely by Spanish entrepreneurs, even though they generally saw coca chewing as repulsive (Gootenberg 2008). Coca helped to facilitate the extraction of surplus value from indigenous laborers. This contrasts with notions of a contained economy of coca production and consumption, and of coca being a strictly spiritual plant embedded solely in precapitalist contexts.

Chewing coca is not a regular daily practice today in Cauca. The chewing of coca had fallen out of common practice by the mid-twentieth century (Henman 1987). Even by the 1950s, Bernal (1954) noted, albeit without much elaboration, that coca cultivations were seen as "for the whites." While in a Tierradentro resguardo, deep in Cauca's mountainous interior, he observed that only elders chewed coca during their work days, speaking little in order to savor the bulges in their lower lip, while younger people passed the days conversing with one another. It is important to note that, even though it is not routinely used in the work day, coca is still regularly used for both ritualistic and medicinal purposes. Full bags of it can still be purchased in local stores and shops in indigenous towns. Cultural activists occasionally chew it during meetings and assemblies. Finally, it still holds an important place in indigenous cosmovision (see Grisaffi, this volume, for an overview of the relationship between coca, indigenous culture, and social reproduction).

It is common for indigenous leaders and cultural activists, such as the youth who spoke at the beginning of this chapter, to romanticize the time before the onset of the drug trade as an idyllic, socially harmonious past when the local economy was rooted in artisanal production, subsistence farming, and local noncapitalist forms of exchange. In these narratives the influx of industrially produced commodities, made affordable by drug crop earnings, corrupted these native systems of production and exchange.

Despite these romanticizations, Cauca's indigenous communities were never isolated from the surrounding economy, class conflicts, and political turmoil. Colombia's renowned indigenous movement is historically rooted in the peasant movement of the 1970s. When indigenous people made culturally distinct demands for land from this period into the 1980s, they won unprecedented rights to it. Yet despite these land gains, indigenous people continued to face economic challenges as small farmers competing with an increasingly industrialized agrarian economy. It was in this context that drug crop cultivation took root (literally) in Colombia's countryside. Drug crop cultivation enabled Caucan indigenous farmers to earn cash and hedge against the anticipated failures of government-led development programs[2] in their territories (Field 1994).

Despite distinctions between a past based on local exchange and a corrupt present dependent on outside goods and nonindigenous entrepreneurs, such a clear historic break is elusive. Before the drug trade, indigenous economic practices were not limited to local artisan production and barter. The drug economy that arrived in Cauca in the 1970s was the latest in a series of cash crop economies in which indigenous people had participated from the nineteenth century onward. These included felling the region's native cinchona trees, the source of quinine, an antimalarial medication, in exchange for cash from external entrepreneurs in the 1870s (Rappaport 1985), followed by coffee and *fique*, a fiber used for making rope, throughout the twentieth century, among other commodities. The small amounts of cash earned with other (legal) cash crops enabled indigenous people to purchase low-value commodities such as salt, clothes, and utensils. Each of these led to social tensions among indigenous communities living on reservations, especially because the cash economy brought by outsiders interfered with the authority of indigenous leaders (Rappaport 1998).

Even though there are various continuities between cultivation of drug crops and other licit cash crops, the drug crop economy differs from these previous cash crop economies in two ways. First, it brought an unprecedented flow of cash and commodities to the region. In this sense, drug crop cultivation was more quantitatively than qualitatively unique in that it amplified the social impact of cash and commodity flows into the region. As I will discuss later, this cash flow irreversibly integrated indigenous communities into a global consumer culture. The second, and more obvious, way is that it operated outside the law. This has made indigenous communities that grow coca targets of political and military repression. It has also extensively shaped how community leaders talk about the drug economy, as I show in the next section.

## TALKING ABOUT DRUG CROPS AT SCHOOL

While increasing household incomes, the drug trade has also brought many social problems to the region. Cash crop economies subject cultivators to boom and bust cycles far out of their control. The illicitness of the drug trade makes them a target for social and political marginalization. It has also brought armed groups that either control or extract taxes from drug production and trade. This has also entrenched the country's armed conflict between the military and insurgent left- and right-wing forces in these rural territories. Many indigenous leaders frame these problems as both cause and effect of a loss of cultural identity. However, this narrative is also at odds with the fact that the drug trade has enabled social mobility and an increase in the quality of life for many indigenous families.

Community leaders and activists are mostly aware of the larger structural factors that compel drug crop production, and the inevitability of the integration with a global consumer culture. However, these structural forces are less often a topic of discussion in public settings, even though it can be a point of tension between indigenous comuneros, who are exasperated with such blame discourses, and indigenous authorities in particular, who wield local power to sanction them. As I argue, this tension between the comuneros and indigenous authorities charged with representing them arises from the fact that the legitimacy of the indigenous movement, vis-à-vis the Colombian state, is constantly threatened by their participation in activities that the state deems illicit, and their proximity to left-wing guerrillas who have long operated in the region.

To present indigenous drug crop cultivation as something indigenous communities do willingly is to risk the gains of the indigenous movement. The far right, notoriously opposed to indigenous people's hard-won multicultural rights, contends that indigenous people who participate in the drug trade are cunning allies or malicious dupes of the drug trade and therefore undeserving of state resources and land. For this reason, liberal-oriented responses to drug crop cultivation have highlighted the lack of viable alternative economic options for poor Andean farmers, indigenous and nonindigenous, as the primary motivator for their participation in this illicit activity, and have funneled scholarly efforts toward supporting economic alternatives that would facilitate the successful integration of these communities into Colombian society (see, for example, Ramírez 2011 on the cocalero movement in Colombia, and Farthing and Ledebur 2015 on the implementation of Bolivia's "social control" policies).

For indigenous communities, these efforts took on an additional cultural feature that aimed to conserve "traditional" indigenous values and lifeways, which drug production is alleged to disrupt. However, these efforts overlook the productive (not to say positive) social effects of the drug trade on these communities—in particular, the transition to a cash-based economy. In the face of this transition, which occurred in tandem with new and exacerbated social problems, many indigenous activists turn inward, lamenting the loss of indigenous values as the source of these social problems associated with the drug economy. Less discussed are structural forces—political hierarchies and drug policy—as a target of change.

As Colombian drug control policies have targeted drug crop growers, the illegality of drug crops has profoundly shaped the way that indigenous leaders and activists talk about the drug trade and its impact on the community. In particular, schoolteachers and community activists whose role has been to focus on and reinforce the "cultural" aspects of indigenous life, have also formed discourses that emphasize the negative impact of the drug trade. Even though, privately, many in the community recognized that drug crop cultivation helped individuals and families to meet their economic needs, in public many emphasized how drug cultivation caused social problems. As I describe below, this has put boundaries on the acceptable ways that comuneros can talk about the drug trade in public settings, its causes, and effects on their lives.

In 2015, I conducted a series of focus groups with indigenous teachers and young adult students in an indigenous youth education program, in which we discussed the impact of drug crop production in the community. Similar to a GED course in the United States, the program was designed to close the generational gap between the majority of younger people enrolled in high school and older people, many of whom had not had the opportunity to graduate. These workshops provided much insight into how discourses about the drug trade were shaped and what was more and less acceptable. Mercedes, the principal of the school, welcomed the workshop analyzing the local trade, saying that the participants would not be pointing fingers about who is involved, because, in perhaps a bit of hyperbole: "Even the Church is involved in that." Still, she wanted participants to focus on discussing the "many problems" that drug crop cultivation has caused in the community.

Omaira, a teacher in the program who volunteered to cofacilitate one of the focus group series, set the tone when she spoke openly about what she saw as the negative impact of drug crop cultivation. Omaira was a single mother of two who, along with her occupation as a teacher, rented out a plot of land to marijuana growers in order to make ends meet. Even though marijuana cultivation played an important role in her household income, she focused on the social hazards of drug crop cultivation:

> Marijuana is cultivated because it helps us with our economy. . . . But this created a lot of dependency, because now, young people don't think about work, saying, for example, "I'm going to plant myself, say, a potato crop." . . . Today young people see illicit crops as a form of surviving. For example, you can see now the kids in the school selling [drugs], because they don't see another way of working; they say that it is easier that way. . . . They don't want to work very hard to earn anything, they want it easy. Even more than that, I have fought to get a woman who will work in the house to take care of

my daughter. They do nothing but *peluqueando* [harvesting marijuana]. And *el señor* (the older man) says no, well, I am in the shade, I eat lunch, I don't get sunburned, I'm in the house, and I'm earning money. . . . The craziest thing is that people prefer to abandon food crops and coffee to plant that plant [marijuana]. . . . Everything that we are eating are flours [imported starches], and they are things brought from outside, not even grown on the farm. It is becoming a problem of eating, of health, of dependency; it is becoming a social problem. . . . You see the one who is growing a little marijuana, you see him drinking [alcohol] every weekend. Having that money has created a worrisome situation.

As Omaira saw it, drug crop cultivation created "dependency," which meant the loss of subsistence crop cultivation such as potatoes. It also made people lazy. She echoed an oft-repeated characterization of young people as wanting things "easy," rather than working hard for them. This extended to older people as well, who could not be troubled with more conventional jobs such as domestic work, when they could earn more harvesting marijuana or renting out their plots. Even worse, money from drug crops contributed to alcoholism and other vices—including drug use.

In the weeks that followed, the young adult participants generally followed suit by continuing to identify the various problems that they saw as rooted in the drug trade. Many focused especially on drug use in the local community as a growing problem. Increasingly, indigenous community members had taken to using drugs themselves, whether smoking marijuana or using cocaine in the bars and *discotecas*. Drug use was openly associated with stigmatizing tropes of urban delinquency. Marijuana made people crazy and/or commit crime, and parents expressed fears that if their children were to use it, the children would end up "living under a bridge." Cocaine was used to extend long nights of drinking at discotecas that could result in conflict and violence. Many saw these problems of drug use and delinquency as a moral consequence of the fact that these drugs were produced in the territory. Curiously, while drug use incited anxiety and stigma from the community in general, there seemed to be a more pronounced moral panic over marijuana use—and exaggerated ideas about its effects—than cocaine use.

For this reason, it was remarkable when a participant pushed back against the "problem-oriented" discourse associated with drug crop cultivation. In the same opening workshop in which Omaira spoke, Marco Evelio, an indigenous student in his thirties, began a long testimony by telling the story of his experience *metiendo vicio*, or using drugs (it was not clear which ones) for what he recounted as about two years. He was proud to say that he eventually stopped at the behest of his wife. Then he concluded with a reflection on drug use and drug crop cultivation:

> The [indigenous] council, the authorities . . . say things about people who cultivate drug crops. They should help those people who need the help, they need it! There are some who do it out of necessity, because at home they are in need of many things, because they have a problem with the economy. . . . So now we ourselves are cultivating it. Why? Because it gives us money, and it allows us to feed our families, to clothe our children. With this, we are helping ourselves get by. Some people have gotten out of it, and now they are teachers! And I see that! It's not just me, it's even the teachers!

Marco Evelio's position was remarkable for how it put him at odds with the prevailing consensus about the problems of the drug trade. Marco Evelio seemed sensitive to this, as it was clear that he sought to head off ridicule from his peers by audaciously pointing out that many people, including teachers, had grown illicit crops. For him, drug cultivation was not a problem, but a solution to household economic troubles. Furthermore, by suggesting that the indigenous council should help people with their economic problems, Marco Evelio also touched on a sensitive nerve in the discourse on the drug trade—that drug crop cultivation, because of its ability to help with such problems, potentially eroded the authority of indigenous leadership. Marco Evelio challenged both the moral discourses that framed the drug trade as bad, but also the moral economy narrative that described the drug trade as disruptive to indigenous values.

There was little follow-up to Marco Evelio's critique, that day or any other. His speech was somewhat garbled and rambling, so it was easier for his peers to not engage, though they did laugh at his stories about getting high and drunk. Omaira responded to his testimony of drug use with curiosity. She and other teachers were generally sympathetic to students' and other community members' needs to grow drug crops to make ends meet. For example, when one student stopped coming to class because he could not pay the tuition, she said to me that he struggled specifically because, as an evangelical Christian, he did not grow coca or marijuana, and noted how unfair it was that such were the conditions under which many had to decide to grow drug crops or not.

The difference between Omaira's and Marco Evelio's approaches is not rooted necessarily in the totality of their outlooks, but of their social position in the community. Even if community leaders and cultural activists might be aware of the greater structural forces beyond the community's control that led them to grow coca and other drug crops, they may not necessarily draw on this insight when speaking with other comuneros. Omaira and many others like her were keenly aware of the indigenous community's subordinate position in the global drug commodity chain and the political forces that shaped it. Yet community leaders and cultural activists are caught between this structural awareness and their duty to confront the very real social problems the drug trade caused. The decades-rehearsed and repeated discourse of the immorality of the drug trade was an accessible one. It made the course of action for comuneros simple and concrete: stop growing drug crops.

On the other hand, Marco Evelio, as a comunero with no stake in leadership, and having shed the aura of self-blame, was more comfortable turning the focus on these structural causes. He did not deny the negative consequences, as he admitted the wrong of spurning his household responsibilities for drug use, but the solution extended beyond individual household decisions to stop growing drug crops, for, as he pointed out more openly than anyone else, meeting economic needs without growing drug crops just was not that easy. It would require the help and political will of indigenous authorities, and others beyond them, to meet those needs. Until then, people would continue to grow drug crops, regardless of the consequences.

The conditions for a moral economy that would allow indigenous people to trade harmoniously among themselves, without a lucrative cash crop such as coca or marijuana, is now gone. The needs of indigenous families have extended beyond commodities that could be locally produced. As I show in the next section, the drug economy was instrumental in accelerating this transition from local commodity consumption to a cash-based economy with a nearly irreversible reliance on global commodities. Now that drug crop production offers one of the few ways to keep abreast of new economic demands, the moral discourses on the drug trade offer little in the way of alternatives to meet these demands.

## MOTOS TORCIDAS, IMMORALITY, AND THE COST OF UNEVEN REGULATION

One afternoon, I took a long *mototaxi* ride to a meeting in a village close to where I was living in in northern Cauca. Mototaxis were the local version of a taxi, except on a motorcycle. For visitors and locals who could afford a ride at roughly two thousand pesos (about one US dollar) for every fifteen minutes, mototaxis were a useful fallback for when buses or trusted acquaintances with motorcycles were unavailable. They also provided an additional source of income for indigenous community members who put their own motorcycles to work.

On the ride to the meeting, my mototaxista, Emilio, an indigenous man in his early forties, told the story of how he had gotten his first motorcycle. Talking over his shoulder, Emilio recounted that he had earned the cash for his first bike when he was fourteen years old by harvesting poppy resin to make heroin. "And what about horses at that time?" I asked him, recalling how, besides buses, horses were the main mode of transport for individuals. "I love horses!" he responded eagerly. And yet, as poppy cultivation and later coca brought more cash to the region, farmers replaced their horses with motorcycles for their speed and to achieve higher social status. Emilio recalled the first man in his home village who bought a motorcycle. "Everyone said that a man with a motorcycle is *el grande*! He has money!" he said nostalgically, "and after that, everyone wanted a motorcycle. . . . Granted, many of them were *torcidas*" (literally "twisted," but in this context, "undocumented").

As in other parts of rural Colombia, motorcycles are now ubiquitous in Cauca. They are the most constant disrupter of the otherwise usually pristine soundscape. While buses, trucks, and chivas are common for transporting large quantities of goods and people, motorcycles are the primary way that individuals and families transport themselves. Faster and requiring less daily maintenance than horses, and more affordable and better suited to narrow and unpaved roads than cars, motorcycles became the vehicle of choice for individuals (though up to three or four riders is not unusual) traveling within and between rural villages. With the occasional scooter exception, the majority of motorcycles are fully manual transmission— more suited to the road conditions. Although these manual transmission motorcycles are typically owned and driven by men, it is not unusual for women to know how to drive them, especially in cases where a motorcycle might be shared by a couple or a household.

*Motos torcidas*, or "twisted motorcycles," referred to motorcycles without proper registration paperwork. Drug gangs, allegedly collaborating with local guerrillas, introduced motorcycles in Cauca in exchange for cash at below market prices or directly for drug crop products. Although the origins of these motorcycles were impossible to trace, indigenous leaders and comuneros believed that most of them had been stolen in nearby cities or towns, or had been used for criminal activity and then had been "dumped" in remote places such as rural Cauca. I did not have access to drug traffickers to inquire further about this, and statistical data were not available, but this narrative was pervasive among indigenous leaders and comuneros.

Motorcycles are distinct from other global commodities that came to Cauca in that, as vehicles of transport, they promoted the development of both licit and illicit markets. An individual could drive to work in a mine or coca plot, attend a public assembly, and pick a child up from school, all in the same day. If needed, one could travel to nearby urban centers such as Cali, or even farther afield. The increased use of motorcycles encouraged road building and the expansion of municipal town centers. One indigenous elder recalled how until recently his town was nothing more than a small strip, but had now expanded up and down the mountain slopes that flanked it. Motorcycles created a whole new consumer market for secondary commodities—gas, spare parts, the occasional helmet—integrating the community directly into the cash economy. As in other parts of the world, motorcycles are both a symbol and a literal vehicle of upward mobility (see Truitt 2008). Following other scholars who examine the articulation between the licit and illicit as cooperative rather than antagonistic (Andreas 1995, 2004; Corva 2008; Arias and Goldstein 2010; Ballvé 2012; Polson 2013), these aspects of motorcycles' now ubiquitous presence in Cauca represent how the illicit drug economy facilitates integration into the licit global capitalist economy.

Despite the marked demand for them, motorcycles were flashpoints for moralizing discourses focused on consumerism and its implications for social ties. As far as some activists were concerned, other comuneros' desire for these commodities was the primary reason for the disruption of what they saw as a socially harmonious past. For example, while I was speaking with Andrés, a twenty-year-old indigenous youth activist, he critiqued the consumer culture that he saw engulfing the young people around him:

Everyone has a motorcycle. It's like one comes out of the womb, and he wants a motorcycle. What has this *generated*? As everyone wants a motorcycle, then, as one doesn't have the money to buy one from the store, at least with updated paperwork, then what do the drug traffickers do? It generates delinquent gangs, and what do they do? They steal motorcycles to take them up to sell there. They say, when you want a motorcycle, we will sell it to you at a lower price. And as you want a motorcycle and you want to grow marijuana, well you can grow the marijuana and I will give you this motorcycle. And so, as young people always want to live the latest trend, so if everyone has a motorcycle, I am going to grow marijuana, and the man will come to me and say,

"Look, I'll give you this motorcycle for that marijuana crop," right? So that's the easy life that the youth wants.

Andrés drew on a common discourse that characterized young people as self-centered. He blamed young people's desire for motorcycles for the illicit activity and delinquent gangs in the community. Young people are practically born wanting a motorcycle, they "always want to live the latest trend," and want to have "the easy life." As he saw it, this vice-like desire of a motorcycle *generated* delinquent gangs who fulfilled that desire by providing stolen motorcycles in exchange for the morally dubious activity of marijuana or coca cultivation. He made no mention of the high demand for motorcycles, or that young people may even need them in order to do their work.

It was evident that Andrés's choice to focus on young people was also shaped by his experience. Like Marco Evelio, he had spent a period of time using drugs, drinking, and partying with friends, but only a year or so prior had decided to leave that life behind at the encouragement of a music teacher who taught him to play the flute. Now Andrés dedicated himself to music and activism with youth in his community. But unlike Marco Evelio, the indigenous authorities and other structural forces were not the focus of his critique. Only twenty years old, and having just overcome a period of what he saw as an improper lifestyle, and finally, taking on a role as a cultural leader in the youth movement, it made sense that Andrés would be more inclined to focus on the moral aspects of his peers' behaviors than the structural causes of them.

Even if Andrés was motivated by personal experience, he still drew on available discourses that highlighted selfishness and individual vice as a cause of social problems brought on by the drug economy and armed groups in the region. Andrés's morally framed discussions about motorcycles shared admonishing tones with similar critiques made by indigenous authorities. Teófilo, a self-taught indigenous legal scholar and member of an indigenous judiciary committee, told me in an interview: "No one has resolved any economic problem [by growing drug crops]. People are incentivized by consumption. In the time of the poppy boom, there were many stolen motorcycles. We don't know what had happened with those bikes, if they were involved in a crime. They used to exchange coca for a motorcycle. And if there was something wrong with the motorcycle, what could the people say? That they did business with the guerrillas? Go ahead and file a complaint!" Teófilo also took an especially judgmental stance toward people growing drug crops. As he saw it, they were deluded by notions that the profits of drug cultivation would solve their financial problems. And if they ran into any problems with their motorcycles, whether mechanical or crime related, it was their own fault for being duped by drug traffickers and guerrillas.

The blame placed on the comuneros and their desire for motorcycles was at odds with the improved quality of life they provided, and the fact that most people could not afford a motorcycle at full market price, even with drug crop incomes. Yet despite these realities, indigenous authorities admonished comuneros for using motos torcidas and sought to regulate their use. During public assemblies, governors and indigenous leaders often made statements about the need to regulate the undocumented motorcycles in the area. Sometimes cabildos, the councils that govern indigenous territories, would set up checkpoints on local roads to verify paperwork.

In recent years, indigenous authorities have taken more aggressive actions to control motos torcidas. In 2017, the national newspaper *El Espectador* published an article headlined: "Indigenous Guards Recuperated 47 Stolen Motorcycles." These motorcycles were reported to have been confiscated from local indigenous comuneros and turned over to police authorities in Cali and Santander de Quilichao. The journalist presented this collaboration with urban police authorities as a laudable turn from what was stereotypically considered to be the uncooperative behavior of indigenous people. The word *recuperate* nods to the indigenous practice of "recuperating" land from wealthy landowners by occupying it from the 1970s into the 2000s, a practice often portrayed as belligerent. Yet in this article, the author resignified "recuperation" to associate it with indigenous conformity with state laws. The report also suggested conflict between indigenous leaders and the community. As the indigenous owners of the motorcycles "recuperated" were likely caught off guard, the confiscations augmented tensions between indigenous authorities and comuneros. By enforcing these regulations, indigenous leaders align themselves with policies that are discordant with the needs of their communities, and as a result, they risk tarnishing their own legitimacy.

Even if authorities sympathize with the needs of their communities, the reason for their actions was obvious. Aside from ethical questions about using stolen property, the association of indigenous communities with yet another illicit activity would put all in a more politically vulnerable position vis-à-vis the state. The regulation of off-market consumer goods draws regular support from conservative urban dwellers, exasperated with street crime, who regularly label buyers of secondhand goods as complicit in grand and petty theft. For such critics who commented on the article's web page, there was an evident connection between urban motorcycle theft and motorcycle use in nearby poorer rural areas, and made indigenous farmers an easy target of further negative stereotyping, on top of already existing ideas that indigenous people were avid collaborators with drug-trafficking guerrillas. Indigenous leaders could not afford further marginalization, and public displays of compliance with state laws could help to mitigate that marginalization.

There are serious potential pitfalls to this approach. Hypothetically, the total regulation of the illicit trade of motorcycles through methods such as confiscation would lessen the gains of drug crop cultivation. Yet it would not erase the problem of economic needs that drug crop cultivation solves for many poor farmers. Regulation of either drug crop cultivation or off-market commodities without a solution would simply make crucial market-price goods inaccessible to indigenous people, and increase the need for even more lucrative crops, and possibly the search for more desperate solutions.

## CONCLUSION

The conditions that make drug crop production one of the most profitable economic decisions for poor indigenous farmers—other than, say, migrating to urban areas—are far out of the control of Colombia's indigenous communities. Yet the moral discourse around the drug trade has made it easy for cultural activists to focus blame for these changes inward, toward the behavior of other indigenous comuneros and their decision to grow drug crops. And because the indigenous movement has borrowed from anthropological notions of an authentic indigenous people as rooted in the (not historically determined) past that predated contact with the West, this blame is set in a narrative of cultural loss, in which the use of global commodities represents a move away from an authentic cultural identity that spurns all things "from outside." But, as I have argued in this chapter, taking motorcycles as the primary example, the abandonment of global commodities is now nearly impossible for many indigenous families.

The problem of motos torcidas, and their moral, social, and political implications, represents the cascade of changes that the cocaine economy brought to rural indigenous Colombia. These changes are not unique to Cauca. Yet the response *is* uniquely shaped by questions of indigenous identity that are typically based on a moral economy, as a meaningful image of the past. This meaningful image, much of which is rooted in real aspects of indigenous social history, is a powerful tool for indigenous comuneros and cultural activists to navigate social problems brought on by the cocaine trade. Indigenous peoples in Latin America have successfully drawn on anthropological notions of contained culture as a tool for building solidarity and raising their profile nationally and internationally (Conklin 1997). Furthermore, cultural loss does not necessarily have to be set against the structural causes of the cocaine trade—the failure of the licit economy, and of the Colombian state, to buffer class inequalities between Colombia's elite and rural poor. However, when the narrative of cultural loss among indigenous comuneros as cause and effect of the cocaine trade is privileged over that of structural causes, it can be politically convenient for the state. The prevalence of this narrative in the indigenous school and among youth activists, I contend, reflects pressure on indigenous leaders and comuneros, historically marginalized by the state, to conform with state drug policy.

Indigenous families' increasing dependence on global commodities has challenged the extent to which indigenous activists and nonindigenous supporters can confront contemporary challenges through identity models rooted in past lifeways. The drug trade has accelerated the shift in Cauca's economy from one based on artisanal production to a cash-based economy. Today, without a dramatic, and likely traumatic, restructuring of the regional economy, many of Cauca's indigenous communities could not sustain themselves without the availability of motorcycles for transport. By introducing motorcycles, the illicit drug economy integrated the indigenous comuneros as consumers and as small-scale entrepreneurs who are now dependent on global commodities for their livelihoods.

The ability of indigenous communities to overcome inequalities that permeate both licit and illicit markets will require an assessment of their new role as consumers *and* producers in the global economy. The drug trade has contributed extensively to that new role, particularly through enabling access to global commodities. In this way, the drug trade has helped to mitigate the effects of class inequalities in rural indigenous regions, much as it has done in other parts of Colombia. Yet this has been achieved through tenuously cooperative relationships between social actors who readily find themselves at odds with one another at the occurrence of the drug trade's political and economic fluctuations, with poor indigenous farmers collectively at the greatest disadvantage. A sustainable solution requires that the state prioritize the needs of indigenous farmers in both long-term agricultural development projects and policies that favor Colombia's indigenous agricultural goods.

NOTES

1  In 1961, the United Nations Single Convention on Narcotics outlawed coca cultivation.
2  Colombian economist Darío Fajardo (2014) argues that national and international agrarian development programs attempted to make up for the failures of land redistribution in rural Colombia.


REFERENCES

Allen, Catherine J. 1981. "To Be Quechua: The Symbolism of Coca Chewing in Highland Peru." *American Ethnologist* 8, no. 1: 157–71.

Allen, Catherine J. 1988. *The Hold Life Has: Coca and Cultural Identity in an Andean Community*. Washington, DC: Smithsonian Institution Press.

Andreas, Peter. 1995. "Free Market Reform and Drug Market Prohibition: US Policies at Cross-Purposes in Latin America." *Third World Quarterly* 16, no. 1: 75–88. https://doi.org/10.1080/01436599550036248.

Andreas, Peter. 2004. "Illicit International Political Economy: The Clandestine Side of Globalization." *Review of International Political Economy* 11, no. 3: 641–52.

Arias, Enrique Desmond, and Daniel M. Goldstein. 2010. *Violent Democracies in Latin America*. Durham, NC: Duke University Press.

Ballvé, Teo. 2012. "Everyday State Formation: Territory, Decentralization, and the Narco Landgrab in Colombia." *Environment and Planning D: Society and Space* 30, no. 4: 603–22. https://doi.org/10.1068/d4611.

Bernal Villa, Segundo. 1954. "Economia de Los Paez." *Revista Colombiana de Antropología* 3: 291–367.

Camacho, Adriana, Alejandro Gaviria, and Catherine Rodriguez 2011. "El consumo de droga en Colombia." Bogotá: Universidad de los Andes.

Conklin, Beth A. 1997. "Body Paint, Feathers, and VCRs: Aesthetics and Authenticity in Amazonian Activism." *American Ethnologist* 24, no. 4: 711–37. https://doi.org/10.2307/646806.

Corva, Dominic. 2008. "Neoliberal Globalization and the War on Drugs: Transnationalizing Illiberal Governance in the Americas." *Political Geography* 27, no. 2: 176–93. https://doi.org/10.1016/j.polgeo.2007.07.008.

Fajardo, Darío. 2014. *Las Guerras de La Agricultura Colombiana, 1980–2010*. Bogotá: ILSA, Instituto Latinoamericano para una Sociedad y un Derecho Alternativos.

Farthing, Linda, and Kathryn Ledebur. 2015. "'Habeas Coca': Bolivia's Community Coca Control." New York: Open Society Foundations.

Ferro, Juan Guillermo. 1999. *Jovenes, Coca, y Amapola: Un Estudio sobre las Transformaciones Socioculturales en Zonas de Cultivos Ilicitos*. Bogotá: Instituto de Estudios Rurales.

Field, Les W. 1994. "Harvesting the Bitter Juice: Contradictions of Páez Resistance in the Changing Colombian Nation-State. *Identities* 1, no. 1: 89–108. https://doi.org/10.1080/1070289X.1994.9962497.

Field, Les W. 1996. "State, Anti-State and Indigenous Entities: Reflections upon a Páez Resguardo and the New Colombian Constitution." *Journal of Latin American and Caribbean Anthropology* 1, no. 2: 98–119.

Fraser, Nancy. 1997. *Justice Interruptus: Critical Reflections on the "Postsocialist" Condition*. New York: Routledge.

Goldberg, David Theo. 1994. *Multiculturalism: A Critical Reader*. Cambridge, MA: Blackwell.

Gootenberg, Paul. 2008. *Andean Cocaine: The Making of a Global Drug*. Chapel Hill: University of North Carolina Press.

Grisaffi, Thomas. 2019. *Coca Yes, Cocaine No: How Bolivia's Coca Growers Reshaped Democracy*. Durham, NC, Duke University Press.

Hale, Charles R. 2002. "Does Multiculturalism Menace? Governance, Cultural Rights and the Politics of Identity in Guatemala." *Journal of Latin American Studies* 34, no. 3: 485–524. https://doi.org/10.2307/3875459.

Hale, Charles R. 2005. "Neoliberal Multiculturalism." *PoLAR: Political and Legal Anthropology Review* 28, no. 1: 10–19. https://doi.org/10.1525/pol.2005.28.1.10.

Henman, Anthony. 1987. *Mama Coca*. London: Hassle Free.

Katz, Cindi. 2004. *Growing Up Global: Economic Restructuring and Children's Everyday Lives*. Minneapolis: University of Minnesota Press.

Pacini, Deborah, and Christine Franquemont, eds. *Coca and Cocaine: Effects on People and Policy in Latin America*. Cultural Survival Report No. 23. Cambridge, MA: Cultural Survival Inc. and Latin American Studies Program, Cornell University, 1986.

Pellegrini, Alessandra. 2016. *Beyond Indigeneity: Coca Growing and the Emergence of a New Middle Class in Bolivia*. Tucson: University of Arizona Press.

Perafán, Carlos Cesar. 1999. "Impacto de Cultivos Ilícitos en Pueblos Indígenas: El Caso de Colombia." Washington, DC: Inter-American Development Bank.

Plowman, Timothy. 1986. *Coca and Cocaine: Effects on People and Policy in Latin America*. Edited by Deborah Pacini and Christine Franquemont. Boston: Cultural Survival.

Polson, Michael. 2013. "Land and Law in Marijuana Country: Clean Capital, Dirty Money, and the Drug War's Rentier Nexus." *PoLAR: Political and Legal Anthropology Review* 36, no. 2: 215–30. https://doi.org/10.1111/plar.12023.

Ramírez, María Clemencia. 2011. *Between the Guerrillas and the State: The Cocalero Movement, Citizenship, and Identity in the Colombian Amazon*. Durham, NC: Duke University Press.

Ramírez, María Clemencia, Kimberly Stanton, and John Walsh. 2005. "Colombia: A Vicious Circle of Drugs and War." In *Drugs and Democracy in Latin America: The Impact of U.S. Policy*, edited by Coletta A. Youngers and Eileen Rosin, 99–142. Boulder, CO: Lynne Rienner.

Rappaport, Joanne. 1985. "History, Myth, and the Dynamics of Territorial Maintenance in Tierradentro, Colombia." *American Ethnologist* 12, no. 1: 27–45.

Rappaport, Joanne. 1998. *The Politics of Memory: Native Historical Interpretation in the Colombian Andes*, 2nd ed. Durham, NC: Duke University Press.

Roseberry, William. 1989. *Anthropologies and Histories: Essays in Culture, History, and Political Economy*. New Brunswick, NJ: Rutgers University Press.

Sanabria, Harry. 1993. *The Coca Boom and Rural Social Change in Bolivia*. Ann Arbor: University of Michigan Press.

Scott, James C. 1976. *The Moral Economy of the Peasant: Rebellion and Subsistence in Southeast Asia*. New Haven, CT: Yale University Press.

Starn, Orin. 1994. "Rethinking the Politics of Anthropology: The Case of the Andes." *Current Anthropology* 35, no. 1: 13–38.

Steinberg, Michael K., Joseph J. Hobbs, and Kent Mathewson, eds. 2004. *Dangerous Harvest: Drug Plants and the Transformation of Indigenous Landscapes*. Oxford: Oxford University Press.

Thompson, Edward P. 1971. "The Moral Economy of the English Crowd in the Eighteenth Century." *Past and Present* 50: 76–136.

Truitt, Allison. 2008. "On the Back of a Motorbike: Middle-Class Mobility in Ho Chi Minh City, Vietnam." *American Ethnologist* 35, no. 1: 3–19.

Williams, Raymond. 1973. *The Country and the City*. New York: Oxford University Press.

Youngers, Coletta A., and Eileen Rosin. 2005. "The U.S. 'War on Drugs': Its Impact in Latin America and the Caribbean." In *Drugs and Democracy in Latin America: The Impact of U.S. Policy*, edited by Coletta A. Youngers and Eileen Rosin. Boulder, CO: Lynne Rienner.

Yule, Marcos. 2004. *Pees Kupx Fxi'zenxi: Nasa USA' s Txi'pnxi = La Metamorfosis de la Vida: Cosmovision Nasa*. Toribío, Colombia: Cabildo Etnoeducativo Proyecto Nasa Municipio.

# 04 FROM CORUMBÁ TO RIO

## AN ETHNOGRAPHY OF TRAFFICKING

In the opening passages of this volume, Arias and Grisaffi claim that while there has been an "explosion" of scholarship on drug-related violence in Latin America, there has been little attention paid to the "broader drug commodity chain as it moves from production to consumption" (Arias and Grisaffi 2016). This is certainly true of the case of Brazil, where the focus has been almost exclusively on the impact of drug-related violence on the lives of the residents of low-income communities, especially in and around the cities of São Paulo and Rio de Janeiro. Very little work has been done, however, on how the drugs that fuel much of this violence get to market, or on the criminal entities that coordinate the procurement, distribution, and marketing process.[1]

There are a number of reasons for this. First, research on the drug trade is extremely difficult and involves a considerable element of personal risk, not only because the entire enterprise is clandestine and illegal, but also because the actors involved, by definition, play by their own rules and settle disputes according to their own sense of "justice." Second, in spite of fact that the entire enterprise is clandestine and illegal, the Brazilian authorities are involved at each and every turn, meaning that, in reality, you can't expect much help from them! And finally, the vast majority of the actors involved know only about the limited and specific role they play in the process, whether it be selling drugs wholesale, laundering money, organizing transportation across country and state lines, or preparing drugs for consumption.

What this means is that access to information about the drug trade—in its broader sense—depends on the existence of guides and informants who are familiar with the different worlds, or "moral economies," within which it is embedded. In my particular case, this guide and informant was a young man I got to know over the course of thirty years of fieldwork who ran a cocaine trafficking business from Corumbá, on the border with Bolivia, to Rio de Janeiro, where he supplied and, following his arrest, eventually joined the criminal faction known as the Comando Vermelho, which, until recently, controlled the majority of the city's favelas (on the field of "convict criminology," see Newbold et al. 2014). Before I discuss his role in this process, however, I wish to revisit the early 1980s, when cocaine made its grand entrance onto the global and local stage.

## THE MARKET: VIDIGAL

My first encounter with benzoylmethylecgonine, otherwise known as cocaine, was in New York City in October 1980. I was on my way from England to Brazil—via the US—when a friend who was studying for a master's degree at Columbia University invited me to accompany her to a party. And there it was—the cocaine, that is—in full view of everyone, in a bowl in the middle of a table, right next to the vodka and gin. My next encounter with cocaine wasn't until five years later, in January 1986, in Rio de Janeiro, where I'd gone to conduct fieldwork for my PhD. As luck would have it, my father's extensive experience as a civil engineer in Brazil meant that I was able to sublet a rent-controlled apartment from a former colleague on Avenida Vieira Souto, one of Rio's most expensive pieces of real estate.

Within a month of my being there, I met an Italian couple who had retired to Rio the year before and were living on the fourth floor. My friends turned out to be partyers, big partyers, and it was through them that I gained access to some of Rio's most exclusive nightclubs. People say that 1986 was Rio's first "white Christmas," and looking back, I can see why. Everyone in the nightclubs we would go to on weekends was high on cocaine, which they snorted in impressive quantities in bathrooms under the watchful eye of a heavily tipped concierge. Hell, my Italian friends even kept a jar of the stuff in their refrigerator!

Now at the time, I didn't know—and quite frankly didn't care—where the substance that was animating Rio's party scene came from. I would soon find out, however, as I became more and more involved with my fieldwork in the favela of Vidigal, which I could see at the end of the beach from my apartment window. When I first started working in Vidigal, in March 1986 (see figure 4.1), the favela was run by an active and well-organized neighborhood association that was born of a failed attempt to remove the community in 1977 (see McCann 2014). I had identified Vidigal as one of two

FIGURE 4.1
Vidigal in 1986.

favelas that I would study over the course of the year because it challenged the logic of so-called clientelist politics, whereby votes were exchanged for favors, and insisted instead that elections were about much broader issues (Gay 1994). Studying so-called new social movements in the context of the transition to democracy was all the rage at the time, at least in the US. The question my adviser kept asking me, however, was whether the neighborhood association's approach had any effect on the mindset and political choices of local residents.

To test this hypothesis, I decided to poll 10 percent of the adult population a week before the elections in November. This meant drawing a 25 percent sample of all of the houses in the favela, despite the fact that there were no maps, registers, or lists. So, instead of preselecting a sample, I decided to walk my way through the favela, picking out every fourth house as I went. Except that, occasionally, the research assistants I had hired to help me would say, "No, not that one," because the house in question had been appropriated by the local drug gang.

It's not that I was unaware that there was a drug gang operating in the favela, or other favelas of the region, it's just that I didn't want them interfering with what I considered, at the time, to be very important research work. Furthermore, the leaders of the neighborhood association assured me—even as I was leaving in December—that the gang posed no threat to their authority. Well, if the gang posed no threat to their authority then, it did by the time I returned three years later to conduct another preelectoral survey in November 1989. On this occasion, the gang had just returned from an unsuccessful military operation in a favela across town and, as a consequence, everyone in Vidigal was expecting a retaliatory strike. As I knocked on people's doors and asked them who they were voting for—and why—I was struck by how reluctant they were to talk and by the number of people who cited public security—or rather the lack of it—as their number one concern.

The other significant thing that happened during my visit was that I got to climb the granite rock outcrop directly behind and to the side of the favela that entailed an hour-long hike up the spine of the hill. Our guide that day was a young man of sixteen named Eduardo whose help my friends had enlisted. Except that when we were about half way up, he reached into the bag he was carrying and produced an enormous joint of marijuana that he proceeded to pass around. Then, a couple of hundred yards further on, out came a plastic bag of cocaine. And then finally, once we reached the top, out came a revolver that my stoned and somewhat distracted companions took turns shooting into the air. Eduardo, it turned out, was a member of the local drug gang, and the current boyfriend of my friend Lucia, who had been one of my research assistants in 1986 (Gay 2005)—see figure 4.2.

Somewhat unnerved by this turn of events, I bided my time until everybody was ready to go back down. Except that on the way we stopped at Eduardo's house, where he poured me a glass of what looked to be fairly expensive imported whisky. And then, while we were sitting there drinking, a police car made its way slowly toward us up the hill. To my surprise, no one moved, least of all Eduardo. And that was because the policeman in question was his uncle, who was paid by the drug gang to provide them with information. And it was then—and only then—that I realized how complicated the situation had become.

The situation became a lot more complicated in the years following my visit in 1989, as the drug gang in Vidigal sought to consolidate its control

FIGURE 4.2  Lucia and Eduardo in 1989.

over the community by undermining the authority of the neighborhood association. Initially, the gang restricted its operations to the upper half of the favela. Now, however, it was looking to move in on the neighborhood association's territory. What this meant was that in each election—held every two years—the gang would back the opposition slate of candidates or, alternatively, attempt to place someone sympathetic to its cause within the neighborhood association's inner circle, to the extent that by the mid-1990s, the original leaders felt they couldn't trust anyone or speak their mind.

The ability of the drug gang to control the neighborhood association in Vidigal became more and more essential as violence in Rio threatened to spiral out of control. In 1980, the official homicide rate—which should be taken with a pinch of salt—stood at thirty per 100,000 people. By the end of the decade, however, it had risen into the mid-sixties.[2] Although it is extremely difficult to quantify, a great deal of the increase in violence in Rio in the 1980s and 1990s can undoubtedly be attributed to conflicts over the spectacular profits to be made from cocaine, conflicts that not only broke out between drug gangs and the police, who went after what they considered their fair share, but also between drug gangs associated with different criminal factions.

For the first twenty years of its existence, the drug gang in Vidigal was associated with a criminal faction known as the Comando Vermelho (cv) that emerged, in the mid-1970s, from inside the walls of the state's penitentiaries. Between 1969 and 1975, the military sought to punish those who took up arms against the regime by banishing them to a prison on the island of Ilha Grande, where they were tortured and in some cases killed (see Sepúlveda dos Santos 2009). While they were there, these educated and largely middle-class political prisoners impressed upon a group of common criminals the importance of organization, loyalty, and discipline and instructed them in the art of guerrilla warfare.[3] The outcome of this unlikely encounter was the aforementioned cv, a criminal faction that continues, on occasion, to employ the revolutionary discourse associated with its roots (see Holston 2008: 300–309).

Initially, the Comando Vermelho sought to impose its control over the prison on Ilha Grande by taking out members of rival factions, introducing strict codes of prisoner conduct, and negotiating for improved conditions with suddenly besieged prison officials. Later on, as its leaders were transferred, the influence of the cv spread to other prisons in the system and, eventually, to cells of operatives in the city that were charged with robbing banks and carrying out kidnappings to finance the purchase of weapons and escapes. Then, around 1982, the leadership of the cv made the critical and strategic decision to fund the organization's activities via the drug trade (Amorim 1993).

Brazil has never been a major producer of illegal drugs, although marijuana is grown fairly extensively in the northeast and the country is an important source of precursor chemicals for illegal drug manufacture.[4] Since the mid-1970s, however, it has become an important transshipment point for cocaine, as the global increase in trade and the US-led war on drugs have prompted producers in Colombia, Bolivia, and Peru to seek alternative markets in Western Europe (see Andreas 1999: 125–41; Gootenberg 2008). Not surprisingly, the emergence of Brazil as a transshipment point has led to a significant increase in local drug use, such that the country is now among the largest consumers of cocaine—and its crack derivative—in the world. And it was the extraordinary profits to be made from the drug trade that the Comando Vermelho sought to capture.[5]

The decision by the Comando Vermelho to move in on the drug trade led to a period of intense and bloody conflict for the territorial control of Rio's favelas, which are—historically—where most of the selling points are located (see, for example, Barcellos 2004). A good number of the leaders and rank-and-file members of the CV were originally from the favelas, and so the relationship between such areas and drug trafficking naturally followed. In addition, the haphazard and impenetrable nature of favela neighborhoods meant that they provided the perfect terrain for drug trade operations. All drug gangs had to do was to arrange for shipments to be made from out of state. The gangs would then mix the drugs with other substances and sell the resulting product to wealthy clients in surrounding neighborhoods and, later on, to users and addicts in their own communities.[6]

Over time, personal disputes, intergenerational rivalries, and changes in the organization of the drug trade caused the Comando Vermelho to split apart. The first of these splits occurred in the late 1980s and gave rise to the Terceiro Comando (TC). The second occurred in the mid-1990s and gave rise to the Amigos dos Amigos (ADA). In both cases, the split in the ranks of the CV greatly increased the level of competition and conflict out on the street, as first the TC and then the ADA competed militarily for their share of the territory and spoils.[7] And it was this increased level of competition and conflict between factions of heavily armed men—and the police—that transformed not just a select few neighborhoods in Rio, but whole areas of the city into a war zone (Aleixo de Souza 2002).

The chaotic and destabilizing nature of these conflicts was brought home to me when I returned for one of my visits in October 1996. I could not help noticing that a large contingent of police was stationed permanently at the foot of the favela as I made my way in. Nobody had said anything to me beforehand, but apparently the violence between rival gangs had reached such a point that the authorities had felt compelled to intervene. And while there was no love lost between the residents of Vidigal and the police, they were happy to have them there if it meant an interruption in what had been weeks of sheer terror. The leader of the drug gang in Vidigal was less than pleased with the situation, however, because it interfered with his ability to sell drugs, which has always been the gang's principal source of revenue. So, in frustration, he called the president of the neighborhood association on his cell phone and ordered him to get everyone on the directorate to sign a petition asking the police to leave, and that if he didn't, he would be executed along with the rest of the members of his family.[8]

The president, after thinking about it, refused to comply with the demand and spent the next few weeks sleeping at a different house every night before packing his bags and moving to another favela. Then, perhaps inevitably, two years later, a group of armed men marched down the hill and into the neighborhood association building and told the last in a long line of democratically elected presidents to leave. From this point on it was the drug gang—and not the residents of the community—who decided who would head up the association. And it was the drug gang that would run things according to its interests.

Now, it goes without saying that the emergence and eventual ascendance of a drug gang in Vidigal changed the day-to-day lives of local residents. Instead of a democratically elected committee of local residents that could be held accountable, there was now a heavily armed and extralegal force. This did not mean, however, that the authority of the drug gang was necessarily enforced at the point of a gun. Far from it. The drug gang in Vidigal depended on the local population for a number of things: first, to provide it with new recruits for any number of roles and positions, including foot soldiers, drug runners, and lookouts (Dowdney 2003: 39–52). Second, the drug gang relied on the local population to provide cover for its operations, in the sense of not providing information that might lead to attacks by rival gangs or the police. It became increasingly common, therefore, for drug gangs to cultivate support by providing social services, such as transportation to and from local hospitals and clinics; by financing public works, such as day care centers and recreational facilities; and by sponsoring parties and cultural events, such as the ubiquitous *bailes funk*.[9] And finally, it also became increasingly common for drug gangs to take advantage of the almost total absence and mistrust of public authorities to punish those who caused trouble (see Leeds 1996). Thus, while the emergence of a drug gang in Vidigal was met with a degree of fear and trepidation, it did provide local residents with a measure of personal security and a means to resolve disputes.[10]

It remains something of a cruel irony that the transition to democracy in Rio was accompanied not by the resurrection of civil society—at least to the extent that some had hoped and predicted—but by waves of violence waged by criminal elements, and the police, over profits to be made from the drug trade (for a historical perspective, see McCann 2014). In Vidigal, the violence associated with the drug trade was directly responsible for the displacement of the neighborhood association by a heavily armed gang associated with Rio de Janeiro's most powerful criminal faction.[11] The question, for our purposes, is: How did this situation come about? More specifically, by what means did the drugs make their way from their places of origin to the favelas of Rio de Janeiro? And how did this reconfigure local social, economic, and power relations? To answer these questions, I now turn to the

FIGURE 4.3 The border with Bolivia.

testimony of an individual who was intimately involved in the procurement and distribution process.

### THE SOURCE: CORUMBÁ

In July 1999, I flew from New York City to Rio to begin interviewing my friend Lucia about her involvement with drug gang life. What I didn't know until I got there was that her then current boyfriend Bruno had just been released from prison. Bruno was a young man of eighteen when he decided to join the navy in 1983.[12] Born on a farm on the outskirts of the city of Recife, in the northeast, he saw the navy as an opportunity to travel and escape his small-town life. After a year at the Naval Academy in Recife, he was transferred to Rio, where he completed his training as a corporal of artillery. Then, upon graduation, he was sent to serve at the naval base in Ladário on the border between Brazil and Bolivia. The base in Ladário is one of seven in Brazil and the only one on the western frontier. Located seven kilometers outside of the town of Corumbá, on the Paraguay River, it has played—and continues to play—a critical role in monitoring one of the major transit routes for drugs and, in particular, cocaine (see figure 4.3).

Soon after he was stationed there, Bruno realized that much of the town's wealth was generated from drug trafficking and that, more importantly, many of his colleagues, including his senior officers, were involved: "I would say that 80 percent of the wealth in that town was generated from drugs. I mean it was as if drugs were listed on the stock exchange. You know, as if there was a set price, like oil, or coffee. And I noticed that some of my friends had stuff that made no sense in terms of their salary. Friends who owned stuff they shouldn't have been able to afford. You know, regular recruits like me, who owned houses, cars, and businesses." (All quotes adapted from Gay 2015.)

And, while they were out on patrol at night, on the river, he and his colleagues would routinely stop and search vessels they suspected of carrying drugs.[13] Instead of reporting such incidents, however, the individuals would be set free and the seized merchandise shared among them: "When the couriers came across to Brazil, they came across the Pantanal in boats.[14] And they'd bring in ten, twenty kilos at a time. And sometimes we'd catch them. And whoever was in charge would say, 'No one saw anything, right?' And we'd all say, 'Right!'" (Gay 2015).

Seizing on an opportunity provided by a colleague at the base, Bruno subsequently agreed to accompany a shipment of ten kilos of cocaine to Rio de Janeiro on board a Brazilian air force plane, for which he was paid ten thousand dollars. The ease with which this initial trip was made prompted him to seek out contacts with suppliers in Bolivia and buyers at the other end of the commodity chain in Rio. These buyers, it turns out, were the leaders of the favelas that, like Vidigal, had become strongholds of the CV.

Bruno's testimony reveals a number of things about the process of getting drugs to market and the relationships this process entails. The first insight is the ease with which drugs cross the border. Talking about his relationship with suppliers, he says: "In those days it was really easy, because the suppliers had lots of drugs and they were always looking for someone to sell them to. I mean it was almost as if drug trafficking was normal. There was even this train that left Santa Cruz de la Sierra, in Bolivia, for Quijarro, which is a town near the border. It was incredible, because you knew that your merchandise was on that train. And you could go to the station and wait for it. I mean, can you believe it?" (Gay 2015).

The ease with which drugs crossed—and continue to cross—the border is a function of two things. The first is the size of frontier itself. The border between Brazil and Bolivia measures 3,423 kilometers, which is longer than the border between Mexico and the US. And then there are the additional thirteen thousand or so kilometers that stretch all the way from Uruguay in the south to French Guiana in the northeast. The second is the extremely small size of the federal force that is charged with monitoring the flow of people and commodities. Both factors have prompted the authorities to consider forming a specialized federal border force and, more ambitiously, constructing a $13 billion "virtual fence" that is to be monitored by electromagnetic signaling, satellites, and drones (Moura and Navarro 2013).

The second insight revealed by Bruno's testimony has to do with the fragmented and disorganized nature of the market for drugs. At least in the early years—and here I am talking about the mid to late 1980s—much of the trafficking of drugs was of the small-scale variety, or what's known locally as *trafico de formigas*.[15] What this means is that there were any number of individuals at the border who were involved with buying small amounts of cocaine and delivering it to clients in Rio. In general, for example, Bruno would buy somewhere between ten and fifteen kilos of cocaine from his suppliers in Bolivia, conceal it in a secret compartment of a car, otherwise known as a *cafofo*, and drive it, or have it driven, the 1,800 kilometers or so from Mato Grosso do Sul, through the state of São Paulo, to its final destination in Rio.

Similarly, the fragmented and disorganized nature of the market for drugs meant that a client in Rio, such as the drug gang in Vidigal, for example, might buy from multiple suppliers at the same time based on individually negotiated verbal contracts. In other words, at least in the early years, no one person, or persons, enjoyed a monopoly over the supply of drugs.

This does not mean, however, that the market was totally chaotic or open, or that there was no relationship or code of ethics between dealers. On the contrary, Bruno's testimony makes clear that traffickers were expected to follow certain rules and, in particular, not to interfere with each other's affairs: "You have to be careful not to create resentment, not to make other people jealous. You have to make sure that no one thinks you're moving in on their territory, understand? Because if you don't, you can end up losing everything, and sitting there wondering, what the hell just happened?!" (Gay 2015). As a matter of fact, while Bruno made a point of being honest and upfront about his business, his original partner in the drug trade did not, and ultimately paid the price:

> My [first] partner Valdoberto was a great guy. And we were in it together from the start. But he had the wrong attitude when it came to crime. You know, he'd lie and say that he brought twenty, thirty kilos with him to Rio,

and that the police arrested him and took it all away. You know, to convince the Bolivians to give him more credit. But he never paid his debts. And he was always asking for more credit. And I didn't think this was the right way to go. And I figured that eventually someone would find out and he'd be killed. And you know what? He didn't last long in this business. (Gay 2015)

The third insight provided by Bruno's testimony has to do with the buying and selling of drugs. During the time in which he was operating his business, between 1985 and 1991, the price of a kilo of cocaine on the Bolivian side of the border was two thousand dollars. The price of a kilo of cocaine in Rio, on the other hand, was five thousand dollars, the markup representing the cost and risk involved with getting the drugs to market. Having said that, the price negotiated also depended on the quantity involved. So, for example, reflecting on his first trip to Rio to sell cocaine to representatives of the Comando Vermelho, Bruno says:

And so [the guy] asked me how much I was asking, and I told him five thousand dollars. And he said that five thousand dollars was a lot, because he wanted to buy more than fifty kilos. So I said, "More than fifty kilos, then it's four thousand dollars." And so we closed the deal at four thousand dollars. Because if a guy buys ten kilos, it's five thousand dollars. But if he buys more, then there's a discount. Because if you buy a lot at the border, there's a discount there too. I mean it's less than two thousand dollars, because you're buying in bulk, understand? (Gay 2015)

Apart from negotiating a price, there was also the matter of negotiating a payment schedule. At both ends of the drug trafficking chain, deals tended to be made at least partially on credit. In other words, Bruno's supplier in Bolivia would provide him with a certain amount of cocaine and ask for only part of the money upfront, on the understanding that he would pay the rest later: "You pay the supplier what you can, with money you've put aside, and you leave your house or your car as security. And then you pay him when you come back. Or sometimes, if he's a good friend, he'll give you the drugs and tell you to pay later. But he has to be a really good friend to do that" (Gay 2015).

The other factor that determined how much money would be paid upfront was the buyer's credit. Over the years, Bruno made innumerable deals with suppliers in Bolivia who were willing to extend him credit based on his reputation as someone they could trust: "There's always someone willing to give you more credit, especially if, like me, you are someone who's known for being honest. I mean I'd sell anything to pay my debts: cars, property, jewelry, anything. Because then I could get more credit. Because you have a line of credit. I mean it's like any business. And my line of credit was pretty much limitless. It had to be, because I had a lot of debts to pay" (Gay 2015).

Just as credit was extended to Bruno by his suppliers in Bolivia, he also extended credit to those he sold to in Rio's favelas. In other words, he'd drop off the merchandise, be paid a certain amount, and be owed the rest. The problem was that because of the presence of a predatory and corrupt police force in Rio, his buyers would often have their merchandise stolen from them:

> Let's say, for example, I supply a favela with thirty kilos of cocaine. And they pay me for fifteen, which means they owe me for another fifteen, which they say they'll pay me the following week. And then the police come in [and take everything]. And they don't have any money, meaning someone's going to have to go out and rob, so they can pay their debt. Or I can give them more credit, so they can pay me from what they make. Because if I'm going to continue selling to them, I'm going to have to give them more credit, understand? Because if I don't, I'll be seen as a Judas. You know, a guy who's your friend when things are good, but who doesn't want to know you when things go wrong. Because then you'll lose that contact. And maybe something will happen to you someplace else. Because word will get around that you're a bad guy, and it's okay to rob you of your stuff. And I didn't want this reputation. I mean I did everything I could to please everyone. (Gay 2015)

The fourth insight from Bruno's testimony has to do with the exchange and movement of money. At the border, all transactions are made in US dollars. In other words, Bruno would buy from his suppliers and pay off his debts in dollars. The problem was that when he was paid by his clients in Rio, he would be paid in Brazilian reais: "Because the guys in the favelas don't do business in dollars. So you have to figure out the exchange rate. You know, someone will say, 'How much is the dollar today?' And then someone else will say, 'It's so much.' Then you do the math and the gang's treasurer works it out on his calculator and pays you the money, understand? Because they don't like to mess with dollars. So it's like, 'Hey, man, just tell me how much it is in reais, okay?' Because this whole business of dollars, and the exchange rate, gets confusing for them" (Gay 2015).

What this means is that Bruno, or someone he has employed, has to transport the money back to the border, oftentimes in the same car and cafofo that the drugs came in, and exchange it there into dollars:

FIGURE 4.4 The hotel Bruno bought in Corumbá.

[In] Bolivia, everything's paid for in dollars, understand? I mean they won't accept reais, because drugs are always commercialized in dollars. And so, we were always at a bit of a disadvantage. Because the dollar kept rising. You know, in terms of its value. And so, if you waited too long, you could end up losing money. So you had to exchange it fast. And where I was stationed, at the border, it was never a problem. Because dollars were sold every day at midday. I mean you had to exchange it in small amounts. You know, six hundred, a thousand dollars, things like that. And then you'd have to go somewhere else to change it, or you'd have to send someone else. Because the federal authorities were always watching. But there are a lot of these guys, especially at the frontier. And the basis of this exchange is mainly drugs, because that's how the system works. (Gay 2015)

Then the question becomes what to do with the money. The first order of business for Bruno was always to pay his debts, to maintain his reputation and credit. Then any money that was left over was invested, in his case in local real estate (see figure 4.4): "Part of the profit that I made from my trips to Rio, I invested in a hotel. Because there was this guy, selling this hotel, in downtown Corumbá, because he was in debt . . . even though the hotel was

on the opposite side of the square from the federal police headquarters!"
(Gay 2015).

But even then, he didn't accumulate much property or live a lavish life-style because, first of all, he was always in debt to creditors and was owed money by his clients. And second, nothing he invested in was in his name, because of the illicit nature of his business. So, while he owned property in town, and a car, and other commodities considered luxuries by those who weren't involved in trafficking, they were never things that he could depend on or truly enjoy:

> Because the money comes and goes real fast. I mean you're able to live a good life and everything. But you never really own anything because noth-ing's ever declared, I mean nothing's ever in your name. Like the hotel wasn't in my name. It was in the name of this lawyer from Rio, who was a friend of a friend. And do you know what he did? He sold the hotel and took off. He double-crossed us. Because a lot of stuff was in his name, so he could move it around. But he took off for Boston, in the US, and we never heard from him again. And so it reached a point where I wanted to quit. Because the whole drug trafficking business was beginning to irritate me. (Gay 2015)

Finally, the fifth insight provided by Bruno's testimony has to do with the issue of widespread corruption and involvement of the authorities. Apart from his colleagues in the navy, the police on both sides of the border—and on the road—were also heavily involved. Talking of the situation in Bolivia, Bruno observes: "There were Bolivians who owed money to other Bolivians. And the Bolivian police were the ones who collected on their debts. What I mean is they arrested people who owed other people, and made them pay" (Gay 2015).

But there again, according to Bruno, the Brazilian police weren't any better. Apart from raiding favelas and confiscating their cocaine, they also made money from arrests (see also Van Dun 2016), such as the time Bruno and his partner Valdoberto were stopped on their way to São Paulo:

> And then, on one of our trips, we were arrested, in São Paulo. Someone must have told them there were drugs in the car, ten kilos in this case. I was driv-ing when they stopped us that morning. Because we were crossing the bor-der between Mato Grosso do Sul and São Paulo. The police took the car and searched it. And then they found the drugs. I only know this because I read about it in the newspaper. But only a small amount was reported, under-stand? Because the police kept the rest. [Because] they were playing a double

game. And after being arrested I stopped traveling with the stuff. I decided I didn't want to do it anymore, I decided I didn't want the risk. (Gay 2015)

Ultimately, it is the uncertainty and riskiness of the drug trafficking business that led Bruno to attempt to make one last deal to get out. Instead of buying cocaine from suppliers in Bolivia, and selling it for five thousand dollars per kilo in Rio, he decided to buy cocaine paste, a cheaper and less refined version of the drug, to distill it in Rio, and to ship it to Italy, where it would sell for five times the price. As the last two kilos of a ten-kilo batch were being dried in a microwave, however, the police broke in and Bruno was arrested. Expelled from the navy and sentenced to eight years in prison, he was subsequently exposed to a very different world associated with the drug trade, a world where most of the decisions that affected his life before his arrest were made.

## COMMAND CENTRAL: PRISON

When Bruno was transferred to a civilian prison, he was given the choice of occupying a cell for former government employees, or a cell for common criminals affiliated with the cv.[16] Given his recent history as a supplier, and his reputation for honesty, he chose the latter and was quickly accepted as a member of the faction. Then, over the course of the next eight years, he spent time in seven different prison facilities where he got to know the leaders of the cv and, as a consequence, the inner workings and scale of their operations. Reflecting back on his role as a trafficker, he says: "[The cv] had a lot of suppliers, supplying a lot more than me. I mean, Jesus Christ, I was a nobody. Because they'd lose one supplier and they'd replace him with another" (Gay 2015). More importantly, he came to realize that almost everything that takes place on the outside was orchestrated by the leadership on the inside, from the buying and selling of drugs to the war against rival factions and the police. "Because they had it all figured out. I mean their ability to manage their affairs was impressive. Because there were favelas bringing in two, three hundred thousand reais a month.[17] And there were leaders there that received three, four visits a day from their lawyers. I mean it was incredible!" (Gay 2015).

And when asked whether these visits were supervised, he said: "No, no they weren't. Because the guard would take the prisoner to this small area at the front of the cellblock, and then he'd leave. And then the lawyer would slide all the paperwork underneath. You know, the accounts from the favela.

I mean they'd get together with their lawyers, and they'd decide which favelas to invade, and how many men it would take. Things like that" (Gay 2015).

When Bruno was arrested in 1991, there were two criminal factions vying for control of the drug trade in Rio: the Comando Vermelho and its recently established rival, the Terceiro Comando. Because of the animosity between them, however, the prison system was organized to keep them apart, meaning that entire cellblocks and prison facilities were set aside for the members of one criminal faction or the other. Then, in 1994, a second split occurred that made Bruno's life in prison a lot more difficult. In July 1994, Ernaldo Pinto de Medeiros, otherwise known as Uê, assassinated a popular figure within the CV known as Orlando da Conceição, or Orlando Jogador. Uê had emerged in the early 1990s as a major supplier of drugs in what was an increasingly consolidated market, which meant that he threatened the power of the CV's leaders in prison, who, whether they liked it or not, had come to depend on him.

The assassination of Orlando Jogador caused Uê to be expelled from the CV, which led him, in turn, to establish a third criminal faction known as the Amigos dos Amigos. Unfortunately for Bruno, this split occurred at the same time that he became the leader of a prison that held over a thousand men. Ordered by the CV to execute those thought to be involved with the assassination of Orlando Jogador, he refused and allowed all the prisoners who came from areas dominated by the newly established faction to be transferred to another prison. As a result, he was declared persona non grata and was in real danger of being killed. Ultimately, however, he managed to clear his name (see Gay 2015, chapter 6 for more) and ended up living with Lucia and her family in the favela of Vidigal following his release from prison in 1999.[18] Then, in 2006, the ADA seized control of Vidigal, which usually meant that anyone associated with the vanquished faction was killed or forced to leave, which led to the following confrontation:

> When the ADA took over, one of their guys called from prison. He called a friend to ask him which side I was on. And so, when I walked out of the neighborhood association one day, there was this guy there with a gun pointed at my head. And he said, "So, Bruno, what's it to be? Which side are you on?" And I said, "All I do is paint houses for a living. All I'm interested in is raising my kids. So, if I'm on anyone's side, it's the side of peace, understand? Now is that good enough for you or were you expecting something else?" And then the guy said, "No, that's fine, Bruno. You can go on your way. You can go your way in peace." (Gay 2015)

When Bruno was arrested in 1991, he knew that he would be well received by the friends of friends he had been supplying drugs to in Rio. What he did not, and could not know, however, was the extent to which the drug trade he had played a small part in was controlled by the leaders of the various criminal factions from within the prison system.[19] As has already been mentioned, the Comando Vermelho began its life in the mid-1970s as a prison-based gang, to be joined a decade or so later by the Terceiro Comando and Amigos dos Amigos. All three factions conduct their operations—and generate their resources—on the outside. Their power, however, remains heavily concentrated on the inside of a chronically overcrowded, medieval prison system whose segregation—by faction—serves only to consolidate their control.[20]

## CONCLUSION

Over the course of the past few decades, research on Brazil has shifted its focus from the transition to democracy and the reorganization of civil society to the violence that is, in large part, fueled by global shifts in the distribution and consumption of drugs. The good news, if there is any, is that we now have an extensive list of meticulously researched monographs that document the ways that drug gangs establish and exercise their authority in low-income communities.[21] Because of the difficulties of field research, however, many if not most of these monographs have focused on a particular neighborhood—or favela—which limits the extent to which they can provide insights as to processes beyond a particular locale.

Drugs, of course, do not appear out of thin air. In the case of cocaine, it has to be cultivated, distilled, procured, transported, marketed, sold, and paid for, while at the same time remaining "hidden" from the authorities. In the absence of any formal contracts or rules of engagement, each stage in this process has to be negotiated on the basis of personal and ultimately unenforceable agreements based on reciprocity and trust. Bruno's survival depended on it, in terms of his dealings both with his suppliers in Bolivia and with his clients in Rio's favelas. In fact, it was Bruno's reputation as someone who would keep his word that led to his rise within the cv—once he was incarcerated—and enabled him to ride out changes in the political landscape once he was released.

Similarly, the gangs that are responsible for selling drugs in Rio do not exist in isolation. Rather, they form part of a network of actors associated with criminal factions that orchestrate each and every aspect of the drug trade. The power of these factions has, from the very beginning, been concentrated within the prison system, a situation that the authorities recognize, but have as yet been unable to control. In fact, if truth be told, most of decisions that have been made by the authorities have only served to exacerbate the situation.

Fortunately for me, I gained the trust and friendship of an individual with intimate knowledge and experience of all three of these very different worlds. Reflecting on his experiences, he said: "If it's one thing at the frontier, it's another thing everyplace else. I mean it's one thing when you're transporting the drugs, and it's another when you're dealing with the favelas. And then it's another thing when you are in prison. Because each situation has its own logic, each situation has its own dynamic, understand?" (Gay 2015).

## NOTES

1 A recent exception to this rule is de Abreu (2017).

2 There are currently fifteen cities in the world that have a homicide rate higher than sixty per 100,000 people. All of them, except for Cape Town (South Africa) and St. Louis (USA), are in Latin America. Five of them are in Brazil, although it should be said that Rio de Janeiro is not one of them. For issues of measurement, see Zdun (2011); Denyer Willis (2016).

3 There is some dispute as to who influenced whom in this regard. The most compelling account of the Comando Vermelho's early years is provided by one of its founding members, William da Silva (1991). See also the documentary by Caco Souza (2004), which is based on interviews with da Silva in prison and the compelling and evocative film by Lúcia Murat (2004).

4 Brazil is party to the 1988 UN Convention against Illicit Traffic in Narcotic Drugs and Psychotropic Substances and introduced an initial chemical control law in 2001, with an updated 2003 decree, imposing strict controls on 146 substances that could be used in the production of narcotics.

5 In its 2002 report on international narcotics, the US Department of State states that "There is currently no widely available, easily renewable commodity more lucrative than illegal drugs. In most cases, they are relatively cheap to produce and offer enormous profit margins that allow the drug trade to generate criminal revenues on a scale without historical precedent" (US Department of State 2002: 4).

6 The purity of the product depends on the economic resources of the client.

7 For the situation in Rio in comparative perspective, see Lessing (2008).

8 For the relationship between neighborhood associations and gangs, see Arias (2006).

9 Bailes funk are dance events featuring "funk carioca," a local hip-hop derivation of Miami bass that became popular in the 1980s. They are also vehicles for the sale of narcotics and demonstrations of drug gang power.

10 To an extent, the imposition of rules and codes of conduct on communities on the outside mirrored the Comando Vermelho's attempt to maintain control of the prison population on the inside. And while it varied from favela to favela, depending on the characteristics of each individual leader, there were consistencies in terms of how local populations were treated. For the relationship between gangs and residents, see Alvito (2001); Penglase (2008).

11 To the extent that by the time my first book came out, in 1994, it bore absolutely no semblance to reality.

12 With bases in the states of Rio de Janeiro, Bahia, Rio Grande do Norte, Pará, Mato Grosso do Sul, Rio Grande do Sul, and Amazonas, the Brazilian navy is currently the largest in Latin America, with sixty thousand active personnel and a hundred ships under its command.

13 While much of the cocaine that enters Brazil crosses the waterways that mark its extensive, 16,885-kilometer western border, a considerable amount also enters via land. Borders between Brazil, Paraguay, Bolivia, and Colombia tend to be open to vehicular and pedestrian traffic and unpoliced. This is certainly true of the border crossings I have visited in Corumbá, Foz do Iguaçu, and Tabatinga.

14 The Pantanal is a vast area of wetlands bordering the countries of Brazil, Paraguay, and Bolivia that is almost completely submerged during the rainy season. The name *Pantanal* comes from the Portuguese word *pântano*, meaning wetland, bog, swamp, quagmire, or marsh.

15 Literally ant traffic.

16 In 1955, a law was passed that granted special privileges to those with a university degree or a government job. Despite being struck down in 1991, however, the law remains in effect. See, for example, "Até preso, rico leva vantagem" (2001).

17 In 2018 it was close to US$100,000.

18 Bruno met Lucia because she used to visit her brother in the same prison.

19 For the situation in neighboring São Paulo, see Biondi (2016); Denyer Willis (2015).

20 Brazil's prison population increased from 90,000 in 1990, to 607,700 in 2014, largely because of the war on drugs.

21 See, for example, Arias (2006); Goldstein (2013); Penglase (2014); Robb Larkins (2015).

**REFERENCES**

Aleixo de Souza, Josinaldo. 2002. "Sociabilidades Emergentes: Implicações da Dominação de Matadors na Periferie e Traficantes nas Favelas." PhD diss., Federal University of Rio de Janeiro.

Alvito, Marcos. 2001. *As Cores de Acari: Uma Favela Carioca*. Rio de Janeiro: Fundação Getulio Vargas.

Amorim, Carlos. 1993. *Comando Vermelho: A história secreta do crime organizado*. Rio de Janeiro: Editora Record.

Andreas, Peter. 1999. "When Policies Collide: Market Reform, Market Prohibition, and the Narcotization of the Mexican Economy." In *The Illicit Global Economy and State Power*, edited by H. Richard Friman and Peter Andreas. Lanham, MD: Rowman and Littlefield.

Arias, Desmond. 2006. *Drugs and Democracy in Rio de Janeiro: Trafficking, Social Networks and Public Security*. Chapel Hill: University of North Carolina Press.

Arias, Desmond, and Thomas Grisaffi. 2016. "The Governance of the Global Narcotics Trade." Paper presented at the annual conference of the Latin American Studies Association, New York, May 27–30.

"Até preso, rico leva vantage: O decreto da prisão especial é de 1955—e já foi revogado." 2001. *Veja* (São Paulo), January 17.

Barcellos, Caco. 2004. *Abusado: O Dono do Morro Dona Marta*. Rio de Janeiro: Editora Record.

Biondi, Karina. 2016. *Sharing This Walk: An Ethnography of Prison Life and the PCC in Brazil*. Chapel Hill: North Carolina University Press.

da Silva, William. 1991. *Quatrocentos contra um*. Rio de Janeiro: Vozes.

de Abreu, Allan. 2017. *Cocaína: A Rota Caipira*. Rio de Janeiro: Editora Record.

Denyer Willis, Graham. 2015. *The Killing Consensus: Police, Organized Crime and the Regulation of Life and Death in Urban Brazil*. Berkeley: University of California Press.

Denyer Willis, Graham. 2016. "Before the Body Count: Homicide Statistics and Everyday Security in Latin America." *Journal of Latin American Studies* 49: 29–54.

Dowdney, Luke. 2003. *Crianças do tráfico: Um estudo de caso de crianças em violência armada organizada no Rio de Janeiro*. Rio de Janeiro: 7 Letras.

Gay, Robert. 1994. *Popular Organization and Democracy in Rio de Janeiro: A Tale of Two Favelas*. Philadelphia: Temple University Press.

Gay, Robert. 2005. *Lucia: Testimonies of a Brazilian Drug Dealer's Woman*. Philadelphia: Temple University Press.

Gay, Robert. 2015. *Bruno: Conversations with a Brazilian Drug Dealer*. Durham, NC: Duke University Press.

Goldstein, Donna. 2013. *Laughter Out of Place: Race, Class, Violence and Sexuality in a Rio Shantytown*. Berkeley: University of California Press.

Gootenberg, Paul. 2008. *Andean Cocaine: The Making of a Global Drug*. Chapel Hill: University of North Carolina Press.

Holston, James. 2008. *Insurgent Citizenship: Disjunctions of Democracy and Modernity in Brazil*. Princeton, NJ: Princeton University Press.

Leeds, Elizabeth. 1996. "Cocaine and Parallel Polities in the Brazilian Urban Periphery." *Latin American Research Review* 31, no. 3: 47–83.

Lessing, Benjamin. 2008. "As Facções Cariocas em Perspectiva Comparativa." *Novos Estudos* 80: 43–62.

McCann, Bryan. 2014. *Hard Times in the Marvelous City: From Dictatorship to Democracy in the Favelas of Rio de Janeiro.* Durham, NC: Duke University Press.

Moura, Paula, and Lulu Garcia Navarro. 2013. "Brazil Looks to Build a 10,000-Mile Virtual Fence." *National Public Radio*, May 16. Accessed October 14, 2018. https://www.npr.org/sections/parallels/2013/05/16/184524306/brazil-looks -to-build-a-10-000-mile-virtual-fence.

Murat, Lúcia, dir. 2004. *Quase Dois Irmãos.* Rio de Janeiro: Taiga Filmes, Ceneca Producciones, TS Productions.

Newbold, Greg, Jeffrey Ian Ross, Richard S. Jones, Stephen C. Richards, and Michael Lenza. 2014. "Prison Research from the Inside: The Role of Convict Autoethnography." *Qualitative Inquiry* 20, no. 4: 439–48.

Penglase, Ben. 2008. "The Bastard Child of the Dictatorship: The Comando Vermelho and the Birth of 'Narco-Culture' in Rio de Janeiro." *Luso-Brazilian Review* 45, no. 1: 118–45.

Penglase, Ben. 2014. *Living with Insecurity in a Brazilian Favela: Urban Violence and Daily Life.* New Brunswick, NJ: Rutgers University Press.

Robb Larkins, Erika. 2015. *The Spectacular Favela: Violence in Modern Brazil.* Berkeley: University of California Press.

Sepúlveda dos Santos, Myrian. 2009. *Os porões da república: A barbárie nas prisões da Ilha Grande, 1894–1945.* Rio de Janeiro: Garamond.

Souza, Caco, dir. 2004. *Senhora Liberdade.* Rio de Janeiro: Mor Produtora; Destiny Internacional, Vira Lata Filmes.

US Department of State. 2002. *International Narcotics Control Strategy Report.* Washington, DC: US Department of State.

Van Dun, Mirella. 2016. "Cocaine Flows and the State in Peru's Amazonian Borderlands." *Journal of Latin American Studies* 48: 509–35.

Zdun, Steffen. 2011. "Difficulties Measuring and Controlling Homicide in Rio de Janeiro." *International Journal of Conflict and Violence* 5, no. 1: 188–99.

ANTHONY W. FONTES

# 05 BORDER, GHETTO, PRISON

## COCAINE AND SOCIAL ORDERS IN GUATEMALA

**PAVÓN PRISON, GUATEMALA CITY, GUATEMALA. MAY 2016**

Trompas, who is now twenty-five years old, was sixteen when he first started working for the woman he would only call "Madam." She was from Zacapa, a province on Guatemala's border with Honduras, and the mother of his friend. Trompas grew up in Zone 6 of Guatemala City, and before starting his employ with Madam, he survived as what he called a "common delinquent." His big chance came when he saved the woman's son from a drug overdose. Out of gratitude, he said, Madam offered him a job and a chance to prove his worth. The job was simple enough: pick up a certain car a few miles from Guatemala's border with Honduras, and drive that car along a prescribed route to the outskirts of El Carmen, a tiny strip of a town on Guatemala's western border with Mexico. Madam provided him with a fake driver's license, car insurance, and registration papers, and promised to pay him a thousand dollars, or about Q8,000. Trompas jumped at the opportunity. "I knew it would be no good to be asking questions. They were paying me a good amount of money to take a car from point $x$ to point $y$, and so I preferred not to get too involved, to not know too much. Because in certain things, information can get one deeper than one wants to get. So it's better not to know. But obviously, it was cocaine, because it couldn't have been anything else. There were secret compartments, because I even went into the trunk to see and . . . nothing."

Over the next several months, Trompas drove a dozen or so cars packed with hidden cocaine across the country. As instructed, he stuck to the backroads rather than main thoroughfares, and navigated well wide of Guatemala City. He was to avoid the nation's capital because of the density of security checkpoints that operate in and around the city, as well as to avoid trespassing on the turf of the mini-cartels that dominate transport and distribution of cocaine and its derivatives within city limits. The money he earned made it possible for him to move his wife and infant to a safer part of Guatemala City, and for this he was grateful. In brief meetings with other employees of Madam, he gleaned that they too must be carrying drugs. Some traveled back and forth from Panama. Others took flights to Europe. And all of them were paid handsomely for their labor. After less than a year working with Madam, she offered him a chance to work as her bodyguard when she came to Guatemala City. But then, when he was nineteen, Trompas was arrested for killing a man in a settling of scores in his old neighborhood. It had nothing to do with the drug business, but nevertheless Madam stepped in to support him through his arrest and subsequent incarceration. She provided him with a stipend of Q2,000 (about $250) a week, and made sure his wife and child had a roof over their heads. Today, he resides in Pavón prison on the outskirts of Guatemala City.

........................

Guatemala has long been a central hub for the transnational transportation of cocaine.[1] Today, most of the cocaine bound for the "insatiable North American nose" passes through Guatemalan territory (Aguilar Camín, quoted in Radden Keefe 2012). The country is a key waystation for cocaine transported from South America via both the Pacific Ocean and the "Caribbean route" through Nicaragua and Honduras (see Rodgers, this volume) and onward into Mexico (see Le Cour Grandmaison, this volume). For most of its cocaine history (from the 1970s through the early 2000s), drug transportation inside Guatemala was monopolized by powerful family networks based in the border regions with Honduras and Mexico. These families (Lorenzana, Leon, Ponce, Zarceño, and others) acted as middlemen between Colombian and Mexican drug trafficking organizations (DTOs) and built cross-border relations with their Honduran and Mexican counterparts. They were often called *los narcos decentes* (the respectable narco-traffickers), mixing largesse with a monopoly over the use of violence within their respective territories. For decades, they were able to carefully limit violence associated with their business by seeking negotiated solutions to conflicts. They also built extensive networks infiltrating local and regional government offices, the police, and the army. Indeed, with the decommissioning of two-thirds of the Guatemalan military in 1996, it is suspected that many former commanders and combatants found employment in the drug trade (Ball, Kobrak, and Spirer 1999; Arnson et al. 2011). National-level politicians have accused these families of causing violence and corruption, but until the last decade, local authorities were never able to touch them. According to Claudia Paz y Paz, the attorney general from 2008 to 2013, "In regions where drug traffickers have a greater presence, they have been able to penetrate the office of public prosecutors, the National Police and the courts" (International Crisis Group 2011: 14). Indeed, some Guatemalan security officials estimate that as much as 60 percent of police are in the pay of local and transnational drug traffickers.

As influential as Guatemalan DTOs are within Guatemala, they have long been subservient to the demands of far richer and more powerful Mexico-based cartels. This, according to many law enforcement agents I have talked to over the years, is a central reason that tracking the logics of violence and change in the Guatemalan cocaine business is so difficult. When it comes to cocaine, "Guatemala is merely the tail of the dragon, while the head is in Mexico" (Chapas 2016). Indeed, in the late 2000s, as the US-backed war on drugs in Mexico surged, Guatemala's family organizations were drawn into the violent turf wars provoked by the Mexican government's crackdown against drug traffickers. In 2011, for example, the paramilitary cartel known as the Zetas initiated tit-for-tat massacres for control over key drug routes in Guatemala.[2] Meanwhile, with deep financial and logistical support from the US government, Guatemalan law enforcement agencies targeted "capos" of the most powerful drug transportation organizations. Along with the anti-corruption investigations against leading members of former President Perez Molina's cabinet, these efforts have revealed how deeply enmeshed the highest echelons of the Guatemalan government are with the business of cocaine trafficking. In 2015, for instance, former Minister of the Interior Mauricio Lopez Bonilla was caught on camera accepting bribes in return for providing protection for cocaine traffickers. He also used police units to provide armed escort for cocaine shipments crossing through Guatemalan territory (Dudley 2016). Such revelations have pushed some to contend that Guatemala is, and has long been, a "narco-state" deeply corrupted by its relationship to cocaine (Newman 2011).

Clearly, in Guatemala the cocaine business blurs any clear distinction between "the law-abiding world and the underworld upon which it rests" (Taussig 1984: 122). However, understanding cocaine's role in Guatemalan society through the normative lens of terms like "narco-state" and "corruption" obscures more than it reveals. After more than thirty years as a cocaine transport hub, the Guatemalan cocaine economy has become deeply embedded in everyday life in an astonishing variety of spaces and communities. As Trompas's account reveals, this illicit substance moves along clandestine but quotidian vectors—beneath the radar of law enforcement and the media, and more often than not in a peaceful, even humdrum manner. Occasional outbreaks of violence reveal fierce competition over the profits and power it makes possible. However, beneath and alongside such violence, the cocaine commodity chain articulates with and helps shape local social orders in important ways, often existing as an open secret for the communities that have come to rely upon the profits it generates. The wealth and influence derived from its trade create essential economic opportunities and governing structures for a wide variety of communities historically abandoned or even abused by state authorities.

As the editors of this volume argue, the best way to understand the value, exchange, and influence of cocaine is to follow the substance itself as it moves through distinct spaces in order to analyze how local actors take part in Guatemala's cocaine commodity chain and make sense of its myriad effects. Toward this end, I will explore three spaces in which the cocaine trade has become deeply integrated into the local moral and political economic milieu in distinctive ways, yet giving rise in each to powerful bonds of reciprocity, trust, and care. Trompas's itinerary provides the roadmap: El Carmen, the border town where he made his first delivery; Barrio El Gallito, a Guatemala City neighborhood from which local cartels have fed the urban crack cocaine market for decades; and Pavón prison, where the drug economy undergirds survival for prisoners, prison officials, and the prison system itself.

## COCAINE AT THE BORDER: EL CARMEN, SAN MARCOS, GUATEMALA

El Carmen is a small town on the Guatemala-Mexico Border across which upward of 80–90 percent of the cocaine consumed in the United States moves (US Department of State 2014). The town is quite a bit smaller than Tecun Uman to the south, where most of the cargo trucks moving commodities of all kinds both north and south along the Pacific coast cross through customs and immigration inspection. It is, however, far more developed than the border checkpoint of La Mesilla several hours to the north, which, according to state officials, is located in "opium poppy (amapola) country" where narcotraffickers are said to cross the border in suvs more or less at will (Chapas 2016).

National borders are typically key spaces of risk and profit for trafficking all things illicit, since navigating past state border defenses requires time, money, and reliable networks.[3] Among the wide variety of commodities smuggled across the Guatemala-Mexico border, cocaine is among the most lucrative because of its high weight-to-volume ratio and easy packing.[4] Over the last decade, drug traffickers in the region have invested considerable time and energy to ensure safe passage for their product northward. For the people of El Carmen and surrounding communities, cocaine has long been an essential feature of the economic and social environment. In a region with virtually no industry beyond sugar cane production, and in an economy in which the availability of cheap goods from Mexico undercuts local trade, the cocaine business is an important source of cash flow. Competition between rivals (and recent government efforts to disrupt transport operations) create an ever-shifting cast of locals and foreigners vying to control cocaine's movement through this region. Such struggles produce intermittent violence and spectacle—a late-model suv riddled with bullets, a young man's corpse, shot execution style, on the side of the road, and so on. Generally, as elsewhere, both the perpetrators and victims of this violence are understood to be directly involved in the cocaine business. Local residents tend to make sense of such violence as a necessary evil, because for many the cocaine business produces a panoply of economic opportunities removed from the lucrative and dangerous business of its transportation.

In El Carmen, a single road curves down toward the bridge over the Suchiate River dividing Mexican and Guatemalan territories (figures 5.1, 5.2). Cheap hotels, cantinas, and restaurants line the road on either side. Men wearing plastic ID cards gesture for attention at cars and buses caught up in the snarl of traffic before the border crossing point. These are *tramitadores*—or "paperwork processors"—men who, for a fee, help travelers fill out—or fake—immigration forms, car registration forms, and so on. In 2014, on my first visit to El Carmen, a particularly persistent tramitador ignored my insistence that I didn't need his help as I wandered around checking the scene. Finally, unable to shake him, I asked him what he knew about undocumented migration, drug trafficking, and all things illicit. As it turned out, he knew a lot about such things.

Valentin, as I will call him, was in his late twenties when we met. He had held a variety of jobs, most of them in the informal economy, on both

FIGURE 5.1 Illicit border crossing, Río Suchiate, Guatemala.

FIGURE 5.2 El Carmen Bridge, Guatemala.

sides of the blurred boundary dividing the licit from the illicit. It is worth mentioning that cocaine is only one of many illegal commodities trafficked across this border—undocumented migrants also move northward, while untaxed black market consumer goods and unregistered firearms (a considerable volume of which originate in the United States) cross south into Guatemala (Goodman 2013). At one point or another, Valentin had tried his luck in all of these markets.

Because he resided so close to the border, Valentin had a special visa that allowed him to cross back and forth across the border and travel up to 150 kilometers into Mexican territory. He had spent much of his teenage years and early twenties following in his father's footsteps as a "coyote," guiding fellow Central Americans—mostly Hondurans, Salvadorans, and fellow Guatemalans—headed for the United States across the Guatemala-Mexico border and delivering them to other coyotes in his network who shepherded his charges farther north (see Slack and Campbell 2016). But after his boss retired and moved elsewhere, Valentin had to find other ways to provide for his wife and four children. A childhood friend of his was linked with a regional cocaine transporter. Because of his intimate knowledge of the border region, Valentin secured employment as a small-scale smuggler, moving backpacks with one or two kilograms of cocaine northward and making between five hundred and eight hundred dollars per trip. But this employment ended after only a few months when a rival group shot and killed his contact.

With little education—he never finished primary school—the only available legal employment was on sugar cane plantations or other fieldwork. Such work is hard and pays no more than Q50 or 60 a day (about eight US dollars). "You work, but you can never make enough to cover your costs," he said. Like many poor rural Guatemalans, Valentin decided to migrate to the US to find work. He managed to live and work in southern California for nearly three years until he was deported back to Guatemala in 2010.

Upon his return, Valentin began what he recalled as the best job he ever had. In the mid-2000s, a Mexican narco-trafficker whom I will call Don Carlos bought a finca with more than a thousand acres of land close to the border. "He brought cars from Mexico," Valentin reminisced, "and they adapted the motor by cutting it in half. One half carried gasoline and the other half cocaine. They moved a lot of material!" Then he sighed. "But he left. He sold the finca and he left."

Don Carlos was connected to Juan "El Chamalé" Ortiz, one of Guatemala's most infamous drug traffickers and a major player in all aspects of political and economic life in the border region. Don Carlos, for his part, was well loved by local communities. He cultivated the communities' good will with public acts of munificence. "Narcos like him give a lot to poor people," Valentin recalled. "So, like, when there would be festivals, they would give away clothes, shoes, balls, and stuff. Because of this, they are well loved here." And it wasn't only acts of charity that earned Don Carlos so much good will. "They give so much work to people who, the truth is, really need it," Valentin explained, "and maybe it's not doing bad things, but simply taking care of cattle, serving food, cleaning out paddocks. . . . Narcos like that are very important for people just trying to earn enough to care for their families. They're central, they help the people a lot."

Don Carlos provided a wide variety of jobs employing a large portion of the local community. Mechanics worked on the fleet of vehicles modified to move cocaine north. He employed local young men as security to guard his cocaine depot against rivals, and of course there were those who worked for him transporting cocaine across the border into Mexico.

But Don Carlos also funneled lots of money into the local economy by providing jobs that had nothing to do with the business of drug trafficking. He employed laborers to work the fields, care for the animals, and clean the stables, and paid a higher than normal rate for such work. He hired locals to build and maintain beehives to produce honey for sale, and carpenters, stonemasons, bricklayers, and so on to build on his vast estate.

Valentin first started with Don Carlos as a gardener, and then worked in the carpentry shop. Since he knew the local terrain well and, he said, had won Don Carlos's trust, Valentin was then put in charge of the man's prize sheep imported from Reynosa, Mexico. "I guided them to the fields to eat, I tended them when they got sick," he recalled with pride, "and the boss's nephew even taught me how to give them injections, treat them, and care for their hooves. Everything." After several months of this, Don Carlos's overseer offered Valentin a new job working security—a job that would require Valentin to carry an automatic weapon and patrol the finca. "But I said no, because I liked what I was doing. I felt good caring for the sheep."

In early 2011, after getting tipped off that Guatemalan law enforcement was closing in, Don Carlos fled the region, selling some of his vast estates and leaving others to his top lieutenants. His sudden departure was a major blow to the local community. It was followed quickly by the arrest of his far richer and more famous colleague, Juan "El Chamalé" Ortiz.

While Don Carlos and his drug money were central to the local community, El Chamalé exercised far deeper and more extensive influence across the entire region. El Chamalé's preeminence on this part of Guatemala's border demonstrates most lucidly how deeply embedded some major narco-traffickers can become in the politics and welfare of the regions where they operate. His organization's territorial reach extended throughout the province of San Marcos, which shares a border with Mexico from the Pacific coast northward into the western highlands. By linking up with fishermen on the coast, Chamalé was able to organize the region's most effective transport system for moving cocaine shipments from South America onward into Mexico. He is also said to have controlled the production and transportation of heroin in the northern part of San Marcos. He worked closely with the Sinaloa Cartel, and for years was dubbed Guatemala's "#1 drug trafficker" by the US Department of Justice ("Juan Alberto Ortiz Lopez" 2017).

Meanwhile, Chamalé cultivated an impressive public profile, becoming a widely respected citizen known for his generosity toward public works programs of all kinds. He served as an honorary pastor in a San Marcos church and supported churches across the region; his licit business empire included cable television channels, agriculture and ranching interests, and construction companies; finally, he sponsored numerous candidates from various major political parties and established several NGOs that operated across the region. Upon his arrest in 2011, communities in several parts of San Marcos, including El Carmen, protested against his extradition to the United States ("Juan Alberto Ortiz Lopez" 2017).

Today, El Chamalé, Don Carlos, and many others linked to their network are gone—fled, arrested, or dead. But the flow of cocaine through the region continues unabated. In 2016, the last time I visited Valentin in El Carmen, I spent a hot afternoon with him and several other tramitadores in one of the cantinas on the road curving down to the border. Work was slow, and the men were maudlin. Several waxed nostalgic about how good life was when El Chamalé reigned in the region. As we idled away the afternoon, they drank beer and occasionally went into a back room to sniff cocaine. Valentin had just returned from another failed effort to get into the United States. I asked him who was in charge of moving cocaine in the wake of Don Carlos's exit and Chamalé's arrest. He shrugged. "I don't know now. There are different groups. There are those who were powerful and who now are dead, while new ones have been born. It's like a stairway. There's one who's bigger than another and they go fighting for territory because many want to control everything but they can't. And so others follow in their footsteps."

San Marcos's proximity to Guatemala's border with Mexico makes it a key territory in cocaine's movement northward. As such, the cocaine commodity chain has become an essential feature of political, economic, and social life at a diversity of scales. El Chamalé exemplifies how powerful drug transporters become conduits by which illicit profits work their way into, and even undergird, the legal economy and the trappings of democratic politics. Cocaine's profits are unevenly concentrated in the hands of those few individuals involved in the business of its transport. However, in the midst of a wide variety of illicit commodities crossing north and south across this border, cocaine's profits make possible dignified licit employment for a generally undereducated and underemployed populace. Indeed, the awe, respect, and wistfulness woven into Valentin's and others' accounts of working with men like Don Carlos speak volumes about cocaine's role in making life livable in this part of Guatemala.

### CRACK COCAINE IN THE CITY: BARRIO "EL GALLITO," ZONE 3, GUATEMALA CITY

Over time, drug transport countries can become drug consuming countries, shifting the flow and even the direction of the cocaine commodity chain.[5] This (d)evolution depends upon several factors, the most important of which is the availability of middle-class consumers able and eager to buy new commodities. In Guatemala, the domestic market for cocaine has not grown as rapidly as in other Latin American transport countries, probably due to the country's extreme economic inequality and the relative smallness of the middle class. But in large urban centers, particularly in Guatemala City, cocaine consumption has grown over the last few decades, if only marginally. Crack cocaine use, on the other hand, has grown at a faster pace, driven by the derivative's low production costs, cheap street prices, and its remarkably powerful, short, and addictive high. The growth of the crack and cocaine markets has had consequences, not least for those communities heavily involved in the drug's production and distribution.

Barrio El Gallito (known simply as "El Gallito" by local residents), is today one of the central points of production and distribution of crack cocaine in Guatemala City (see figure 5.3). The reach and influence of the "mini-cartels" that dominate the neighborhood make up one reason that Trompas's boss instructed him to avoid the capital on his cross-country trips. El Gallito begins on the westernmost edge of Zone 3, demarcated by

FIGURE 5.3 Barrio El Gallito, 2010.

the Avenida Elena on its eastern border, the general cemetery to the south, the city dump to the west, and Belice Bridge to the north.

During the 1930s and 1940s, El Gallito became a working-class "beachhead" and the site of union organization and political resistance to militarized tyranny (Way 2012: 204). However, more than thirty years of social cleansing operations targeting union leadership and other "subversives" for disappearance, torture, and execution terrorized the community and tore the social fabric apart (Way; see also Levenson 2013). In the wake of the political terror and social upheaval of the 1960s, 1970s, and 1980s, El Gallito became known as a particularly insecure and dangerous neighborhood.

Emerging in the midst of long-standing state terror and abandonment, cocaine has become key to the lives and livelihoods of everyone in El Gallito (Feilding and Giacomello 2013). El Gallito's role in the urban cocaine market is said to have begun in the 1980s, and ramped up through the end of the country's long civil war. By the 1990s, the neighborhood had become Guatemala City's primary point of crack production and distribution. In addition to distributing powder cocaine to a smattering of high-end night clubs, the mini-cartels that ruled Gallito also cooked and distributed crack through local points of sale and in the prison system. Through their profits, they were able to establish and maintain deep ties with Guatemalan law enforcement, paying for protection from rival groups and from the law itself (Feilding and Giacomello 2013: 204).

Like the traffickers working in a wide variety of state-abandoned spaces (see Gay, this volume, for further examples), these groups have also exercised considerable influence over the lives of their neighbors.[6] Juanga, who turned thirty-five in 2015, grew up in El Gallito just as the early cocaine trafficking organizations were getting a foothold in the neighborhood. His father was a bus driver and his mother worked at home picking up whatever work—cleaning clothes, cooking food—she could find to make ends meet. Juanga was eight years old when he first came in contact with men involved in the cocaine business. On their way to school each day, he and his twin brothers walked by the corner where men selling crack cocaine set up shop, and the men would call out to them, invite them over, and give them presents. The three brothers began skipping school and hanging out on the corner. "They would tell us that we were their lucky children, their lucky totems, because when we were with them the police never came around. They gave us little toys and money, but we had to stay there with them. They didn't give us any material, or ask us to do anything illegal, and we would use the money to buy my little sisters food."

As noted in this volume's introduction, and in Grisaffi's contribution on the Bolivian cocaine industry, also in this volume, through its incorporation into family survival strategies the drug business can become extremely vital for poor communities with little access to formal economies. The income from involvement in the production, transport, and distribution of crack cocaine can make it possible for families to avoid deep poverty, and can even allow a degree of prosperity. That such involvement is almost inevitably a Faustian pact is part of the price of survival.

A few months after Juanga and his siblings began hanging out with neighborhood crack dealers, a cartel lieutenant named Juan Carlos approached him on the corner. "He asked us about my mom and my dad, and we told him our dad worked as a bus driver. And my mom stayed at home and was looking for some kind of work. He asked if he could speak with our mom, and we said yes, but please don't tell her that we were hanging out on the corner! 'It's all good,' Juan Carlos said. 'Don't worry! We just really need to talk to her. Let's go!'"

Juanga's family's home was located on the edge of El Gallito, at the dead end of a street overlooking a deep ravine where the city dumps its trash. From a real estate point of view, its location on a sharp decline and proximity to the city dump put its value at the lower end of the neighborhood spectrum. But for the cartel, it was ideal, because it backed onto the last street before the ravine, was within spitting distance of the house where they cooked crack, and through the back door one could easily escape into unpaved and makeshift alleyways, and from there lose oneself in Zone 3.

"After they talked with my mom, she explained to us that they were going to rent half our house," Juanga recalled. "We locked and covered a door leading to the back of the house. They bought us a king-size bed, a stove, furniture, and a home entertainment system. And they paid for electricity and water as well as rent and provided lunch for the kids each day. That was the deal my mom made, and they used half our house, not for a laboratory, but for their accounting. Every Monday they would do their accounting, counting and stacking money from seven at night to two, three in the morning."

For Juanga and his family, their entrance into the cocaine business irrevocably transformed their lives. His father stopped working as a bus driver, and instead used the profits to buy and sell gold and silver jewelry. Juanga never went to school again. As he and his siblings grew up, they took on a variety of jobs in the production and distribution of cocaine. Along with their mother, they managed a crack *punto*—point of sale— on the edge of an outdoor market in the heart of El Gallito. Later, they spent eight hours a day packing baggies of crack. The crack business grew through the 1990s, and the cartel of El Gallito grew with it. By the time Juanga was fifteen he was transporting packages of cocaine and crack across the city, and making as much as Q1,000 (US$135) a day. "From eight years old until I was eighteen I sold drugs," he said as we spoke in courtyard of Pavón prison. "They arrested me when I was eighteen, and I had a Ninja [motorcycle] and all kinds of things. We had a Dodge Ram, and like four other cars."

In 1999, Juanga was arrested and imprisoned for murder after he shot a man who was attempting to steal a cocaine shipment from a safehouse that was under his care. He received a twenty-year sentence. For the first five years of his confinement, the cartel continued to care for him, his children, and his family. He received regular installments of food, a stipend of Q500 (US$65) a week, and was paid additional money for helping to manage crack distribution in the various prisons he occupied. The cartel also provided for his wife and children with monthly payments, and even gave them a home in El Gallito, demonstrating just how dedicated they remained to the family.

"They kicked out a family from their home," Juanga said, shaking his head, "and gave it to us to live in as our own, that is, to my woman and my children."

But then, one by one, the leaders of his cartel were killed in shootouts with rivals or arrested by the law, and members of his family also suffered the consequences of the violence so often associated with the drug trade. Competitors shot and killed his father, and his mother took a bullet to the spine that left her paralyzed. Today, Juanga's siblings remain in the game, managing their own crack sale points for the cartels that today hold sway in El Gallito, but they, like other members of the cartel, no longer help Juanga. Since his father's death, he has struggled with his own crack addiction, smoking up all the money and goods he received from the outside. To collect on the drugs that Juanga was supposed to have sold, the cartel raided his wife's home in El Gallito, taking away their washing machine, stove, refrigerator, and television. "They even took her motorbike," Juanga said, shaking his head. "Now she says she wants nothing to do with [the cartel], and if I go back to using crack, she says I will never see her or my children again."

Juanga's boom-and-bust life story may appear a cautionary tale for those tempted by the potential riches of the cocaine business. But for residents of El Gallito, this business continues to weave itself into the fabric of everyday life, forming a significant and unavoidable part of the social and physical environment. Today, though the names of the cartels and personalities at the top have changed over the years, the business continues unabated. These groups pay rent and mortgage for residents in return for silence and service. Whole families work on behalf of the cartel, manufacturing and sometimes selling drugs out of their homes. Women and children transport product and money from crack factories set up in family basements to points of sale in El Gallito and beyond. Elderly widows stash arms and drugs for the cartel. Boys and veteran addicts patrol the neighborhood on motorbikes or bicycles, and report police movements, the presence of strangers, and so on. Young men work as security and salesmen. The more skilled or determined might, like Juanga and his siblings, become managers of their own punto, or freelance *sicarios*—hitmen for hire—and enjoy the short-lived riches and glitz such a lifestyle can afford (see also Baird 2018).

In late 2016, the last time I visited El Gallito, the main street was a bustling marketplace, and seemed far more lively than its counterparts in other poor urban neighborhoods I have visited over the years. This is because, according to longtime residents, the cartel provides security against petty thieves and gangs that would prey on the community. These are businessmen who do not want to see their operations disturbed by local violence.

State police and military units operate parallel to (or is it in conjunction with?) the cartels' embedded networks here. Police pickup trucks drive a regular route through the neighborhood, rarely slowing down, simply showing the flag of state authority. Since 2005, military patrols have been installed in a permanent "civilian defense force" depot along the main street. Their base is a sheet metal construction, painted slate gray, protected by a sandbag barricade. The troops—young men, most of indigenous descent recruited from poor farming communities—stand guard on street corners radiating out from their base. They wear fatigues and bulletproof vests, heavy boots, and stand with AK-47s for six- to twelve-hour stretches. They are here to protect (or is to perform protection's charade?).

All about them, business goes on as usual. On several afternoons, I met with drug dealers operating a stone's throw from the army barracks down narrow alleyways cutting away from the main street. Stairways of chipped concrete descend between long rows of ramshackle homes toward the steep precipice overlooking the ravine of trash. Patrons in search of Q5 (US$.75) bags of marijuana or Q10 (US$1.50) pebbles of crack need only beckon an adolescent boy slouched against a jacaranda tree pushing up the pavement of one of the narrow alleys off the main street. After quickly inspecting his customer, the boy nods and flicks his hand in a gestured question, informs the patron of the price, and takes the payment palmed into his hand. Then he disappears down the alley. A minute or two later, he returns, and transfers the product in a quick handshake. A steady flow of customers repeat the ritual throughout the day.

There is only one way to drive in or out of Barrio El Gallito. Makeshift roadblocks of concrete and rebar impede every other thoroughfare. A military spokesman told me security forces erected them to ensure that all traffic in and out of El Gallito must pass before the civilian security barracks. Juanga claimed that the cartel erected these barriers years ago to protect itself from incursions by rival traffickers and police. I tried to confirm this with Gallito residents. But none I spoke with could—or would—say for sure.

In El Gallito, cocaine and the profits and power linked to its commodification became an essential economic and social lifeline for a community suffering long histories of state terror and abandonment. It has become a source of risk and profit while also indirectly contributing to communal security strategies, as those profiting most from it seek to keep out criminals who would prey directly on their neighbors. The drug's influence is deep and multigenerational, shaping residents' housing strategies, employment opportunities, relationship to the law, life trajectories, and so on. Under these circumstances, cocaine's capacity to become a key part of family survival strategies is especially visible and widespread. In the burgeoning urban distribution end of Guatemala's cocaine market, entire families have been drawn into the labor market for moving, storing, cooking, and selling crack cocaine. As Juanga's experience demonstrates, this involvement entangles people in complex relationships of debt and remuneration that can free them from perennial poverty. Such intimate involvement in the cocaine business illuminates the intense moral, social, and economic contradictions of this unique commodity. Even as participating in this market provides families like Juanga's with a taste of prosperity unavailable otherwise, addiction and violence can corrode these gains so thoroughly as to destroy whatever value they might once have had.

## COCAINE AND THE CARCERAL: GRANJA PENITENCIARIA PAVÓN, GUATEMALA

Today, like Trompas, Juanga resides in Pavón prison, located on the outskirts of Guatemala City, about ten kilometers up the winding Carretera El Salvador (see figure 5.4). It is one of a half dozen prison facilities built on the grounds of a military base. Completed in 1976, Pavón is Guatemala's oldest and largest prison complex.[7] Here, too, cocaine has become interwoven with the basic maintenance of daily life. In fact, the drug economy has become absolutely essential to the survival of both prisoners and the prison itself. The transport and distribution networks that control its flow into the prison give rise to much-needed cash flow in a prison economy perpetually in need of liquid currency. That is, the cocaine business is a key pillar supporting imprisoned populations and a prison system that otherwise could not sustain themselves.

At different moments in its history, life in Pavón itself has been governed by men whose power and wealth flow directly from the cocaine trade. Over the years, the power of such individuals has waxed and waned, but has always remained an essential element in prison governing structures.

FIGURE 5.4 Pavón Prison, Guatemala.

For example, in the early 2000s, a group of powerful men known as the Comité de Orden y Disciplina (COD) ruled over Pavón with little meaningful state oversight. Prison guards patrolled the outer perimeter only, while the COD established and maintained the law on the inside. Many of the COD's leading personalities had gained their wealth and authority from their involvement in transporting and distributing cocaine across Central America. Under the COD's reign, resource-rich prisoners built comfortable residences for themselves, and the facility became known as "the Hilton" of the prison system. One prisoner even installed a Jacuzzi bathtub in his residence. Prisoners also built a nightclub, a mechanics' shop that refurbished stolen vehicles, and one enterprising prisoner ran a crack factory from which he distributed the drug to other prisons. In 2006, in an effort to regain at least a façade of control, the government took back the prison in a spectacular operation dubbed Pavo Real (Peacock). Five thousand heavily armed soldiers and policemen raided the grounds. In the midst of the chaos, government agents executed seven, five of whom were leading members of the COD (Washington Office on Latin America 2015; see also McDonald 2012). The military and police ultimately demolished the residences and

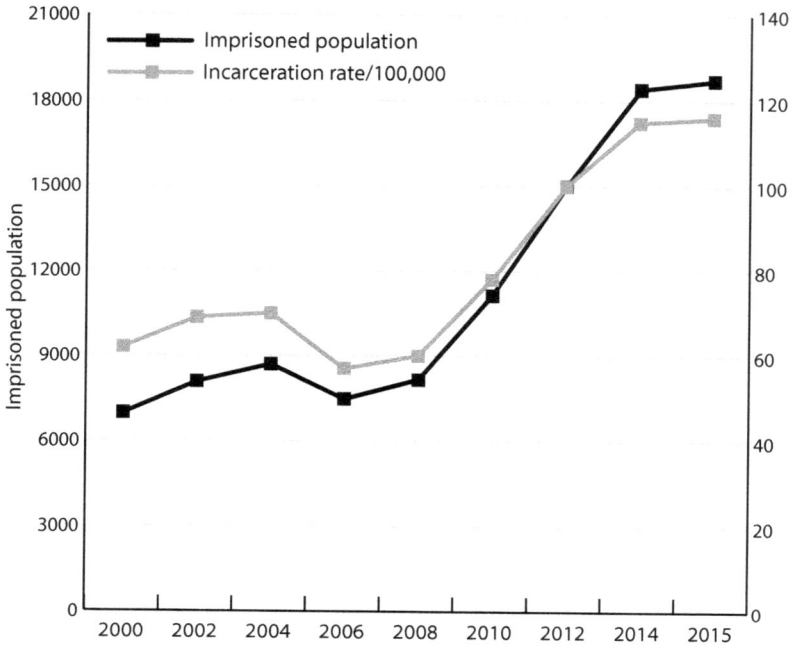

FIGURE 5.5 Graph showing the evolution of the Prison Population, 2000–2015.
Source: International Centre for Prison Studies, 2016.

other prisoner-built structures, and attempted to reestablish government rule.

In the years since, Pavón has become a more peaceful but decidedly less comfortable place to reside. Originally built to serve some 1,200 inmates, today more than 4,000 men live within Pavón's walls. Such severe over-crowding is not unique to Pavón.[8] Over the last couple of decades, prohibitionist drug policies have helped pack the nation's prison system to bursting.[9] While prosecution rates for violent crimes have remained less than 10 percent over the last twenty years, during this time the prison population has tripled—see figure 5.5 (International Centre for Prison Studies 2016b; OAS n.d.).

Even so, it seems that the Guatemalan state has had little motivation for investing the time and money needed to revamp the prison system. Spending on prisons equals 0.739 percent of the state's annual budget (Guatemalan Ministry of Interior 2015), with an overpopulation rate of above 500 percent in facilities housing pretrial detainees (see Centro de Investigaciones Económicas Nacionales 2012a, 2012b). More than half of the twenty-two prisons were built between 1950 and 1980. None have been improved to keep up with growing prison populations or technological advances, such as cell phones.[10] Most lack even rudimentary security technologies, such as functional metal detectors, body scanners, and drug dogs. Lack of state investment, of course, also curtails the provision of care to prisoners. The entire system employs a meager twenty-one educators, twelve psychologists, sixteen medical doctors, and eighteen social workers across the twenty-two geographically dispersed prison structures. The vast majority of these employees serving those structures live in or around the capital city (Guatemalan Ministry of Interior 2015; see also Castañón 2017).

The severe lack of state investment in prisons has made prisoners dependent upon other sources of support. Inmates must work for themselves and/or rely on outside help, in the name of survival. To earn money, prisoners operate restaurants, bakeries, barbershops, exercise gyms, laundry services, shoe repair shops, and painting studios inside these facilities. They raise pigs, chickens, goats, fighting cocks, and raccoons for sale. Many even grow their own food on small farm plots. In Pavón, there are inmate-run pig and chicken feed stores, carpentry workshops, tortilla vendors, and hammock-weaving factories.

Inmates trying to run their own businesses in prison all face a significant roadblock: the prison economy is perpetually starved of liquid cash. This is a central reason that the flow of illicit drugs into prison has become woven into the very fabric of prison life. A liberal visiting policy allows a constant flow of visitors—mostly the prisoners' wives, mothers, and lovers—who are important vectors for the entrance of cash as well as licit goods and essential illicit goods, the most lucrative of which is, of course, drugs.[11] These visitors uphold a prison economy that functions through a complex system of exchange and barter linking licit and illicit markets into an unruly whole. In addition to cell phones, redeemable cell-phone minutes, and marijuana, cocaine and crack cocaine markets form a central pillar of this system.

This is a thriving market. Driven by the risky logistics of prison drug smuggling, marijuana and cocaine in prison are priced at least three times higher than Guatemala City street value and, according to prison officials, 60 percent of Guatemalan prisoners use drugs (see also Pressly 2014).

Marijuana is by far the most commonly used and most widely welcomed drug in prison. Prison officials even consider marijuana "not only necessary but required" to maintain a tranquil and orderly prison population. As one prison director stated, "I know how much marijuana gets smuggled in here. But let them smoke their joints. It calms them down, makes the time pass. If I were to seize all the marijuana tomorrow, I would have an immediate riot on my hands" (Fontes 2018).

Though frowned upon by prison authorities as a source of prisoner conflict, cocaine and crack cocaine are also widely available inside Pavón and every other prison in Guatemala.[12] "On certain days," explained another Pavón prisoner, "it is easier to find crack in here than bread." Juanga, who as you will recall has struggled with crack addiction much of his life, said, "Drugs is what surrounds you here. When I was in [pretrial detention], there'd be a guy cooking crack next to me, another guy selling further down the corridor, and another guy high as shit in the corner." Cocaine's pervasiveness within prison walls makes it pivotal to the entire prison economy. The profits it generates allow imprisoned drug dealers to invest in any number of prison-run businesses, which in turn provides employment for other prisoners lacking sufficient support from the outside.

As in Barrio El Gallito and the border region, the business of transporting and distributing cocaine has become an essential source of income for a wide variety of individuals removed from the violence so often associated with drug trafficking. More than 30 percent of prison guards pad their paltry salaries by collaborating with prison drug traffickers. This makes smuggling drugs into prison relatively routine, but does not eliminate the legal and health-related risks for the female visitors responsible for physically bringing the cocaine for consumption inside. The most common means of entry is via their bodies: some female prison visitors earn their livelihoods by hiding cocaine in their vaginas and smuggling it through prison gates. To repeat: The Guatemalan prison system has no X-ray scanners, drug dogs, or other means of detecting illicit substances except for cavity checks. To enter the prison, every woman must wear a skirt and submit to being searched by a female guard wearing a latex glove. "They wear the same glove on every girl," complained a woman who supported her children by smuggling crack, marijuana, and cell phones into prison. "It feels like a kind of rape." And, of course, prohibitionist drug legislation mandates that anyone caught trafficking illicit substances receive a minimum five-year sentence.

The risks of cocaine trafficking have always been what makes it so lucrative, and the gendered nature of prison visitation and prison trafficking has turned male prisons into spaces of considerable opportunity for some women. Given sky-high unemployment rates, poor wages, and the fact that Guatemalan women generally receive less than 60 percent of what men receive for the same labor, poor women can make exponentially more money from prison drug smuggling than they might make in the licit economy (US Department of State 2017). Typically, a woman smuggling drugs gets paid for quantity.[13] Tono, a longtime Pavón prisoner, grew up working for his grandmother's prison smuggling network. He then took over the family business. "If a lady smuggles a half pound of marijuana [into the prison]," he explained, "she gets a hundred fifty quetzales [US$28]. If she smuggles a pound for me, she gets three hundred to three hundred fifty quetzales [US$55]. Now, if she enters a pound and a telephone, she'll be getting three hundred fifty plus the value of the phone. And if you replace the telephone with a packet of cocaine, she'll be making like seven hundred quetzales [US$100]" (Fontes and O'Neill, 2019).

The potential profits draw in women who otherwise struggle to make ends meet, and the vast majority take on the risks in order to provide support for their children and families. A woman known as La Shadow, who was serving out a five-year sentence for trafficking, said, "Smuggling drugs into prison was the only way I could support my kids and also care for them," she shrugged and smiled sadly. "But look where it got me."

Indeed, the business of smuggling cocaine and other illicit substances into Guatemalan prisons reveals the glaring contradictions that create but also destabilize social order in the prison system and beyond. Prohibitionist drug policies have helped pack the national prison system to the point of catastrophe, while a weak state has proven unwilling or unable to provide for those it incarcerates. Meanwhile, as families and communities rely upon cocaine profits, and the penitentiary system itself depends upon such illicit markets to triage an extreme lack of state investment, official state laws and practices make such transactions a source of unending risk for all involved.

Nevertheless, the networks feeding and feeding off of the prison cocaine economy extend beyond prisoners to include prison guards, directors, and the highest echelons of prison administration. Trafficking networks also link the exigencies of prison life to the business of survival for the women who move cocaine and other illicit commodities into the prison setting.

In this way, the cocaine commodity chain connects state agents, incarcerated men, and families getting by in poor urban neighborhoods, weaving these disparate spaces and actors together in ways that cannot be easily disentangled.

## CONCLUSION

Driven by the tantalizing profits and power it makes possible, cocaine moves across Guatemalan territory along myriad vectors, drawing in individuals and communities from across the economic and social spectrum. Along the way, as I have shown, it articulates with and (re)orders local social worlds in distinctive ways. Straddling the border, powerful regional DTOs leverage transnational profits to infiltrate and reshape state governing structures, providing opportunities for both licit and illicit employment for entire communities. In Guatemala City, involvement in the growing crack cocaine market has set the life trajectories for generations of El Gallito residents, providing new chances for prosperity and exposure to risks of death, incarceration, and addiction. And in Guatemala's prisons, the markets for cocaine and other illicit commodities undergird survival for prisoners, visitors, and the penal institution itself. In each of these spaces, the cocaine market supports licit livelihoods, weaving into the fabric of communal relations, the operation of state institutions, and the exercise of power and politics. Those who benefit most from the drug's flow through Guatemala—narco-traffickers like El Chamalé, or high-ranking officials like Lopez Bonilla—can earn enormous profits and gain remarkable influence. For those surviving at the lower end of cocaine-trafficking hierarchies—people like Trompas, Valentin, Juanga, and their communities—involvement in the drug business can provide the chance for dignified employment and prosperity in the midst of overwhelming poverty. Notwithstanding the vast inequalities in wealth and power between these two groups, they are tied together by relationships of trust, reciprocity, and mutual care that emerge out of and go well beyond cocaine's flow through the region. Valentin and his community relied upon the likes of Don Carlos and El Chamalé to support their families, and publicly protested Chamalé's arrest and extradition. Madam trusted Trompas to guard her life, and lent him help when he was incarcerated. The Gallito cartel provided Juanga with everything he and his family might need until, finally, his addiction broke their trust. It is these relationships and the realities they expose that have made cocaine an essential part of lives and livelihoods in Guatemala for decades, and that supersede, even when overshadowed by, the violence that prohibitionist policies force upon the cocaine commodity chain.

**NOTES**

1   For a long view of cocaine trafficking in the region, see Gootenberg (2008).
2   See, for example, Quinn (2011).
3   For a historical overview of illicit narcotics crossing state-boundaries, see Gootenberg (2009).
4   Marijuana, in comparison, is far easier to detect and much more difficult to densely pack than cocaine, as are firearms, timber, wildlife, and undocumented humans. According to state officials and local residents, the only illicit commodity that can earn comparable returns is locally sourced heroin.
5   See Gootenberg, chapter 11, this volume.
6   See Arias and Grisaffi, introduction to this volume; Gay, chapter 4, this volume; and Strange (1996).
7   For a detailed history of Pavón prison, see Ordoñez (2007). For a deeper look at the history and logic of incarceration in Latin America, see Salvatore and Aguirre (1996).
8   Such massive overpopulation characterizes prison systems across the region. See, for example, Bergman, Fondevilla, and Vilalta (2015). For comparable trends in Honduras, see Carter (2014). And for a global perspective, see Cheliotis (2014).
9   A central reason for the growth in the prison system has been an impressive rise in violent crime. See Wacquant (2009); UNODC (2011); Council on Hemispheric Affairs (2016); Washington Office on Latin America (2017).
10  In the last ten years, the Guatemalan government has made numerous attempts to block cell phone signals in prison facilities. In 2015, for example, the government contracted mobile phone companies to construct signal-blocking towers located on the perimeter of several medium- and maximum-security prisons. While they initially functioned in at least some facilities, recent reports from inmates and prison directors indicate that rain and wind have limited their reach and made possible cell phone communication between inmates and the outside world once again.
11  See also Fontes and O'Neill (2019). For analysis of gender and drug trafficking, see Feilding and Giacomello (2013).
12  In 2016, one of Pavón's most powerful cocaine traffickers was involved in the assassination of Byron Lima, the former "king" of the Guatemala prison system. See Fontes (2016).
13  See also Garces, Martin, and Darke (2013). For one of the most insightful analyses available, see Garces (2014).

Arnson, Cynthia J., James Bosworth, Steven S. Dudley, Douglas Farah, Julie López, and Eric L. Olson. 2011. *Organized Crime in Central America: The Northern Triangle*. Washington, DC: Woodrow Wilson International Center for Scholars. https://www.wilsoncenter.org/publication/organized-crime -central-america-the-northern-triangle-no-29.

Baird, Adam. 2018. "Becoming the 'Baddest': Masculine Trajectories of Gang Violence in Medellín." *Journal of Latin American Studies* 50, no. 1: 183–210.

Ball, Patrick, Paul Kobrak, and Herbert F. Spirer. 1999. *State Violence in Guatemala, 1960–1996: A Quantitative Reflection*. Washington, DC: American Association for the Advancement of Science, Science and Human Rights Program, and International Center for Human Rights Research.

Bergman, Marcelo, Gustavo Fondevilla, and Carlos Vilalta. 2015. *Reporte de cárceles en El Salvador: Perfiles generales, contexto familiar, delitos, circunstancias del proceso penal y condiciones de vida en la cárcel*. San Salvador: Universidad Francisco Gavidia.

Carter, Jon Horne. 2014. "Gothic Sovereignty: Gangs and Criminal Community in a Honduran Prison." *South Atlantic Quarterly* 113, no. 3: 475–502.

Castañón, Mariela. 2017. "Policía: 13 cárceles públicas en ocho departamentos albergan a 1,678 detenidos." *La Hora*, January 4. Accessed February 13, 2017. http://lahora.gt/policia-13-carceles-publicas-en-ocho-departamentos -albergan-1678-detenidos/.

Centro de Investigaciones Económicas Nacionales. 2012a. *Un mejor futuro para los adolescentes privados de libertad*. Guatemala City: CIEN. Accessed January 23, 2016. https://es.scribd.com/doc/147267680/Postura-6-Un-mejor-futuro -para-los-adolescentes-privados-de-libertad.

Centro de Investigaciones Económicas Nacionales. 2012b. *El sistema penitenciario Guatemalteco: Un diagnostico*. Guatemala City: CIEN.

Chapas, Aldo. 2016. Interview with Chief of Guatemalan Counternarcotics Police by author. Guatemala City, Guatemala, March 12.

Cheliotis, Leonidas K. 2014. "Prison Realities: Views from around the World." *South Atlantic Quarterly* 113, no. 4.

Council on Hemispheric Affairs. 2016. "Guatemala—Central American Crime Capital." http://www.coha.org/guatemala-central-american-crime-capital/.

Dudley, Steven. 2016. "Guatemala's Mafia State and the Case of Mauricio López Bonilla." *InSight Crime*, December 15. https://www.insightcrime.org /investigations/guatemala-mafia-state-case-of-lopez-bonilla/.

Feilding, Amanda, and Corina Giacomello. 2013. *Illicit Drugs Markets and Dimensions of Violence in Guatemala*. Oxford: Beckley Foundation.

Fontes, Anthony W. 2016. "The Demise of a Prison Lord." *New York Times*, August 16. https://www.nytimes.com/2016/08/17/opinion/the-demise-of-a -guatemalan-prison-lord.html.

Fontes, Anthony W. 2018. *Mortal Doubt: Transnational Gangs and Social Order in Guatemala City*. Berkeley: University of California Press.

Fontes, Anthony W., and Kevin O'Neill. 2019. "*La Visita*: Prison and Survival in Guatemala." *Journal of Latin American Studies* 51, no. 1: 85–107.

Garces, Chris. 2014. "Denuding Surveillance at the Carceral Boundary." *South Atlantic Quarterly* 113, no. 3: 447–73.

Garces, Chris, Sacha Darke, Luis Duno-Gottberg, and Andrés Antillano, eds. Forthcoming. *Carceral Community: Troubling 21st Century Prisons in Latin America*. Philadelphia: University of Pennsylvania Press.

Garces, Chris, Tomas Martin, and Sacha Darke. 2013. "Informal Prison Dynamics in Africa and Latin America." *Criminal Justice Matters* 91, no. 1: 26–27.

Goodman, Colby. 2013. "US Firearms Trafficking to Guatemala and Mexico." Washington, DC: Wilson Center.

Gootenberg, Paul. 2008. *Andean Cocaine: The Making of a Global Drug*. Chapel Hill: University of North Carolina Press.

Gootenberg, Paul. 2009. "Talking about the Flow: Drugs, Borders, and the Discourse of Drug Control." *Cultural Critique* 71: 13–46.

Guatemalan Ministry of the Interior. 2015. "Request for Information #546." June 1.

International Centre for Prison Studies. 2016a. "Highest to Lowest: Prison Population Rate." http://www.prisonstudies.org/highest-to-lowest/prison _population_rate?field_region_taxonomy_tid=18.

International Centre for Prison Studies. 2016b. "World Prison Brief Data: Guatemala." http://www.prisonstudies.org/country/guatemala.

International Crisis Group. 2011. *Guatemala: Drug Trafficking and Violence*. Washington, DC: International Crisis Group. https://reliefweb.int/sites/reliefweb .int/files/resources/Full_Report_2623.pdf.

"Juan Alberto Ortiz Lopez, alias 'Juan Chamale.'" 2017. *InSight Crime*, May 9. https://www.insightcrime.org/guatemala-organized-crime-news/juan -alberto-ortiz-lopez-juan-chamale/.

Levenson, Deborah. 2013. *Adiós Niño: The Gangs of Guatemala City and the Politics of Death*. Durham, NC: Duke University Press.

McDonald, Mike. 2012. "Caging in Central America." *Global Post*, May 14. Accessed February 13, 2017. http://www.globalpost.com/dispatch/news /regions/americas/120513/honduras-prison-fire-central-america-jail-crisis.

Newman, Lucia. 2011. "Guatemala: A Narco State?" *Al Jazeera*, August 14. http:// www.aljazeera.com/blogs/americas/2011/08/60291.html.

Ordoñez, Edison Roderico Tello. 2007. "Planificación de una granja modelo de rehabilitación penal: La rehabilitación en el sistema penitenciario." PhD diss., Universidad de San Carlos de Guatemala.

Organization of American States. n.d. "Situación actual del sistema carcelario Guatemalteco." Washington, DC: Organization of American States. https:// www.oas.org/dsp/Observatorio/Tablas/Guatemala/sistema%20peniten- ciario-Guatemala.pdf.

Pressly, Linda. 2014. "Guatemala's Addicts behind Bars." *Crossing Continents*, BBC Radio 4, August 28. http://www.bbc.co.uk/programmes/b04fc8yq.

Quinn, Ben. 2011. "Guatemala Massacre Leaves at Least 27 People Dead." *Guardian*, May 15. https://www.theguardian.com/world/2011/may/16/guatemala -massacre-leaves-27-dead.

Radden Keefe, Patrick. 2012. "Cocaine Incorporated." *New York Times Magazine*, June 17. https://www.nytimes.com/2012/06/17/magazine/how-a-mexican -drug-cartel-makes-its-billions.html.

Salvatore, Ricardo D., and Carlos Aguirre. 1996. *The Birth of the Penitentiary in Latin America: Essays on Criminology*. Austin: University of Texas Press.

Slack, Jeremy, and Howard Campbell. 2016. "On Narco-Coyotaje: Illicit Regimes and Their Impacts on the US-Mexico Border." *Antipode* 48, no. 5.

Strange, Susan. 1996. *The Retreat of the State: The Diffusion of Power in the World Economy*. Cambridge: Cambridge University Press.

Taussig, Michael. 1984. "Culture of Terror—Space of Death: Roger Casement's Putumayo Report and the Explanation of Torture." *Comparative Studies in Society and History* 26, no. 3: 467–97.

UNODC. 2011. "Prison Reform and Alternatives to Imprisonment." Vienna: United Nations Office on Drugs and Crime. Accessed January 23, 2016. http://www.unodc.org/documents/justice-and-prison-reform/UNODC _Prison_reform_concept_note.pdf.

US Department of State. 2014. *Guatemala Country Report: 2014 International Narcotics Control Strategy Report*, vol. I: *Drug and Chemical Control*. Washington, DC: US Department of State. https://www.state.gov/j/inl/rls/nrcrpt/2014/vol1 /222894.htm.

US Department of State. 2017. *Guatemala 2016 Human Rights Report*. Washington, DC: US Department of State. https://www.state.gov/documents /organization/265802.pdf.

Wacquant, Loïc. 2009. *Prisons of Poverty*. Minneapolis: University of Minnesota Press.

Washington Office on Latin America. 2015. "La comision internacional contra la impunidad en Guatemala: Un estudio de investigacion de WOLA sobre la experiencia de la CICIG." Washington, DC: WOLA. Accessed February 13, 2017. https://www.wola.org/sites/default/files/CICIG%203.25.pdf.

Way, J. T. 2012. *The Mayan in the Mall: Globalization, Development, and the Making of Modern Guatemala*. Durham, NC: Duke University Press.

# 06 DRUG CARTELS, FROM POLITICAL TO CRIMINAL INTERMEDIATION

THE CABALLEROS TEMPLARIOS' MIRROR SOVEREIGNTY
IN MICHOACÁN, MEXICO

September 6, 2006, marked a turning point in the political and criminal life of the Mexican state of Michoacán. That night, an armed commando unit assaulted a nightclub in Uruapan, the state's second largest city. Approximately twenty men equipped with military gear and carrying assault rifles entered the disco and closed the doors behind them. Once inside, they forced the people to sit or lie down and threw five severed human heads onto the dance floor. They then hung a large *manta* [blanket] that read: "La Familia does not kill for money, does not kill women, does not kill innocents. Those who have to die, die. Everybody must understand: this is Divine Justice" (RELEA 2006).

At that time, Mexicans were not yet accustomed to the spectacles of criminal violence that were so commonplace by the late 2000s. The act shocked commentators in the press and society at large (Durán-Martínez 2015). Over the following days, La Familia Michoacana (The Michoacán Family) presented itself to the local population through public events, speeches, and flyers. These documents presented the group as a force for good: able to restore security, promote economic development, and act as a bulwark against the "invasion" of other criminal actors from elsewhere in Mexico, labeled as foreigners (*gente de fuera*)—notably the Zetas and Sinaloa Cartel. The Caballeros Templarios (Knights Templar), a cartel created in

March 2011 by a schism within La Familia, later used similar rhetoric and tactics.

The arrival of cocaine in Michoacán in the 1980s changed the state from being exclusively a zone of marijuana and poppy production into a dynamic narcotics production and transit hub. Although this chapter will not focus on the cocaine trade itself, it will build on this territorial change in the commodity chain of trafficking to introduce an example of how drug money provided immense resources that allowed criminal groups to transform local political, social, and economic interactions. This shift in Michoacán's economic niche occurred in the 1990s, and it accelerated the professionalization of the narcos, allowing established traffickers to consolidate their status as an economic elite, and therefore to become important political players in the region.

As crime bosses centralized an increasingly complex drug trade that involved production, import, protection, and export, the accumulated economic and social capital enabled them to control sectors of the licit economy, enforce social norms, and control political structures and public budgets. This shift transformed Mexico's historic clientelist mechanisms, displacing state officials and informal intermediaries, as well as giving criminals a dominant position at the center of these interactions (Malkin 2001; Mendoza 2017; Pansters 2018). My hypothesis is that drug cartels in Michoacán transformed patronage relations and brokerage practices by displacing, replacing, or mirroring brokers that lie at the center of political and social mediation. In so doing, they were able to impose a new moral and political economy in the territories they socially and geographically control. This territorial control is not merely an occupation of land. It lies at the base of their ability to transform social relationships and hierarchies, to impose alternative social orders, and to build governance models that extract resources from the drug trade, as well as the public and private sectors.

This chapter focuses on the role of the Caballeros Templarios cartel in local governance from 2011 to 2013. I conducted thirteen months of fieldwork in Michoacán, spread out over five visits between 2013 and 2017. The research coincided with a conflict between the Templarios and local Autodefensas (self-defense groups). The presence of Autodefensas enabled the inhabitants to speak more freely, and I was able to conduct more than sixty formal interviews with local state officials, residents of the zone, members of armed groups and criminal organizations, as well as numerous informal conversations and observations. I also interviewed former members of the Caballeros Templarios who had joined the self-defense groups.

Drug cartels qualitatively transform patronage relations through their access to private organized violence and the economic resources they derive from the international drug trade. This shift radically alters clientelist practices in some locales, as drug trafficking organizations displace state-connected brokers at the center of political and social mediation. Criminal-political relationships "do not follow the same rules as more conventional—that is, more open—forms of patron/broker relationships" (Gayer 2014: 136), because they are driven by non-state armed organizations not bound by prevailing social norms, and these brokerage relationships are often "too unstable to become fully institutionalized" (Gayer 2014: 137–38). This situation produces a social dynamic in which cartel leaders tend to acquire more autonomy, and sometimes more authority, than the informal brokers or the elected politicians who used to act as political bosses (Sives 2002; Gayer 2014). The result is a set of flexible political exchanges in which the criminal actor injects significant new resources into clientelist exchanges and negotiates simultaneously with social actors, state officials, and other brokers while exercising a high degree of dominance in those relationships, which it can exploit to control social, economic, and political relations.

Broadly speaking, clientelism is a reciprocal asymmetric relationship characterized by "the distribution of resources (or promise of) by political office holders or political candidates in exchange for political support, primarily—although not exclusively—in the form of a vote" (Gay 1990: 648). This is key to the concept of clientelism: Although it admits an unequal relation between two individuals, it simultaneously introduces the idea of reciprocal exchange. Two broad concepts of clientelism drive scholarly understandings of the insertion of criminal actors into political and social dynamics. The first sees criminally inflected clientelism or brokerage as a relationship in which political patrons dominate criminal clients in relatively rigid schemes of protection (Andreas 1998; Snyder and Durán-Martínez 2009). This model often confuses brokerage with market-based zero-sum transactions that separate political patrons from criminal clients and fuel violence, which is considered to be "the main survival strategy of drug-traffickers" (Snyder and Durán-Martínez 2009: 267). The second view is that clientelistic relationships are actually quite flexible and usually not part of a zero-sum game. Such approaches focus on the moral economy and symbolic mechanisms that underlie "the everyday dealings of political brokers, the practices and perspectives of so-called clients, and the problem-solving network that links clients, brokers, and political patrons" (Auyero 2000: 58). Scholars see these relationships as ongoing negotiations and conflicts that constitute and reconstitute patron–client relations.[1]

Neither of these approaches offers a complete picture of how the emergence of powerful criminal actors transforms clientelist exchanges. The ability of criminals to use violence and disruptive illicit economic resources to change the nature of political reciprocity or to exit reciprocity altogether lies at the heart of this difference. Criminal actors in Michoacán have access, through fierce competition among them and against public armed forces, to almost unlimited financial resources via their participation in the international drug trade. The drug trade, then, represents what Christian Geffray has referred to as a providential resource that enables its holder to transform political intermediation and social relationships.[2] In Michoacán, I will show how the sheer economic power of criminal organizations involved in the illicit narcotics trade places them in competition with the state in order to claim "de facto sovereignty" over a territory, including "the right over life—to protect or to kill with impunity" (Hansen and Stepputat 2006: 296), as well as a "project of rule . . . that [goes] beyond criminal force and violence only" (Pansters 2015: 153). Building on these models, I argue that criminal organizations become the guarantors of the social order amid, through, and also, in spite of violence, establishing violent social orders that encompass state, economy, and society.[3]

This de facto sovereignty enables a very different form of clientelism and moral economy to emerge than those that are described in the existing literature. Drug trafficking organizations in Mexico invert standard models of clientelism and political brokerage by using coercion to move resources from clients to patrons, even as they also provide some limited patronage to the exploited clients. This model of clientelism represents a hierarchical set of relationships, in that criminals can use their access to violence to ensure compliance with many of their decisions about how exchanges will work. Critically, one of the key goods provided by criminals under these circumstances is the provision of protection as an alternative to effective state-provided security.

The growing power of drug gangs has had particular effects on the nature of political brokerage in Mexico, where informal authorities such as caciques[4] used to "monitor the crucial junctures or synapses of relationships which connect the local system to the larger whole" (Wolf 1956: 1075). These political intermediation networks are based on personal connections, including "friendship and face to face relations" (Montes Vega 2011; also see Maldonado 2010) and often compadrazgo, a system of fictive kinship. Through these connections, the system of "caciquismo" (or bossism) articulates "different societal domains" to construct "intermediation, protective networks and [control access to] the means of violence" (Pansters 2018: 5). The emergence of contemporary criminal organizations that look to illicit markets as a key source of resources that they can distribute as "patronage"—rather than acquiring these resources through the state—has altered both formal and informal governance arrangements (Knight and Pansters 2006). Leaders of criminal organizations have supplanted traditional political brokers, in that today it is the criminal actors who are able to control access to public institutions and political resources, as well as the connections between elected officials and the social bases. Thus, in Michoacán since the 1990s, increasing competition from socially, economically, and territorially powerful criminal organizations that use illicit violence as a key political tool has displaced the state as "the sole center for rewards and privileges" (Barkey 1994: 13).[5] Criminal organizations now monopolize mediation between citizens and the state in some locales and, as a result, they have "come to symbolize many aspects of modernity that challenge older social relations," as well as a vector for social mobility (Malkin 2001: 103).

This evidence is consistent with Arias and Goldstein's (2010) claim that criminal organizations form part of a "violent pluralism," in which "armed groups are incorporated into wider political processes and become part of the political system" (Arias 2010: 116). This approach also makes clear the evolution of practices of political intermediation of public and private authority and sovereignty, and how state formation is affected by contact with private armed actors.[6] At the same time, my argument goes beyond these analyses by showing the effect of how the centrality of armed actors in these patronage networks transforms the ways of mediating exchanges and political support. I argue that criminal actors use the dramatically different scale of resources at their disposal to redefine local sociopolitical relationships, as well as the notion of political reciprocity. In order to do so, this chapter will focus on the closing of intermediation channels between local society and regional public authorities by the Templarios cartel, as well as the group's modalities of governance, rather than on the relationships between the state and the criminal group. It will provide an example of construction of local authority, social order, and competing moral economies in a region of cocaine reception and bulk drug trafficking.

The state of Michoacán, and especially the central Tierra Caliente region, has been a focus of the illicit drug trade since at least the 1940s, when marijuana and poppy production dominated the area. However, in the 1990s it became a major route for South American cocaine destined for US markets. While the central region of Tierra Caliente offered an excellent climate for marijuana and opium poppy growing, the isolated two hundred–kilometer coast, as well as the deepwater port of Lázaro Cárdenas, offered comparative advantages for Michoacán to become a hub for cocaine reception and transportation (Maldonado 2010). It also helped to make it one of the world's top producers of methamphetamines for the US market as the chemical precursors from China and India are imported and processed there.[7]

In 1999, Operation Millennium, a DEA-led counter-narcotics operation in collaboration with the governments of Colombia and Mexico, revealed that Armando Valencia, the leader of the Michoacán-based Valencia-Milenio Cartel, was a crucial ally of Fabio Ochoa, an important Medellín Cartel leader.[8] According to DEA reports, "this group was able to ship 20 to 30 metric tons of cocaine every month to the United States and Europe."[9] Ten years later, in 2009, the "largest US law enforcement action ever undertaken against a Mexican drug cartel," called "Project Coronado," ended up with the dismantling of a nationwide trafficking network working for the Michoacán cartel of La Familia Michoacana.[10] The investigation, which led to the arrest of 1,186 individuals, the seizure of approximately $32.8 million in US currency, and the seizure of approximately 2,710 pounds of methamphetamine and 1,999 kilograms of cocaine, offered a vivid picture of the importance and the resilience of Michoacán drug trafficking organizations through recent history.

Michoacán has hosted various drug trafficking organizations since the 1990s. The first was the Valencia-Milenio Cartel, run by local criminal actors but connected to Colombian traffickers and the Juarez Cartel. The Cartel del Golfo (from Mexico's east coast) and their allies the Zetas then defeated the Valencia-Milenio group and took control of Michoacán with the initial help of local criminal operators. The Zetas and the Cartel del Golfo were then ousted by La Familia Michoacana, which dominated the local drug trade between 2006 and 2011. The Caballeros Templarios, which I will refer to simply as the Templarios, formed in March 2011 as a result of a split in La Familia. They controlled the local drug trade until 2014–15. Finally, a coalition of self-defense militias, the Autodefensas de Michoacán, overthrew the Templarios in a violent conflict that lasted from February 2013 to the summer of 2015.[11]

Drug cartels in contemporary Michoacán have been able to build on their autochthonous and localist protection rhetoric, as well as their increasingly powerful territorial control in order to transform the political and moral economy of drug trafficking. The progressive integration and consolidation of the region as a strategic territory for cocaine transshipment in the late 1990s and early 2000s transformed DTOs in Michoacán through a process of professionalization, militarization, and bureaucratization that Natalia Mendoza has called "cartelization" (Mendoza 2017). Her work allows us to consider the construction of "drug cartels" as a social process that goes from local, open networks of traffickers to monopolistic, regional, and strictly organized structures that are able to centralize functions of drug trafficking, territorial control, and governance.

The cartelization process entailed a professionalization of drug trafficking activities, the creation of a strict hierarchy and labeling in relation to groups, and a militarization of them. This regional evolution—connected to the international drug trade—shook up the drug economy's forms of integration and participation. Marijuana growing did not necessarily involve membership in an established criminal group. Above all, it was not always a full-time activity for producers, who combined it with other farming or commercial activities. Moreover, marijuana and opium production did not require local traffickers to build strong international connections.

The introduction of cocaine changed matters and encouraged the cartelization process. In particular, it required an international network and coercive means to protect routes, shipments, and territories. The development of these drugs, which are infinitely more profitable than marijuana, accelerated the professionalization of local traffickers, who began to serve a structured criminal organization. This evolution was accompanied by a transformation in traffickers' social representations: these individuals were now identified exclusively as professional "narcos," belonging to and obeying one specific drug cartel.

Here, the flow of revenue produced by the drug trade, and especially cocaine, is key to the cartels' ability to challenge existing schemes of moral economies: it provides the bedrock for the construction of alternative social, economic, and political orders in which cartel members, and especially the leaders, progressively become political actors. In doing so, drug cartels have become more than a violent challenger to the state; they have managed to transform political loyalties, exchange mechanisms, and channels of resource allocation in order to become a key player in local governance. This chapter will focus on one aspect of this new social order by analyzing the political, administrative, and taxation system that was put in place by the Caballeros Templarios cartel in Michoacán between 2011 and 2013. I argue that this period represents an ephemeral moment of criminal intermediation and sovereignty that deeply transformed the moral economy of politico-criminal relations in Michoacán by altering the patronage systems that were previously in place.

## MICHOACÁN DRUG CARTELS: THE CABALLEROS TEMPLARIOS EXTORTION SYSTEM

In Michoacán, La Familia Michoacana and the Caballeros Templarios, after their creation in March 2011, have publicly justified their existence by claiming to provide protection against threats coming from internal or external criminal groups, as well as from the state apparatus. The Templarios, led by La Familia's ex-leader Nazario Moreno González, also known as "El Chayo" or "El Más Loco," and Servando Gómez Martínez, "La Tuta," announced the group's creation through messages they disseminated in the regional press, leaflets, and on billboards all over Tierra Caliente. One such press release stated: "To the Michoacán society: we today announce that from now on we will be active in the region. We will take over the altruistic activities formerly conducted by La Familia. We remain under the authority of the Michoacán society, in order to take care of any situation that could threaten the integrity of its inhabitants. Our commitment toward society aims at maintaining order, preventing robberies, kidnappings, extortion, and to armor our state against possible rival invasions. The Knights Templar" (Univision Noticias 2011).

According to several interviewees, the Templarios were initially relatively well received, especially in Tierra Caliente, for several reasons. First, La Familia's racket of extracting money from local businesses immediately stopped. Second, the Templarios proceeded with a social cleansing operation against La Familia's operatives. Third, the strict hierarchy of the newly formed cartel effectively ensured the vertical control of local operators, hit men, drivers, lookouts, and drug producers, as well as the regulation of the violence these low-level actors exerted against ordinary citizens not involved in criminal activities. Finally, their military capabilities, combined with their territorial control and social embeddedness, allowed them to "lock down" Michoacán. As a result, the region became impervious to rival groups' intrusions.

This domination progressively expanded to public authorities, at both the state and federal levels, through collusion, corruption, and coercion.[12]

During the first interviews I conducted in Michoacán in the summer of 2013, locals said, "the Templarios are the government." Even in Morelia, the state capital, a city of more than one million, located several hours from cartel strongholds, people avoided publicly naming the organization or its leaders, since they feared someone may be watching or listening. In Tierra Caliente, where the leaders exercised the strongest control, their social domination was total. As one person from near Apatzingán, a Tierra Caliente municipality, told me, "They controlled everything. It was forbidden to gather on the main square at night. Forbidden to play music too loud. Forbidden to hunt. If you had a problem with a neighbor, you had to go to them. If you wanted to get a divorce, you would go to them. They were in charge of everything!"[13]

The Templarios distinguished themselves from other Mexican criminal organizations by the level of their social control practices. This section will analyze these social control activities along three dimensions: (1) the regulation of daily life; (2) the exploitation of markets through extortion; and (3) the exercise of control over the public sector, including the creation of a governance system that developed its own territorial administrative subdivisions.

### The Regulation of Daily Life

Within the municipalities I studied, the cartel's domination had direct consequences for the lives and daily practices of the inhabitants. The moralistic discourse of the Templarios, directly inherited from ideas developed by La Familia, first materialized in a series of bans on daily social interactions. These norms were sometimes written and enforced through fines and receipts. The ban imposed on socializing in the main squares of towns helped to create a climate of distrust and fear among the inhabitants by preventing people from socializing with one another. As a woman from Coalcomán in her mid-sixties recalled:

> With the Templarios, we didn't go out anymore. I did the groceries but I didn't talk to the storekeepers, although they were lifetime friends! And I wouldn't go to see my friends anymore! Can you imagine? I love going to see my friends . . . going to the *mitote* [an expression that designates the activity of going to hear the town's rumors and latest news in the shops, at friends', and so on]. You had to be very careful of who was listening to you, even at home. Family or friends . . . were best avoided, especially if you

were known as not being a very good "friend" [she quotes] of the cartel. We stopped living for two years.[14]

When people gathered at night, the Templarios' "patrols" dispersed them. Juan, a university employee in his early thirties, born and raised in the town of Paracuaro, said:

> There is a big park in the town, where we used to go to play soccer, eat an ice cream with a girlfriend. . . . That kind of stuff. But the Templarios started going against that, prohibiting the meetings, the music. . . . If you were in the park, they would come and threaten you. They would tell you to leave. . . . But you know, these guys, I knew them! They were with me at school! But [now] they act this way, they're in the cartel, you can't say anything. . . . When I used to meet one cartel guy in the streets, I saluted him with respect, quietly, I don't go crazy [no me paso de lanza], especially with the nervous ones, the younger ones.[15]

The Templarios patrolled in pickup trucks carrying armed young men who cruised around the streets of the towns and villages. According to interviewees, the men would not hesitate to show their weapons except in front of the army or the federal police. Their vehicles bore the logo of the organization, a red Maltese cross. More importantly, as the evidence from the interviews suggests, the local population knew who was part of the organization and what role they had. And, of course, cartel members also knew the local population. In cases of repeated disobedience, the members of the cartel would administer punishment. An interview conducted with a man in Tierra Caliente during the winter of 2014 illustrates such practices and their effect as social control mechanisms:

> Back then, I wasn't able to control my teenage son. . . . He wouldn't come to work with me. One night, he was in the town's square, with friends. The patrol [la patrulla] passed by them several times, but they did not leave. So they took them. . . . They put them on the ground and started beating them. Then they took them to the town's outskirts, next to a small river. They made them dig a grave, hit them again, made them kneel, pretended to shoot them in the head. . . . Then they took them back. The narcos woke me up, gave me my son back, and told me that this was the last warning. . . . The next day, my son was standing, ready to come work with me.[16]

Exemplary punishments by the Templarios included *tablizas* (caning on the back, thighs, or backside), sometimes in public. In certain cases, the punishment followed a graded scale in which a specific fault would lead to a designated number of blows. Templarios entered homes in order to "arrest" individuals for purported misconduct or "treason" against the cartel. Those who were targeted were at risk of being kidnapped and, in the Templarios' hands, might endure physical abuse, torture, or even death.[17] The body might be given back to the family, left in a public space to set an example, or be simply "disappeared."[18]

### The Closed-Circuit Extortion System

The cartel's law was in the hands of the local boss: the *jefe de plaza*. The jefe de plaza, a concept central to contemporary Mexican narco-trafficking organizations, refers to the chief of a drug trafficking organization's operations in a particular territory, town, or strategic zone. In the case of the Templarios, the jefe de plaza reflects the territorial and social embeddedness of the organization as well as the way that the organization seeks to mirror formal state sovereignty and governance practices. In most municipalities the jefe was a well-known figure, and local inhabitants knew both his name and nickname. In certain cases the jefe had been installed by the cartel during a formal public meeting that immediately followed their takeover in 2011. Carlos (a pseudonym), a former mayor of a municipality in Tierra Caliente, explained: "Here, they arrived with eighty pickups, heavily armed. They circled around town a couple of times, and then went to the main square. They rang the church bells in order to gather the population. Then a Templario leader presented who was to be the jefe de plaza. He told us that he would be at the service of the community. Any problem, we could go to him! They even gave us his cell phone number!"[19] The jefe thus became a parallel mayor through whom local disputes were resolved. The latter may include divorces, land conflicts, or favors asked of the cartel, such as money lending. The former mayor noted a great deal of ambivalence about Templarios' governance, which oscillated between timely and efficient service and coercion: "La Familia had started to do this kind of conflict resolution stuff. . . . You knew that you could always find someone from the cartel whom you could go to and try to arrange certain things. But now the jefe was always here, easy to find. And honestly, they were much more efficient than the local government or any public authority."[20]

Under this system, the jefe de plaza led the cartel's extortion racket. While the Templarios had publicly claimed that they would fiercely combat such practices, going as far as to execute local racketeers, they nevertheless put in place one of the most sophisticated extortion systems in Mexico, targeting individuals, shops, and industries.[21] This racket differed slightly from municipality to municipality, depending on the local commercial activities, as well as on the personality of the jefe de plaza or the strategic importance of the locality. However, several common practices tied them together. First, the Templarios taxed certain goods, including corn tortillas, a staple food throughout Mexico. Under the Templarios' rule, the price of a kilo of tortillas went up around 30 percent in the Tierra Caliente region of Michoacán, going from eleven to twelve pesos to sixteen to seventeen pesos due to the levy imposed by the cartel on the shopkeepers through a cut of the monthly revenue or a percentage of retail sales. In order to remain profitable, local shops had to raise prices. In the case of tortillas, the cartel's extortion almost worked as a value-added tax since tortillas are a staple, and therefore most people contributed to the cartel's earnings. The same mechanism was in place for other products including meat, fruit, and bread.

This contributed to a general rise in the cost of living. In some Tierra Caliente villages, local products could be more expensive than in markets in Mexico City. The cost of living became unbearable for a large chunk of the population, as Juan recalls: "The shop owners, you know, they could at least get along because they would push the prices according to the tax. But what about us? The consumers? If you work for eighty or a hundred pesos a day, how can you pay a kilo of tortillas at seventeen? Meat at eighty-five? Tomatoes at twenty-five? It's simply impossible."[22] Eventually, these practices were extended to land property and real estate, as a protection tax called *derecho de piso*, an equivalent to the *pizzo* imposed by mafia-type organizations in Italy (Gambetta 1996; Sciarrone 2000). Given this configuration, all social classes were affected by the extortion regime and, in contrast with the statement above, even small-scale shopkeepers suffered since many consumers saw them as the only beneficiary of the situation because they raised prices to match the illicit levies. Consequently, they found themselves in a very difficult situation, as one shopkeeper from Parácuaro recalled: "We were between a rock and a hard place [*entre la espada y la pared*], as they say. People hated us! And if we did not respect the cartel's instructions, of course, we would get killed, or someone from our family would. . . . That's how they destroyed the social fabric here."[23]

Simultaneously, the Templarios extorted local commercial agriculture, especially avocado, lime, and timber production. As a result of ongoing extortion, kidnappings, and murders, these industries would eventually turn against them.[24] According to interviews in one municipality of Tierra

Caliente, as well as press reports about lime producers, the Templarios succeeded in organizing and regulating production and retail prices through the control of labor organizations, harvesting, transportation, and packaging. According to the Templarios' rules, farmers were forced to pick limes on Monday, Wednesday, and Friday until a fixed hour. They had to dedicate the other days of the week to packing the fruit for export. The Templarios strictly controlled the harvesting cycles in order to maintain the flow to packing plants and avoid losses due to overproduction. In this context, factories received clear instructions: when the price of the limes went up, they had to buy selectively. More precisely, the more the price rose, the more they had to buy from producers, who were also members of the cartel. In addition, the packaging companies paid a tax to the Templarios. Eventually, the cartel took control of them, too, as occurred in Apatzingán, in the heart of the Templarios' territory. If the producers did not respect the picking days, punishments included fines, tablizas, and even executions. Several interviews I recorded with residents after the fall of the Templarios discussed the expropriation of producers as well as the disappearance of owners who were in conflict with the cartel.

According to interviews, producers at first welcomed the regulation. Indeed, prices went from 2,250 pesos per ton in 2008 to 3,500 pesos per ton by 2011 in some municipalities. Although it is difficult to corroborate such information, several interviewees indicated that narcos' investment and money laundering had fueled the boom in the lime sector since the early 2000s, creating more work and more business in the region.

Progressively, however, the Templarios became increasingly coercive and extended their racket to every step of the local production chain. Mayor Carlos explained, "Here, the tax was two hundred pesos for three tons of production. It doesn't sound like a lot when you say it like this, but in the area we pick up to 1,400 tons per day. So do the math!"[25] At the peak of the Templarios' domination in 2013, the cartel managed to extort both the truck owners who transport day laborers from the towns to the fields, and the workers. The truckers are a key intermediary actor in the agricultural production chain, in charge of transporting the workforce according to the producers' needs.[26] Then the day laborers were also taxed and monitored, similar to practices found in other business sectors. It affected them in two ways. First, the transporters passed on their losses to the workers, charging them an extra ten pesos per day in order to take them. Second, since the Templarios increasingly forbade the workers to pick limes on certain farms in order to favor their own properties, this drastically cut the demand for labor. In one town of Tierra Caliente, a lime picker told me: "It got to the point where we had to pay to work. . . . You make a hundred pesos per day, and you have to give away 10 percent. If you don't pay, you don't work. And in certain cases, even if you paid, you couldn't work. It was as simple as that.[27] Thus, the cartel managed to build a closed market, excluding an important part of the producers in order to buy and export only their own merchandise.

### Political Control and the "Mirror" of Governance

Similar to the extortion schemes discussed above, the Templarios were able to put in place a racket system for public finance and the administration of the regions they controlled. In fact, beyond his direct relations with the population and his role as a criminal boss, the jefe de plaza was the person most directly in contact with the local administration and public authorities, in this case the mayors. The jefe, as a local broker, embodied the authority of the cartel and served as the intermediary between the organization's hierarchy and local politicians. Through him, the cartel extracted 10 percent of the municipal budgets in the territories under their control, as Mayor Carlos argues: "Here again, La Familia did this as well. But they usually only controlled local public security institutions, municipal police. . . . The Templarios completely took over. They controlled the mayor, the public security department, the public works department, the social services department. . . . They had their own people inside, managing security, administration, and finance. It's the first time they managed to do this."[28]

In order to describe this administrative extortion, I will build on several interviews conducted with mayors who were in place during the Templarios' rule, as well as with local administrators, citizens who had participated in local politics, and ex-mayors. These interviews were conducted in five municipalities in Tierra Caliente and the Sierra Costa regions of Michoacán between 2013 and 2017.

The municipal elections of 2011 marked a turning point in how criminal organizations participated in Michoacán politics. According to public opinion as expressed in the press, as well as legal testimony collected after the fall of the cartel, the Caballeros Templarios and the Partido Revolucionario Institucional (PRI) conspired to determine the outcome of the 2011 state and municipal elections. In spite of this, a couple of mayors from opposition parties managed to win elections in the region where I conducted fieldwork. To maintain confidentiality, I will refer to my main informants as Mayor Pablo and Mayor Fernando, and I will not mention the municipalities they represented or their political party. Both were in office between 2012 and 2015, serving under the Templarios' rule, as well as under the Autodefensas armed movement, which overthrew them starting in winter and spring 2013. Both had public responsibilities in their counties before running and being elected in 2012.

In 2011, during his party's local general assembly, Mayor Pablo had been nominated to run for mayor:

> The very same day, the local jefe de plaza called me. He told me: "I know you've been appointed by the party, but you're not going to win. Everything is arranged with the PRI." So I went back to my party to see what we were going to do. We decided to run anyway, but without registering us officially, you see. . . . Running but without the official documents, we thought it would more discreet. After knowing that I was going to run anyway, the jefe called me again: "I know you. I have been living here for many years, I know where your family is. We will destroy you." The thing is, this municipality had already been ruled by the [party] for almost ten years. So if we were not going to run officially, if the [party] was not on the campaign lists, even the federal government might have looked into the situation, because it's weird, you know. . . . I think this is what made the Templarios change their minds. Anyhow, the jefe called me once again: "Okay, you can run. Go for it, I don't care. But you will never win.[29]

Yet, apparently because of internal local divisions within the PRI in the municipality, and also because the army occupied the municipality on the day of the election, thus limiting the ability of the criminal group to move around freely and intimidate voters, Pablo eventually won and became mayor. The next day he was called to a meeting in the mountains where the jefe told him that his victory was "a mistake," and an "anomaly" in the state's election results. Yet, since there was "nothing [he] could do now, it was better to start working closely together." He went on:

> The jefe told me who was going to be appointed to public security, public works, and accountability. I knew these people! They were all from around here. He told me that from then on, my link to the administration was him, and that if I disobeyed, my family would disappear. Then we sat down in my office and he asked me to take out the public records so we could start working. He had in his possession the exact copies of my official files. We were discussing and working from the same documents. The cartel wanted

10 percent of the municipal budget, as well as 10 percent of any construction expenses. And I had to contract and buy machines from only one company, which he indicated to me.[30]

As this interview reveals, the jefe de plaza became what was in effect a shadow mayor (see also Annette Idler's chapter, this volume, for an example of shadow governance). At the local level, the jefe did not replace the mayor, but Pablo had to obey him at all times. Moreover, the Templarios implemented a similar system of "mirror" governance at the state level. At this time, the municipality that Pablo represented was under the command of the city of Apatzingán, which functioned as the cartel's capital, replacing the official state capital, Morelia. The cartel had reorganized what I will call the "western zone" of Michoacán under new cartel-led administrative rules. In this case, both Pablo and Fernando fell under the control of the jefe de plaza in Apatzingán. Every month, the mayors of this region had to go to Apatzingán, regardless of which party they belonged to, in order to report to a cartel coordinator. Mayor Pablo recalled that at the time the municipal budget was 40 million pesos per year (equivalent to US$3 million in 2012):

> In Apatzingán, we were received by a woman. Today she's in the state government! She was running a team of a dozen people, accountants and administrators mostly. They were in charge of checking what we were bringing, the money, but also how we were running our districts. Besides the money, every month I had to bring a pen drive that contained all the budget details of the municipality. If they found "irregularities," stuff that I would hide from them, they would investigate. They were threatening us all the time. . . . Back then, they never killed a mayor, but several public administrators got tortured. . . . We obeyed.[31]

Mayor Fernando also recalls the level of coercion and surveillance imposed by the Templarios through different concrete examples. Once, he decided to go to the military base in Apatzingán, where the 43rd Military Command Zone, charged with carrying out army operations in Tierra Caliente, is headquartered. Mayor Fernando wanted to speak directly to the general in command in order to tell him what was happening with the Caballeros Templarios:

> I didn't even tell my wife that I was going. Honestly, I didn't think I would make it back. . . . You had to pass several cartel checkpoints before reaching Apatzingán. Some of the guys at the checkpoints knew who I was, they looked at me. . . . So I got there. I already knew the general, so I tried to

go directly to him, not to present myself to anybody else in the base. I told him my story, but I also told him that he was the only one that was aware of my presence, that he was the only one to know about our meeting, that no one else was aware of my trip. . . . And you know what? When I got back home, there was a guy from the cartel waiting for me. He took me to the jefe, who asked me: "What the fuck were you doing with the general in Apatzingán?"[32]

According to the interviews conducted in this part of Michoacán, from 2012 until the summer of 2013, when the Autodefensas actually took control of this zone, the mayors had no contact with the official state administration in Morelia, "For me the authority was Apatzingán, and the local representation of the Templarios [the jefe]. Period."[33] These examples were a key moment of criminal political dominance. While under the Templarios' rule, most of Tierra Caliente was directly administered by the cartel, which was extorting public budgets and private enterprise.

### CRIMINAL MEDIATION AND PATRONAGE: THE END OF RECIPROCITY?

In this chapter we have seen how the Templarios managed to turn political and patronage loyalty into obedience. Such domination relies on building power through patronage and dependency, without requiring the disappearance of the state. Indeed, within this configuration of politico-criminal collusion, the Templarios redefined the interactions between the population and state institutions by introducing "a disequilibrium in interdependencies, which makes [them] less dependent on others, than others towards [them]" (Gayer 2014: 17). In that sense, more than a transformation, what we observe in Michoacán between 2011 and 2013 is a rare and brief moment of full appropriation of political mediation channels by criminal actors.

During this period, the Templarios transformed patronage dynamics and the hierarchies that prevailed between local bosses, elected officials, and criminal brokers. Here, existing Mexican political patronage schemes, premised on the use of public resources to constitute a clientele, fell under the domination of criminal organizations that controlled and organized the political and economic activities it claimed to "protect." This configuration installed a system of favors that competed with and eventually eclipsed traditional state-centric patronage networks. If in the past, especially with the PRI, and as Elisabeth Picard suggests occurred with Syria's Baath Party, local politics and "the party apparatus [were] the preferential channel towards powerful positions or even social ascent for families or clans" (Picard 1994: 218), I argue that the consolidation of contemporary drug cartels alters the forms of political mediation, social mobility, and moral economy by establishing the criminal groups as central patronage alternatives to the historic bosses and the state. Therefore, the criminal organizations in Michoacán can at least in part be described by their capacity to appropriate the political patronage schemes through collusion and coercion, as well as by their tendency to monopolize the channels that tie state institutions to the population, and vice versa.

The emergence of this type of drug cartel brings conflict into the political sphere. Under these circumstances, violence can become a source of belonging for a population wary of other criminal threats or state security forces, as well as an instrument for territorial control to protect drug trafficking or dominate markets. Moreover, organized violence constitutes "a preferential modality of access to the spaces of political decision-making" (Grajales 2014: 46). This can take place through threats to or the abuse or murder of political candidates, elected officials, or public forces, as we have seen with Pablo and Fernando.

This has direct political implications in that it transfers the clientelist reciprocity relationship toward a regime of coercion and domination. Even though the cartels create a social base by providing certain social services, as well as by presenting themselves as providers of protection, the population living under their rule remains captive within this political configuration, reducing space for negotiation and the need, on the part of the criminal group, for reciprocity in the form of compliance.[34] Noncompliance with cartel demands is violently sanctioned. Locals cannot, for example, enjoy the relative freedom to choose the most generous patron suggested in some writing on clientelism (see, for example, Gay 1994). In the Templarios' regime, locals had only one option for a patron. Therefore, drug cartels did not need loyalty or full compliance with their domination. Rather, they demanded and imposed obedience. Similarly, with regard to the public and state actors, including the armed forces, criminals' capacity to corrupt cannot be understood without the constant backing of organized violence as a sanction, as well as a means of selecting partners and eliminating enemies.

In more typical forms of clientelism, disloyalty, such as disobeying the party's or the broker's orders, for example, would not necessarily lead to a physical threat or death. Under the Templarios' rule, disobedience was sanctioned by both. Following Geffray's notion of "impossible reciprocity," the political configuration created by the Templarios excluded almost any type of reciprocity, since the Templarios obliged "clients," the local population and the politicians, to follow their instructions. In that sense, the Templarios' period of domination represented a paradigmatic example of a clientelist configuration that fully stands outside of most reciprocal exchanges or, building on Claudio Lomnitz's work on "negative asymmetric reciprocity," that the nature of their domination is based on practices in which social and political exchanges begin with "an act of coercion or exploitation" and rely on "unidirectional flows of gifts and services [that go] from the have-nots to their patrons" (Lomnitz 2005: 323). When the cartels achieve the kind of authority that the Templarios did, the fact that the "clients" cannot give back to the cartel is not really central "as long as [the clients] remain faithful" (Geffray 2000: 250).

And yet, while the 2011–13 period represents a moment of domination on the part of criminal brokers over political bosses, the Autodefensas, which later built on a coalition of private and public forces to overthrow the cartel, confirms the inherent instability of politico-criminal dominance. This becomes clear when considering the context of fierce competition that reigns in Michoacán, and in Mexico in general, where dozens of different armed actors compete for control of the drug trade. In that sense, the Templarios' moment of domination is a parenthesis within a broader regime of "discontinuous, overlapping sovereignties" (Gayer 2014: 160). In fact, the ephemeral project of sovereignty constructed by the cartel must be understood as a juncture within the conflicts that constitute the political reality of contemporary Michoacán as a "twilight zone of multiple, indeterminate configurations of power and authority" (Hansen and Stepputat 2006: 302).

In fact, the rapid collapse of a structure seemingly as strong as that of the Templarios can be explained by the convergence of interests opposed to the criminal system in place. By alienating itself from the set of social groups that it initially claimed to "protect," the cartel caused an armed mobilization that began in Tierra Caliente and rapidly spread between February 2013 and the winter of 2014. For populations that had been left exasperated by the cartel's predatory practices and abuses, the self-defense movement indicated a will to change the moral economy of drug trafficking in Michoacán. To put it another way, it was not so much that local populations were opposed to drug trafficking as a local economic and social activity. Rather, they rejected one particular configuration of the moral and political economy of drug trafficking that I have illustrated through the study of their governance system.

## CONCLUSION

We cannot understand Michoacán's political dynamics without considering the role of drug trafficking in those interactions. As a crucial territory for the importation, production, and transportation of cocaine, methamphetamines, and marijuana, Michoacán represents an important case for the analysis of drugs as both an economic and a political resource. Here, and following Geffray again, drugs, and especially cocaine, represent a providential economic resource that disrupts a local socioeconomic equilibrium by providing one actor with an unmatchable economic power. In Michoacán, this has contributed to the evolution of horizontal criminal networks into hierarchical organizations.

Yet, since drugs are illegal, organized violence often plays a role in controlling its trade. At the same time, the simple use of violence, without the articulation of disruptive economic resources, would not differentiate the Caballeros Templarios from other criminal operators or violent entrepreneurs. In fact, the Templarios distinguished themselves through their ability to articulate and organize violence, extract resources, and control territory in order to build an encompassing political economy of violence in the region that served as a basis for their position as politico-criminal brokers.

This chapter illustrates one specific configuration of moral economy in the drug trade. It builds on a specific ephemeral moment of criminal sovereignty. The moral and political economy of drug trafficking, understood as the articulation between a disruptive economic resource, organized violence, and the social control of a territory, allows for unprecedented levels of criminal autonomy from the state, and is therefore at the basis of the transformation of social relationships, hierarchy, and norms. Yet this autonomy is not necessarily a formal opposition to the state since cartels are not interested in overthrowing state power, or in changing economic and social relations, but rather in constantly instantiating a space of tolerance for their ongoing illegal activity. This chapter illustrates how criminal organizations can act as builders of social order amid, through, and also, in spite of violence within a peculiar politico-criminal configuration, in which reciprocity is no longer at the core of political exchange.

1 See Lazar (2004); Arias (2006b); Auyero (2007); Auyero, Lapegna, and Poma (2009); Piliavsky (2014); Combes and Vommaro (2015).

2 See Geffray (2000: 249). The term *manna* is used by Christian Geffray in order to make a first distinction between "two non-market forms of circulation of wealth: civic entitlements and clientelistic manna." Geffray uses *manna* in order to describe a "wealth coming from elsewhere which inflected the course of regional economic life in the same manner as a subsidy would have. Yet, unlike a subsidy, wealth did not come from Public Treasury but from a criminal activity, and it was allocated . . . according to an outlaw authority" (Geffray 2000: 247). Geffray here follows Alain Morice's use of the word in order to "qualify the nature of the wealth that circulates within clientelistic networks" (see Morice 1995).

3 See Geffray (2000); Das and Poole (2004); Arias (2006a, 2006b); Maldonado (2010); Gayer (2014).

4 A cacique, in the Mexican context, is "a political patron . . . working as a mediator, a broker." See Knight and Pansters (2005).

5 Amanda Sives (2002) exposes a similar argument in her work on political patrons and drugs dons in Kingston, Jamaica. Sives shows that a double configuration of neoliberal reforms and a massive entry of cocaine money into Jamaica changed the clientelist equilibrium.

6 See Tilly (1985); Das and Poole (2004); Gayer (2014); Grajales (2016); Hansen and Stepputat (2016); Lund (2016).

7 See Cochet 1993; Grayson 2010; Maldonado 2012.

8 More information on Ochoa and Bernal can be found on the DEA website, https://www.dea.gov/pubs/pressrel/pr103001.html.

9 See Farah (1999); also see https://www.dea.gov/pubs/pressrel/pr101399.htm.

10 More information on this operation can be found on the US Department of Justice website, https://www.justice.gov/opa/pr/more-300-alleged-la-familia-cartel-members-and-associates-arrested-two-day-nationwide.

11 In February 2013, a coalition of Tierra Caliente's inhabitants took up arms against the Caballeros Templarios under the label of "Autodefensas de Michoacán." This armed coalition claimed that its raison d'être was to defeat the Templarios, principally in order to make extortion disappear. It gathered a local yet socially heterogeneous crowd of farmers, small businessmen, industrial and agro-business actors, as well as members of the Templarios who sought to topple the cartel in order to control its market. Active between February 2013 and the summer of 2015, the Autodefensas managed to topple the cartel. Yet many of the traffickers who took part in the armed movement have re-created small criminal cells, which are still fighting for control of the Michoacán territory in 2018, thus feeding the current state of fragmentation and increasing violence in the region. For more information on the Autodefensas movement, see Guerra Manzo (2015); Pansters (2015); Le Cour Grandmaison (2016).

12 Since 2006, ninety-six federal police officers have been murdered in Michoacán, thus making it the most violent state in Mexico. Moreover, the total
homicide figure for the period that is covered by this chapter is 7,253 dead
(figures added by the author, based on the National Security System).

13 Interview in Tierra Caliente, February 2014.

14 Interview in Coalcomán, February 2014.

15 Interviews conducted with Juan (name changed) in Morelia, August 2013, and
in February 2014.

16 Interview in Tierra Caliente, February 2014.

17 Literally, in Spanish, the term means "to get someone on his feet." In contemporary Mexico, it designates the kidnapping and forced disappearance
practices carried out by a criminal group or public forces. The word is now
common vocabulary.

18 According to official figures, 1,044 persons are reported missing in Michoacán since 2006. Data available at http://personasdesaparecidas.org.mx/db
/db. If analyzed through the light of the *cifra negra* (the dark figure of crime),
which describes the amount of unreported or undiscovered crime, the total of
missing persons is probably much higher. The Mexican cifra negra, according to the official figures of the National Institute of Statistics and Geography
(INEGI), was 92.8 percent (2015). Data available at http://www.inegi.org.mx
/saladeprensa/boletines/2015/especiales/especiales2015_09_7.pdf.

19 Author interview with Mayor Carlos (name changed) in March 2014.

20 Interview with Mayor Carlos, March 2014.

21 It should be noted that certain municipalities in Michoacán have not been victims of extortion. In Arteaga and Tumbiscatio, for example, the territory of
one of the cartel's top leaders, testimonies indicate that there was no racket.
Other municipalities that lay outside of the Templarios territory—mainly outside of Tierra Caliente—also avoided such practices. Yet, within Tierra Caliente, almost every municipality was under racket between 2011 and 2013, or
even early 2014.

22 Author interviews with Juan (name changed) in Morelia, August 2013, and in
February 2014.

23 Interview in Parácuaro, February 2014.

24 In 2015, Mexico represented 30 percent of the world's entire lime and avocado
productions. At the national level, Michoacán represented 80 percent of the
avocado production, for revenues estimated at more than a billion dollars per
year in 2012, and almost the same for lime. The agricultural sector is Michoacán's first employer, as well as its leading economic sector. According to official figures, agriculture employed more than 23 percent of the legally declared
active population. In reality, these figures are much higher if one takes into
account the daily workers who are not declared, as well as the children and
underage employees who work in the fields.

25 Author interview with Mayor Carlos, March 2014.

26 The Templarios had established a directory of these intermediaries based on a census conducted in the municipality.
27 Author interview in Tierra Caliente, March 2014.
28 Author interview with Mayor Carlos, March 2014.
29 Author interview with Mayor Pablo, October 2015.
30 Interview with Mayor Pablo, October 2015.
31 Same interview with Mayor Pablo, October 2015.
32 Author interview conducted with Mayor Fernando, October 2015.
33 Interview with Mayor Pablo, October 2015.
34 One crucial exception would be a collective armed uprising, precisely such as the one that occurred in Michoacán against the Templarios from February 2013 onward. Here, the Autodefensas movement could be understood as a social movement that rises from within its "embededness" in criminal intermediation. Following Auyero, Lapegna, and Page Poma (2009), the Autodefensas could be seen as a criminal patronage "breakdown scenario," as a collective action that emerged in order to reestablish preexisting clientelist schemes. For a study of the Autodefensas through this lens, see Le Cour Grandmaison (2016, 2019).

**REFERENCES**

Andreas, Peter. 1988. "The Political-Economy of Narco-Corruption in Mexico." *Current History* 97: 160–65.
Arias, Enrique Desmond. 2006a. *Drugs and Democracy in Rio de Janeiro: Trafficking, Social Networks and Public Security*. Chapel Hill: University of North Carolina Press.
Arias, Enrique Desmond. 2006b. "Trouble en Route: Drug Trafficking and Clientelism in Rio de Janeiro Shantytowns." *Qualitative Sociology* 29: 427–45.
Arias, Enrique Desmond. 2010. "Understanding Criminal Networks, Political Order, and Politics in Latin America." In *Ungoverned Spaces: Alternatives to State Authority in an Era of Softened Sovereignty*, edited by Anne L. Clunan and Harold A. Trinkunas, 115–35. Stanford, CA: Stanford University Press.
Arias, Enrique Desmond, and Daniel Goldstein. 2010. *Violent Democracies in Latin America*. Durham, NC: Duke University Press.
Auyero, Javier. 2000. "The Logic of Clientelism in Argentina: An Ethnographic Account." *Latin American Research Review* 35: 55–81.
Auyero, Javier. 2007. *Routine Politics and Violence in Argentina: The Gray Zone of State Power*. Cambridge: Cambridge University Press.
Auyero, Javier, Pablo Lapegna, and Fernanda Page Poma. 2009. "Patronage Politics and Contentious Collective Action: A Recursive Relationship." *Latin American Politics and Society* 51: 1–31.
Barkey, Karen. 1994. *Bandits and Bureaucrats: The Ottoman Route to State Centralization*. Ithaca, NY: Cornell University Press.

Cochet, Hubert. 1993. *Des barbelés dans la Sierra: Origine et transformation d'un système agraire au Mexique*. Paris: Editions de l'Orstom.

Combes, Hélène, and Gabriel Vommaro. 2015. *Sociologie du clientélisme*. Paris: La Découverte.

Das, Veena, and Deborah Poole, eds. 2004. *Anthropology in the Margins of the State*. Santa Fe, NM: School of American Research Press.

Durán-Martínez, Angélica. 2015. "To Kill and Tell? State Power, Criminal Competition, and Drug Violence." *Journal of Conflict Resolution* 27: 1377–402.

Farah, Douglas. 1999. "New Drug Smugglers Hold Tech Advantage." *Washington Post*, November 15. http://www.washingtonpost.com/wp-srv/WPcap/1999-11/15/052r-111599-idx.html.

Gambetta, Diego. 1996. *The Sicilian Mafia: The Business of Private Protection*. Cambridge, MA: Harvard University Press.

Gay, Robert. 1990. "Community Organization and Clientelist Politics in Contemporary Brazil: A Case Study from Suburban Rio de Janeiro." *International Journal of Urban and Regional Research* 14: 648–66.

Gay, Robert. 1994. *Popular Organization and Democracy in Rio de Janeiro: A Tale of Two Favelas*. Philadelphia: Temple University Press.

Gayer, Laurent. 2014. *Karachi: Ordered Disorder and the Struggle for the City*. London: Hurst.

Geffray, Christian. 2000. "Etat, Richesse et Criminels." *Mondes en développement* 28: 15–30.

Grajales, Jacobo. 2014. "Le pouvoir des armes, le pouvoir de la loi: Groupes paramilitaires et formation de l'Etat en Colombie." PhD diss., Sciences Po Paris.

Grajales, Jacobo. 2016. *Gouverner dans la violence: Le paramilitarisme en Colombie*. Paris: Karthala.

Grayson, George W. 2010. *La Familia Drug Cartel: Implications for U.S.-Mexican Security*. Carlisle, PA: Strategic Studies Institute.

Guerra Manzo, Enrique. 2015. "Las autodefensas de Michoacán: Movimiento social, paramilitarismo y neocaciquismo." *Política y Cultura* 44: 7–31.

Hansen, Thomas B., and Finn Stepputat. 2006. "Sovereignty Revisited." *Annual Review of Anthropology* 35: 295–315.

Knight, Alan, and Wil G. Pansters. 2005. *Caciquismo in Twentieth-Century Mexico*. London: Institute for the Study of the Americas.

Lazar, Sian. 2004. "Personalist Politics, Clientelism and Citizenship: Local Elections in El Alto, Bolivia." *Bulletin of Latin American Research* 23: 228–43.

Le Cour Grandmaison, Romain. 2016. "Vigilar y Limpiar: Identification and Self-Help Justice-Making in Michoacán, Mexico." *Politix* 115: 103–25.

Le Cour Grandmaison, Romain. 2019. "Etre vus pour être reconnus: Organiser la violence, des Autodéfenses à l'Etat dans le Michoacán, Mexique." In *L'Etat malgré tout: Produire l'autorité dans la violence*, edited by Jacobo Grajales and Romain Le Cour Grandmaison. Paris: Khartala.

Lomnitz, Claudio. 2005. "Sobre reciprocidad negativa." *Revista de antropología social* 14: 311–39.

Lund, Christian. 2016. "Rule and Rupture: State Formation through the Production of Property and Citizenship." *Development and Change* 47: 1199–228.

Maldonado, Salvador. 2010. *Los márgenes del Estado mexicano: Territorios ilegales, desarrollo y violencia en Michoacán, México*. Zamora: El Colegio de Michoacán.

Malkin, Victoria. 2001. "Narcotrafficking, Migration and Modernity in Rural Mexico." *Latin American Perspectives* 28: 101–28.

Mendoza, Natalia. 2017. *Conversaciones en el desierto: Cultura y tráfico de drogas*. Mexico City: CIDE.

Montes Vega, Octavio. 2011. *Héroes pioneros, padres y patrones: Construcción de la cultura política en los pueblos del Medio Balsas*. Zamora: Colegio de Michoacán.

Morice, Alain. 1995. "Corruption, loi et société: Quelques propositions." *Revue Tiers Monde* 36: 41–65.

Pansters, Wil G. 2015. "'We Had to Pay to Live!' Competing Sovereignties in Violent Mexico." *Conflict and Society: Advances in Research* 1: 144–64.

Pansters, Wil G. 2018. "Drug Trafficking, the Informal Order, and Caciques: Reflections on the Crime-Governance Nexus in Mexico." *Global Crime* 19: 315–38.

Picard, Elizabeth. 1996. "Fin de partis en Syrie." *Revue du monde musulman et de la Méditerrannée* 81–82: 207–29.

Piliavsky, Anastasia, ed. 2014. *Patronage as Politics in South Asia*. Cambridge: Cambridge University Press.

Relea, Francesc. 2006. "Cuando las cabezas ruedan en Michoacán." *El País*, October 8. https://elpais.com/diario/2006/10/08/domingo/1160279554 _850215.html.

Sciarrone, Rocco. 2000. "Réseaux mafieux et capital social." *Politix* 49: 35–56.

Sives, Amanda. 2002. "Changing Patrons, from Politician to Drug Don: Clientelism in Downtown Kingston, Jamaica." *Latin American Perspectives* 29: 66–89.

Snyder, Richard, and Angélica Durán-Martínez. 2009. "Does Illegality Breed Violence? Drug Trafficking and State-Sponsored Protection Rackets." *Crime, Law, and Social Change* 52: 253–73.

Tilly, Charles. 1985. "War and State-Making as Organized Crime." In *Bringing the State Back In*, edited by Peter B. Evans, Dietrich Rueschmeyer, and Theda Skocpol, 169–91. Cambridge: Cambridge University Press.

Univision Noticias. 2011. "'Los caballeros Templarios': El nuevo cartel del narco que siembra terror en México." June 23. https://www.univision.com /noticias/narcotrafico/los-caballeros-templarios-el-nuevo-cartel-del-narco -que-siembra-terror-en-mexico.

Wolf, Eric R. 1956. "Aspects of Group Relations in a Complex Society: Mexico." *American Anthropologist* 58: 1065–78.

# <u>07</u> OF DRUGS, TORTILLAS, AND REAL ESTATE

ON THE TANGIBLE AND INTANGIBLE BENEFITS
OF DRUG DEALING IN NICARAGUA

As Steven Levitt and Stephen Dubner (2005: 103) famously highlighted in their popular book *Freakonomics*, numerous myths and misconceptions exist concerning the benefits of drug dealing. In the chapter drolly titled "Why Do Drug Dealers Still Live with Their Moms?" for example, they described how, contrary to what is generally thought, the overwhelming majority of those involved in the drug trade in the US earn "less than the minimum wage," with only drug gang leaders receiving anything in the way of substantial material returns. This is not necessarily the case everywhere, however—see Rodgers (2017b)—partly because the profits of drug trafficking do not occur solely at the end point of the commodity chain that the endeavor constitutes, but all along it. At the same time, there is no doubt that the benefits of drug dealing can often be unevenly distributed, highly contingent, and volatile, and that different accumulation regimes exist along the drug commodity chain writ large. Certainly, the nature of the drug trade in Colombia, where it is produced—and as described by Idler in this volume—is quite different from that at other points along the trafficking route to North America—as the contrasting chapters in this volume by Bobea and Veeser on the one hand, and Le Cour Grandmaison on the other, highlight well.

Having said this, as the volume editors point out in their introduction, such localized political economies of drug trafficking have mainly been discussed either in relation to the broader policy and institutional regimes within which the drug trade operates, or else through a narrow focus on what might be termed the tangible, material benefits of the movement and sale of drugs, that is to say, the financial wealth that drugs can generate (or not), and the way that this is (conspicuously) spent and invested (or not). Economic accumulation involves more than just physical capital, however; there are also more intangible advantages associated with the drug trade, including in particular the way that drug dealing and trafficking can generate nonmaterial forms of economic value.

More specifically, the drug trade can impart particular knowledges and skill sets to those involved that can potentially have further-ranging economic consequences than more tangible, material returns, partly because they are less prone to being eroded or dissipating due to their intangible nature, but also because they clearly have the potential to influence non-drug-related forms of accumulation and exchange. This obviously raises critical questions regarding both the sustainability of drug dealing and trafficking and their long-term advantages that are generally not taken into account, at least partly due to the generically negative connotations associated with the drug trade that are well reflected in the opening anecdote of the editors' introduction to this volume. Indeed, most analyses of the long-term consequences of drug dealing and trafficking have focused on normative questions of power (see, for example, Varese 2001; Volkov 2002; Glenny 2009) or morality (see, for example, Karandinos et al. 2014; Rodgers 2015), rather than how they might instrumentally shape the underlying nature of other forms of economic exchange or determine non-drug-related accumulation regimes.

Drawing on Pierre Bourdieu's (1986) deconstruction of the notion of capital in order to characterize its forms beyond the material, this chapter explores how the more intangible benefits generated by the drug trade can impact on non-drug-related exchanges and accumulation in ways that are potentially more meaningful than their more tangible equivalents (see also Le Cour Grandmaison, this volume). More specifically, it builds on Bourdieu's distinction between "embodied" and "objectified" capital in order to explain the contrasting trajectories of Bismarck and Milton, two former drug dealers in Barrio Luis Fanor Hernández,[1] a poor neighborhood in Managua, the capital city of Nicaragua, where I have been carrying out longitudinal ethnographic research since 1996. While Bismarck initially seemed to have successfully drawn on capital accumulated through drug dealing in order to build a real estate business, its objectified nature meant that his post-dealing economic activities were highly vulnerable to changing circumstances. By contrast, Milton's use of embodied capital in developing a tortilla business meant that his new accumulation strategy was much more sustainable. At the same time, however, Bismarck's and Milton's stories also highlight how it is not just the difference between the underlying natures of the benefits of drug dealing that is important to take into account, but also the nature of the field of activity to which they are "transferred," and more specifically, their moral underpinnings.

## VARIETIES OF CAPITAL AND CAPITAL ACCUMULATION

In his classic article "The Forms of Capital," Pierre Bourdieu (1986) distinguishes between three different types of capital—economic, social, and cultural—but also three different forms that these can take: "embodied," "objectified," and "institutionalized." The notion of economic capital refers to material resources (that is to say, money, physical assets, or property), that of social capital to resources linked to an individual's social relations, while the idea of cultural capital refers to an individual's knowledge and skills acquired through education and social status. Different types of capital are accumulated by social agents in different "social fields," but Bourdieu argues that it is the form of the capital that determines the impact and the consequences of its accumulation, especially over the long term, and this in relation to all three types of capital. Embodied forms of capital are skills and knowledge acquired through socialization, objectified capital refers to material goods and property, while institutionalized capital is related to the broader formal recognition of different types of capital as well as the process of capital accumulation itself. A perhaps simpler way of thinking about the differences between embodied, objectified, and institutionalized capital is in terms of their materiality, with embodied capital being intangible, objectified capital tangible, and institutionalized capital about contextual recognition.

In the case of economic capital—which is the type most relevant to this discussion on the benefits of drug dealing—Bourdieu (1986) argues that it can either take the form of embodied capital, that is, particular practices and ways of being that enable or enhance capital accumulation; objectified capital, that is to say the monetary profits or commodities bought with the latter; or, finally, become institutionalized capital, for example, in the form of property rights. Although economists frequently consider different forms of capital to be interchangeable, Bourdieu argues that this is not the case, stressing that different forms of capital can underpin capital accumulation differently. In particular, he contends that long-term economic accumulation is based on the institutionalization of capital. As the work of other social scientists such as North and Weingast (1989), Acemoglu, Johnson, and Robinson (2001), or Angeles (2011), for example, highlights well, this certainly

seems to be the case, but that is not to say that the differing natures of embodied and objectified capital cannot also have potentially important consequences for the sustainability of economic accumulation. Certainly, this is an
issue that has implicitly come to the fore in some of the critiques of Thomas
Piketty's (2014) magisterial *Capital in the Twenty-First Century*, most notably by
Savage (2014) and Friedman et al. (2015). The latter highlight how the former
not only focuses almost exclusively on the role played by economic capital
accumulation in the generation of persistent inequality—ignoring the critical importance of cultural capital, for example—but also limits himself to
considering only objectified forms of capital (in particular, conflating capital
with wealth). As a result, Piketty's analysis of global and historical inequality
trends is arguably rather deterministic, based on a limited and one-sided
model of the dynamics of capitalism (Pettifor and Tily 2014).

This problem is something that becomes evident when we consider the
varying trajectories of former drug dealers in the Managua neighborhood of
Barrio Luis Fanor Hernández. As I have described in more detail elsewhere
(Rodgers 2018), drug dealing was one of the few economic activities that allowed for significant capital accumulation in the neighborhood, and while
there were significant differences between different categories of drug
dealers—for example, between street dealers and wholesalers—within categories, individuals tended to accrue comparable amounts of wealth. Their
post–drug dealing trajectories display significant variation, however, even
within categories. To a certain extent this was due to the personal choices of
individuals, but the variation can also be linked to the form of accumulated
economic capital deployed in different post–drug dealing economic activities, and more specifically whether they drew on embodied or objectified
capital, as the contrasting trajectories of Bismarck and Milton demonstrate
very well. Before considering these in detail, the next section offers a brief
overview of the rise and fall of the Barrio Luis Fanor Hernández drug trade,
in order to provide some context to the lives of these two individuals.

## THE RISE AND FALL OF THE BARRIO LUIS FANOR HERNÁNDEZ
## COCAINE ECONOMY

Although drugs were by no means unknown in Barrio Luis Fanor Hernández prior to 1999, cocaine was extremely rare, and those who consumed
drugs mainly smoked marijuana, sniffed glue, or drank boiled *floripón* (a
flower native to Nicaragua that has hallucinogenic properties when in-
gested).[2] The latter were all sourced locally on a very artisanal basis, and,

perhaps not surprisingly, the neighborhood cocaine trade initially also developed in an informal, ad hoc manner, around a single individual known as *el Indio Viejo* (the Old Indian). He had been a member of the first postwar local gang in the early 1990s, and after leaving the gang had started growing marijuana with his brother on communal land near their house in the barrio, selling the crop mainly to a regular clientele of local gang members, but also to a small number of individuals from outside the neighborhood. Although he himself had lived in Barrio Luis Fanor Hernández all his life, el Indio Viejo's family was originally from the Caribbean coast of Nicaragua, and in 1999, a fisherman cousin from Bluefields, knowing of his involvement in the marijuana business, sent him a bale of cocaine (or *langosta blanca*—"white lobster") that he had picked up at sea, presumably thrown overboard by drug traffickers as they had sought to avoid arrest after being intercepted by the US or Nicaraguan navy, and asked him to sell it for him. Through one of his non-neighborhood clients, el Indio Viejo sold the cocaine to a drug dealer in another neighborhood,[3] and in doing so realized that the profit margins on cocaine were much higher than on marijuana.

He consequently immediately set about actively organizing his Caribbean networks of family and friends to send him any bales of cocaine they might find, initially offering to sell them for a commission but rapidly simply buying them directly. He soon found out that he had to sell most of the cocaine in the form of crack—known in Nicaragua as *la piedra*, or "the rock"—due to local market conditions. Crack is a made by boiling cocaine (cocaine hydrochloride) and sodium bicarbonate in water, and is much less expensive than cocaine, being obviously diluted and far less pure, to the extent that it is widely known as "the poor man's cocaine," meaning that it was affordable in the generally impoverished context of Barrio Luis Fanor Hernández. Making crack is, however, quite labor intensive, and el Indio Viejo decided to recruit collaborators in order to share the workload, and the Barrio Luis Fanor Hernández drug economy became a three-tiered pyramid as a result. At the apex was el Indio Viejo—also known as the "narco"—who brought the cocaine into the neighborhood and mainly wholesaled it, principally, but not exclusively, to half a dozen *púsheres* in the neighborhood. Púsheres "cooked" the cocaine they bought from the narco into crack, which they then sold from their houses—*expendios*—to a regular clientele that included *muleros*, the bottom rung of the drug dealing pyramid. Muleros sold crack in small doses to all comers on barrio street corners, generally in the form of *paquetes* containing two "fixes," known as *tuquitos*.

In total, then, by 2002 the Barrio Luis Fanor Hernández drug economy directly involved twenty-nine individuals: one narco, nine púsheres, and nineteen muleros. The narco, púsheres, and muleros were all from the barrio, and were, moreover, all gang members or ex-gang members. The narco and púsheres, however, also often hired non-gang members—generally members of their household—to help them out, but a large number of barrio inhabitants were also indirectly involved in the drug economy by acting as *bodegueros*, stashing drugs in their houses for the narco or for púsheres in exchange of payment, generally between fifteen and seventy dollars, depending on the quantity and the length of time they had to be stored. This constituted a substantial sum of money in a context where the monthly median wage was around a hundred dollars, but paled in comparison to the sums earned by those more directly involved in the drug trade, which emerged as the single most significant form of local economic capital accumulation in Barrio Luis Fanor Hernández. As I have described in more detail elsewhere (Rodgers 2006, 2007a, 2007b, 2016, 2017a, 2018), in 2002, local neighborhood muleros made between US$350 and US$600 per month from their drug dealing, while púsheres made between US$1,050 and US$2,400 per month (depending on whether they bought one or two kilos of cocaine from el Indio Viejo). I have no direct information about the narco's income, although this was clearly much higher. He owned two houses in Barrio Luis Fanor Hernández—one of which had two stories, something that was relatively rare and a sign of conspicuous affluence in earthquake-prone Managua—two motorbikes, and a fleet of ten cars, eight of which were taxis.

The financial benefits of the drug trade also trickled beyond the "narco-bourgeoisie" of those directly involved, as these shared their bounty with extended family, to the extent that about 40 percent of households in Barrio Luis Fanor Hernández could be observed to be visibly better off as a result of drug dealing compared to surrounding non-drug-dealing neighborhoods. At the same time, however, as many studies have highlighted, drug dealing is as much about status generation as it is about income (see, for example, Bourgois 1995; Contreras 2013; Baird 2015; Zellers-León, this volume), and all those involved in the Barrio Luis Fanor Hernández drug trade were also engaged in various forms of "conspicuous consumption," including wearing ostentatious jewelry, buying brand-name clothes, drinking imported alcohol, or shopping in supermarkets rather than the local market. This accumulation of objectified capital was particularly striking at an infrastructural level, as drug dealers materially transformed their homes from the drab wooden shacks that were the characteristic neighborhood dwellings into ostentatious, gaudily painted brick houses with extravagant fittings—in one case, real crystal chandeliers!—and filled with exotic furniture such as rococo full-length Louis XIV mirrors, handmade hardwood chairs and sofas, as well as luxurious home appliances such as wide-screen televisions, mega-wattage sound systems, and Nintendo game consoles.

The political economy of the narcotics trade in Barrio Luis Fanor Hernández began to change from 2003 onward, however, as el Indio Viejo sought to professionalize his operations. On the one hand, this was due to most of the current gang members he'd recruited to be street dealers—and who also provided a ready-made security apparatus for the drug economy—having become crack addicts and therefore being increasingly unreliable. On the other hand, the ad hoc nature of his supply meant that it was not always dependable, something that obviously impacted negatively on dealing. Through his Caribbean coast networks, he consequently developed links with a Colombian drug cartel—the Norte del Valle Cartel, according to two former púsheres whom I interviewed in 2007—that was moving drugs from Colombia to Nicaragua in order to ensure a more regular, less contingent supply of cocaine, and also began to be more selective in his choice of associates as a result. By 2006, el Indio Viejo was leading a rather shadowy, tight-knit group that was locally referred to as the *cartelito*, or "little cartel," and was highly feared, partly because it was something of an unknown quantity, since it involved individuals from outside the neighborhood, although Barrio Luis Fanor Hernández remained their main dealing territory.

Although el Indio Viejo continued to supply some local pushers—who effectively became members of the cartelito—he cut others off, and actively discouraging the latter from attempting to pursue any drug dealing activities by dramatically killing a pusher after he attempted to secure an alternative source of cocaine for himself. During this period, members of the cartelito also increasingly clashed with the local Barrio Luis Fanor Hernández gang, muscling them out of the street drug trade by generally intimidating and sometimes shooting randomly at any gang members they saw hanging around in the streets. After a few months of enduring such acts, the Barrio Luis Fanor Hernández gang decided to retaliate and attacked el Indio Viejo's house one evening in mid-2006, which led to a shootout between the gang and members of the cartelito, during which a gang member called Charola was badly wounded. The other gang members fled, leaving him behind, and a member of the cartelito called Mayuyu went up to Charola and killed him, shooting him in the head, execution style, "as a warning to the others," as he put it during an interview a few years later (see Rodgers 2015 for more details).

Following this event, the Barrio Luis Fanor Hernández gang effectively ceased to exist and local drug dealing was fully and exclusively controlled by the cartelito. On the basis of exchanges that I had with former drug dealers—as well as one member of the cartelito—during a visit in 2007, it was clear that the number of people involved in the drugs trade in Barrio Luis Fanor Hernández had shrunk, and also that the material benefits of the trade consequently no longer trickled down into the non-drug-dealing population as much as previously, despite 2006–7 being by all accounts the high point of drug dealing in the neighborhood in terms of volume.[4] From late 2007 onward, however, the Barrio Luis Fanor Hernández cartelito began to reduce its involvement in local drug dealing activities and refocused on drug trafficking—that is, moving drugs across Nicaragua—instead. The initial impulse for this was el Indio Viejo being arrested and deciding this had been linked to the visibility of drug dealing in the barrio.[5] At the same time, though, el Indio Viejo had increasingly come to realize that the profit margins of drug trafficking were much higher than those associated with drug dealing, and so while in prison, he institutionalized his existing Colombian cartel links, brokering an agreement to become their exclusive "man in Nicaragua," so to speak, and the Barrio Luis Fanor Hernández cartelito began to take charge of transporting regular shipments of cocaine from the Caribbean coast of the country to the Honduran border.

This further reduced the number of people benefiting from the drug trade in Barrio Luis Fanor Hernández as the cartelito's operations became increasingly spread across the country, and there was less need for local bodegueros and other indirect workers. Members were rarely seen, however, even after el Indio Viejo was released from prison in 2010, although Barrio Luis Fanor Hernández was the theater of frequent acts of unpredictable and extreme violence, largely related to the increasing monopolization of the narcotics trade in Nicaragua that took place during this period, whereby rival cartelitos fought each other for control over drug trafficking routes and shipment rights. Although at the height of its success, the Barrio Luis Fanor Hernández cartelito by all accounts became one of the four most important native drug trafficking organizations in Nicaragua, in 2011 el Indio Viejo was arrested again, along with most other members of the cartelito, reportedly at the behest of a rival cartelito that had developed close links to certain members of the Nicaraguan government.[6] Although what remained of the Barrio Luis Fanor Hernández cartelito subsequently reorganized in a much-reduced manner around el Indio Viejo's former number two, another ex-gang member from the first postwar generation known as "Pac-Man" (due to his voracious appetite), they constituted little more than a loose group of local dealers sharing the benefits of economies of scale, and by 2014 had effectively dissipated as an organized concern.

Four individuals subsequently continued to operate in Barrio Luis Fanor Hernández as low-level street dealers, buying their drugs from bigger dealers in other neighborhoods. One of these was Pac-Man's daughter, another was a former pusher from the early 2000s who had subsequently integrated the cartelito, and the other two had been muleros in the early 2000s. All principally sold crack, although it should be noted that the neighborhood drug market had by then shrunk substantially compared to the past. This was partly related to the fact that when the Barrio Luis Fanor Hernández cartelito moved from dealing to trafficking in the late 2000s, they not only reduced the local supply of crack dramatically, but also cracked down (so to speak) on local addicts in order to avoid drawing police attention to the neighborhood. By November 2016, marijuana had in fact supplanted crack cocaine as the main drug being sold in Barrio Luis Fanor Hernández, and there were only two local dealers left—one of the former muleros died, while Pac-Man's daughter left the neighborhood—although a growing number of local delinquent youth were dealing in an "amateur" manner (see Kessler 2004), that is to say, selling sporadically on an occasional basis, generally motivated by immediate financial desires, although it should be noted that these tended to remain modest (i.e., needing to buy a new pair of shoes or a formal shirt for a birthday party, for example).

## THE BENEFITS OF DRUG DEALING: CONTRASTING PERSPECTIVES

Many individuals in Barrio Luis Fanor Hernández have benefited materially from the drug trade over the course of the past two decades, whether directly as dealers, or indirectly, employed as helpers or bodegueros, or as extended family members benefiting from the largesse of drug dealers. The particular evolutionary arc of the Barrio Luis Fanor Hernández drug trade, however, raises the question of what happens after a drug "boom," once the drug trade has changed or moved on. Or, put another way, what happens to drug dealers when they become unemployed? Do they benefit from having been drug dealers, or is this a drawback? In a recent article, I explore the different economic trajectories of former drug dealers, identifying three typical pathways: "downsizing," "destitution," and "diversification" (Rodgers 2018).

The first involved reverting to a non-drug-dealing—or in other words, a more modest—lifestyle. This was well summarized by a drug dealer called Espinaca during an interview in November 2016, when he responded to my queries about his visible impoverishment compared to a few years before with a rather philosophical *"cuando hay, hay, y se tiene que disfrutar, y cuando no hay, no hay, y se tiene que aguantar"* (when you have money, you've got to enjoy it, and when you don't, you've just got to make do).

Downsizing more often than not involved the lowest rung of drug dealing, the muleros, as they rarely accumulated much in the way of economic capital. This was not the case for púsheres, however, and the latter two pathways, destitution and diversification, represented two different ways in which these made use of the material benefits that they accumulated during drug dealing, or in other words, what they did with the monetary capital that their drug dealing had generated. Those who ended up destitute did so because they tried unsustainably to maintain the conspicuous consumption habits that they had developed when drug dealing, despite no longer having a consequent revenue stream. They would rapidly run out of money, and then pawn off the luxury furniture, electronic appliances, and motorbikes they had bought when dealing drugs, ironically often in order to buy and consume the drugs to which they had become addicted during their dealing. Those who diversified, on the other hand, invested the economic capital that they accumulated while drug dealing in new businesses, including in particular real estate. A case in point in this respect is Bismarck, who was a pusher-level drug dealer in Barrio Luis Fanor Hernández between 2000 and 2006. Bismarck regularly saved a significant proportion of his drug dealing profits, and when he stopped dealing drugs in 2006—partly at my urging— he invested his accumulated economic capital in real estate, becoming something of a "slum lord" in Barrio Luis Fanor Hernández. He started off by buying a shop at the local market in 2006 (which he subsequently sold in 2010), and rapidly expanded his property portfolio, buying a local *pulpería* (corner store) in Barrio Luis Fanor Hernández in 2007, setting up a motorcycle mechanic's workshop in 2008, as well as purchasing three adjacent houses in the neighborhood, which he had joined together and converted into flophouse rental accommodations in 2009. In addition, drawing on the profits of his real estate empire, he bought four more houses in the neighborhood between 2010 and 2014, which he rented out.

Bismarck's real estate investments ensured him a monthly revenue of around US$600, equivalent to a little more than 50 percent of what he'd earned per month when drug dealing, but about four times the monthly median wage within Nicaragua's formal economy, according to official Nicaraguan Central Bank statistics.[7] By November 2016, however, Bismarck had lost all of his property portfolio except for his own home. This downfall began when one of his houses was commandeered by the Barrio Luis Fanor Hernández cartelito in 2011, and then confiscated by police when the cartelito fell. Subsequently, another two houses were taken over by two interrelated families who banded together to beat Bismarck up when he tried to collect rent, and he has since then considered them "lost." Bismarck also sold one of his houses in 2014 to pay off debts linked to having a gastric bypass operation, and his motorcycle workshop was closed down by the police after he stopped paying local officers a regular bribe that he had been paying them since his drug dealing days, thinking that these were sufficiently far in the past that they would not be able to do anything to him. Bismarck's flophouse was burned down by ex-military staying there who did not take well to being threatened by Bismarck when they failed to pay their rent, and finally, his pulpería closed because of a lack of cash flow, which meant that he could not stock it properly, and his regular clientele deserted him as a result. Since the middle of 2016, Bismarck has worked as a personal chauffeur for the director of a Taiwanese clothing company operating in one of Managua's free trade zones, earning US$180 a month, about 15 percent of what he earned a month as a drug dealer.

Bismarck's trajectory highlights the highly volatile and unpredictable nature of economic accumulation based on the tangible, objectified capital benefits of drug dealing, that is to say, the material advantages that the activity procures, whether in the form of accumulated financial resources or its investment in real estate. Although initially very successful, Bismarck's investments were vulnerable to broader contextual factors that he could not control, with their objectified form meaning that they could be confiscated, destroyed, or sold off in order to respond to noneconomic imperatives (in this case, a gastric bypass operation). Because it was ultimately based on having invested objectified capital in the form of savings in an alternative form of objectified capital (property), losing this property fundamentally undermined his real estate business, and he was unable to reestablish it. At the same time, however, drug dealing can also impart a variety of more intangible benefits in the form of embodied capital, which is arguably less susceptible to the unpredictability of tangible forms of objectified capital. This is something that is well highlighted by the experience of Milton, who was also a drug dealer in Barrio Luis Fanor Hernández between 2010 and 2011. Contrary to Bismarck, Milton did not save much money while dealing drugs, preferring to spend conspicuously. After he ceased his involvement in the drug trade, however, he drew on the more intangible advantages of his experience dealing drugs in order to set up what became a very successful tortilla-making business. What follows is a combination of extracts from two interviews, one conducted in 2012 and the other in 2016, where he explains this:

I spent seven years in Costa Rica, first in Alajuela, then in San José, and finally in Liberia. I went *mojado* [illegally], through San Carlos. It's easy, that place is puro coyotes,[8] it's like a market. There's a place there where you can talk to different coyotes, ask around, and negotiate a price. It's cheap, not like going to the US, you only pay 200, 300, 500 córdobas per person, depending on whether the coyote likes you or not. When he's got a good-sized group, you then cross the river and he takes you through the forest to a road where buses come by, and you just hop on. Costa Rica is *pura vida*, that's what they say there. It's more developed than here, and there are lots of jobs, so you can work, not like here, where there's nothing. I worked in all sorts of things, construction, a packing factory, I even picked coffee! I earned good money, US$120 a week, and I was able to save up US$5,000 during my seven years there. . . . I would have saved more, but I drank a lot then, and drinking really sucks you dry. . . . I've now given it up, though—I haven't drunk anything since November! And US$5,000 is still a lot of money, and you can really do things with that amount of money here in Nicaragua! When I came back in 2004, I first used some of it to buy some land in a new barrio, and built a house there, which I then rented out, but there were too many complications, so I sold it all after only a few months. Luckily, I didn't lose anything, and I used my money to set up a pulpería [corner store] in my home here in the barrio.

The problem, though, is that a pulpería is a dead-end business, you can't expand, there's already lots of pulperías here in the barrio, and people go to the same one all the time, and don't like changing. It doesn't make you any money, so after a few years, I got into drug dealing, which was the thing to do then. Because I was a member of the first barrio gang, you know, one of the two young ones, with Bismarck, I went to see el Indio Viejo, you know, el narco, who had been in the first gang too, and I asked him whether he'd let me sell. Although the cartelito had taken out the gang by then, because they were always high and couldn't be trusted, and they wanted to stop sales in the barrio, el Indio Viejo was my friend, and he trusted me, so he was okay with selling me some cocaine every month so that I could cook it into crack to sell, so long as I wasn't obvious about it, because they didn't want to attract attention. I told him that I wouldn't sell on the streets but would only sell to regular clients and that I would deliver drugs to them directly, whenever they wanted it instead of having them come to the barrio. He said that was fine, and so for a year I sold drugs, which was pretty good money. I had a good number of clients, who would text me whenever they wanted some crack, which I'd then deliver to them on my bicycle. But then the cartelito got taken out, and el Indio Viejo was imprisoned, so I didn't have a supplier anymore, and I decided to start a tortilla-making business instead.

Why a tortilla-making business, you ask? Well, my mum was a *tortillera*, but she was getting old and wanted to give it up, so I told her, why don't you let me take over? You see, I had an idea about how to make tortillas differently. Tortillas are great, everybody likes tortillas, but they're only really good if they're fresh, so I thought that what would be really good business would be to make them and distribute them as soon as they're made. . . . Normally tortilleras make a whole bunch of tortillas early in the morning and then distribute them afterward, so you get them cold. Sometimes they'll do another batch in the afternoon, but it's the same thing; unless you live next door to the tortillera you'll always get cold tortillas. So I thought to myself, why don't I do like I did with drugs, get people to text me when they want tortillas, and I'd then make them and deliver them straight away? So what I did was go around the barrio and the market with some samples, and told people that if they wanted fresh, hot tortillas, they should just text me and I'd have them delivered real fast. At first only a few people did so, but word got around, and pretty quickly I was getting more orders than I could cope with! At first it was just my wife and me doing everything, but I had to hire help, and now I have five people making tortillas for me. The trick is to be able to make them fast, and then deliver them fast. Initially I delivered on a bicycle, but now I've bought a motorcycle, and I'm delivering over three thousand tortillas a day.

Milton's rather remarkable "just-in-time" tortilla delivery business has been extremely successful, and in 2016 provided him with a monthly profit of approximately US$800, a huge sum in the Nicaraguan context. This success is clearly very much due to Milton having drawn on his drug dealing experience in structuring his new business. In particular, the use of mobile technology and the just-in-time delivery enabled him to gain an edge on existing tortilla sellers, and established the basis for an exceptionally profitable mode of financial capital accumulation within a field that normally has very low profit margins and also had a very traditional means of operating. As a result, Milton completely dominates the local tortilla market in Barrio Luis Fanor Hernández and its surroundings, including the nearby market.[9] Milton's success has enabled him to revive the lifestyle that he engaged in while dealing drugs, including in particular engaging in the "infrastructural conspicuous consumption" characteristic of drug dealers in Barrio Luis Fanor Hernández during the 2010s by building a second story on his house, something that was originally only associated with the most successful drug dealers in the neighborhood (see Rodgers 2017a). Although Milton has suffered several robberies since setting up his business, none of these have brought his tortilla-making business to a halt, mainly because its major investment is the embodied capital—the particular skills and knowledge—that he accumulated from his drug dealing rather than any form of objectified capital. Each time the robbers have simply taken as much cash as they could extort from Milton, as well as occasionally some of his consumer goods, but they have not been able to take any of the fixed investments of his business, in the form of the ovens, nor have the robberies prevented Milton from starting his successful business model again, as it is based on an intangible rather than a tangible benefit of his drug dealing.

## CONCLUSION

Bismarck and Milton's contrasting trajectories respectively illustrate the potentially different implications of economic capital based on the tangible and intangible benefits of drug dealing. This can be said to effectively correspond to accumulation based on objectified versus embodied forms of economic capital. Milton drew on particular practices that he had learned as a drug dealer in order to structure his tortilla-making business, while Bismarck invested the financial profits from his drug dealing in real estate. Milton's economic accumulation has clearly suffered much less volatility and unpredictability than Bismarck's, and one could interpret this as suggesting that the accumulation based on objectified capital is more uncertain than accumulation based on embodied capital, precisely due to its material or tangible nature. At the same time, however, not all embodied capitals are equivalent. In many ways, Bismarck also drew on embodied capital accumulated during his drug dealing in order to run his property empire in what was, for a time, a very effective manner. In particular, he regularly resorted to violence, frequently beating up rent defaulters, for example, something that most other landlords in Barrio Luis

Fanor Hernández did not do, partly because it is formally illegal, but also because a majority of those renting out individual rooms in Barrio Luis Fanor Hernández are women, and most did not have the same capacity for violence as Bismarck.

His resorting to extreme brutality in a very targeted way in order to ensure prompt rental payments was reminiscent of the way that drug dealers in Barrio Luis Fanor Hernández would never allow their clients to build up large outstanding debts, beating up and intimidating recalcitrant clients in a contextually hyper-violent manner (see Rodgers 2006, 2015). Having said this, it was also arguably the cause of Bismarck's downfall, with the burning down of his flophouse, in particular, unlikely to have occurred had he not beaten up and publicly humiliated some of his ex-military tenants. These tenants would more likely have simply left surreptitiously one night, and he would simply have had to find new tenants, but the moral outrage they felt at having been treated unfairly was what pushed them to take such dramatic action. To this extent, it could be argued that Bismarck's intangible benefits were less useful to him than his material benefits, and the contrasting trajectories of Bismarck and Milton therefore do not just suggest that there are intrinsic differences between the long-term sustainability of economic capital accumulation based on embodied versus objectified forms of capital, but that these also depend on the way that an embodied capital "transfers" from one field of economic activity to another. Bourdieu (1986) argued that "the real logic of the functioning of capital, the conversions from one type to another," was governed "in accordance with a principle which is the equivalent of the principle of the conservation of energy, profits in one area are necessarily paid for by costs in another." This observation, which he made in relation to conversion between capital types, arguably also applies to capital forms, and, seen from this perspective, what Bismarck's and Milton's stories also highlight is how it is not just the difference between the underlying natures of tangible and intangible benefits that are important to consider, but also how particular forms of embodied capital are "transferred" from one type of economic activity to another, with certain intangible benefits from drug dealing clearly less transferrable than others.

The reason for this was clearly linked to the underlying moral framework within which a particular field of economic activity operated. The violence that Bismarck engaged in relative to his rental business was widely considered in Barrio Luis Fanor Hernández to be morally dubious in nature. Due to his physical strength, gang member past, and reputation as a former drug dealer, he had always had the upper hand over individuals who rented from him, as they generally felt unable to challenge him, but this was not the case for the two interrelated families who "expropriated" him of two of his houses (who had strength in numbers), and even less so of the ex-military tenants of his flophouse, who responded to his threatening them by taking the dramatic action of burning down the flophouse. By contrast, Milton's transfer of drug-selling practices to his tortilla-making business was deemed socially acceptable because it was not seen to undermine anybody, whether socially, economically, culturally, or morally.

Seen from this perspective, it is clear that while economic capital needs to be disaggregated, and we need to understand the different effects that different forms can have, these also need to be considered in relation to the diverse social, political, cultural, and moral contexts within which they are embedded. In relation to the drug trade, the forms of capital that it generates often operate within particular regulatory frameworks that mean that they do not necessarily always transfer well into other fields of economic activity. At the same time, the drug trade also has the potential to fundamentally reorder social relations, shift political economies, and generate secondary markets, and so the key question for future research is therefore how, why, and when it does so in a way that allows for the emergence of forms of embodied and objectified capital that can promote new and more complex forms of capital accumulation beyond drug dealing—whether economic or otherwise—and under what conditions drugs lead to much more segmented and parochial economic activities. The answer in this regard clearly lies at least partly in relation to the perceived moral legitimacy of capital transfers within new fields of capital accumulation.

## NOTES

An early version of this chapter was presented to the ERC Social Dynamics of Civil War project seminar in Paris, France, on October 25, 2017. I am grateful to Gilles Dorronsoro and seminar participants for their constructive comments.

1   This name is a pseudonym, as are the names of all the individuals mentioned in the chapter.
2   This section draws on Rodgers (2018). Due to its proximity to the Colombian island of San Andrés, Nicaragua is geographically a natural transshipment point for drugs moving from South to North America. It was underexploited until the turn of the century because of the patchy nature of its transport infrastructure, including in particular the lack of connection between the Caribbean and

Pacific coasts of the country. In late 1998, however, Nicaragua was devastated by Hurricane Mitch, suffering major infrastructure damage and resource drainage. This negatively affected the (already limited) capabilities of local law enforcement institutions, thereby facilitating the importation of drugs, but at the same time, post-Mitch reconstruction efforts focused largely on rebuilding transport links, including building a road between the Caribbean and Pacific coasts, and generally improving the whole of the country's transport network, which had a knock-on effect of increasing the volume of traffic and making moving drug shipments easier. A sizable proportion of the Western Hemisphere's south–north drug trade has consequently been transiting through Nicaragua since the early 2000s.

3  This dealer was interested in the cocaine because, contrary to most other drug dealers in Managua at the time, who mainly sold marijuana, he had a regular clientele of foreigners, mostly NGO workers, who could afford to buy cocaine.

4  I based this observation on the fact that on a daily basis there were visibly at least 20–30 percent more individuals coming to buy drugs in Barrio Luis Fanor Hernández in 2007 than in 2002 or 2003.

5  In actual fact, it seems to have been bad luck—he was arrested by transport police officers who detained him due to a traffic violation but subsequently discovered significant amounts of drugs in his car.

6  The latter subsequently consolidated monopoly control over the country's narcotics trade, to the extent that we can plausibly talk of Nicaragua now being a "narco-state" (see Rocha, Rodgers, and Weegels n.d.).

7  See statistics on income from the Nicaraguan Central Bank, http://www.bcn .gob.ni/estadisticas/sector_real/mercado_laboral/3-3B06.htm, accessed February 10, 2018.

8  A "coyote" is an individual who smuggles migrants across borders, generally in exchange for remuneration.

9  Milton has, moreover, adapted to evolving technology, moving on from texting to WhatsApp as cheap smartphones have begun to become more widespread in Nicaragua.

REFERENCES

Acemoglu, Daron, Simon Johnson, and James A. Robinson. 2001. "The Colonial Origins of Comparative Development: An Empirical Investigation." *American Economic Review* 91, no. 5: 1369–401.

Angeles, Luis. 2011. "Institutions, Property Rights, and Economic Development in Historical Perspective." *Kyklos* 64, no. 2: 157–77.

Baird, Adam. 2015. "*Duros* and Gangland Girlfriends: Male Identity, Gang Socialisation and Rape in Medellín." In *Violence at the Urban Margins*, edited by Javier Auyero, Philippe Bourgois, and Nancy Scheper-Hughes, 112–32. Oxford: Oxford University Press.

Bourdieu, Pierre. 1986. "The Forms of Capital." In *Handbook of Theory and Research for the Sociology of Education*, edited by John Richardson, 241–58. Westport, CT: Greenwood.

Bourgois, Philippe. 1995. *In Search of Respect: Selling Crack in El Barrio*. Cambridge: Cambridge University Press.

Contreras, Randol. 2013. *The Stickup Kids: Race, Drugs, Violence, and the American Dream*. Berkeley: University of California Press.

Friedman, Sam, Mike Savage, Laurie Hanquinet, and Andrew Miles. 2015. "Cultural Sociology and New Forms of Distinction." *Poetics* 53: 1–8.

Glenny, Misha. 2009. *McMafia: Seriously Organised Crime*. London: Vintage.

Karandinos, George, Laurie Kain Hart, Fernando Montero Castrillo, and Philippe Bourgois. 2014. "The Moral Economy of Violence in the US Inner City." *Current Anthropology* 55, no. 1: 1–22.

Kessler, Gabriel. 2004. *Sociología del Delito Amateur*. Buenos Aires: Editorial Paidos.

Levitt, Steven B., and Stephen J. Dubner. 2005. *Freakonomics: A Rogue Economist Explores the Hidden Side of Everything*. London: Penguin.

North, Douglass C., and Barry R. Weingast. 1989. "Constitutions and Commitment: The Evolution of Institutions Governing Public Choice in Seventeenth-Century England." *Journal of Economic History* 49, no. 4: 803–32.

Pettifor, Ann, and Geoff Tily. 2014. "Piketty's Determinism?" *Real-World Economics Review* 69: 44–50.

Piketty, Thomas. 2014. *Capital in the Twenty-First Century*. Cambridge, MA: Harvard University Press.

Rocha, José-Luis, Dennis Rodgers, and Julienne Weegels. n.d. "Myths and Realities of Nicaraguan Exceptionalism: Drugs, Policing, and the Political Economy of Violence." Unpublished paper in progress.

Rodgers, Dennis. 2006. "Living in the Shadow of Death: Gangs, Violence, and Social Order in Urban Nicaragua, 1996–2002." *Journal of Latin American Studies* 38, no. 2: 267–92.

Rodgers, Dennis. 2007a. "Managua." In *Fractured Cities: Social Exclusion, Urban Violence and Contested Spaces in Latin America*, edited by Kees Koonings and Dirk Kruijt, 71–85. London: Zed.

Rodgers, Dennis. 2007b. "When Vigilantes Turn Bad: Gangs, Violence, and Social Change in Urban Nicaragua." In *Global Vigilantes: Anthropological Perspectives*, edited by David Pratten and Atreyee Sen, 349–70. London: Hurst.

Rodgers, Dennis. 2015. "The Moral Economy of Murder: Violence, Death, and Social Order in Gangland Nicaragua." In *Violence at the Urban Margins*, edited by Javier Auyero, Philippe Bourgois, and Nancy Scheper-Hughes, 21–40. Oxford: Oxford University Press.

Rodgers, Dennis. 2016. "Critique of Urban Violence: Bismarckian Transformations in Contemporary Nicaragua." *Theory, Culture, and Society* 33, nos. 7–8: 85–109.

Rodgers, Dennis. 2017a. "Micro-Volumetric Urbanism: The Socio-Symbolic Political Economy of Multi-Storied Construction in Poor Urban Neighbourhoods in Managua, Nicaragua." Paper presented at the international workshop on Volumetric Urbanism: Charting New Urban Divisions, University of Sheffield, UK, May 24–26.

Rodgers, Dennis. 2017b. "Why Do Drug Dealers Live with Their Moms? Contrasting Views from Chicago and Managua." *Focaal: Journal of Global and Historical Anthropology* 78: 102–14.

Rodgers, Dennis. 2018. "Drug Booms and Busts: Poverty and Prosperity in a Nicaraguan Narco-*Barrio*." *Third World Quarterly* 39, no. 2: 261–76.

Savage, Mike. 2014. "Piketty's Challenge for Sociology." *British Journal of Sociology* 65, no. 4: 591–606.

Varese, Federico. 2001. *The Russian Mafia: Private Protection in a New Market Economy*. Oxford: Oxford University Press.

Volkov, Vadim. 2002. *Violent Entrepreneurs: The Use of Force in the Making of Russian Capitalism*. Ithaca, NY: Cornell University Press.

# 08 "A VERY WELL-ESTABLISHED CULTURE"

COCAINE MARKET SELF-REGULATION AS ALTERNATIVE
GOVERNANCE IN SAN JUAN, PUERTO RICO

San Juan's morning paper brings the news that drug traffickers are using exotic animals, such as caimans, serpents, and poisonous toads, to punish *chotas*, as squealers are called there. Rumor has it that drug lords eliminate their rivals—or rather, their cadavers—by throwing them into caiman-infested waters in poor neighborhoods. The stories are part of San Juan's urban mythology: drug lords have twisted nature to serve their needs.

Puerto Rico's popular culture also reveals the deep penetration of the drug trade. Hip-hop lyrics denounce politicians like Jorge Santini of the conservative Nuevo Progresista party. As mayor of San Juan from 2001 to 2012, Santini waged a war on drugs, even though he had the reputation of being a cocaine user. "I'm going to make you famous," a song by the group Calle 13 warned Santini, "for being a drug-addicted mayor with the face of a moron" (Calle 13 2010).

This study of the impact of the cocaine supply chain on San Juan is based on three months of research conducted in 2012.[1] The data draw on a survey of 117 adults in various neighborhoods, as well as interviews with community leaders, former drug traffickers, journalists, lawyers, academics, politicians, members of NGOs, and teachers. Finally, we organized eight focus groups with local residents, community leaders, and young people in low-income neighborhoods.[2] These informants explained in detail how the cocaine commodity chain's self-regulation has restructured life in San Juan's poorer neighborhoods.

Puerto Rico's position in the drug commodity chain has evolved from a transshipment point to an area of retail consumption, part of what Paul Gootenberg in this volume identifies as the "shift south." Puerto Rico has always played a peripheral role in the global economy (Santiago-Valles 1994; Ayala 1999; Grosfoguel 2003). A colonial subject and provider of raw materials earlier in the twentieth century, Puerto Rico became the home of low-wage sweatshops and pharmaceutical production, while US corporations benefited from a 1976 law exempting them from federal corporate income tax. The phase-out of the tax exemption in 2005 undercut Puerto Rico's industries and led to the loss of manufacturing jobs.

As the formal economy declined, a buoyant illicit economy emerged, confirming the failure of globalization's promise of inclusion, as the introduction to this volume notes. The island's location between drug producers in South America and consumers in North America, as well as its status as a US territory, allowed Puerto Rico to articulate itself as a critical link in the cocaine commodity chain (Arias and Grisaffi, this volume).

At first Puerto Rico served mainly as a bridge between global suppliers and users, but over time traffickers expanded the island's consumer markets, in part by paying their operatives in kind.[3] Thus, Puerto Rico shares traits of both transshipment and consumption sites along the drug commodity chain, as shown in the introduction to this volume. Drug traffickers, originally focused on exporting cocaine to the United States and Europe, gave rise to local dealers who have captured many poor neighborhoods, even as they sold their product to wealthier consumers. In the process, retail sellers transformed "marginal" urban spaces and a "disposable" workforce into assets in their value chain. As a critical transshipment point, Puerto Rico continues to permit high-level traffickers to accumulate significant amounts of capital, while at the local level the retail business is characterized by low-skilled workers competing in dangerous markets for smaller, widely dispersed profits.

Like other participants in this volume, we ask why the drug trade becomes embedded in some communities and not others, how the trade transforms relationships within communities, and how those communities in turn shape the contours of the drug trade. We pay special attention to the ways that illicit markets impact collective value systems (Bair and Werner 2011). As the introduction to this volume notes, "transnational production and consumption generate particular social and economic interactions among people and places." We attempt to elucidate the growth of "moral economies" in San Juan that transcend mere economic calculation through non-market values such as mutual obligations and dependencies.

Our research confirms that the impact of illegal commodities extends well beyond a core of active traffickers to include entire communities. One explanation for these multiple but subterranean impacts is that the illicit trade produces a range of beneficial outcomes to the local population. In areas where the state has an ambiguous presence, transgressive actors create forms of self-regulation that residents experience as an alternative value system and rival mode of governance. The power of criminal actors is based not only on violence and intimidation, but also on accommodation and co-optation. Vulnerable populations adapt in ways that are essential to the reproduction of illicit markets. In the process, the spatial dimension of the barrios is reconfigured and the meaning of authority and legitimate violence redefined. As the introduction to this volume asserts, the drug commodity change encourages the emergence of new social contracts based on webs of reciprocity and self-regulation operating beyond the reach of state authorities.

## SAN JUAN: AN OVERVIEW

If Puerto Rico's geographical position and juridical status first allowed it to emerge as an ideal cocaine transshipment point, San Juan's built environment also offered a rich landscape for the growth of a local drug market. San Juan's physical and social spaces have been constructed through conflicts over many decades (Fuller Marvel 2008; Cotto Morales 2011). The contest over urban space produced several distinct categories of housing in San Juan. First are the *barriadas*, which became ubiquitous by the mid-1930s as replacements for the infamous *arrabales* or *villas miserias*. Barriada is a term commonly used to describe multifamily housing complexes. Many barriadas were created through squatter movements that occupied public or private lands, leading to confrontations with the authorities.

*Residenciales públicos* are more recent constructions. Residenciales, or public housing projects, were the government's response to housing the city's low-income families after 1960.[4] They are large, enclosed, and thus spatially segregated developments. Among the oldest are Llorens Torres in Santurce, with 2,000 units, and Nemesio Canales in Rio Piedras, with 1,500 units. These massive projects provided housing, but planners also saw the physical segregation of the poor as a way to "sanitize" the urban center. Politicians and bureaucrats applauded the new projects, but many in San Juan felt the residenciales broke up communities and disrupted traditional values.[5] The enclosed design, with limited points of entry and exit, would shield the violent groups that later took control of the public housing projects.

In addition to the smaller barriadas and massive residenciales, a third and less intentional spatial configuration is formed by the abandoned and ruined residences that today are visible all over San Juan, and especially within marginal communities. A result of the city's declining population, these existential hollows attract *deambulantes* or the homeless, drug addicts, and alcoholics, as well as a growing nomadic population of unemployed youth.

San Juan's physical landscape is thus the product of decades of urban policy, private investment, and popular struggle. As the drug commodity chain grew, a new logic undermined the intentions of state planners and private builders. The reordering of social space in San Juan shows how the drug market has repurposed a built environment originally intended to shelter, but also to isolate, the poor. Where the state envisioned modern, affordable residences, drug dealers found gated fortresses that protected a new elite empowered by the cocaine trade. And within those fortresses, dealers inspired both a new "moral economy" and an alternative form of governance for those living adjacent to the emerging drug market.

In what follows, we will introduce a number of key informants: Ricardo, a former cocaine dealer in the neighborhood of Cantera, now married to a local community activist and retired on disability allowance; Jaimito, another former dealer, in his fifties, who was working for an NGO that helps young people at risk; Max, in his late thirties, a trafficker who became an evangelical Christian; and Ray, a teacher and activist who has lived for many years in drug-plagued San Juan neighborhoods. These and other informants are all identified by pseudonyms; the names of the communities, however, are real. Their lived experience illustrates the fusion of the local retail markets with global commodity flows.

## THE BEGINNING OF EVERYTHING

Drug dealing is essential enough to poor communities in San Juan that the business even has its own origin myths. The transition of Puerto Rico from transshipment to consumption can be traced back to the 1980s. Informants often hearken back to this earlier period as a "golden age."

The essential locus of the retail drug trade in San Juan is the punto, as it is universally known—that is, the "point of sale" where street-level drug dealers meet with their retail clients. The puntos became the nucleus around which the emerging retail trade organized itself, and from which a new moral economy radiated outward. In the early years, informants noted, dealers at puntos carried guns only during turf wars. "The less you had at the punto the better, because if the police caught you, they couldn't take your paraphernalia; and besides, at the time it was all about mutual trust," Ricardo, a former dealer, told us. "We really didn't have issues with anybody; we sold drugs during the day, and at night we went to the punto . . . to *vacilar*, that is, to party."

If there was a problem between different puntos it wasn't uncommon for somebody to mediate the issue. "We were a punto that resolved issues, because we understood that the aim of any confrontation was always to eliminate the competition."[6] In the early days, competition among rivals could still be settled through negotiations rather than annihilation.

At the age of thirteen, Ricardo convinced the "owner" of a punto to give him a job. The dealer knew his turf intimately, Ricardo reported. "He was somebody I knew from growing up in the area . . . and he knew my mother. He was afraid about her reaction if she found out that he let me get into the drug business. 'Are you crazy?' he told me, sort of alarmed. 'If I do that Nina will come here and kill us all.' My mother was super strict, and she had high moral standards." Ricardo remembers telling the dealer that because he was a minor, nobody would give him a job, and his single-parent household needed the money. He noted, "That's how I started, and I don't regret it, although that first day I was shitting myself. I was scared because the police were patrolling the area. They looked at me and said, 'So, you are the new one.' The punto was a family-friendly place, it was the best environment that I have seen in my entire life, it could take you wherever you wanted."

Another former dealer also recalled the "golden age" of the drug trade. Max began selling in a small public housing project, where nobody else was doing it. "Then I started little by little carrying cocaine from Puerto Rico to the US." Max eventually got caught and went to prison. After getting out, he moved up in the business.

Max explained how dealers were recruited in the 1980s. In places like Ramon Antonini, one of San Juan's oldest residenciales, young men affiliated with the street gangs from an early age. "There were several [gangs], but Netas was the most important one; they had strict rules and were more structured." Max mentioned other groups, such as the Veinticinco in Mayaguez and in Manati and the Veintisiete in Aguadilla. "They were always competing against each other, but Netas were by far the best organized and least troublesome."[7]

By affiliating with a gang, the individuals became enmeshed in the supply chain of cocaine and other drugs. This chain functioned both on the street and in prison. In the 1990s, many young people were locked up for minor crimes. Once in jail, they fell in with the gang from their barrio. Affiliating with a gang, Max said, afforded protection against prison guards as well as other gangs. The protection model that started in jail extended outside into the communities—a similar pattern to that noted by Fontes in this volume.

Gangs changed the logic of the cocaine commodity chain, taking it out of the hands of the small-time, locally organized groups of earlier decades. As the market grew and competition increased, rival groups used lethal violence to raise "entry costs" for newcomers. The relationship of dealers to their communities also changed.

The respect was lost as well as the control that was established in society, because competition proliferated. This competition was fierce and ubiquitous, and massacres became the most spectacular way to establish domination. "Before, the understanding among the gangs' members was that if I had a problem with somebody, I went to the projects and executed that person, but spreading violence openly and killing innocent people, that was unacceptable" (interview with Max).

When reconstructing the "before" and "after" of the drug market in Barrio Obrero and Buena Vista, members of a focus group expressed nostalgia for a "benevolent" social order that was broken at some point. One participant in a focus group said: "I used to live in Villa Palmera, and the guys that ran the puntos were the ones that guarded my mother when she came home from work . . . back then, the type of drugs that were sold were mostly pills, marijuana, and heroin, and the selling was more discreet, they used more concealed means to let people know where the punto was located."[8] When asked why "the good old days" ended, some informants talked about the introduction of more and different types of drugs. But the deeper change was structural. "I think what happened had to do with the appearance of more structured groups. . . . There were some puntos that started looking more like an organization, and then, when the leader of that organization was killed or locked up, small groups started competing for his place. When the authorities cut the head off, everybody tried to take the control of the organization" (Focus Group 1 participant). Other informants agreed that a key factor in the increasingly violent form of drug market self-regulation was the state's strategy of policing. In the words of one public housing manager: "The government and the DEA [US Drug Enforcement Administration] attacked the leadership. Across the whole island, the big traffickers, the owners of the puntos, were arrested or killed, and that resulted in an open war among rivals, eager to take control from those that were eliminated. Now it is different, because the previous ones, they had rules, they did not allow robbery or violence. When they were taken down, the power became fragmented, and many young dealers wanted to move up fast, no matter what; now, there is no leadership, no one to negotiate with."[9] By attempting to eradicate large suppliers, authorities failed to realize that the commodification of drugs is a dynamic phenomenon that is constantly creating new centers of power and new relationships with the community. Where previously there had been informal cartelization, division of territories, respect for innocent bystanders, and negotiation among rivals, the state's "zero tolerance" policy perpetually renewed bare-knuckle competition among traffickers. As noted in the introduction to this volume, "repressive policies may remove particular actors from the drug trade but leave in place a local economic ecology that favors the emergence of new criminal actors to take their place." In Puerto Rico and elsewhere, state policies of prohibition, interdiction, and incarceration succeeded only in bringing more violent actors to the fore, increasing competition and dismantling prior structures imbued with a relatively benign moral economy. Like a radical antitrust policy, the actions of the authorities served to drive the drug market toward a condition of primitive accumulation, of each against all.

### "THE STORY MUST BE TOLD FROM ALL SIDES"

Confirming the fact that Puerto Rico is now as much a retail consumption site as it is a transshipment point, a newcomer to San Juan has little trouble finding the city's drug micro-markets. The puntos are visible as points of encounter, often street corners or building entrances where young men are ever present and always ready to serve their customers.

Puntos are the lowest rung of the drug trade. Those who operate puntos receive drugs from higher-level suppliers. Drugs that come from Colombia follow a detailed plan: "It comes into the barrios, then it is placed at several points and stashed in the barrios; the prices go up as the stocks circulate through the island" (Ricardo interview). At the puntos, *tiradores* (runners) nervously glance at potential buyers, as the *velons* (lookouts) announce their arrival. The owner of the punto moves between the stash houses and the punto, bringing drugs and taking away money. The *bichotes*, a corruption of the English term *big shot*, are those who operate more than one punto.

Like legal businesses, puntos have a life cycle, from start-up and growth to maturity and decline. Jaimito explained that "an organized punto would never let their people get out of control or have people begging for work." He remembers that the punto in Cantera developed in stages: "There was a moment when we had a benevolent dictator as the leader of the punto; he had a vision of maintaining peace. The community was in a developmental phase, but there were few job opportunities, so one day the owner of the punto called me. He wanted to know what local organizations were doing with young people in the community. He was concerned and wanted to help because, as he said, there were too many young guys asking him for a job."[10] Puntos and the communities where they operate evolve together. Some puntos change because the community itself is in transition, with older residents leaving and new ones arriving. One example is Parque Victoria, a barriada founded in 2002 by people displaced from elsewhere and thus with few local ties. There were many conflicts among residents, and "because they were only supposed to be there for a short time, until relocated to a permanent setting, there was little effort to forge a sense of community," according to Pedro, a resident of Parque Victoria.[11] The lack of solidarity among residents distinguished Parque Victoria from more established communities.

Government policy also shaped the landscape in which entrepreneurial drug dealers established themselves. Public housing projects became fertile ground for the flourishing of alternative social orders that protected drug entrepreneurs. In addition to the unintended consequences of public housing initiatives, other government policies also impacted the trajectory of the drug commodity chain.

The differing ties to a community in fact determine the nature of the punto. Although puntos may all seem similar, they are in fact quite different in terms of their levels of organization, maturation, and relations with local residents. Though operating furtively in some neighborhoods, in others the puntos carry out their business in the open. It all depends on the level of competition, collaboration, and fear among a diverse set of stakeholders. The more the residents know about the punto, who the traffickers are, and how they will behave, the better they can influence situations that could easily get out of control.

Self-regulation of the drug trade has its own logic. Obviously, no formal regulation exists for illegal drugs as it does for legal industries such as pharmaceuticals, tourism, or agro-industry. Total prohibition rather than nuanced regulation is the policy of the US government. Therefore, traffickers avoid enforcement of draconian drug laws by undermining the integrity of police and elected officials.[12]

Former drug dealers in San Juan confirmed the significance of state–criminal contacts. Jaimito notes the relationship of dealers with state officials in Cantera. "Originally when we were growing up there, the drug business was under the control of the police . . . but they all got arrested for corruption and those in the street gained more power." The breakdown of cooperation with the police often leads to increased violence, with the resurgence of "unregulated" market competition. As Max put it: "You need to know how to negotiate with them. In Puerto Rico it is a common practice that judges extort lawyers, and vice versa."

## FROM "FAMILY FRIENDLY" TO NO MAN'S LAND

The evolution of the drug trade toward a more rationalized, corporate structure had an impact on those in the trade and beyond it. Max reveals how the changing market transformed the life trajectories and identities of young people involved in the trade: "Before, the puntos were located in specific sectors, not like now, where they are all over, on every corner. There were also understood rules: not to invade anyone's territory, no selling on the main avenues, no single thing that gave preference to one punto over another was allowed, the owners of each location communicated with the others, and no matter what, you tried not to mess up the locations by attracting the police." Like mom-and-pop store owners describing the invasion of Walmart, the men detailed what happened when large-scale operations replaced the personalized, small-scale drug retailers. "Things started changing around '98," Max continued. "Among other factors, the respect and legitimacy of the people toward the police was lost. The punto changed radically because now the consumption of drugs was higher, it was purely pecuniary and about making fast money. Bigger locations need more employees, you cannot open for only a few hours, that freedom that you felt before, that you go to bed confident that somebody is running your punto, that vanished. Now you needed guns, trust was minimal, the street was a no man's land."

The government only worsened drug-related violence. Ricardo insists that the upsurge of violence started with the police: "They [the police] used to come to the barrio and abuse people, and that was a disruption of an established arrangement. What brought on the crisis was that before, everybody avoided trouble in order not to give the police an excuse to enter. The problems began when the police started coming into the barrios to shut down everybody's business; they came by surprise at night, the SWAT teams, to sweep the floor with you." The evolution of the drug market brought with it a generational change, as the old guard was replaced by a younger, less risk-averse leadership. Ricardo remembers a well-known bichote of the old school:

> He was a killer, but he was tired of fighting and killing people, so he decided to sort of retire and rent his puntos to the younger guys. Those kids started paying him a "mortgage," but then they realized that they could make the money themselves. They defied him to come and get his money, at the risk of being killed. Today these young guys kill by hiring a sicario, they make no distinction, the mentality is "if a fight breaks out I will take advantage of it to expand my business." What this new generation wants is absolute control, it's not only about the point anymore.

As these testimonies suggest, as the drug market became established as the "new normal," it also "professionalized," in the sense of becoming more structured, self-regulated, and interconnected around the island, rather than simply localized. Its personnel raised entry costs for newcomers through intimidation and lethal violence. At the same time, as in any market, the existence of lucrative opportunities draws newcomers into the market, often young people who are less risk-averse. In the next section we explore how communities react to the violent self-regulation of the cocaine market.

### HOW COMMUNITIES VIEW THE DRUG MARKET

Evidence from different San Juan neighborhoods confirms a changing level of violence surrounding the drug business. We asked over a hundred survey respondents if they knew firsthand a murder victim, and they overwhelmingly said yes, usually linking the deaths directly to drugs.[13] Twenty-four percent knew someone who was killed because of a drug debt; another 12 percent knew people killed as a result of competition between drug gangs; 6 percent knew individuals who had been executed by contract killers; 18 percent mentioned people killed directly by drug traffickers; and 9 percent knew someone killed by the police. The predominance of drug violence is suggested by the fact that only 6 percent of respondents said they knew of the death of an individual in a fight among neighbors, and only 11 percent knew someone killed in non-drug-related violence.

Residents believe that elected officials and the police are complicit in the drug trade. When asked who is involved in drug trafficking, 53 percent of those surveyed said that the mayor was very much or somewhat involved. Similarly, 21 percent considered the police to be very involved, and 41 percent said they were somewhat involved in the drug trade. While these opinions do not necessarily correlate with clear evidence of wrongdoing by officials, they reveal a strong sense among those surveyed that corruption spawned by drug trafficking has infected both the police and elected officials. A woman in her seventies who had lived for years in public housing articulated the connection between the drug business and politics. "The prosperous life that comes with the drug business benefits the narco-trafficker, the owner of the point, and politicians. But what happens when the politician that promised the drug dealer he is not going to be jailed fails to accomplish that? That's why you see so many politicians getting charged with crimes, because narco-traffickers are very smart" (resident of Nemesio Canales). Survey data also suggest that many small businesses and residents are involved in the drug trade. Five percent and 34 percent of respondents, respectively, thought that small businesses were very or somewhat involved in drug dealing and other illicit activities, while 12 percent and 28 percent of respondents gave the same answers for residents of the communities.

The data highlight three issues. First, contrary to the usual narrative about the impact of the drug market, drug dealing is not perceived as a zero-sum activity involving a small, violent minority. On the contrary, the widespread perception of the involvement of politicians, police, small businesses, and residents suggests that the drug trade directly or indirectly benefits different stakeholders. Ricardo describes the "multiplier effect" of drug revenue. "Houses are bought with that money, new businesses appear, and by being invested in the community, that money also benefits the government of Puerto Rico." Ricardo states that drug dealers tend to invest money rather than, for example, buying a car, because it is easier to conceal. It is important to recognize, of course, that not everybody benefits equally from the cocaine market.

Second, as the editors of this volume state in their introduction, any alteration in the commodity chain will have widespread impacts. Given the multiplicity of stakeholders, the government's simplistic idea of trying to "fix local dynamics" through SWAT raids, residential occupations, and disruption of drug puntos has unintended economic and social consequences.

Among these effects are a more anarchic violence, a diversification of criminal activities and actors, leadership struggles within gangs, and accommodation with government officials. Third, the exchanges that take place along the cocaine chain produce social connections with a meaning that goes beyond the purely economic. The existence of these noneconomic bonds adds layers of complexity to the social environment in neighborhoods significantly penetrated by drug trafficking. Ricardo alluded to this phenomenon when he declared that he is still respected in his community, despite the fact that he was a drug dealer, and indeed a murderer. But, in the past, he also did lots of favors for those in the community, and he believes that his bad actions are counterbalanced by his good work now as an educator. Yet he still feels indebted to the bichote who hired him when he was only thirteen and still visits him regularly. The rules imposed by drug dealers—not to rob neighbors, not to abuse old people, not to rape, not to bring in stolen cars—are designed by the punto to avoid drawing the police, but they also benefit the community. Furthermore, as Enrique Desmond Arias and Robert Gay both note in the Brazilian context, drug dealing creates bonds of interconnection with the mainstream population who go to the barrios to buy drugs (Arias 2006; Gay 2015).

The extent to which different sectors of the population involve themselves as sellers and buyers of drugs undermines the prohibitionist framework imposed by the state and makes self-regulation the primary form of control. The assumption of regulatory responsibilities by illicit agents ultimately contributes to the blossoming of alternative, plural social orders (Arias and Barnes 2017) and, as Hechter (1988) has suggested, contributes to the maintenance of a certain kind of national order. In what follows, we examine different modalities of self-regulation that have evolved among stakeholders in the cocaine business of Puerto Rico.

## MECHANISMS OF SELF-REGULATION

Unlike in legal markets, illicit actors deploy violence and intimidation as regulatory mechanisms (Reuter 1983). In Cantera, focus group participants noted that violence occurred when "something is out of place." Residents understand violence as an instrument that reestablished the balance of things, whether that was power that stakeholders had lost, or respect that they wished to acquire. Locals saw violence as "a result of the scarcity or the disappearance of supplies" (Pedro, Focus Group 2),[14] "a surge in competition"

(Beto, Focus Group 2), or "disorganization and vacuums created by the police" (Rosa, Focus Group 1).

These respondents identify specific disruptions of market equilibrium—a scarcity, an upsurge in competition, and power vacuums—as triggers of violence. The fact that residents interpreted violence as a response to particular conditions rather than intrinsic to the drug trade suggests a moral economy at variance with the official, prohibitionist view.

Not all residents accept the new moral economy. The idea that violence erupts to restore "balance" is strongly disputed by Helena, who works in a local NGO dedicated to the economic development of Cantera. "Residents don't see the punto as a problem, as long as there is no overt violence. Nevertheless, what they feel is a false sense of stability. The notion that violence is under control makes no sense." She categorically refutes the view that violence happened only in the past as a myth that disguises the true nature of the current drug regime. "It is often said that lethal violence is something that happened many years ago, but then you find out that just recently somebody was killed," she notes. "Then one morning a guy shows ups with a bloody machete in his hand, which tells us that this is happening here and now, the intimidation is right there!" (Helena, Focus Group 2).

Violence is a critical resource to maintain market share, but for violent acts to be seen as legitimate they must reflect a collective purpose. People in the community see violent actors as the end product of a process happening gradually at the local level, one conditioned by structural factors such as a lack of education, unemployment, and access to guns, rather than as an individual pathology. In focus groups in Barrio Obrero and Buena Vista, local activists and professionals situated the alienation of the current generation of "lost boys" in a timeless framework of the search for masculine identity (Ramírez 1999; Rodgers 2009; Baird 2012). One focus group participant noted: "They are drop-outs. They are ignorant; they are not focused. They don't value life and they want to let everybody know that they are not afraid and that they should be feared. They want everybody to see what they are doing [imposing control], because that gives them standing . . . like they want to say something, getting our attention, saying we are here! And we are doing this because this is the way that things are going to be run here" (Focus Group 1 participant). The drug economy, in other words, gives "normal" masculine violence a special utility. That violence can become a resource for the larger community. Manuela, a community leader from

Barrio Obrero, observed: "Here, those from the punto also want to impose their laws, and people agree with it as a way to restore the respect of the barrio [in relation to other barrios]. Right now, if someone has a problem with somebody else, the aggravated person goes to punto x and complains. Then the guys from the punto search for that person and hit him hard, leaving him dead."[15] As noted in the introduction to this volume, not all street violence is mindless; it can reflect a broader moral framework and foster a web of reciprocity in the community. The self-regulation of the drug market, in other words, can create a new social contract between dealers and residents. Ricardo describes an act of vigilantism that demonstrates the alternative governance deployed by the drug regime.

> One day I was resting at home, and one of the guys from the punto came in, agitated, looking for me because there was a guy in the neighborhood that was caught molesting a little girl. My friend told me "right now he is being held by a bunch of people." I was like . . . what?? Wait, I am going to take care of that; I went to my room and get my 9 mm. . . . I was so furious, man, I couldn't contain myself, the guy was crying on the floor and I came in, and bang, bang, bang, *pa' que aprenda!* [to teach him a lesson]. (Ricardo, September 2012)

The violent act described here is the "lynching" of a suspected pedophile who had no connection to the drug trade. The punto simply supplies the angry, armed young men who are more than willing to carry out an extrajudicial death sentence. In the process, they create solidarity with an irate community that endorses cold-blooded murder in this case. As anthropologist Insa Koch has noted in the context of an English housing project, "where the state fails to provide residents with the protection they want, residents can fall back on informal violence that gets condemned as unlawful action by the state" (Goldstein 2003; Koch 2017: 4). By acting as executioners on behalf of the larger community, the dealers blur the line between legitimate and illegitimate violence, making residents indebted to them rather than to the authorities.

## REMAPPING NEIGHBORHOODS

The instrumental violence of the puntos creates a new equilibrium and provides the "fringe benefit" of protection for the community, but it also reconfigures spatial relations in the barrios. The process of spatial reconfiguration imposes new norms of behavior by basing freedom of movement on loyalty and familiarity. Once installed, it becomes another form of self-regulation.

The data show that drug dealers influence the way that residents live, circulate, and relate to each other. Of the population surveyed, 19 and 18 percent, respectively, considered that drug dealers had either a great deal of or some power over residents' freedom of movement and interactions. Only 13 percent of those surveyed believed that the police had a great deal of influence over their communities, while 24 percent recognized that they do have some influence. Fully 38 percent said the police had either little or no influence on the lives of community residents.

We know that the creation and re-creation of space plays a crucial role in the proliferation of different types of social orders, as Arias and Barnes (2017) have recently reminded us. But the production of a new order depends on obtaining some form of collective acceptance of the alternative form of control. Among the competing stakeholders who try to win the passive or active assent of the community, drug dealers are often the ones who are tolerated the most. One reason for that toleration is that drug dealers are not external to the community. "Communities adapt themselves," one informant said, "and it is a very difficult situation to manage, because those involved in the drug business are their own children, their grandchildren, their friends from school, or somebody that I, as a resident, saw growing up within the barrio. On the other hand, that kid has the power to cut lives short, to kill and torture, so people need to find ways to confront the owner of the punto."[16]

The recognition that the drug problem is internal leads some communities to take positive actions to improve conditions rather than prophylactic steps to contain the dealers. The same informant pointed out how some communities are dealing with the drug issue:

I have seen how organized and disorganized communities deal with those issues. For example, in Puente Blanco, Catano, a community with a long political history, there is a major punto there, but what the residents did was to concentrate on the young people, attending to their needs and offering support at school. A community leader there told me the other day, "When we started working here, 75 percent of the young people dropped out of school, but now 75 percent of the kids manage to stay at least until the fourth grade." Everybody in the community has different motivations to cooperate. Many women do it because they have young kids growing up in the community. Another became a leader because her son was killed and she decided to dedicate her energies to promoting development among the youth. In Villa Canona, Loiza, they are also working, developing initiatives within the community, and there are lots of problems with the police because they are really oppressive, but that community has a long history of fighting back, and they don't let intimidation stop their efforts to develop Villa Canona. (Ryan 2012)

The push and pull between dealers and residents reveals a framework in which drug activity responds to community demands. In the barriadas, for example, residents and drug dealers compete for public spaces. In many barriadas the *cancha* or basketball court serves as a multiuse space for the community to hold meetings and parties and as a hangout for young people. Because drug dealers use the canchas as a place for recruitment, it becomes a space that must be negotiated. In the words of Amparo, a resident of Barrio Obrero: "When the community is planning to put on some social or cultural activity, we do inform the head of the puntos about the event. However, that doesn't mean that we are asking for their permission, we are just informing them, in order to avoid any conflict or violent act on their part" (Amparo, Focus Group 1). Amparo clarifies that the community doesn't ask to use the basketball court of La Luisa anymore because the bichotes have taken possession already, and that would imply trespassing on their territory. "We used to have some arrangements with previous capos [kingpins], but that can change if the leadership also changes." The layout of a typical barriada is different from a large public housing project but still accommodates the needs of drug traffickers, as the director of a school who was a longtime resident of Cantera noted: "This is a good place for a punto, in a barriada like this. Here, there are several entries and exits that allow traffickers to move freely when the police come. There are houses where they can hide the drugs and themselves. People do not call the police to denounce them because they fear retaliation. Within the community there is also money laundering, which benefits the bodegas. . . . In general, small businesses benefit a lot from drug commerce" (Focus Group 2 participant). Residents of drug-engaged communities often take on roles made available to them by the dealers. A resident of the residential Nemesio Canales said:

> People keep things in their apartments, guns, drugs. . . . I personally do not resist, because I have been living here for many years and I don't want to be thrown out of my apartment [by the traffickers]. So it is better that they don't see you seeing them. . . . The police came one day at four a.m. and went apartment by apartment looking for somebody; they came without a

search warrant. The rule here is nobody says anything. When the SWAT force comes to arrest somebody, all the women give them hell. But at night, people shut themselves in their house and leave the street to them [the dealers].[17]

The authority of the drug dealers is quasi-official: as noted above, they have the power to evict residents they don't trust. In fact, in Nemesio Canales several building managers have been fired for not following the bichotes' rules. In one focus group, social workers and employees at a public housing project made clear that their work is directly impacted by the drug dealers. One of the participants put it this way, "If for some reason you get in trouble with some of those guys, they could hit you, and if you complain, they have the power to throw you out of your job. . . . It also happens that sometimes when we have to evict somebody you could be in a risky situation if that person is related to the drug dealer" (building manager, Focus Group 3).[18] Other housing officials mentioned how sometimes the dealers come to them, defiant, to tell them that they have to leave the project. When that happens, the dealers usually start harassing the administrative employees; they find out about them, their family, where they live, as a way to intimidate them. To avoid such ultimatums, employees may negotiate with the bichotes. An employee in Nemesio Canales said: "Today I have a meeting with them, because they shut off all the lights in the public areas of the project, and now we have to be in the dark because they don't want anybody to see them, but that is not right" (Focus Group 3 participant). Another employee interrupted to say, "That, and the issue of the numbers." She explained:

> We had an inspection by the federal officials, and they demanded that we put numbers on each building, and we put them up, but the drug dealers took them down. We explained to them that we need to reinstall the numbers because we receive federal money, and the federal government requires us to put the numbers back up, and we did it! But as soon as the inspection happened, they took them away again, as if they were telling us, "We allowed you that moment but be clear that we are going to erase them."

Residents freely acknowledge that runners from the punto control everyone that enters their territory. As one explained:

> I said, look, if you see a police car in front of my house it is because they are coming to pick me up to attend a meeting about the residential, and they told me, "Yes, that's okay, we understand that you are the administrator and have to attend meetings." Also, when I have family visiting me, I go to them in advance and tell them: "Look, this is a relative of mine; just in case, because

that is how we are here." Since everybody here knows everyone else, they pay attention if they see a new face, they come to ask you and because you are afraid you have to find out who that person is. (Focus Group 3 participant)

Space also becomes a signifier of the social relations that are built along the drug value chain. In localities that have a strong presence of drug dealers, spaces and people that were discarded, underutilized, or marginalized are recovered and "recycled" by the dealers. They are, of course, then subjected to a new form of control and regulation. The fate of the homeless, universally known as deambulantes, is a good illustration of this dynamic.

Because public housing projects are gated developments, they do not offer space for the homeless. For that reason, the deambulantes tend to circulate in the older neighborhoods, the barriadas. By default, then, responsibility for the homeless and the addicted population falls to the residents of the barriadas, including the drug dealers. Residents assimilate deambulantes and drug addicts by allowing them to occupy empty spaces that become *conventillos* or shooting galleries, where addicts go to inject drugs. In exchange, the homeless and drug users are hired to clean vacant lots, pick up garbage, and do other chores for residents, as well as serving as eyes and ears for the punto. The coexistence of community residents, drug dealers, and the homeless and addicted creates reciprocal relationships and dependencies (see also Rui, this volume).

The sense of reciprocal dependence and obligation is epitomized by the informal but rigidly observed policy of "no snitching." For drug dealers, earning the loyalty of the communities in which they operate is critical to their business, whether that loyalty is won through gift giving, employment, negotiation, tolerance, intimidation, or outright violence. The barriadas, like Cantera, Barrio Obrero, Las Monjas, and Caimito, are more open than housing projects and therefore invite incursions by competitive groups willing to challenge the incumbent drug leadership, fomenting violence. Residents of the barriadas respond to high levels of competition and violence by playing selectively on both sides—drug dealers and the police—depending on their calculation of the risks and benefits in a given situation. Residents adapt to higher levels of violence in the barriadas. "I saw that those at the punto surprised somebody who was stealing, and they started striking him with a stick. Suddenly, several residents came out and also hit the guy," says Ray, a social promotor in Cantera. "It is like for Puerto Ricans those power structures are valid and they must turn to them."[19]

What makes some communities more inclined to be subject to regulation than others? "It's all circumstantial," Ray explains. "Cantera passed through a stage of maturation regarding the puntos, just to experience a fallback later. . . . There is an absolute institutional abandonment; nobody in Barrio Obrero believes in the police! We've seen the police arresting somebody from the punto, and then calling the runner of the punto to extort them." Again and again, the failure of the police to win the confidence of the community—due to corruption, violence, incompetence—enhanced the legitimacy of the drug dealers' system of self-regulation and spatial control.

In the absence of "public goods" provided by government, locally embedded drug dealers "provide a modicum of security and limited norm enforcement" in exchange for the active or passive collaboration of the community, as the introduction to this volume notes. Yet the fragmentation and violence of the local market mean that genuine social mobility for low-level drug operatives is exceptional. For that reason, Ray is skeptical about the future and thinks that things will get worse before they get better. "The problem is that there is no upward mobility at the punto. It's not like people make millions, and the mobility is achieved at gunpoint; somebody must disappear for another one to enter. And the police also enter into that game." He also felt that if people cannot enter into the lucrative field of drugs, they will commit other crimes. "Rich people are becoming increasingly aware that even in their exclusive neighborhoods they could have a punto with runners; they realize that the world they thought to be exclusive is not like that anymore."

In the absence of a larger plan for the development and well-being of the poor barrios of San Juan, drug dealers have stepped forward with their own proactive and inclusive strategy for economic advancement. As Ray says, "As an advocate for development, I want to include people from the punto in the development plan for the community, because they are in fact part of the community, they are the sons of the community even if they are whores, fags, fuckers; we need to work with all of them, because if we exclude them from the negotiations, we would be doing exactly the same thing that the government does, marginalizing them." The business model of the drug dealers, from this perspective, is more realistic, ambitious, and encompassing than that of Puerto Rico's government. The ability of the cocaine commodity chain to create an advantageous macro-environment for itself is essential, as Ray explains: "The main mistake that authorities or even researchers make is to think of this as a subculture, as something marginal to the island's reality. In fact, selling drugs, cutting and distributing drugs, is a very well-established culture, very present in the lives of Puerto Ricans. People find this difficult to accept. . . . But a punto where addicts, homeless, and community people go to buy does not produce millions, those runners can barely live from it; the important transactions are made in the big hotels and in the rich neighborhoods." Ray was one of the few informants who clearly connected the two sides of Puerto Rico's hybrid place in the drug commodity chain—as both a transshipment bridge and a retail market. Arrest of small-time dealers, Ray continues, is a game of smoke and mirrors that conceals the big operators, who remain out of reach. "The big companies are engaged in the business, the banking system is involved, also the airlines. The federal police play the game: let's give something to society to make them feel safe, and give the perception that we are doing something. They go to one barrio and disarticulate twenty or thirty drug puntos, but the real business is untouchable. . . . They don't go beyond the distributors and intermediaries."

## CONCLUSIONS

We have seen how an illicit commodity chain reorganizes social space, affecting the lives of ordinary people. The Puerto Rican case shows in detail how the drug commodity chain articulates congenial social relations and instrumental spatial configurations.

First, armed transgressive groups repurpose natural and built environments and change the rules to suit their priorities, thereby creating new forms of social control. Dealers reorganize territories to their advantage, creating no-go zones and appropriating public spaces, but also helping small businesses with new cash flows and offering a variety of jobs to residents. At the same time, they privilege local residents over strangers and offer some protection against the anarchy of "all against all."

Second, however ruthless drug dealers at times may be, they ultimately rely on a system of interpersonal networks that gives rise to a peculiar moral economy. Dealers learn the community's diverse needs and invest in them to nurture loyalty and trust, although they are also perfectly willing to gain cooperation through intimidation and violence if necessary. Most residents tacitly accept the presence of the drug commodity chain in their neighborhoods, refusing to rat out dealers to the police. When communities do respond, it is often by providing greater opportunities to the children of the barrio as alternatives to entering the drug trade.

Third, by exercising hard and soft power, drug dealers become a quasi-official regulatory mechanism that suppresses disorganized street crime within the communities. In the absence of effective and popularly approved action by the state, the actors in the drug commodity chain enforce social control by mediating disputes, establishing collectively sanctioned forms of behavior, and protecting residents from outside attacks. When they offer protection to residents in exchange for active or passive collusion with their enterprise, they are breaking the monopoly of power and violence that the state theoretically enjoys in those communities. As our interviews showed, many residents see the drug dealers as filling a vacuum left by an ineffective, indifferent, and corrupt government.

Recent events in Puerto Rico, including the arrest of dozens of high-level government officials followed by the resignation of Governor Ricardo Roselló in August 2019, tend to confirm the pervasiveness of alternative moral economies on the island. While none of those officials have been charged specifically with drug trafficking, their alleged crimes include conspiracy, money laundering, and obstruction of justice. In the context of the competing moral economies described in this chapter, the travails of the Roselló government underscore the weakness and hypocrisy of the official narrative. Corruption at the top of the political system undermines the legal and moral authority of all the island's officials, suggesting that a "well-established culture" of criminality is the mainstream, not the margin, in Puerto Rico.

**NOTES**

Lilian Bobea wishes to dedicate this essay to her mentors, Immanuel M. Wallerstein and Giovanni Arrighi, who were both grand theory builders and practitioners and whose transformative and inspiring influence lives on.

1 Lilian Bobea thanks Open Society and SSRC for supporting this research with a Drugs, Security and Democracy fellowship, as well as Dr. Humberto Garcia-Muniz, director of the Center for Caribbean Studies at the Universidad de Puerto Rico, and Dr. Jorge Rodriguez Beruff for their time and dedication. This research was accomplished thanks to a team of assistants, especially Wilfredo Mattos, whose help was invaluable. Thanks also to Lisa McGirr for commenting on a draft of this essay.
2 The survey was conducted in the San Juan neighborhoods of Caimito, Las Monjas, a subsector of Hato Rey Central; El Caño de Martin Peña in Hato Rey Norte; Bella Vista and Israel-Bitamul in Hato Rey Sur; and Las Marias, Loiza, Barrio Obrero, 27 de Febrero, Condado, and Condadito in Santurce.

3 The island is still a bridge for drugs en route to the US and Europe. As one
   ex-dealer explained: "You can hardly talk about a superabundance of kilos of
   cocaine circulating on the streets of San Juan. Puerto Rico is essentially a bridge;
   what goes to the street is a residual amount of the gigantic traffic that goes
   through the island" (author interview with Jorge Rodriguez Beruff, San Juan,
   October 2012).
4 Public housing projects were the epitome of urban renewal under Luis Muñoz
   Marin. During the 1960s around 54,000 units were built, 60 percent of them
   in metropolitan San Juan (Picó 1969: 257).
5 Author interview with historian Fernando Picó, San Juan, October 2012.
6 Author interview with Ricardo (pseudonym), San Juan, October 2012.
7 Author interview with Max (pseudonym), San Juan, October 2012.
8 Author interview with participants in Focus Group 1, Barrio Obrero, San Juan,
   October 2012.
9 Author interview with a public housing administrator, San Juan, November 2012.
10 Author interview with Jaimito (pseudonym), San Juan, October 2012.
11 Author interview with Pedro (pseudonym), San Juan, October 2012.
12 Lilian Bobea has coined the term *statetropism* to describe the attraction of
   criminal actors toward state officials (Bobea 2015).
13 Inteviews were conducted all over the municipality of San Juan, which includes
   the neighborhoods of Caimito, El Cinco, Rio Piedras, Hato Rey Norte, Hato
   Rey Central and Hato Rey Sur, Cupey, Santurce, Viejo San Juan, and Nonacillo
   Urbano. On the other hand, Barrio Obrero, Martin Pena, Cantera, Llorens
   Torres, Las Monjas, and 27 de Febrero are subneighborhoods located in the
   northern part of San Juan. Of the random sample of 117 adults, 44.6 percent
   reported an annual household income under US$14,999, including salary and
   remittances.
14 Author interview with participants in Focus Group 2, Cantera, San Juan,
   October 2012.
15 Author interview with Manuela (pseudonym), San Juan, October 2012.
16 Author interview with Ryan (pseudonym), San Juan, October 2012.
17 Author interview with participants in Focus Group 4, Nemesio Canales, San
   Juan, October 2012.
18 Author interview with participants in Focus Group 3, Nemesio Canales, San
   Juan, October 2012.
19 Author interview with Ray (pseudonym), San Juan, October 2012.

REFERENCES

Arias, Enrique Desmond. 2006. *Drugs and Democracy in Rio: Trafficking, Social
   Networks, and Public Security*. Chapel Hill: University of North Carolina Press.

Arias, Enrique Desmond, and Nicholas Barnes. 2017. "Crime and Plural Orders in Rio de Janeiro, Brazil." *Current Sociology* 63, no. 3: 448–65.

Ayala, Cesar J. 1999. *American Sugar Kingdom: The Plantation Economy of the Spanish Caribbean, 1898–1919.* Chapel Hill: University of North Carolina Press.

Bair, Jennifer, and Marion Werner. 2011. "The Place of Disarticulations: Global Commodity Production in La Laguna, Mexico." *Environment and Planning* 43, no. 5: 998–1015.

Baird, Adam. 2012. "The Violent Gang and the Construction of Masculinity amongst Socially Excluded Young Men." *Safer Communities* 11, no. 4: 179–90.

Bobea, Lilian. 2015. "Seeking Out the State: Organized Crime, Violence and Statetropism in the Caribbean." In *Gangs in the Caribbean*, edited by C. Katz and A. Harriott. Kingston: West Indies University Press.

Calle 13. 2010. "Digo Lo Que Pienso." *Genius.* Accessed June 6, 2018. https://genius.com/Calle-13-digo-lo-que-pienso-lyrics.

Cotto Morales, Liliana. 2011. *Desalambrar: Orígenes de los Rescates de Terreno en Puerto Rico y Su Pertinencia en los Movimientos Sociales Contemporaneos.* San Juan: Tal Cual.

Fuller Marvel, Lucilla. 2008. *Listen to What They Say: Planning and Community Development in Puerto Rico.* San Juan: Universidad de Puerto Rico.

Gay, Robert. 2015. *Conversations with a Brazilian Drug Dealer.* Durham, NC: Duke University Press.

Goldstein, Daniel M. 2003. "'In Our Own Hands': Lynching, Justice, and the Law in Bolivia." *American Ethnologist* 30, no. 1: 22–43.

Grosfoguel, Ramon. 2003. *Colonial Subjects: Puerto Ricans in a Global Perspective.* Berkeley: University of California Press.

Hechter, Michael. 1988. *Principles of Group Solidarity.* Berkeley: University of California Press.

Koch, Insa. 2017. "Moving beyond Punitivism: Punishment, State Failure and Democracy at the Margins." *Punishment and Society* 19, no. 2: 203–20.

Picó, Rafael, et al. 1969. *Nueva geografía de Puerto Rico: Física, económica y social.* Río Piedras: Editorial Universitaria.

Ramírez, Rafael L. 1999. *What It Means to Be a Man: Reflections on Puerto Rican Masculinity.* New Brunswick, NJ: Rutgers University Press.

Reuter, Peter. 1983. *Disorganized Crime: Economics of the Visible Hand.* Cambridge, MA: MIT Press.

Rodgers, Dennis. 2009. "Living in the Shadow of Death: Gangs, Violence, and Social Order in Urban Nicaragua, 1996–2002." In *Youth Violence in Latin America: Gangs and Juvenile Justice in Perspective*, edited by G. A. Jones and D. Rodgers. New York: Palgrave Macmillan.

Santiago-Valles, Kevin. 1994. *"Subject People" and Colonial Discourses: Economic Transformation and Social Disorder in Puerto Rico, 1898–1947.* Albany: State University of New York Press.

# <u>09</u> VISIBLE AND INVISIBLE "CRACKLANDS" IN BRAZIL

MORAL DRUG COMMERCE AND THE PRODUCTION OF
SPACE IN SÃO PAULO AND RIO DE JANEIRO (1990–2017)

Since the 2000s, following the "shift south" of the cocaine trade noted by Gootenberg in this volume, crack use in Brazil caused a big stir, with the media classifying it as an "epidemic" (see, for example, Freire 2010; Forero 2012; Laranjeira 2016). The clusters of emaciated and dirty consumers attracted attention to the sites of consumption and commerce, which the press stigmatized as *"cracolândia"* (cracklands).

The visibility of these "cracklands" and the media attention they drew pushed Dilma Rousseff's government (2010–14) to spend approximately US$1 billion on an anti-crack campaign known as *Crack É Possível Vencer* (Crack Can Be Defeated) (Richard 2015). Some of this money supported a national survey conducted by the FIOCRUZ-Oswaldo Cruz Foundation, a public health research center. The survey estimated that in 2013 there were 370,000 crack consumers across Brazil's state capitals, accounting for just 0.81 percent of the population of these cities—far less than the "millions of consumers" ("Epidemia de crack" 2015) suggested by the mainstream press. As Gootenberg explains (this volume), crack use in Brazil reflects what happened in the US over the decade 1985 to 1995: a cycle of oversupply, low prices, racialization, and the associated large-scale public health problem.

I have studied crack consumption in Brazil for more than ten years (see Rui 2014). The big news about crack in this country is not so much the number of consumers, but their visibility. Drug gangs regulate the mobility and presence of crack users in the city. Thus, in order to comprehend Brazil's crack cocaine phenomenon, its territorial patterns, and public responses to it, we first need to understand how the drug gangs evaluate, engage with, and govern users.

This chapter focuses on drug consumption spaces in two of Brazil's largest cities—São Paulo and Rio de Janeiro. Within São Paulo, I consider two distinct cocaine consumption zones—the peripheral neighborhoods and the center—focused on the Estação da Luz train station. In Rio de Janeiro, I focus on consumption in a restricted part of the Maré favela complex. These two cities experience very different territorial patterns of drug consumption. In São Paulo, drug use is highly visible on the streets downtown and is widely commented on in the media. In Rio, drug use has mostly been contained inside favelas; it is therefore less visible and elicits less media attention, although, as we will see, in 2010 this changed when large numbers of crack users began appearing on public thoroughfares.

I argue that these different patterns of crack consumption can be traced to the operating logics of each city's drug trafficking organizations. Hirata and Grillo (2017) have shown how in both Rio de Janeiro and São Paulo, criminal organizations are based in prisons. These penitentiary-based "comandos" or *facções*—who are important players in the local drug trade—exert de facto control over poor urban territories (see Gay, this volume). They represent "a new type of political actor." Their preeminent position in poor communities stems from an appropriation of state power made possible by their engagement with the international illegal drug markets (Arias 2006: 298).

In São Paulo the crack trade has been consolidated for three decades and the cracolândia has been a feature of the urban landscape for at least twenty years. If in the first decade there was an open market violently disputed by various criminal groups, in the last two decades the criminal faction Primeiro Comando da Capital (First Command of the Capital; PCC) has exerted hegemonic power, managing elements of the governance of poor neighborhoods throughout the city. Because of this, the PCC deliberately drives problematic crack users out of the city's PCC-controlled favelas for what many perceive as antisocial behaviors, and into downtown spaces, which are not under the PCC's control.

In contrast, even though Rio de Janeiro has a long history of powder cocaine use, dating back to the early 1980s, it is only since 2000 that the crack market has expanded. Here, three criminal factions compete for control: the Comando Vermelho (Red Command; CV), Terceiro Comando Puro (Pure Third Command; TCP), and Amigos dos Amigos (Friends of Friends; ADA).[1] Unlike their counterparts in São Paulo, Rio's gangs have no immediate interest in regulating consumption because they are forced to compete with one another for access to consumers.[2]

In this chapter I provide an overview of these local crack markets and how they are morally regulated, and I reflect on their effects on and repercussions for territorial production. I describe how the decisions made by criminal organizations regarding the structure of retail drug markets produce specific territorial arrangements for consumers. For this study I have employed both historical and ethnographic methodologies in order to make sense of the dynamics of the drug trade in both sites. This chapter builds on and contributes to an emerging literature on how criminal organizations promote norms that impact on the everyday life of residents of the territories that they manage (Barbosa 2012; Feltran 2012; Grillo 2013; Biondi 2016; Arias and Barnes 2017; Hirata and Grillo 2017; Arias in the conclusion to this volume). From this vantage point, I emphasize how the market differences and forms of illegal governance produce specific moralities and territories of crack consumption.

## FRAGMENTED CITIES, CRACK USERS, AND CRACKLANDS

The contemporary Latin American city is characterized by high levels of unemployment, declining opportunity, and social exclusion. Academics talk of the "new poverty," "advanced marginality," and "the underclass" (Auyero 2000; Gonzalez de la Rocha et al. 2004; Portes and Roberts 2005; Wacquant 2008; Auyero and Sobering 2017). One of the harshest realities is the sharp increase in violence, crime, and insecurity.

Researchers have argued that violence is no longer the sole domain of the state; rather, it has become something that can be used by a variety of actors to meet their own goals (Koonings and Kruijt 1999; Arias and Goldstein 2010; Auyero, Bourgois, and Scheper-Hughes 2015). The most prominent actors within the new panorama of urban violence are the youth gangs and drug gangs that act as para-state organizations in certain locales, as discussed in this chapter and other contributions to this volume (Arias 2006; Rodgers, Beall, and Kanbur 2012).

Researchers have confirmed that as a result of these processes Latin American cities are fragmenting (Rodgers 2004; Koonings and Kruijt 2007). On the one hand, slums and shantytowns have become ever more cut off from the rest of the metropolis (Perlman 2010), while the rich live protected by CCTV, high walls, electrified fences, bulletproof glass, and private security (Caldeira 2000). This reorganization of urban space has profound implications for citizenship and democracy (Caldeira and Holston 1999; Holston 1999). Teresa Caldeira (2000) has documented the decreasing participation in public democratic life in Brazil and the rise of support for antidemocratic measures—including the use of death squads (Wacquant 2003; Wacquant 2008). This illiberal backlash carried Bolsonaro to power (Hunter and Power 2019).

But if the main analytical frame to understand urban space in the current literature has been on fragmentation, this chapter tells a slightly different story. Here we see urban zoning as an ongoing process that involves constant negotiation between various actors—chief among them the drug gangs. The population of crack users move around, and in so doing make what were considered to be respectable areas less attractive. The kind of decisions drug traffickers make, then, which are rooted in deeper social logics about protecting their own communities, businesses, and relationships, reconfigure space in the Latin American city.

## SÃO PAULO (1990–2017)

Criminality and the crack trade in São Paulo can be divided into two critical historical periods. The first occurred during the 1990s when, amid wider gang conflict in the city, crack was cooked near downtown areas. Later, a second period emerged as the PCC consolidated its power in the metropolitan area and dealers drove problematic consumers out of peripheral neighborhoods and into the city center.

### An Overview of the History of Crack in São Paulo

There is little information about how and when crack first emerged in Brazil. The most reliable records from newspapers indicate that the drug initially took root in the eastern periphery of the city of São Paulo. In the early 1990s, the São Mateus neighborhood was the site with the city's most intense crack trade. In June 1992, *Folha de São Paulo*, a major national newspaper, referred to São Mateus as "the Bronx of São Paulo,"[3] associating the area with the notorious New York borough that was at the center of the crack trade in the 1980s. Marcos Uchoa, in one of the first books on the subject, wrote: "Let's go to São Mateus, . . . one of the first 'safe havens' of crack in São Paulo. . . . About 600,000 people live in this poor neighborhood in the East Zone, a caricature of the Bronx alleys in New York City. . . . Children and teenagers use drugs sitting on the sidewalk, there are drug dealers on the street corners and around the schools" (Uchoa 1996: 34).[4]

Similarly, a June 1991 report in *Folha de São Paulo* stated that "crack is sold in the region" ("Crack é vendido na região") and that children aged between seven and twelve years old were "addicted" to the drug. In June of the following year, a half-page story in the same newspaper, titled "Crack Addict Youth Is Killed by the Police" ("Jovem viciado em crack é morto pela PM"), reported that the police had shot dead a seventeen-year-old boy in the locality. The family and the local Child Protection Center reported that the boy, who was said to be "addicted to crack," was last seen getting into a police car following his arrest. According to the story, this was the thirteenth recorded death of a child in the region between December 1991 and April 1992. All of them were crack users.

It took another four years, however, for the term *cracolândia* to appear in the press. The first time the word appeared in the newspaper *O Estado de São Paulo*, another leading national newspaper, was in August of 1995 ("Polícia reforça combate a traficantes"), while in *Folha de São Paulo* its first mention was in May 1996 ("PM afirma ter recapturado 2 dos fugitivos"). The area was described as a "point of sale" (Uchoa 1996: 73), as a "drug point," or even as a place for preparing crack. Mingardi and Goulart's research corroborates this. They write: "Most of the crack marketed in the area is prepared in the 'kitchens,' . . . we have data that indicates that these kitchens operate in the area of cracolândia itself, this suggests that much of the crack sold in this area is also prepared there. According to interviews with former DENARC agents (the police investigation department) until a few years ago practically all the crack consumed was manufactured in the area. . . . With the increase in demand, much of the crack is now manufactured outside of the area" (Mingardi and Goulart 2001: 34).[5]

As Mingardi and Goulart note, the area was named cracolândia because of the preparation and sale of drugs in the area. It was only in the 2000s, especially in the second half of the decade, that the place became a site for consumption and gained national and international notoriety. At its peak, between 2008 and 2009, the area attracted more than a thousand drug users each night—a number that occupied an entire city block.

These reports are important sources of information about what occurred on the outskirts of the city with the advent of crack consumption. There are other sources too. Alessandra Teixeira (2012) and Bruno Paes Manso (2012) have examined the homicides of children and adolescents who used crack cocaine in São Paulo in the early 1990s. Both observed how the arrival of crack helped to change both the scale and the shape of drug trafficking in the metropolis. In Teixeira's formulation (2012: 16), crack was "a destabilizing element on a (drug) market still being consolidated." For Manso, the sale of crack accelerated and deepened social conflict. It was during this period that the *noia* (junkie) emerged in popular discourse as a person who is unable to follow rules and who has no rights, not even the right to life (Manso 2012: 228). Thus, "more than perpetrators of violence, addicts appear in the 1990s as preferential victims of those who kill" (Manso 2012: 228). These deaths have to be understood in the context of intense conflict between police, ex-police groups, gangs, and dealers for monopoly control over the territory. Crack users were accused of disturbing the flow of everyday life, accruing large debts, stealing from community members, and bringing the place into disrepute. Killing them was a way to signal power and local control.

In the early 1990s, Brazil experienced formal redemocratization, economic restructuring, and the deregulation of import markets, opening the country to international commerce. This experience included greater trade in illicit goods, specifically cocaine and crack (consumption of crack had already stagnated in the United States; see Reinarman and Levine 1997). At this time there was an upsurge of violent crime in the city of São Paulo, which scholars have linked to the shift to open markets. In the words of sociologist Gabriel Feltran: "'A lot of mothers cried' in the early hours in hospital lobbies, and cemeteries. A generation still bears the marks of this period, perhaps for a long time. . . . In the peripheries it is common for the 1990s . . . to be remembered as 'the time of war'"[6] (Feltran 2012: 238–39).

The cracolândias of Brazil and their associated violence and crime, then, initially grew alongside neoliberal restructuring and the transition to democracy. They are part of the "disjunctive democracy" that combines extensive formal freedoms with elevated violence and rights abuses, particularly against the poor, that Caldeira and Holston (1999) have argued has emerged in the years since.

### The Shift in Criminal Structures and the Transformation of the Cracolândia

In São Paulo, amid numerous gang wars on the outskirts of the city, the PCC crime faction emerged in the wake of the 1992 Carandiru Massacre, when police murdered 111 prisoners while suppressing a riot at the Casa de Detenção de São Paulo.[7] The faction's members demanded improvements in prison conditions and also formed a prisoners' alliance that reduced violence and promoted alternative dispute resolution between inmates. This massacre had significant repercussions and, among other effects, contributed to restructuring the state penitentiary system. The Carandiru prison was demolished and the government began to build new prisons. At the same time, São Paulo moved to a mass incarceration policy. Two decades later, there are 171 prison buildings and 170,000 prisoners.

All of this strengthened the PCC. In 2001, the PCC orchestrated rebellions in penitentiaries, which offered a public demonstration of the PCC's control over São Paulo's prisons, and since 2006 it has exercised hegemony over criminal activities throughout the state. The drug market workers, who were incarcerated in large numbers under São Paulo's emerging mass incarceration policy, were socialized in the prisons by the PCC. In Feltran's (2012: 242) analyses, "Incarceration removed from the streets boys at war with each other and returned them, a few years later, socialized into a logic of internal peace."[8] Over the course of two decades, the PCC consolidated its grip on power, changing the organization of the drug market and the way gangs managed problematic crack users.

Throughout the 1990s, the violent conflicts among police, ex-police, and dealers and the growing consolidation of the PCC's power in the city's peripheral areas pushed out crack users, who migrated to the center of São Paulo, congregating at the Estação da Luz railway station. There they mingled with homeless people, prostitutes, and former prison inmates, a kind of "moral region" (Park 1915) of the city. This region underwent a significant transformation, as "the economy of prostitution began to decline and the drug trade slowly began to gain traction as a criminal business in the city, spreading across multiple territories and actors" (Teixeira 2012: 10–11).[9] The hotels and hostels that formerly housed travelers and prostitutes became the domain of crack consumers and vendors who came from other parts of the city on the run from the "war" between traffickers and police officers in the peripheries. And so the cracolândia was born.

Today, crack users' motivation to migrate to cracolândia are very different from those of the 1990s. By 2010 the peripheral areas of São Paulo had become far safer as a result of the hegemony of the PCC, which promoted a more ordered approach to drug sales, explicitly stating that "one can no longer kill." The PCC outlawed crack in state prisons (Biondi 2011), and its members strictly manage crack around the metropolitan area.

Lacking any serious competition, the PCC was able to build norms that offered poor residential neighborhoods some protection against problematic drug users. More than marijuana or cocaine, PCC associates crack with moral degradation, lack of control, and disrespect for community ties. Indeed, area residents had significant concerns that drug users might commit crimes such as theft and muggings. Drug traffickers are motivated to minimize conflict at their distribution points to avoid police attention and maintain positive relations with area neighbors. In addition, they have respect for the communities where they live and work. In this sense, the crack commerce forms part of an alternative moral economy that prioritizes good relations between criminal actors and local residents. Criminal actors make efforts to limit the disturbance associated with crack use. For instance, they will not sell drugs to people who they believe to be a nuisance, and can expel particularly troublesome individuals (Biondi 2011). This logic circumscribes the sites that crack users can occupy. In other words, street-level drug dealers exert a certain control and have an impact on the movement of users throughout the city. When an abusive user is banned from one *biqueira* (crack selling point), he or she has to look for another place to buy and consume drugs. If banned from a second biqueira, he or she will then look for a third, and so on.

Dealers, then, will eventually force some users out of a cluster of neighborhoods and into the city center, the location of São Paulo's cracolândia. It is not, however, simple to retrace one's steps and go back to where one came from, because this involves negotiations with the dealers, and sometimes punishment. This often one-way migratory pattern illustrates how practices and decisions made by drug dealers are morally informed and over the course of the 2000s are connected with the displacement of problematic crack users toward the center of the city. This movement is in no way random, and can explain why São Paulo's cracolândia has been a matter of great public and media interest since 2008.

I situate my ethnographic research in this milieu. Over the years I have met locals and built networks of friendship, exchange, and affection. This space produces a dynamic of territorial occupation and drug sales that is different from those observed at the city's peripheral neighborhoods (Rui 2013, 2014, 2016). In the urban margins, consumers congregate in shacks, out of sight of acquaintances and relatives. In these places, dealers manage the trade by only selling the drug as an entire three- to five-dollar rock rather than as cheaper fragments. Dealers require users to make these purchases with bills rather than coins.

But in the cracolândia of central São Paulo, where drug use happens in public view, consumers can, at any time of the day, buy a large crack rock, break it down, and resell the pieces for as little as a few cents each (a practice that gang members would not permit in the urban peripheries).[10] Not only is crack much cheaper here, but it has also become a currency, used to buy everyday necessities such as shoes, clothes, cigarettes, and food. This reflects the sad reality of what is one of the "most competitive and fragmented markets" in which "autonomous individual resellers, living on the verge of extinction, [operate] with very low profit margins and are incapable of generating any surplus"[11] (Lessing 2008: 46). This dynamic blurs the boundaries between drug traffickers and drug users, as the police frequently arrest users for reselling fragments of cocaine, leading to a revolving door between the streets and prison (Mallart and Rui 2017).

The cracolândia exists as a result of the exercise of social control within the norms set by the PCC in an array of poor residential neighborhoods around the city. It is the cracolândia (rather than the favela) that then becomes the focus for state action. Health services and social assistance operate in the area, as do NGOs, churches, activists, journalists, and researchers. The police frequently enter the cracolândia through spectacular and violent operations that lead to mass incarcerations. And yet, despite this repression, the cracolândia has survived for more than twenty years in the heart of the continent's largest metropolis.

São Paulo's cracôlandia has emerged, too, as a result of how the PCC controls urban space. The consolidations of gang control under the auspices of one group throughout the metropolitan area decreases competition and allows the PCC to establish relatively strong social control in the poor neighborhoods where most of their members and their members' families live. These same locales are important staging areas for other larger-scale criminal activities such as drug wholesaling. Thus, not having to compete with other groups over retail drug sales enables the PCC to provide some protection and to force more difficult addicts to other areas of the city where the PCC is more comfortable having their behavior attract police attention.

### RIO DE JANEIRO (2000–2017)

Crack arrived in Rio de Janeiro much later than São Paulo. Here the first news reports of crack use date only to 2000. Researchers have linked the emergence of this illicit market to the splintering of the criminal factions that have controlled retail cocaine sales in the city since the late 1980s (Barbosa 1998; Misse 2003; Arias 2006; Grillo 2013). There are three phases to the history of crack in Rio. The first was in the 1990s when crack was virtually nonexistent. During the second period, crack became more common as a core group in the Comando Vermelho (Red Command; CV) fractured and a new criminal organization, the Amigos dos Amigos (Friends of Friends; ADA) emerged. During the most recent phase, dating from 2010, growing police activity suppressed certain types of criminal territorial control ahead of the 2014 World Cup and 2016 Olympics, driving crack users out of the favelas and into public view.

### Crack in Rio in the 1990s

Rio de Janeiro first emerged as an important transshipment point for Bolivian and Peruvian cocaine en route to Europe in the 1990s (Misse 2003; see also Gay and Gootenberg, this volume).[12] In the words of Arias (2006: 297), "the density of favelas and corrupt policing that characterized these areas made them ideal places for the storage of cocaine in preparation for transshipment." This story shows that "it was not the demand, but the huge supply and the reduction of retail prices"[13] (Misse 2003) that led to the growth of the cocaine market in the city.

At that time the criminal factions in the city were waging a "private war" (Salles 1999) to control the cocaine trade. But, curiously, they were less interested in the crack trade. The anthropologist Antônio Rafael Barbosa (1998) has referred to Rio de Janeiro's late uptake of the drug as "the Carioca mystery." The reason Rio was a late adopter is due to a series of moral and economic considerations on the part of drug traffickers. Initially, many looked down on crack; it had a low price, generating small profit margins, and traffickers worried that street-level dealers would consume the drug and disrupt business at the *boca* (drug selling point) where other drugs, such as marijuana and powder cocaine, were for sale.[14] Moreover, criminal factions thought that the drug would destroy their relations with the neighborhood as a result of petty thefts by consumers, whom many considered untrustworthy. These are moral perceptions that, over the course of the 2000s, came into conflict with the increasingly high capital turnover generated by this trade. This delicate moral and monetary calculation was critical to the emerging crack consumption scene in the city.

For example, in the Maré favela complex, where I conducted research, a member of the CV criminal organization told me that he had urged other members of the organization to stop the sale of crack cocaine in Rio's slums altogether—"this is not like São Paulo," he said. "Morals have to prevail, not the market." He acknowledged, however, that his opinion was not shared by other members of the *facção*, who were more concerned about the revenue generated by the crack business. He said, "You know, right? Nobody thinks it's good to sell, but they've seen [that] the trade makes money. You have to think like a company too."

### Crack Consumption and Territorial Order in the 2000s

Crack became available in Rio in the early 2000s at a moment when the CV was weakened and there was a glut in supply (see also Gay, this volume). At this time, the CV made commercial agreements with the PCC after it had disrupted long-standing supply agreements and alliances.[15] Michel Misse sums this up, writing:

> The weakening of the main faction of the CV, at the time that the PCC emerged and [was] getting stronger in São Paulo, allowed agreements to be established between these networks, but very little is known about their extension. One of the indicators that this link exists is the entry of crack into Rio de Janeiro, which the CV had hitherto avoided when it was stronger. Another indicator of the weakening of the CV was the emergence of the ADA . . . , which intervened in the old and permanent dispute between the CV and the so-called Terceiro Comando [Third Command].[16] (Misse 2011)

From 2005 to 2006, public consumption of crack became more visible on Rio's streets (Rosales and Barnes 2011), and the figure of the *cracudo* ("crackhead") embodied the type of immoral and damaging drug use that neighborhood residents wanted to avoid (Brandão 2015; Veríssimo 2015). As Frúgoli and Cavalcanti noted: "the sale and consumption of crack rapidly transformed the dynamics of trafficking in the areas in which it was established, generating a new structure for drug management and sales, but also daily efforts by the traffickers themselves to organize the spaces under their influence, in view of the new territorialities produced by the tensions between the movements and the [spatial] persistence of crack users" (Frúgoli and Cavalcanti 2013: 74).[17]

Thus, unlike São Paulo, where crack consumption is more evident in a central cracolândia, a situation that has existed there for more than twenty years, crack consumption in Rio de Janeiro has not yet territorially consolidated (Frúgoli and Cavalcanti 2013). The small-scale drug scenes, which do not exceed two hundred people, are only ever temporary and can be found in Rio's poorer neighborhoods and favelas. The users who are part of these scenes shift locality and reorganize themselves whenever they face a hostile reception.

### Growing Crack Visibility in the 2010s

Public outcry about crack use in Rio was pronounced when the media observed hundreds of drug users on and around the Avenida Brasil, a major artery running through the northern part of the city, as occurred most significantly between 2012 and 2013 ("Imagens mostram usuários" 2012; "Usuário de crack" 2012). Heightened concern over drug use was also linked to the fact that Rio was preparing to host several major sporting events, including the 2013 FIFA Confederations Cup, important portions of the 2014 World Cup, and the 2016 Olympics. The backdrop to these events included the implementation of the Pacifying Police Units (UPPs),[18] a militarized and repressive policing program focused on the state establishing public territorial control of some shantytowns, as well as some infrastructural and architectural investment in those same neighborhoods.

According to Frúgoli and Cavalcanti (2013), the military occupation of a favela such as the Complexo do Alemão, which occurred in December 2010, produced a surge in the number of crack users in the crack consumption spaces of Jacarezinho and Manguinhos, two favelas located near Maré and close to the Avenida Brasil. Nearly two years later, in October 2012, drug use in and around Avenida Brasil became visible as a result of the actions of the UPP, which weakened gang territorial control in those areas and also drove crack users out of the favelas.

Due to the fact that they were expelled from regions where the UPP program had been implemented, and given their tense relations with the traffickers, the drug users migrated to Avenida Brasil. By occupying such a public space, they became visible to the press, which was hungry for stories about Rio's underbelly. Displaced, the drug users initiated their "territorializing efforts" (Frúgoli and Cavalcanti 2013), camping out in flowerbeds on the Avenida Brasil and along its extensive embankments.[19] The visibility of drug users provoked an official response that included police incursions and the compulsory hospitalization of users (Marinho 2013).

The Residents' Association (a powerful local community group) in the favelas bordering Avenida Brasil, in collaboration with the CV, agreed that the users should leave Avenida Brasil and move to a less visible space located inside the Maré favela, in the hope that this would reduce police incursions and media attention. The corner where the drug users were taken was a former industrial area away from residential and commercial streets. Initially, the site consisted of no more than fifteen shacks made from tarpaulins stretched over wooden frames. The consumers, many of whom were not from Maré, stayed there during the day, but returned to the avenue at night because the site was located on the border between cv- and tcp-controlled territory. As such, it was the site of frequent violent conflicts between members of the opposing groups, and was particularly dangerous at night.

While conducting ethnographic fieldwork at the site in 2014 and 2015, I documented drug users' daily routines, including the precarious conditions in which they lived migrating between the "corner" by day and Avenida Brasil each night. The users faced another challenge with the arrival of the police Batalhão de Operações Especiais (Special Operations Battalion; bope) in March 2014[20] and, later, the army, both of which were part of an embryonic but never fully realized pacification process.

At first, users feared the presence of the bope and the military, and some left the neighborhood altogether. However, in response to negotiations between the Residents' Association and the ngo Redes da Maré, the military and the police did not harass the users. In fact, over time the security forces inadvertently promoted the local drug scene inasmuch as their presence caused a decrease in confrontations between cv and tcp, making the area safer for the users. The important point here, then, is that the state-led pacification actually reinforced the presence of crack users in this territory.

Throughout 2014, the improvised shacks gave way to more elaborate wooden structures, minimally furnished but with electricity powering small refrigerators, televisions, radios, and dvd players. Some crack users make their money from scavenging for aluminum cans and recyclable material, repairing electronics, acting as porters, sweeping the streets, and gardening. Some also engage in petty crime. While the local authorities put up with crack users, their position is by no means secure. The president of the Residents' Association told me that while all the bocas in Maré sell crack, "whenever the traffickers wish it, so the cracolândia will end." However, in the meantime the criminal factions turn a blind eye and allow it to continue.

The territorial persistence of drug users in the favela had some positive repercussions, including state-implemented basic health and welfare projects targeted at drug users. In addition, between January and July 2015 the Redes da Maré consolidated a range of ngos with the aim of assisting local drug users. In partnership with the Centro de Estudos da Segurança e Cidadania (Center for Security and Citizenship Studies; CESeC), the Núcleo Interdisciplinar de Ação Para a Cidadania of the Universidade Federal do Rio de Janeiro (Interdisciplinary Nucleus of Action and Citizenship;

NIAC/UFRJ), and with financial support from the Open Society Foundations (OSF), a team started to work at the site, initially researching the population and running activities including photo workshops and a movie club for drug users (see Redes da Maré and CESeC 2016). The census revealed that in 2015 there were about seventy permanent residents living in sixteen different shacks, the maximum allowed by the traffickers and Residents' Association. The president of the local Residents' Association had made clear that there was no possibility that the local drug scene would be allowed to expand, because it would be difficult to manage.

Public service providers, including health and social assistance agencies, agreed that the crack user population was now permanently resident and that they had not caused a major problem for the city or conflicts within Maré. Given the relatively "peaceful" and "controlled" management of the site, some public services were withdrawn. This provoked a reaction from NGO staff, who complained that city agencies were abandoning users in an effort to prioritize other, more politically "urgent" cases. Those who remain in the locale depend on the good will of the traffickers, whose territorial control has been resurgent as the UPP program has unwound after the 2016 Summer Olympics.

## CONCLUSIONS

This chapter has examined how the specific urban illicit market histories of Rio and São Paulo have shaped where and how drug consumers locate themselves within the urban landscape. Thus, this chapter coincides with Arias and Grisaffi's observation in the introduction to this volume about the limited attention paid to the broader drug commodity chain as it moves from production to consumption. My focus is on the moral economies of the local crack commerce, considering its effects on the sociability and spaces of consumption.

Starting from how the most visible cracolândia of the country, in São Paulo, was formed and moving to the "invisible" consumption sites of Rio de Janeiro (Hart, Sousa Silva, and Lemgruber 2014), we have seen two different urban and criminal histories, two possible commercial dynamics, and thus two different ways that crack consumption takes root in and defines territory. Both case studies reveal that the illegal drug trade produces and regulates user scenes in the city, but not in the same way.

The consolidation of this market in São Paulo is connected with the monopolization of the distribution and sale of drugs by a single criminal faction and how this organization manages the conflicts that the trade inevitably generates. Illicit markets are not necessarily violent. Mercantile and moral dynamics displace problematic users from various locations within the city, leading to the concentration of drug users in specific "hot spots." Downtown São Paulo, in this respect, is the final destination for thousands of people, and because of this it becomes a significant problem for government. Repressive and punitive policies are implemented, ignoring the reasons why people ended up there in the first place. Such approaches are shortsighted; more state repression will only increase the number of crack users in prisons that, as we have seen, are governed by the PCC. Thus, over time, this state strategy has strengthened the criminal organization by providing new recruits.

The Rio de Janeiro case presents a different situation, in which state actions have displaced drug users to many different parts of the city—often in highly visible locales. This displacement becomes a problem for the state and for the criminal organizations. The gang's actions seek to contain drug users inside the favela's territory to reduce public attention and resulting police incursions. This strategy benefits not only competing illegal armed actors who benefit from selling drugs in the areas where they operate, but also the state since, in a city that has been a focus of major international events, it hides the problem from view. As a result, the media, tourists, the international press, and the wealthy—in sum, people who matter to government—do not see the consumption sites and, as a result, there is little pressure on the government to deal with the causes and consequences of the rising tide of drug use. The activities of drug factions and state responses shift, rather than resolve, the problem of drug consumption in each city, and in so doing continually reconfigure urban spaces in accord with the concerns of the criminal groups operating in those spaces.

This chapter fits with the broader themes of this book by showing how the drug trade is not simply driven by crude economic consideration. If crack sales generate a great deal of profit, it also is balanced by moral considerations. Criminal organizations carefully manage (problematic) drug users, and prioritize relations with neighborhood committees and agents of the state (including the police and local government officials) over and above profit maximization. Moreover, drug trafficking organizations in both Rio and São Paulo view aspects of the crack trade as damaging—and something that they do not want on their doorstep. The decisions that criminal organizations make regarding the distribution of drugs, including the kind of drugs they are prepared to market—and to whom—have implications not just for the areas where they hold sway, but for the city as a whole. In this commerce, moral economies have spatial consequences.

The crack trade is not the same everywhere, and it does not easily follow the capitalist logic of the market. If policy makers are ever to come up with effective strategies to help problematic drug users and stem the negative impacts of the crack trade, it is essential they understand the logic by which criminal organizations operate—the kinds of judgments they make and their impact on vulnerable consumers.

## NOTES

I thank the Drugs, Security and Democracy Fellowship for funding the Rio de Janeiro–São Paulo comparative research between 2014 and 2015. Concerning this paper, I thank the critical comments made by Gabriel Feltran, Carolina Grillo, and by the organizers of this volume, Desmond Arias and Thomas Grisaffi.

1 To read in more detail on how differences among organizations manifest in retail drug activities, see Hirata and Grillo (2017).
2 Growing police activity against gangs ahead of the 2014 World Cup and the 2016 Summer Olympics led to crack users appearing in downtown areas when they were temporarily forced out of the favelas by police actions.
3 See "Jovem viciado em crack é morto pela PM: Polícia diz que S.O.P., 17, trocou tiros com soldados; colegas de São Mateus, o 'bronx paulistano,' negam tiroteio," *Folha de São Paulo*, June 25, 1992 (my emphasis).
4 Translated by author. In the original: "Vamos a São Mateus, . . . um dos primeiros 'portos seguros' do crack em São Paulo. . . . Cerca de 600 mil pessoas moram neste bairro pobre da Zona Leste, uma caricatura dos becos do Bronx, em Nova York . . . Crianças e adolescentes usam drogas sentados na calçada, traficantes nas esquinas e nas imediações das escolas. Fácil acreditar que não podia haver cenário mais apropriado para os primeiros passos do crack em São Paulo" (Uchoa 1996: 34).
5 Translated by author. In the original: "a maioria do crack comercializado na área é preparado nas 'cozinhas', locais da região ou proximidade onde a mistura é feita numa escala maior, mais industrial. . . . Temos dados que indicam que muitas delas funcionam nas proximidades, ou seja, na própria área da cracolândia, o que indica que boa parte do crack vendido nesta área é também aí preparado. Segundo entrevistas com antigos funcionários do DENARC, até poucos anos atrás praticamente todo o crack consumido era fabricado na área. . . . Com o aumento da demanda, parte do crack já é fabricado fora da área."
6 Translated by author. In the original: "O desemprego estrutural que chegou a 22% na região Metropolitana de São Paulo no final dos anos 1990, a informalização

dos mercados e as altíssimas taxas de lucro das atividades ilegais elevaram os índices de criminalidade violenta. O controle desses mercados emergentes gerava corrida armamentista e uma guerra aberta nas periferias da cidade. 'Muita mãe chorou' nas madrugadas de saguões de hospitais, Institutos Médico-Legais e cemitérios. Uma geração traz ainda hoje as marcas desse período, talvez por ainda muito tempo. . . . Nas periferias é comum que os anos 1990 . . . sejam lembrados como 'a época das guerras'" (Feltran 2012: 238–39).

7 In October 1992, to contain a rebellion, military police invaded the Carandiru prison and killed 111 people (official figures). To read more about the subject and its current developments, see Machado and Machado (2015).

8 Author's translation; in the original: "o encarceramento retirava das ruas meninos em guerra entre si e os devolvia, alguns anos depois, socializados numa lógica de paz interna."

9 Author's translation, in the original: "a economia da prostituição entrava em declínio e o comércio de drogas começava lentamente a ganhar alguma referência como negócio criminal no plano da cidade, difundindo-se em múltiplos territórios e agenciamentos."

10 The fractionation of the drug is more feasible in the drug retail market of Rio de Janeiro than in São Paulo, due to important differences in their territorializations. For more details about this, read the excellent article by Hirata and Grillo (2017), which compares drug retailing activities in the two cities. For the purposes of this text, I indicate that what was seen in cracolândia was completely different from the rest of the city of São Paulo.

11 Translated by author; in the original: "mercados mais competitivos e fragmentados," no qual "revendedores individuais autônomos, vivendo à beira da extinção, [operam] com margens de lucro ínfimas e incapazes de gerar qualquer superávit."

12 As well noted by Lessing (2008: 59), "At this historic moment, most Brazilian cities did not offer international drug dealers large enough criminal organizations with infrastructure capable of establishing a hierarchical distribution network (most of the time they operated with the sale to innumerable medium distributors that, in their turn, supplied fragmented local markets). The CV, on the contrary, seems to have deliberately sought out international traffickers, presenting itself as a capillary criminal organization with a ready-made distribution network." For Lessing, the domination of the penitentiary system was central to this strengthening.

13 Translated by author; in the original: "não foi a demanda, mas a enorme oferta e a redução dos preços a varejo."

14 *Boca* is a term for a drug selling point. Note the contrast to the term *biqueira*, which usually refers specifically to the crack selling points. For a better description of the boca, see Grillo (2013: 80–94).

15 It was in the early 2000s, precisely in 2001, that there occurred what was known as the "Massacre of Captain Bado" (on the Brazil-Paraguay border),

when trafficker Fernandinho Beira-Mar ordered the deaths of João Morel and his sons, João being Beira-Mar's former distributor and ally. This is an important fact in understanding the change in the drug trade agreements in Rio, as well as the possible but still little studied CV–CCP relationship. In June 2016, the execution of Jorge Rafaat on this same frontier started the rumor of the breakup of the CV–CCP relationship and, therefore, the beginning of new disputes.

16  Translated by author. In the original: "O enfraquecimento da principal facção, o CV, na época em que surgia e se fortalecia em São Paulo o PCC permitiu que acordos se estabelecessem entre essas redes, mas sabe-se muito pouco sobre sua extensão. Um dos indicadores de que existe essa ligação é a entrada do crack no Rio de Janeiro, sempre evitada pelo CV quando este estava fortalecido. Outro indicador do enfraquecimento do CV foi o surgimento da ADA (Amigos dos Amigos), que se interpôs na antiga e permanente disputa entre o CV e o chamado Terceiro Comando." The Terceiro Comando was an earlier version of the Terceiro Comando Puro.

17  Translated by author. In the original: "a venda e o consumo de crack rapidamente transformaram as próprias dinâmicas do tráfico nas áreas em que se instauraram, gerando uma nova estrutura de gestão e de vendas da droga, mas também esforços cotidianos do próprio tráfico na ordenação dos espaços sob a sua influência, tendo em vista as novas territorialidades produzidas pelas tensões entre os fluxos e as permanências dos usuários de crack."

18  For critical analysis of UPPs, see Machado da Silva (2010); Barbosa (2012); and the dossier "Unidades de Polícia Pacificadora—CEVIS," organized by Machado da Silva and Leite (2014, 2015). The most consistent and long-lasting work on UPPs is that of Palloma Menezes (2015).

19  It is important to note, therefore, that the research does not extend to the entire Maré, considered the largest complex of favelas in Rio de Janeiro (sixteen), with a population of approximately 130,000 inhabitants. One resident once warned me that "Maré is an invention for outsiders; people who live here say that they are from Parque União, Nova Holanda, Baixa do Sapateiro."

20  An insightful description of this occupation can be read in Barnes (2014).

**REFERENCES**

Arias, Enrique Desmond. 2006. "The Dynamics of Criminal Governance: Networks and Social Order in Rio de Janeiro." *Journal of Latin American Studies* 38, no. 2: 293–325.

Arias, Enrique Desmond, and Nicholas Barnes. 2017. "Crime and Plural Orders in Rio de Janeiro, Brazil." *Current Sociology* 63, no. 3: 448–65.

Arias, Enrique Desmond, and Daniel Goldstein, eds. 2010. *Violent Democracies in Latin America*. Durham, NC: Duke University Press.

Auyero, Javier. 2000. "Hyper-Shantytown: Neo-Liberal Violence(s) in the Argentine Slum." *Ethnography* 1, no. 1: 93–116.

Auyero, Javier, Philippe Bourgois, and Nancy Scheper-Hughes, eds. 2015. *Violence at the Urban Margins*. Oxford: Oxford University Press.

Auyero, Javier, and Katherine Sobering. 2017. "Violence, the State, and the Poor: A View from the South." *Sociological Forum* 32: 1018–31.

Barbosa, Antônio Rafael. 1998. *Um abraço para todos os amigos: Algumas considerações sobre o tráfico de drogas no Rio de Janeiro*. Niterói: EDUFF.

Barbosa, Antônio Rafael. 2012. "Considerações introdutórias sobre territorialidade e mercado na conformação das Unidades de Polícia Pacificadora no Rio de Janeiro." *Revista Brasileira de Segurança Pública* 6, no. 2: 256–65.

Barnes, Nicholas. 2014. "Rio de Janeiro's BOPE and Police Pacification: Fear and Intimidation in Complexo da Maré." *Anthropoliteia*, June 6. http://anthropoliteia.net/2014/06/06/rio-de-janeiros-bope-and-police-pacification-fear-and-intimidation-in-complexo-da-mare/.

Biondi, Karina. 2011. "Consumo de drogas na Política do PCC." *Coletivo DAR*, March 14. https://www.academia.edu/5666346/Consumo_de_drogas_na_pol%C3%ADtica_do_PCC.

Biondi, Karina. 2016. *Sharing This Walk: An Ethnography of Prison Life and the PCC in Brazil*. Chapel Hill: University of North Carolina Press.

Brandão, Beatriz. 2015. "Usos do crack na cidade: Antropologizando sinais do corpo." *Anais da V Reunião Equatorial de Antropologia*. Maceió: Edufal.

Caldeira, Teresa. 2000. *City of Walls: Crime, Segregation and Citizenship in São Paulo*. Berkeley: University of California Press.

Caldeira, Teresa, and James Holston. 1999. "Democracy and Violence in Brazil." *Comparative Studies in Society and History* 41, no. 4: 691–729.

"Crack é vendido na região." 1991. *Folha de São Paulo*, June 3.

"Epidemia de crack atinge dois milhões e coloca Brasil no topo do ranking de consumo da droga." 2015. *Noticias R7*, September 22. Accessed January 2, 2019. https://noticias.r7.com/saude/epidemia-de-crack-atinge-dois-milhoes-e-coloca-brasil-no-topo-do-ranking-de-consumo-da-droga-29052017.

Feltran, Gabriel. 2012. "Crime que produz governo, governo que produz crime." *Revista Brasileira de Segurança Pública* 6, no. 2: 232–55.

Fiocruz. 2014. "Pesquisa Nacional sobre o uso de crack: Quem são os usuários de crack e/ou similares do Brasil? Quantos são nas capitais brasileiras?" Edited by Francisco Inácio Bastos and Neilane Bertoni. Rio de Janeiro: Editora ICICT/FIOCRUZ.

Forero, Juan. 2012. "Epidemia de crack no Brasil lembra os EUA." *O Estado de Sao Paulo*, December 28. Accessed January 2, 2019. https://sao-paulo.estadao.com.br/noticias/geral,epidemia-de-crack-no-brasil-lembra-os-eua-imp-,978290.

Freire, Aluizio. 2010. "Epidemia de crack está fora de controle, adverte especialista." *Globo.com*, June 8. http://g1.globo.com/rio-de-janeiro/noticia/2010/06/epidemia-de-crack-esta-fora-de-controle-adverte-especialista.html.

Frúgoli, Heitor, Jr., and Mariana Cavalcanti. 2013. "Territorialidades da(s) cracolândia(s) em São Paulo e Rio de Janeiro." *Anuário Antropológico/2012* 38, no. 2.

Gonzalez de la Rocha, Mercedes, Janice Perlman, Helen Safa, Elizabeth Jelin, Bryan Roberts, and Peter Ward. 2004. "From the Marginality of the 1960s to the 'New Poverty' of Today: A LARR Research Forum." *Latin American Research Review* 39, no. 1: 184–203.

Grillo, Carolina C. 2013. "Coisas da vida no crime: Tráfico e roubo em favelas cariocas." PhD diss., Instituto de Filosofia e Ciências Sociais, Rio de Janeiro.

Hart, Carl, Eliana Sousa Silva, and Julita Lemgruber. 2014. "Favelas e cracolândias que ninguém vê." *O Globo*, June 7. https://oglobo.globo.com/opiniao/favelas-cracolandias-que-ninguem-ve-12751986.

Hirata, Daniel, and Carolina Grillo. 2017. "Sintonia e Amizade entre patrões e donos de morro: Perspectivas comparativas entre o comércio varejista de drogas em São Paulo e no Rio de Janeiro." *Tempo Social* 29, no. 2: 75–98.

Holston, James, ed. 1999. *Cities and Citizenship*. Durham, NC: Duke University Press.

Hunter, Wendy, and Timothy Power. 2019. "Bolsonaro and Brazil's Illiberal Backlash." *Journal of Democracy* 30, no. 1: 68–82.

"Imagens mostram usuários de crack às margens da Avenida Brasil, no Rio." 2012. *Globo.com*, December 13. http://g1.globo.com/rio-de-janeiro/noticia/2012/12/imagens-mostram-usuarios-de-crack-margens-da-avenida-brasil-no-rio.html.

"Jovem viciado em crack é morto pela PM." 1992. *Folha de São Paulo*, June 25.

Koonings, Kees, and Dirk Kruijt, eds. 1999. *Societies of Fear: The Legacy of Civil War, Violence and Terror in Latin America*. London: Zed.

Koonings, Kees, and Dirk Kruijt, eds. 2007. *Fractured Cities: Social Exclusion, Urban Violence and Contested Spaces in Latin America*. London: Zed.

Laranjeira, Ronaldo. 2016. "Crack: Como acabar com essa epidemia que devasta o país." *Veja*, September 23. https://veja.abril.com.br/blog/letra-de-medico/crack-como-acabar-com-essa-epidemia-que-devasta-o-pais/.

Lessing, Benjamin. 2008. "As facções cariocas em perspectiva comparativa." *Revista Novos Estudos* 80: 43–62.

Machado, Maira, and Marta Machado, eds. 2015. *Carandiru não é coisa do passado: Um balanço sobre os processos, as instituições e as narrativas 23 anos depois*. São Paulo: FGV, Direito.

Machado da Silva, Luís Antonio. 2010. "Afinal, qual é a das UPPs?" *Observatório das Metropóles*, March. http://www.observatoriodasmetropoles.ufrj.br/artigo_machado_UPPs.pdf.

Machado da Silva, Luís Antonio, and Marcia Leite, eds. 2014. "Dossiê Unidades de Polícia Pacificadora—CEVIS." *Revista Dilemas* 7, no. 4.

Machado da Silva, Luís Antonio, and Marcia Leite, eds. 2015. "Dossiê Unidades de Polícia Pacificadora—CEVIS." *Revista Dilemas* 8, no. 1.

Mallart, Fábio, and Taniele Rui. 2017. "Cadeia ping-pong: Entre o dentro e o fora das muralhas." *Ponto Urbe* 21. https://doi.org/10.4000/pontourbe.3620.

Manso, Bruno Paes. 2012. "Crescimento e queda dos homicídios em São Paulo entre 1960 e 2012." PhD diss., University of São Paulo.

Marinho, Isabela. 2013. "Prefeitura faz internação involuntária de 29 adultos usuários de crack no RJ." *Globo.com*, February 19. http://g1.globo.com/rio -de-janeiro/noticia/2013/02/prefeitura-faz-internacao-compulsoria-de -adultos-usuarios-de-crack-no-rio.html.

Menezes, Palloma. 2015. "Entre o 'fogo cruzado' e o 'campo minado': Uma etno-grafia do processo de 'pacificação' de favelas cariocas." PhD diss., Instituto de Estudos Sociais e Políticos da Universidade do Estado do Rio de Janeiro.

Minguardi, Guaraci, and Sandra Goulart. 2001. "As drogas ilícitas em São Paulo: O caso da cracolândia." *Revista do ILANUD* (São Paulo) 15.

Misse, Michel. 2003. "O Movimento: A constituição e reprodução das redes do mercado informal ilegal de drogas a varejo no Rio de Janeiro e seus efeitos de violência." In *Drogas e pós modernidade*, vol. 2, edited by Marcos Baptista, Marcelo Santos Cruz, and Regina Matias, 147–56. Rio de Janeiro: EDUERJ.

Misse, Michel. 2011. "Os rearranjos de poder no Rio de Janeiro." *Le Monde Diplo-matique Brasil*, July 1.

Park, Robert. 1915. "The City: Suggestions for the Investigation of Human Behav-ior in the City Environment." *American Journal of Sociology* 20, no. 5: 577–612.

Perlman, Janice. 2010. *Favela: Four Decades of Living on the Edge in Rio de Janeiro.* Oxford: Oxford University Press.

"PM afirma ter recapturado 2 dos fugitivos." 1996. *Folha de São Paulo*, May 14. Ac-cessed June 2014. http://www1.folha.uol.com.br/fsp/1996/5/14/cotidiano/23 .html.

"Polícia reforça combate a traficantes." 1995. *O Estado de São Paulo*, August 7.

Portes, Alejandro, and B. R. Roberts. 2005. "The Free-Market City: Latin Ameri-can Urbanization in the Years of the Neoliberal Experiment." *Studies in Comparative International Development* 40, no. 1: 43–82.

Redes da Maré and CESeC. 2016. "Meu nome não é cracudo: A cena aberta de consumo de drogas da rua Flavia Farnese, na Maré, Rio de Janeiro." *Boletim Segurança e Cidadania* (Rio de Janeiro) 22 (March).

Reinarman, Craig, and Harry Levine. 1997. "The Crack Attack: Politics and Media in the Crack Scare." In *Crack in America: Demon Drugs and Social Justice*, edited by Craig Reinarman and Harry Levine. Berkeley: University of California Press.

Richard, Ivan. 2015. "Governo investiu em 4 anos R$3,6 bilhões no combate às drogas, diz Senado." *EBC*, April 23. http://www.ebc.com.br/noticias/2015/04 /governo-investiu-em-quatro-anos-r-36-bilhoes-no-combate-drogas-diz -senad.

Rodgers, Dennis. 2004. "Disembedding the City: Crime, Insecurity and Spatial Organisation in Managua, Nicaragua." *Environment and Urbanization* 16, no. 2: 113–24.

Rodgers, Dennis, Jo Beall, and Ravi Kanbur, eds. 2012. *Latin American Urban Development into the 21st Century: Towards a Renewed Perspective on the City.* Basingstoke, UK: Palgrave Macmillan.

Rosales, Kristina, and Taylor Barnes. 2011. "New Jack Rio." *Foreign Policy*, September 14. Accessed March 11, 2016. http://foreignpolicy.com/2011/09/14/new -jack-rio/.

Ruggiero, Vicenzo, and Nigel South. 1997. "The Late Modern City as a Bazaar: Drug Market, Illegal Enterprise and the Barricades." *British Journal of Sociology* 48, no. 1: 54–70.

Rui, Taniele. 2013. "Fronteiras, espaços e usos do crack." In *Sobre Periferias: Novos conflitos no Brasil Contemporân*, edited by Neiva Vieira da Cunha and Gabriel de Santis Feltran. Rio de Janeiro: Lamparina/FAPERJ.

Rui, Taniele. 2014. *Nas tramas do crack: Etnografia da abjeção.* São Paulo: Editora Terceiro Nome.

Rui, Taniele. 2016. "Fluxos de uma territorialidade: Duas décadas de 'cracolândia' (1995–2014)." In *Pluralidade Urbana em São Paulo: Vulnerabilidade, marginalidade, ativismos sociais*, edited by Lucio Kowarick and Heitor Frúgoli Jr. São Paulo: Editora 34.

Salles, João, dir. 1999. *Notícias de uma guerra particular.* Rio de Janeiro: VideoFilmes.

Teixeira, Alessandra. 2012. "Economias criminais urbanas e gestão dos ilegalismos na cidade de São Paulo." Paper presented at the 36th meeting of ANPOCS.

Uchoa, Marcos. 1996. *Crack: O caminho das pedras.* São Paulo: Editora Ática.

"Usuário de crack morre atropelado na Avenida Brasil, no Rio." 2012. *Globo.com*, November 20. Accessed January 2019. http://g1.globo.com/rio-de-janeiro /noticia/2012/11/usuario-de-crack-morre-atropelado-na-avenida-brasil-no -rio.html.

Veríssimo, Marcos. 2015. "Quem são os 'cracudos'? Apontamentos para o estudo antropológico de um 'problema social.'" *Dilemas: Revista de Estudos de Conflito e Controle Social* 8, no. 2.

Wacquant, Loïc. 2003. "Toward a Dictatorship over the Poor? Notes on the Penalization of Poverty in Brazil." *Punishment and Society* 5, no. 2: 197–205.

Wacquant, Loïc. 2008. "The Militarization of Urban Marginality: Lessons from the Brazilian Metropolis." *International Political Sociology* 2, no. 1: 56–74.

PHILIPPE BOURGOIS, LAURIE KAIN HART,
GEORGE KARANDINOS, AND
FERNANDO MONTERO

# 10 THE VIOLENCE OF THE AMERICAN DREAM IN THE SEGREGATED US INNER-CITY NARCOTICS MARKETS OF THE PUERTO RICAN COLONIAL DIASPORA

Raffy, the *bichote* [Puerto Rican Spanglish double entendre for "big shot"/"drug boss"/large phallus] is out on the corner tonight and invites Tito and me to sit next to him on the stoop of an abandoned row home. Tito is Raffy's "caseworker," the local term for a bichote's second-in-command, who is responsible for managing the shifts of sellers and lookouts on a drug corner. Soon we are surrounded by half-a-dozen of his off-and-on-duty heroin and cocaine sellers, wannabe sellers, and teenage and pre-teenage bored kids. They are all eager—like me—to be around the big shot boss. When he shows up on the block, Raffy becomes the charismatic nexus for action, money, power, potential, and risk. Perhaps most importantly, he is also the only provider of local employment in this desolate, almost all Puerto Rican, formerly industrial inner city neighborhood.

A police car cruises slowly down the block. We tense up and avoid eye contact while simultaneously trying to look bored and indifferent. The passenger-side officer rolls down his window and yells out, "Betta get off the block right now fatass!" Raffy jumps to his feet, muttering "dickhead!" His riposte—meant for our ears only—is, however, a little too loud. The officer jumps out of the car, flushes red, and slaps his baton in his palm. "I heard that, fatass. Get the fuck outta here! A buncha' people I locked up been telling me about you. His voice rises to a shout: "Go home, bitch . . . right now!" Residents of the block's cramped two-story row homes have raised their windows and some are cautiously stepping out onto their stoops to watch the volatile spectacle of a police raid at sunset.

Raffy snaps his mouth shut, spins around, and obediently starts walking away from the officer. I hold my breath, hoping the escalation will defuse, but after only a few steps, Raffy stops. A grin spreads across his face, and he slowly raises his fists above his head, pumping them in a boxer's victory salute. He is evoking the character of Rocky Balboa, Philadelphia's beloved working class Italian-American movie icon whose billion-dollar series of eight-plus blockbuster films spanning the 1970s through the late 2010s was set and filmed in this very same neighborhood as it transitioned from all white to nearly all Puerto Rican. The crowd of employees, wannabes, young admirers, and curious or concerned neighbors breaks into laughter and starts following Raffy as he continues walking—but in slow motion now—up the block. Fists raised above his head, Raffy defiantly pumps the Rocky salute in rhythm with each of his now deliberately slow steps.

The irate officer flushes a deeper shade of red and, spittle flying from his mouth, explodes in another slew of "fatasses" and "bitches." He reholsters his baton and, lunging forward to follow Raffy, raises his arms to pump his fists to match the challenge, sputtering, "I'll fight you right now. . . . Right now." His barely contained potbelly bursts through the bottom button of his uniform and spills onto his holster belt laden with pistol, taser, baton, walkie-talkie, and other bulky, standard, police officer public order peace-keeping accessories. The momentum of his belly and overloaded belt almost makes him fall on his face in the middle of the street, prompting roars of laughter from the growing crowd. Someone starts a chant: "Dickhead! Dickhead!"

I notice that the caseworker, Tito, is not joining the chanting. He is hanging back at the edge of the crowd, calling out to the youths in front of him: "Yo, stop! Shut up. You don't know what you're doin'. . . ." I'm impressed, Tito is clearly trying to de-escalate this confrontation that I fear will end in a brutal police beatdown on charges of resisting arrest or assaulting an officer.

The driver of the patrol car has now also reluctantly jumped out into the middle of the street. He is loudly calling for reinforcements into a walkie-talkie pinned to his left shoulder, making sure the crowd can hear the threat of potential disaster awaiting anyone out on the street right now. He glares and palm-slaps his baton for emphasis. The chanters, however, have turned their back on him to follow behind Raffy in a spontaneous parade of support. Still trying to catch up, his irate partner continues to pursue Raffy, fists raised in his awkward imitation of Raffy; but his taunts, "bitch . . . fatass," are drowned out by the crowd's now louder chorus of "dickheads."

Raffy reaches the corner first. The crowd assembles around him but backs away when the two officers catch up and barge through, batons raised, reaching for Raffy. The crowd then immediately recloses around the officers into a tighter circle and, disconcerted, the officers lower their batons. Several youths are holding up cell phones to video-record the confrontation. Raffy drops into a squat and goose-steps around the irate officer in a chicken dance, clucking and flapping his elbows, stunning all of us into a momentary awed silence. I can't believe what I am seeing. Raffy stands up suddenly and, maintaining a dignified, bichote-like demeanor in stark contrast to the sputtering officer, then announces in an authoritative voice, "Meet me in the gym. We'll put on gloves. . . . Not out here on the street like bitches."

Three patrol cars screech around the corner and six more officers jump out, batons in hand. The police/crowd stalemate has suddenly broken. The youths closest to the patrol cars jump backward and the calmer officer takes advantage of their retreat to grab Raffy's left elbow, twisting it expertly behind Raffy's back into handcuffs. He then yanks Raffy up off his feet by his hand-cuffed wrists, presumably trying to dislocate his shoulders, but Raffy adroitly uses the momentum to dive forward through the open back door of the patrol car awaiting his arrest. He ducks his head just in time under the doorframe and avoids a blow to his head but lands face down on the backseat. Gasping for breath, he squirms upright in the seat with his handcuffed arms tightly pinned behind him and manages to regain his composure. In fact, still playing to the crowd, Raffy opens his mouth widely in what looks like a full-throated, full belly laugh, but we cannot hear him because another officer has already slammed the door shut, regained the driver's seat, and revved the motor.

The crowd's solidarity, the plethora of cell phones videoing, and Raffy's charismatic agility saved him from the standard on-the-spot retaliatory outcomes of such confrontational arrests [e.g., sprained handcuffed wrists, a dislocated shoulder, a concussed head, fractured ribs, multiple tazerings, or just another routine black-and-blue, tooth-splintering inner-city police beatdown]—if not a deadly blaze of bullets.

The irate officer is on a roll now, and lunges after Wiwi, a sixteen-year-old wheelchair-bound hustler who makes the mistake of trying to rush to his home across the street. Wiwi has a juvenile sunset "curfew condition" imposed on him from an arrest earlier in the week and the moon has already risen overhead in the now pitch-black sky. The officer grabs the right handle of Wiwi's wheelchair and drags him to the far side of the patrol car as another officer flings open the rear door. He tries to throw the disabled adolescent directly from his wheelchair into the back seat next to Raffy, but Wiwi is wearing a seatbelt and the entire chair lifts into the air. Both the officer and the disabled adolescent curfew violator fall backward on the pavement.

Aghast, none of us laugh—even the "dickheads" chorus falls silent. Several adult onlookers have the courage to raise their voices in protest, "Nah nah, Officer! He ain't doin' nothin'. He's just goin' home. The young 'bol' [Philadelphia slang for young man] lives right here [pointing to a house across the street]." The cop yells back, "I got every right to arrest him! I got him with bundles [wholesale packets of drugs prepackaged for retail sale] just last week." Wiwi adds his teenager's cracking voice to the melee, "You got no right to arrest me in front of my own house." The officer laughs, "You cried like a little bitch in your cell last week. You gonna cry again now?" Sixteen-year-old Wiwi has, indeed, burst into flowing tears of rage and frustration.

Wiwi's mother has rushed out of her house and is pushing through the crowd, asking in a surprisingly calm but loud voice, "What seems to be the problem, Officer?" Without pausing for a response, she turns to Wiwi, raises her hand as if to slap him, but instead yells, "*Callate, hijo* [shut up, son]." Her motherly disciplinary intervention appears to temporarily pacify the irate officer.

Wiwi, obviously mortified, has broken into sobs. He undoes his seatbelt and tries to throw himself from his chair directly into the back of the open patrol car door next to Raffy. He shouts hoarsely, "Okay, okay, arrest me, dickheads. My lawyer's gonna. . . ." His arms, however, are not strong enough and his wheelchair tips over. His mother catches him just in time, jams him back down behind his seatbelt, and wheels him home rapidly.

Two more patrol cars skid to a stop and we disperse onto stoops and inside houses. The police, however, make no more arrests. Instead, they rapidly cram back into their vehicles and screech off, with Raffy, in a stench of burnt rubber.

I am standing next to Tito, the young caseworker, and hear him making multiple urgent phone calls to "re-up product." Sweating and barking out orders, he announces with bichote-style authority, "We openin' back up." This is his exciting break, a chance to rise in the "food chain," as he later explains it to us. Anticipating that a district attorney prosecutor might throw the book at Raffy, Tito is hoping he can take over as interim bichote on this profitable block without having to pay rent, or fight for control.

Only minutes after the police have left, the usual stream of customers—most of them white—is already flowing again, cash in hand. Many are emaciated, limping, and covered in scabs and rags, conjuring images of concentration-camp survivors on a final death march. I hear a scrawny young white youth with a filthy bloodstained bandage wrapped around his forehead bargaining with Tito to exchange a "nine millimeter Glock" for "a bundle [fourteen ten-dollar packets] of dope [heroin] and a bundle of powder [cocaine] in the mornin'."

During a lull in the selling, one of the hottest-headed "dickhead" chanters, perhaps jealous of Tito's opportunistic commandeering of the corner, or maybe just hedging his bets, hoping to be hired by Tito's caseworker, raises his hand to slap Tito a high-five, bragging, "The cops was drawlin' [acting inappropriately]. We should'a beaten 'em up." This prompts an almost conventional businessman's rebuke from Tito about the stupidity of their having taunted the police, "Nah, nah! They gonna be on our ass now. Hittin' the block. It's gonna be hot. We won't even be able to smoke a blunt on this block no more."

The hothead ripostes, laughing: "Nah, they just angry at us 'cause we the outlaws and they can't be." Tito cracks up laughing too and fist-bumps the hothead's still hanging high five. A white customer interrupts them in an impatient rush for his fix and they go right back to the mundane business of retail drug sales, exchanging packets, play-boxing, counting money, replenishing from the stash, periodically pausing to roll blunts and play-box, releasing the tension and the boredom. Clouds of marijuana waft into the chill of the late autumn night. Dollars, dope, and powder are passing dizzyingly fast hand to hand, and there are no police sirens or police helicopter motors audible, no searchlights or rooftop strobe lightbars in sight. The night shift is back in full gear.

To our surprise, a few days after the police confrontation described in this field note, a sympathetic judge dismissed the bogus assault charges filed against Raffy by the wannabe-Rocky officer. Raffy immediately returned to the block and took back control of sales from his caseworker Tito. To our further surprise, he started hanging out even more conspicuously, and generously treating his sellers, us, and the other neighbors to sodas and hoagies [mid-Atlantic slang for overstuffed lunchmeat sandwich roll]. He also deepened his relationship to us, agreeing to tape-record his life history.

Tito strategically quit as Raffy's second-in-command because the humiliated police were raiding nearly every day and sometimes several times a day. We followed his example, staying inside more and peering cautiously through the window of the subdivided row-home apartment we rented. All members of our ethnographic team fit the profiles of the kind of people the narcotics teams routinely targeted in their dragnets. Indeed, within two weeks, Raffy was arrested on narcotics charges two more times and a notoriously draconian judge sentenced him to a completely unanticipated sentence of twelve and a half to twenty-five years in prison on a probation-violation technicality (no option for a jury trial), because of an outstanding drug sales conviction, compounding this with the maximum sentences for each of the two new arrests, "stacking" [adding] them consecutively rather than overlapping them "concurrently." We were rapidly forced to learn the inscrutably complex machinations of the Philadelphia courts.

Raising the stakes even higher, another former bichote, Panama Red, burst onto the scene. Newly released from prison, he had a reputation for "liking to play with guns." Everyone anticipated that Panama Red would try to take over direct control over the block, and that, as an elderly grandmother warned Fernando and George, "a body is going to fall." Astutely, Panama Red stepped back from direct supervision, and rented out the corner for $5,000 a week to a subcontractor, yet another ambitious younger wannabe-bichote from the block who quickly seized the opportunity, but was arrested within a few months in an FBI sting facilitated by a jilted girlfriend while fetching a kilo of cocaine from Miami. We never heard from him again; rumors circulated that he had fled just in time to Puerto Rico and set up a barber shop with his remaining capital.

The tempo of arrests inexplicably slowed down, as it always did in the mysterious ebbs and flows of the incompetent offensives of inner-city police narcotics patrol teams. In Philadelphia, as in many large cities across the United States, narcotics units have to be purposefully rotated out of neighborhoods every few weeks or months to prevent the inevitable institutionalization of corruption. The easy money and high profits associated with illegal drugs and arbitrary discretionary power of officers blur the boundary between criminal perpetrator and law enforcement agent. Philadelphia newspapers documented hundreds of examples of egregious police corruption and brutality scandals during our core fieldwork years, 2007–2021. The coverage includes a Pulitzer Prize–winning series on a notorious narcotics team in our micro-neighborhood that combined theft of legal storekeepers as well as street sellers with sexual abuse (Denvir 2013; Ruderman and Laker 2015). Corruption extended to the highest levels of criminal justice in the city. In 2017, Philadelphia's head district attorney, Seth Williams, was indicted on corruption and bribery charges (Roebuck 2017). In 2019, the police commissioner, Richard Ross, who was hired to reform abuses in the department, was forced to resign for sexually harassing an officer (Marin et al. 2019). During those same years, multiple beat level police officers—sometimes several dozen at a time—were charged with crimes and abuses (Bender and Gambacorta 2019).

Since its origin in the 1800s the Philadelphia Police Department has been systemically unable to rid itself of corruption and scandal and has failed to hold officers accountable, even when caught flagrantly in illegal acts (Pennsylvania Crime Commission 1974; Green-Ceisler 2003). The department's multiple class-action suits and federal consent decrees and attempts to hire reformist police commissioners since at least the 1970s have not remediated the problem. Philadelphia's Home-Rule Charter—which itself was an attempt to give crucial City agencies autonomy from abusive manipulation by the machine politics plaguing most US big cities—gives the police union ("Fraternal Order of Police"), de facto veto power over firings and sanctions through arbitration processes. Union-controlled arbiters routinely reinstate officers convicted of crimes. Ironically, arbiters even order the city to reimburse delinquent guilty officers for the "theoretical overtime" they "hypothetically lost" during the months or years they were removed from desk duty or fired while they were on trial or under arbitration review (Denvir 2014; Ruderman and Laker 2011).

Systemic police corruption and abuse is good for the retail level narcotics industry. In 2008 when Panama Red's interim wannabe-bichote subcontractor/renter was arrested, narcotics units' arrests ceased on the block because the officers were rotated to another poor neighborhood of the city. Panama Red judged it safe enough for him to take back direct control of sales on the block and extend shift hours, hiring two new caseworkers: one for a 12-hour day shift and the other for a 12-hour graveyard shift. Over the next eighteen months, Panama Red managed to keep the block open 24/7 in a flagrant cat-and-rooster dance with the police, who intermittently continued to raid but focused primarily on arresting the addicted customers and the lowest-level sellers. They rarely even managed to locate the temporary "stashes" where the sellers on duty temporarily hide their shift's wholesale supply of heroin and/or cocaine prepackaged for retail sales.

### SCRAMBLING FOR UPWARD MOBILITY ON THE CORNER

We were initially baffled by Raffy's provocative response to the abusive police officer on the night of his arrest. In fact, it took us years to unravel the "everyday emergencies" (transporting philosopher Walter Benjamin's phrase from the Nazi era to the contemporary US inner city) of violence and arrests besetting our neighborhood (Taussig 2014). Commonsensically, seasoned bichotes usually avoid spending time at their retail sales points lest they attract police attention or over-expose themselves to attacks by rivals. Consequently, we had been even more surprised when Raffy insisted on continuing to hang out so visibly at his sales spot, despite the likelihood of police revenge after his release by the sympathetic judge. At the time we did not yet understand the economic, cultural, and personal stakes propelling Raffy to take such spectacular risks and be so generous and outgoing to us and so many of the neighbors. We came to understand that Raffy's performative visibility and risk taking was actually a desperate attempt to retain his fragile bid to control this valuable territory through his charismatic reputation in the moral economy. He was under violent siege, not only by Panama Red, who ultimately did seize control, but also by his estranged business partner, Lucas, who had formerly been his primary cocaine supplier, and also lived on the block.

We also did not yet fully understand the importance to narcotics profits—or the complexity—of the Philadelphia slang term *rider*. Riders provide violent backup for one another in times of conflict. A rider's reputation accrues from engaging in especially brutal violence performed in a culturally appropriate, dignified manner. Bichotes, caseworkers, and even entry-level hand-to-hand sellers cultivate obligations for mutually assistive violence among networks of riders as a protection against betrayal and victimization. We have referred to this as the "moral economy of violence," to communicate its crucial valence to pragmatic material/personal interests and his physical/emotional security in the absence of public state legal services and sanctions for mediating economic disputes peacefully (Karandinos et al. 2014). The ability to rapidly mobilize loyal, violent minions is most obviously the best way to enforce cash-only contracts in the multibillion-dollar narcotics industry. More subtly, it also intimidates potentially disgruntled neighbors, rivals, and jealous friends who might be tempted (or coerced) by the police to serve as informants.

Amid this generalized violence, however, the bichote must establish a *pax narcotica* (Bourgois and Hart 2016), because peace is good for business, and facilitates a steadier flow of retail customers. Peace also keeps a street corner under the radar screen of the police. The moral economy of violence, consequently, counterintuitively is transformed into a reputation for being able to "keep the peace" because the legitimation of violent hegemony ensures: 1) prompt payments of debts; 2) labor discipline; 3) product integrity; 4) cash flow, and 5) freedom from snitching and incarceration.

## FIELDWORK, THE NEIGHBORHOOD AND ITS NARCOTICS MARKETS
## IN THE HISTORICAL CONTEXT OF DEINDUSTRIALIZATION

Our impoverished block was a cash cow. On days when the police did not raid our block, one hundred "bundles" of heroin and forty of cocaine were sold per shift. Bundles usually consisted of fourteen ten-dollar retail packets of product. For heroin, this represented less than 0.003 grams of product. Cocaine packets varied more, because its pure form weighs more than heroin, as do many of its cuts, and it absorbs moisture more readily. Furthermore, cocaine wholesale markets appear to be more diversified and directly accessible to the island of Puerto Rico and Puerto Rican neighborhoods in the US Rust Belt, usually mediated by undocumented Dominican and Colombian suppliers higher up in the smuggling chains (Bourgois 2018; Contreras 2013; Rosenblum et al. 2014). Ultimately, on many—if not most—days on our block at least $14,000 worth of cash in untraceable ten-dollar bills was changing hands every twelve hours without a single dollar going missing. Our block had a decent reputation for drug potency and a higher Puerto Rican segregation-level than most other census tracts, but many dozens, if not hundreds of other blocks in Philadelphia's Puerto Rican-majority blocks had equally good (or better) reputations (Volk 2011). The whirlwind of drug boss arrests and successions described thus far occurred early in the long-term participant observation fieldwork project we carried out as a team in Philadelphia from the fall of 2007 through the summer of 2013 with frequent onsite follow-up fieldwork through 2015, and periodic interviews/ visits ongoing through the date of this publication. We had rented an apartment in the heart of the city's approximately three hundred square block Puerto Rican inner city, a zone of decaying subdivided two-story row homes clustered tightly around huge abandoned red-brick factories interspersed by vacant lots and piles of rubble. Two members of our ethnographic team (George Karandinos and Fernando Montero Castrillo) lived in the apartment, on a block with active drug sales, full-time (2008–13). We socialized with our neighbors, hanging out on stoops, in homes, and at the sales points. We accompanied arrestees through the criminal justice system, and visited them when they were incarcerated.

Referred to as "North Philadelphia" by local Puerto Ricans and African Americans and as "Kensington" by whites and the press, the neighborhood has hosted Philadelphia's most consistently active open-air narcotics markets since at least the 1980s (Richards 1994; Rosenblum et al. 2014), when Puerto Ricans had the bad luck of immigrating in search of factory employment at the height of deindustrialization. Instead of factory work they found themselves shunted into the burgeoning global narcotics industry. For over half a century, this end point in the global narcotics market has been serving low-cost, high-potency heroin and cocaine to primarily white customers from the four-state region of southern New Jersey, Delaware, Maryland, and Pennsylvania (Bourgois and Hart 2011; Rosenblum et al. 2014).

The larger neighborhood had been Philadelphia's nineteenth-century industrial heartland, and its infrastructure was devastated by public- and private services-sector abandonment, and an exponential rise in public investment in punitive policing and hyper-incarceration (Wacquant 2010). Manufacturing jobs decreased more than twelvefold between the early 1950s and the mid-2010s (US Bureau of Labor Statistics Database), and court sentences were dramatically lengthened (Gottschalk 2015; Alexander 2010). The streets around us were riddled with abandoned factories, decaying row homes, vacant lots, defunct railroad lines, and random piles of rubble and garbage. Throughout our fieldwork years, there were virtually no legal businesses offering any significant source of legal employment within ten blocks of our apartment, and almost half of the households in our census tract had annual incomes below the US federal poverty line. The multibillion-dollar global narcotics industry had flooded into this economic vacuum during the late 1980s, when the powder cocaine epidemic morphed into the infamous crack epidemic. Through the 1990s and 2000s the price of both heroin and cocaine dropped even lower, and their potencies continued to rise. In 2013–14, potency further spiked with the entry of fentanyl into the supply chain, wreaking havoc along its path. Our neighborhood became a national epicenter of the US overdose epidemic. Youth growing up on our block, unable to find legal jobs, found themselves selling opiates and cocaine in the shadows of the factories that used to employ their grandparents. The state's punitive response of law enforcement brutality and chronic hyper-incarceration further compounded the routinized occupational injuries of addiction and interpersonal violence that accompany illegal drug sales.

Drawing from several thousand pages of fieldwork notes and transcriptions of interviews, we are trying to make sense of the maelstrom of deadly violence engulfing the young men we befriended. We are interested in linking the intimate experience of violence in the US inner city to the larger political, economic, and historical forces that turn US inner cities into concrete killing fields. These forces include, most importantly, (1) neoliberal globalization and financialization that has dramatically increased income inequality, (2) narcotics monopoly profits that are artificially elevated by illegality, (3) a global arms industry that thrives on ineffective US gun control laws, and, most visibly, (4) the carceral mismanagement of racialized poverty and unemployment. What follows is an account of how these forces play out in the lives of two brothers, Tito (Raffy's caseworker in the opening field note) and Tito's little brother, Leo, as they both came of age on our block. From their perspective, they were ambitiously seizing the only "actually existing" opportunities for a sliver of the "American dream" in the segregated inner city into which they were born.

## CHURNING THROUGH CHRONIC INCARCERATION

Virtually every "hustler" who made "hand-to-hand" retail sales on the regular six- to twelve-hour shifts, and most caseworkers in the spatially enclaved economic niche we studied were arrested—often multiple times—within a few months of being hired. The police relied on racial profiling (customers = whites/sellers = Puerto Ricans) and primarily targeted hand-to-hand sellers and customers during their frequent raids. This maximized the number of low-level arrests with the least amount of effort, thereby increasing opportunities for officers to generate overtime pay as witnesses in multiple court appearances. The city's court and jail system were overwhelmed by this volume of nonviolent, low-level misdemeanor arrests (primarily "narcotics possession" and petty sales of ten-dollar packets of heroin or cocaine). The criminal justice system was incapable of following due process by bringing so many arrestees to a jury trial. Consequently, judges routinely temporarily released narcotics misdemeanants on low bails pending arraignment and prolonged plea bargaining arrangements. Police officers, in response, systematically overcharged misdemeanants with a litany of false or exaggerated felony accusations, enabling the District Attorney's prosecutors to offer a "reduced" plea bargain that carried shorter prison terms of two-to-four years, so long as arrestees waived their right to "trial."

Most corners in the neighborhood were controlled by a bichote who hired caseworkers who managed six- to twelve-hour hour shifts staffed by hand-to-hand sellers called hustlers or *joseadores*, an onomatopoeic Spanglish rendition of the English slang word. The caseworkers and the hustlers were at highest risk of arrest, and were paid only a commission of their sales. They usually shared between ten and forty dollars of every $140 worth of product sold (depending upon their negotiated arrangements with a particular bichote) in response to market shifts, personal venalities, and/or shifts in supply and demand of available workers following police raids. To further decrease their risk of arrest and/or assault, caseworkers and sometimes also hustlers proactively paid part of their commission to a "runner" who transported the prepackaged wholesale bundles for shifts from a supplier or a "packing house." They often also shared another portion of their commission with part-time "lookouts." Most corners closed before midnight, but the most profitable ones, like Panama Red's, operated 24/7, employing dozens of local residents in multiple hierarchically remunerated and differentially risky labor roles.

Ironically, the confusing array of specific roles in the labor hierarchy was chameleon-like, flexibly contracting or expanding to accommodate the inevitable disruptions of police raids, which foment yet more opportunities for temporary windfall earnings or seizures of new territory. Distinct tasks could be temporarily combined on an emergency just-in-time basis, depending upon who was suddenly arrested, shot, AWOL on a shift, or might need to generate extra income.

The flexibility and pragmatic adaptability of diversified, hierarchical positions at sales points enabled sales to persist despite frequent police raids. More subtly, on the level of subjectivity formation, the differentially remunerated risk-inflected roles of this high-stakes, illegal, but often profitable labor market resonated culturally with charismatic, masculine patronage tures. Even more ironic, it was also consistent with the quintessential hard-working American immigrant dream of upward mobility—promising a meteoric rise in the local labor force for those ambitious youths blessed by good luck, courage, and astute entrepreneurial skills.

A profound "symbolic violence" (invoking Bourdieu 2000) consequently pervaded this inner-city version of the Horatio Alger "rags to riches" dream (Contreras 2013). It confused underlings into respecting or accommodating the profit-making hierarchies that victimized them and benefited bichotes. Both bichotes and peers alike publicly blamed arrested hustlers for being careless "knuckleheads," ridiculing them for smoking too much marijuana, taking too many opioid pills, or becoming distracted by sexual flirtations.

Perversely, turnover from arrests and occupational violence/substance use disorder was so prevalent that it was not unrealistic for street sellers and lookouts to suddenly have an opportunity to ascend the local labor hierarchy on their corner. We witnessed several cases of meteoric upward mobility like Tito's—usually followed or preceded by a murder, a shoot-out, or an arrest. The younger members of a crew would convince themselves that they could sell more adeptly than their careless predecessors and could rise to become the next caseworker, bichote, or supplier. The inevitability of their arrest in the context of the US drug war and hyper-incarceration was invisible. Sadly, the everyday emergencies of police raids were interpreted as moments of opportunity to be seized, rather than a forewarning of the likelihood of their own future incarceration. Most parents, even those involved in the narcotics economy, lamented having to raise their children on the block because of the appeal of hand-to-hand selling to their teenagers, who were tempted to drop out of their neighborhood's dysfunctional high schools and scramble in the entry-level retail narcotics markets.

## TERRITORIAL CONTROL AND CULTIVATING "VIRTUOUS POWER"

We documented well over a dozen bichote transitions within our micro-neighborhood during our fieldwork. These territorial successions became pressure cookers for violent confrontations that sometimes lasted several weeks or months, with multiple rivals jockeying for control, like the tug-of-war between Raffy/Panama Red/Lucas. As noted, however, aspiring bichotes could not rely on brute force alone. Their longevity ultimately hinged on their ability to be recognized as a respected "leader among equals" who was beneficial for everyone. Bichotes consequently needed to cultivate a hegemony of what Venezuelan criminologist and social critic Andres Antillano calls "virtuous power" (personal communication). This moral economy of violence dynamic of legitimizing territorial control requires continuous and innumerable sociable assertions of generosity. The most resilient bichotes intersperse acts of expressive brutality and masculine bravado—such as Raffy's reckless displays of comic provocation against the irate police officer—with acts of charismatic generosity and combined counterintuitively, with expressions of personal humility to defuse envy or resentment over hierarchy.

Had Raffy not been imprisoned with a twelve-and-a-half- to twenty-five-year sentence, he would likely have maintained control of the block, because he was respected by many of our neighbors. Many admired him for preferring old-fashioned fisticuffs to the spectacularly murderous gunplay at which Panama Red excelled. During the three-way divide-and-conquer tug of war between Panama Red, Raffy, and Lucas, Tito eloquently communicated his genuine respect for Raffy's physical courage, and proved it by loyally siding with Raffy as one of his loyal riders (even though he had astutely already quit as his caseworker to avoid arrest).

TITO: First, Panama Red's bols started taking the coke off of Lucas's sellers. Raffy was ready to fight but Lucas didn't want to ride and he started bitchin' to Raffy, "I'm just going to pay rent to Panama Red."

But when Panama Red started taking the dope off of Raffy's hustlers too, Raffy beat him up. No gunplay! Just knocked him to the ground with his hands [shadow boxing enthusiastically]. Knocked him right under his own truck!

After that, Raffy said, "Fuck this, Lucas ain't riding, so I'm going to take the powder from him too." 'Cause he didn't really have no respect for Lucas at that point. So beef started bubbling up between Raffy and Lucas too.

Lucas got powdered up [high on cocaine] and came out the house at Raffy with his AK. At first he had the jawn [Philadelphia slang for an indefinite noun defined by context, in this case "jawn" refers to Lucas's AK-47 machine gun] pointed to the side and Raffy was like, "Yo, n—, don't point that shit at me." But Lucas, I guess he had some courage from all that powder, and kept it pointed at Raffy, and that n— started dancing. Like, "Oh shit!"—Ducking around, scared as hell, ready to dive.

Reenacting the scene, Tito opened his eyes wide and feigned a terrified adrenaline rush. He hopped from foot to foot, swayed his body, waving his arms, and ducking his head.

TITO: But instead, Lucas went back into his house. I grabbed my ratchet [gun], and so did my brother Leo. It was me, Raffy, and Leo waiting for Lucas up the block, ready to put that shit full of holes.

Lucas came out and saw us waiting at the corner and he went right back in the house and didn't come out for days. But by then it was too late, Raffy was already locked up and Panama Red had this block poppin' with the fire dope. That n— Lucas don't have no heart [spitting in disgust].

### VIOLENCE AND INCARCERATION: TITO'S EXPERIENCE

None of this mortal risk turmoil dissuaded Tito from his ongoing pursuit of upward mobility.

TITO: I don't even know what stamp [brand name of heroin] Panama Red's peoples be sellin' now because the cops been raidin' and I've gone up the food chain puttin' out my own work [drugs] on a corner over there [motioning vaguely with his chin toward a nearby block with multiple active salespoints parallel to us].

Tito was thrilled about having just seized yet another chance opportunity that opened up when a bichote who ran a nearby corner was suddenly shot dead by the little brother of one of his caseworkers, whom the slain bichote had failed to bail out after an arrest. The murdered bichote's widow trusted Tito, having known him since he was a little boy. She also needed to act fast because one of her late husband's cousins, an unknown outsider, was trying to take over the block by brute force. Consequently, she offered Tito an exceptionally low rent, only $500 a week—a tenth of what Panama Red was receiving at that time from his temporary subcontractor/renter on our block. Tito immediately partnered with a childhood friend who had just purchased a brand-new .357 Magnum, and they eagerly agreed to an arrangement with the widow, promising to also defend her right to her husband's corner from her cousin-in-law, in addition to paying the discounted rent. Business immediately boomed, only to come to a disastrous end three months later when Tito accidentally killed his best-friend/partner during a drunken and benzodiazepine-addled celebration of their three-month anniversary as fledgling bichotes on such a bargain-priced drug corner. Tito's judge, yet another notorious hard-liner, initially insisted on charging Tito with homicide—carrying a seventeen- to thirty-four-year sentence—despite the fact that everyone, including the arresting police officers, Tito's public defender, and even the mother of the slain youth, knew the shooting had been a genuine accident, and should have qualified Tito for the much shorter "involuntary manslaughter" charge of two and a half to five years.

We visited Tito in the county jail on multiple occasions. On the first visit, Tito walked into the visitors' room with his face covered in scratches.

TITO: I just got in a fight with some black bol and look, [raising his shirt to reveal a deep crimson circular bruise in the center of his chest] the motherfucker bit me! We had words earlier at the phones, and he kept runnin' his mouth. But I let it go. I wanted to be peaceful, you know, I have a lot on my mind. I have to go to court tomorrow. But the n— came into my cell and [making a punching motion] snuck me in the back of the head. Then he stood there lookin' at me like I wasn't gonna' do nothin'. Like I'm some kinda' pussy.

I guess 'cause I'm small and I'm Puerto Rican, and I came in here quiet, minding my business, people think they can fuck with you. That's what I get for trying to keep to myself. I know if I came in here like a savage then he wouldn'a done that.

Now I might end up killing this n—, 'cus when I get mad I don't really know what I'm doing. And I get mad at any little thing. I just lose it; go into a rage.

The over-fourfold explosion in the size of the incarcerated population in the United States since 1980 has turned prisons into de facto gladiator schools that hone the fighting skills and transform the habitus of inmates, sabotaging their future ability to find legal employment when they are released (Contreras 2013: 69–83). The structural brutality of overcrowded US jails dramatically raises the stakes for cultivating violent reputations and propagates racist prison gangs as each ethnic group scrambles for self-protection. Inmates often become aggressively violent in order to avoid victimization, and are then trapped in a catch-22 feedback loop of solitary confinement, extended prison sentences, and punitive lockdowns that damage their mental health. These cycles of fury and frustration are further exacerbated by the institutionalization of routine arbitrary bullying by often poorly trained and overwhelmed guards (Bauer 2018). Describing his first fight in jail, for example, Tito mentioned with a shrug, "When I saw the bol was trying to stab me I asked the CO [Correctional Officer] 'don't lock us in' [the cell together] but the CO did anyway."

In the routinized context of institutionalized carceral brutality, it is easy to understand the survival utility of Tito learning how to fly into a "blind rage" and beat a fellow inmate insensate inside his locked jail cell. Tito is Puerto Rican and, as he points out, "small," in an African American–dominated, overcrowded county jail supervised primarily by white guards in a racist institutional culture. As a baby-faced nineteen-year-old facing a long-term prison sentence, Tito must ensure, for his survival, self- respect, and sanity, that he does not become a mark for bullies, whether inmates or correctional officials.

Tito has no difficulty identifying the infrastructural context generating the extreme levels of interpersonal violence among his fellow inmates in his maximum-security "lockdown" unit. Violence in this institutional context becomes a "social fact" (invoking Durkheim 1951). Each individual act may appear to be precipitated by the idiosyncrasy of the personalities of perpetrators but, from a sociological perspective, the systemic phenomenon of carceral interpersonal violence cannot usefully be understood as being the "choice" of individuals. Tito's fight is more usefully interpreted as the product of what anthropologist Paul Farmer and others have called "structural violence" (Farmer 2003), or alternatively what Philippe Bourgois and Nancy Scheper-Hughes have categorized as "everyday violence" or "normalized violence" (Scheper-Hughes and Bourgois 2004; Bourgois 2010). These approaches to violence highlight the invisible forces of political-economic inequality and the institutional and bureaucratic frameworks that generate the spectacularly visible interpersonal criminal violence that has become normalized in the United States, where the firearm murder rate in 2010 was ten times higher than that of comparably wealthy nations (Geneva Small Arms Survey 2012).

Tito recognized the oppressive effects of structural forces, but his critical insight on the normalization of abuse in US jails did not stop the institutionalized brutality from seeping into his subjectivity to become a core component of his own conception of masculine self-respect:

TITO: This unit is crazy, man. A lot of people don't know what's going on yet with their case. They stressin'. They have that uncertainty. They don't know if they going home soon, or if they ain't ever goin' home. Plus, we in close custody. They got us on lockdown half the time because of some shanking [stabbing]. There ain't shit to do. You just sit in your cell all day bored and frustrated. That's half the reason there be so many problems. We might kill each other over ten minutes on the phone. Or hot water in the shower, or whatever.

Out in the street I knew how to resolve a situation. You could talk to someone out there and maybe it didn't have to come to any violence. In here there is no choice. You can't just let them treat you like a bitch 'cause then everyone be sayin', "He a pussy. Ain't gonna do anything." And walk up in your cell, "Look n—, gimme all that, or I'm'a fuck you up." I done seen it too many times, man.

No one is going to talk about me like that. All I have in here . . . [choking back tears] is my pride. I'm not letting nobody take that away from me! My mama didn't raise no pussy.

We were concerned that Tito might not survive in the county jail waiting for trial, so we sought out Don Ricardo—another charismatic former bichote who had completed a fifteen-year sentence for a road-rage murder he committed in his early twenties. Against all odds, Don Ricardo had managed to reintegrate himself into the legal labor market in his early forties. He prided himself on his redemption as a just-above-minimum-wage, part-time janitor cleaning offices, but he also cultivated his prominent retired, "OG" Original gangster presence on the block surrounded by his extended family and loyal riders. He frequently doled out advice to the young street hustlers, who respected him for his history as a successful, violent, and generous bichote. We were hoping to persuade Don Ricardo to call Tito and advise him to refrain from engaging in such excessive violence in jail, but Don Ricardo cut us short:

DON RICARDO: Naaahh! I don't see nothing wrong with what Tito did. Tito did right to fight. He is going to have to fight a lot, especially in his weight class. Tito gotta show that he don't care how little he is. You can't show that you fear nobody.

If Tito keeps fighting like that, trust me, he'll be all right. He ain't gonna win all his fights, but he'll get his respect . . . make a reputation.

It's not just Tito's problem. The black people in the county [jail]—especially the Muslims [a racialized Philadelphia prison gang]—try to take your heart. Can't let them bully you or they're gonna call you Maytag [term for a feminized inmate]. You gonna be washing their underwear, dirty shitty underwear, and then you gotta be givin' that booty up. I seen smaller guys than Tito kill guys real quick during a prison lockdown. Yo! I remember one. It was a major riot. The whole prison went wild.

Caught in the momentum of a carceral riot flashback, Don Ricardo was suddenly on his feet, animated, slashing the air in front of him as if he had a "Gilette [razor]" in his hand.

The profit margins of narcotics sales, dramatically inflated by illegality, are what most proximately fuel high levels of violence on inner-city streets, awash with automatic weapons and untraceable cash. Less proximally, but no less important, is the structural political-economic reality of Puerto Rican vulnerability to violence and narcotics has been historically driven by the island of Puerto Rico's status as a former colony of the United States ever since its invasion by US Marines in 1898. The hijacking of the island's political administrative system disarticulated its economy, expelling over half of its population as cheap wage laborers to the US mainland (Dietz 1982; Bonilla et al. 1986; Caban 2002; Santory Jorge and Quintero Rivera 2018). Literally driven by hunger, formerly rural or shantytown-dwelling unemployed Puerto Ricans have been desperately emigrating to segregated inner cities like Philadelphia, seeking sweatshop jobs precisely when factories in those cities were moving overseas, as industrial corporations sought tax-free (and labor- and environmental regulation-free) offshore production sites (Bourgois 2003). This "globalization" process devastated "rustbelt" cities of the Northeast and Midwest who Puerto Ricans migrated as colonized subjects especially vulnerable to drug epidemics.

Formal colonies are an anomaly in the twenty-first century and normally represent an international embarrassment to their imperial, military-economic masters. Nevertheless, more than a century after its occupation, Puerto Rico remains (as of 2021) an "unincorporated overseas territory" of the United States. Although residents of Puerto Rico have US citizenship and must obey federal laws and regulations, they cannot vote in US elections and, lacking states' rights, their economy is subject to involuntary US federal oversight. Typical of the perversity of colonial regimes of unequal status, Puerto Ricans receive the full legal rights of US citizenship only if they take up permanent residence on the US mainland.

In the 2000s, Puerto Rico's dysfunctional colonial status imploded economically. After a decade-long decline in the island's domestic economy, the US Supreme Court thwarted a desperate attempt by the Puerto Rican governor to file for public-sector bankruptcy in 2016. Worse yet, US Congress also imposed a seven-member Control Board, nicknamed the "junta," which imposed an economic austerity plan prioritizing debt payments to US hedge funds and vulture capital creditors. Meanwhile, social welfare services including public employee retirement pensions for Puerto Rican

residents were slashed, and the Puerto Rican domestic economy continued to decline while residents desperately emigrated in search of employment in ever larger numbers (Epps 2016; Williams Walsh 2017a, 2017b).
According to US Department of Labor reports, in the mid-2010s at the
height of our fieldwork, over 46.2 percent of Puerto Ricans on the island
lived below the US poverty line. This is more than three times the US mainland's poverty rate. Most important, legal labor force participation rates in
2017 dropped to 40 percent—more than one-third lower than that of the
US mainland's already low rate of 62 percent. These economic dislocations
pushed even higher proportions of the working-age population into the island's increasingly violent underground economy. Murder rates in Puerto
Rico are approximately five times higher than those on the US mainland
(Bourgois 2015).

Ironically, it is precisely the peculiarity of Puerto Rico's anachronistic
colonial status, with its US-imposed export/import model of corporate
economic development (misnomered "free trade") that has turned both the
island and its inner-city US mainland diaspora into predatory profit in-
cubators for the global narcotics industry. Unable to support themselves
in their colony's disarticulated economy, Puerto Rican youth are disproportionately shunted into the riskiest, most visible echelons of the global
narcotics arket.

## THE LEGACY OF CHRONIC INCARCERATION: LITTLE BROTHER LEO

Puerto Rico's bleak, ongoing colonial history in 2021 is the invisible driving structural political economy force generating the tremendous human
burden of useless suffering on US inner-city streets that we are document-
ing ethnographically. We watched helplessly as this played out in the life of
Tito's little brother, Leo, when he turned eighteen. He ambitiously followed
in the footsteps of his older brother, whom he admired. Immediately upon
Tito's incarceration, Leo took full responsibility for the outstanding rent
owed on his brother's former corner. He put out his own new "stamp" of
heroin, and it sold like hotcakes. Four months later Leo, like his brother, was
in jail, awaiting trial for shooting one of his employees. As an overly preco-
cious teenager way out of his league, like his brother, he had overreached in
pursuit of fledgling bichote status. Surrounded by guns, money, cash, and
an abundant supply of potent cocaine- and fentanyl-laced heroin, he over-
reacted to the pressure of being bullied, threatened, and disrespected by
the slightly older and tougher peers he was attempting to discipline as his

retail sellers. In the anxious boredom of his jail cell, Leo reflected for long hours on why he had pulled the trigger. He was honestly befuddled over how he could have so stupidly shot a street-smart neighbor when all he had meant to do was intimidate him into returning $500 worth of a "misplaced" stash of narcotics.

LEO: Oh man, I got into some dumb-ass shit. Real stupid! It was all over some nut shit. It wasn't even supposed to happen like that. I was gonna smack the shit out of him with the gun, but he kept talking. I wasn't even gonna shoot him, but it just happened too fast man. I don't know, this the dumbest thing I ever did in my life.

I was rentin' the block and I had this young bol, Adrian, out there hustling for me. I went around the corner to advertise my stamp [shout out his heroin's brand name to passersby]. And when I go back, the work [supply of cocaine and heroin] ain't there, so I'm like, "Adrian, damn, you're the only person sittin' here, like, what's up? Where the work go?"

[Imitating ostentatious innocence] "Oh, I didn't touch nothin'" . . . this-an'-that. Then he wanted to get all hype, so he called his peoples: Bobo, Bambam, Ninito . . . all of his cousins. So I go back to my crib and I grab the strap [gun] and I come back.

[Putting his head into his hands] I don't know, everything was just moving so fast, like. [His voice cracking] I ain't really know what to do. I was gonna smack the shit out of him. But he kept talking. I raised my hand at him but he dipped back.

And all his peoples was standin' there, I was thinkin' in my head, like [setting his face into a threatening frown], "Damn, if one of his peoples got a gun. . . ." And Adrian like [taunting voice]. "You a nut-ass n—! You ain't gonna be treating me like a nut." . . . This-an'-that . . .

I'm like, "What!" And I pulled the jawn out.

But he was just like, "N—, you not gonna do shit." And he came at me. So I shot him, but just once so he could get away from me. That was the first time I ever shot somebody. And I thought I was gonna be like hesitant. But I didn't even hesitate. It was just like a spur of the moment thing.

Afterward, from my crib I had called one of his peoples. He told me they found the dope and I told him, "Look, when Adrian get better, we could rumble [fist fight]."

But they told me Adrian was like almost dying in the hospital 'cause the bullet almost hit his main artery. I'm thinking in the back of my head, "Damn, I didn't want all that to happen. . . . I just did some dumb shit."

Next thing I know, the police come running up in my crib. "Where the gun at?" And started rippin' the house apart.

Six months later Leo was in shackles awaiting transfer to a western Pennsylvania prison on a five- to ten-year, plea-bargained sentence. As an eighteen-year-old he was objectively terrified that he would find himself cycling through prison for the rest of his life, trapped in the dead-end logic of the inner-city narcotics market in which he had tried so hard to be an overachiever.

Like his brother Tito, he was acutely aware of the structural forces propelling him to self-destruction. Terrified, as a high school dropout who had never held a legal job in his life, with a predicate felony record that extended back into his early adolescence, all he could do is blame himself for being "weak-minded":

LEO: There's old-ass people in here with white hairs. And them n—s ain't changed. You really gotta be strong to change. And I ain't gonna hold [lie to] you, I'm kinda weak in my mind. I get sucked into doing dumb stuff.

'Cause it's like a chain reaction. You come home [from prison] and you go back right to the same thing. This lifestyle is just so addictive. Every little thing about it—especially when you got a corner. You just wake up and you got money. You walk around the block and your workers passin' you some money. Next thing you know [cocking his neck as if cradling a cell phone], "Yo, I'm done, come pick this money up." It's so easy. But it don't lead nowhere. Next thing you know, you wind up killin' somebody 'cause he tried to kill you and you in this situation [shaking his shackles] ready to do more time. That's why I know I ain't gonna change if I come back to Philly.

## THE DENSE POSTADOLESCENT SOCIALITY OF INNER-CITY
## CONCRETE KILLING FIELDS

If being in prison was a scary prospect, being on the street had been just as terrifying for Leo. On another one of our prison visits, he expressed ambivalent relief about having been incarcerated just in time to save his life. "If I wasn't in this predicament I probably would've got killed, not even knowing that they was looking for me to kill me." In an emotional confessional outpouring—barely stopping for breath—Leo poured out the dizzying details of multiple overlapping murders and threats of murder among his

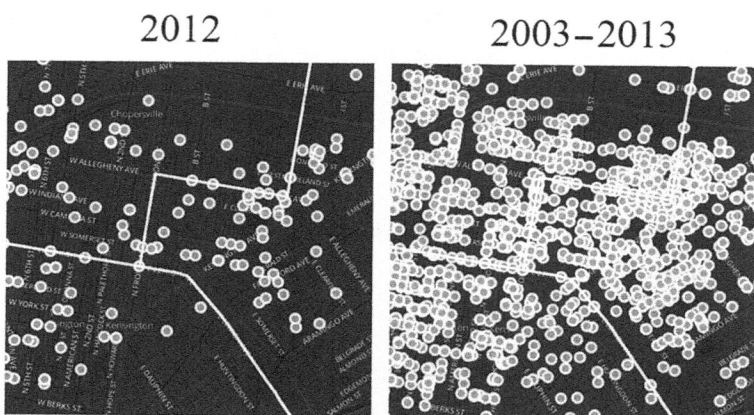

FIGURE 10.1 Shootings in the dozen square blocks surrounding our apartment.

close-knit peer group of late-teenage and early-twenties wannabe-bichotes. They were trapped in the fickle camaraderie of their early childhood rider relationships that now embroiled them in murderous conflicts, with often contradictory obligations for assistive violence across crisscrossing friendships that were polarized by immature and ill-coordinated jockeying for fragile control of corners, or derailed by momentary acts of jealous rage over jilted love.

It is impossible to keep track of the tumble of names of victims and perpetrators in Leo's account. Touchingly, despite their premature transition into early adulthood as bona fide lethal gangsters, both victims and perpetrators still bear the affectionate diminutive baby boy nicknames bestowed on them by their mothers and grandmothers when they were— not so long ago—adorable toddlers. Their nicknames resonate as an objective linguistic trace of the tragedy of growing up too poor, too fast, amid too many guns, drugs, and chronic unemployment. What should have been drug-addled impulsive postadolescent petty squabbles exploded into irrevocable acts of murder. Each shooting or insult traps a wider net of these highly sociable and ambitious young men into obligations of solidary, rider violence. Figure 10.1 illustrates graphically the statistical tragedy of excessive access to unlicensed, inexpensive automatic weapons, primarily among postadolescents scrambling for cash and prestige through retail drug sales. In a collaboration with epidemiologists drawing on publicly available law enforcement firearm violence data, we calculated that Puerto

Ricans in Philadelphia had a six times higher rate of firearm deaths than whites and a 1.3 times higher rate than African Americans. In our immediate neighborhood, the per capita firearm death rate was even worse, a mind-boggling 59 percent higher than the city's overall Puerto Rican average (Friedman et al. 2019).

These murder rate disparities come alive in Leo's tear-choked account of the firearm violence that landed him in jail. He begins—almost as a non sequitur—with two additional unrelated, mistaken-identity violent emergency life threats crashing down on him at the time of his arrest. Gordo, an older, big-time narcotics supplier had put out a $50,000 murder contract on Leo's head when two kilos of coke "came up missing" from Gordo's garage. Gordo was a former boyfriend of Leo's mother, and Leo had eagerly run errands for him. As an adult Leo remained affectionately respectful of Gordo, and frequently passed by his house to say hello. Unfortunately, one of those casual visits coincided with the timing of the two stolen kilos.

> LEO: But Gordo not my only problem. I was chillin' with Wiwi in his new car and we see my bols Dito and Nano in the Crown Vic [car]. Dito jump out, "Yo, let me get the gun, let me get the gun." Wiwi give him the ratchet, and Dito jump back into the car.
>
> Twenty minutes later all you hear is bam, bam, bam, bam. And Dito come back around. He chillin', "Yeah, I just shot bitch-ass Lolo, because he wanna be smacking my baby mom. I hope that n— die."
>
> I'm like thinking, "Damn! You a vicious bol, Dito. You crazy!" And that n— look innocent as a motherfucker with his hazel eyes, but he got the devil in him, for real! Dito shot Lolo six times. But Lolo didn't die and he didn't tell [the police] on Dito. He just walked in that bol's garage and shot him in front of everybody.
>
> And Izzi too, that bol always be smilin'. He got big-ass teeth, just a funny-lookin' goofy-ass n—. But he one of the n—s that don't play either. He took his own man out on Somerset with a .357 [Magnum], and it wasn't over no bread, it was over some beef, "Oh, you tried to holler at my girl. . . ."
>
> They was walking and Izzi played cool with his bol and pulled back, and let his bol walk ahead of him. Now he's doin' life upstate. My other bol Litito got kilt over nothin' too. It was just the tension. . . . Words got thick.

Leo then reenacted a phone call he had received a week before his arrest from a close friend warning him that he and two of their other mutual

FIGURE 10.2  North Philadelphia cemetery.

friends were out to kill him. A few days earlier, bored, Leo had again inadvertently provoked their lethal anger by going cruising with an acquaintance simply to pass the time of day. Unbeknownst to Leo, that acquaintance was competing for control of the drug corner employing several of Leo's friends. When those friends saw Leo passing by in their rival's car, they assumed Leo was riding for an enemy of their bichote, Chinito:

> LEO: [Imitating a gruff voice] "Why you lookin' to kill Chinito?" I'm like [confused voice], "What you mean?" [Gruff voice again] "Oh, then, why you runnin' around with a n— that lookin' for [trying to kill] Chinito?"
>
> I told him [frustrated tone], "What's up with that nut-ass shit! Y'all don't communicate. I didn't know nothin' about Chinito! I didn't know ya'll n—s was goin' through shit. Next time, let a n— know somethin' before I get shot for no reason!"
>
> [Gruff voice again] "Alright. But Chinito's lookin' to kill you. And Lolo lookin' too. And I'm just keepin' it real, I was slidin' through your block every day 'cause I was tryna' check you out [plan your murder] too."

George and Fernando, who were visiting Leo on this occasion, sat back in the uncomfortable plastic chairs of the jail's visiting room, exhausted by the high stakes of teenage intrigue, evocatively punctuated by a dizzying swirl of baby boy nicknames. They did not know how to respond. Before they had a chance to restabilize their emotions, Leo poured out two more stories of even more horrific recent internecine shootings that had occurred in the past few months among his childhood friends. Despite Leo's self-reflexive critique of the senselessness of "bein' kilt over nothin' nut-ass shit," and "words got thick," the primary lesson he drew from the kaleidoscope of deadly gun violence engulfing everyone around him was his need for more firepower, and his employee became the next collateral damage.:

LEO: I don't wanna be caught slippin'. You can't let people think you sweet [weak]. That's why I was carrying my gun on me all day.

He had also been stalking Gordo, "the bol who had put $50,000 on me":

LEO: I used to go to his [Gordo's] girl's crib every night, strapped up, ready to kill him. But he never showed up. I kept it on the tip [secret]. 'Cause if he know I know, he gonna be more of a fuckin' Jedi about killin' me first.

George purposefully shifted the conversation to the easy accessibility of firearms in the inner city by asking Leo where he had obtained this last gun, opening the Pandora's box of gun fetishism among adolescent males in neighborhoods flooded with cheap, unlicensed, and very powerful automatic weapons. Leo's intimate account might initially appear to register sociopathic levels of irrational interpersonal deadly violence, but it is important to link this murderous mayhem to the political economy undergirding it and to identify specific public policies and corporate actors: the "predatory accumulation" logic (Bourgois 2018) of the global small firearms industry which lobbies (mostly right-wing) US politicians against common-sensical gun-control laws. In other words the white collar legal activities of the firearm corporations and rightwing politicians (to invoke Appel's (2019) work on the "licit economy" of oil and mining corporations devastating the natural resources and economy of equatorial Africa) are the most proximate force propelling high rates of murder and suicide in the United States. Both legal and illegal firearms trafficking follow the same paths, in the reverse direction, as illegal drug traffic. The United States also has the highest rate of automatic small-firearm ownership in the world. Once again, the formal colonial status of Puerto Rico imposes this the murderous mayhem on its population, situating it geographically, juridically, and economically as a profitable conduit for "free flow" of US small fire-arms both locally and

FIGURE 10.3 Half-brothers at the memorial to their father, who was shot on their block.

throughout the rest of Latin America, the Caribbean, and beyond. The island of Puerto Rico bears the tragic burden of having the highest proportion of homicides committed by firearms of any nation in the world (96 percent in the 2010s) simply because it is a conduit for both legal and illegal trafficking of US small firearms along with narcotics(Geneva Small Arms Survey 2012; Bourgois 2015). Again, Leo's relationship to corporately propagated firearm violence is an extension of the logic of colonial injustice affecting the Puerto Rican diaspora on the US mainland that finds itself confined to enclaves overwhelmed by narcotics markets. Poignantly for Leo, these deadly, structurally imposed risks are intimately embedded in his childhood friendship-based social networks.

LEO: I bought the jawn [weapon] off one of my homies. It was a big-ass chrome forty [.40 mm]. I put $300 and my bol Freddo put $300. We was sharin' it. It was real cheap 'cause somebody probably already done did something [killed someone] with it.

I'm a gun freak, I love them too much. Before this one, I had this shotgun that this bol had tossed on Allegheny Street when he was runnin' from the cops. Later I sold it to Benny for like $80.

GEORGE: How do you get so many guns so easily?

LEO: I don't know. They just come to me. Like, [imitating a sales pitch] "Yo, I got a shotgun $100. Real cheap! . . . [Voice filling with energy] a nine [9 mm] . . . a forty. . . ." And, I'm like [eyes lighting up], "I need that!"

GEORGE: You like guns too much.

LEO: [Nodding] I don't know why. I got to leave them alone. . . . I had so many guns in the house, I'm surprised that my mom didn't just get rid of me [burying his face in his hands as tears well up].

## CONCLUSION: THE LICIT AND ILLICIT POLITICAL ECONOMY OF PREDATORY ACCUMULATION PROPELLING PROFITS IN US INNER-CITY NARCOTICS MARKETS

In the United States, we tend to blame violent, addictive, or socially destructive behavior on the individual victims who engage in it, framing population-level behaviors as "poor choices." Indeed, young men like Leo and Tito in North Philadelphia also share in the reproduction of this symbolic violence, blaming themselves for their incarceration and murderous acts. From a social science perspective it is more accurate, and from a practical policy and political/humanitarian outcome perspective more productive, to situate their destructive behaviors in the historically grounded structural context that constrains their life chances growing up in such infrastructurally devastated neighborhoods, devoid of legal employment and overrun by narcotics and firearms. They find themselves trapped in a destructive dead end. Unemployed Puerto Ricans living both on the island of Puerto Rico and in its US mainland inner-city diasporas are burdened with what needs to be recognized as politically imposed suffering.

More immediately, as we framed the problem in the introduction, the fourfold punch of high rates of firearm injury, substance-use disorders, mental/physical disabilities, and the "mass incarceration"— or more accurately "hyper-incarceration" of poor urban African Americans and Latinos (Wacquant 2010), are specific policy outcomes that can be changed. The United States imprisons more of its inhabitants than any nation ever has in all of world history. US gun control policies are so dysfunctional that inner-city streets are flooded with automatic weapons that sell at well below their market rate and no doubt often well below their cost of production. Overcrowded carceral facilities are objectively institutionally brutal. They turn rageful interpersonal violence into a necessity for survival and self-respect. They also decrease the social capital and employability of inmates.

"Ex-offenders" stained by their felony and misdemeanor carceral records enter the legal labor market at a tremendous disadvantage. Desperate to support themselves and find some kind of esteem, they often slide back into the highest-risk, lowest-level echelons of the global narcotics industry's retail labor force. On inner-city streets, the state's response of punitive law enforcement and zero tolerance for drugs, exacerbated by racial profiling and police brutality, ironically fails to protect the physical security of inner-city residents. As a result, the violently enforced *pax narcotica* of bichotes metamorphoses their profitable brutality into what appears to be virtuous power. They maintain provisional order in an environment of systemic precarity. Neighbors, consequently, find themselves obliged to seek out their block's bichotes as the only available brokers capable of reducing the violent collateral fallout of their narcotics profiteering. Norbert Elias's landmark analysis of how a "civilizing process" heralded the emergence of the modern European state (Elias 1978) has been turned on its head by South American political theorists in the "era of predatory accumulation" (Bourgois 2018), whereby punitive warlordism, narcotics racketeering, and environmental disaster become business-as-usual (Bourgois 2018). The state becomes a "de-civilizing" or "de-pacification" force (O'Donnell 1993; Arias 2006; Goldstein 2004; Auyero and Berti 2015) that decreases the security of civil society and turns substance-use disorders, repression, and disability into profits extracted from the inner-city poor, legal taxpayers, and from the premature death of vulnerable populations. Although the specifics of police corruption, physical insecurity, and state repression differ dramatically between the US and Latin America nations, in the US the routinization of police brutality, malfeasance, and especially mass incarceration is a central force sustaining crime, violence, and plentiful cheap narcotics inside US inner cities.

Youth on the street are seduced into bichote dreams because the war on drugs vastly inflates profit margins. They struggle for a piece of the pie through expressive performances of lethal violence. For ambitious young men like Tito and Leo, the classic second-generation immigrant's American dream of upward mobility through intrepid entrepreneurship backfire into an 'Amerikan' nightmare of destructive cycles of violence that they reproduce even as they also insightfully condemn them. Incarcerated as teenagers, they strive to pick themselves up by their bootstraps in their early twenties, but stumble on the reality of their exclusion from the legal labor market and backslide into substance-use disorders, or as they put it, "my addiction to money." On a structural level, they have become superfluous, legal labor power. Their irrelevance to the productive, wage-earning, legal economy comes crashing down on them:

> LEO: I just don't want to go back to the same nut shit when I get home. Philly is like the fuckin' devil. I need to figure out a game plan to keep me away from the streets. I need to have a job before I get out of here. And I don't know how that's goin' to work. I ain't never had no job before.

## EPILOGUE

As this article goes to press, Leo is serving time in a federal penitentiary for gun possession, and his older brother Tito couch surfs between his mother's and his girlfriend's houses, in and out of stints of narcotics sales and occasional day labor jobs in demolition construction work.

## ACKNOWLEDGMENTS

Figure 10.2 courtesy of Fernando Montero. Figure 10.3 courtesy of George Karandinos. Research and analysis were partially funded by National Institutes of Health grants: UL1TR001881, DA049644, DA010164. Early versions of the ethnography and preliminary version of the analysis were adapted from: Philippe Bourgois and Laurie Hart (trans. Simon Bourdieu), "Pax narcotica: Le marché de la drogue dans le ghetto portoricain de Philadelphie," *L'Homme* 219–20 (2016): 31–62; Philippe Bourgois, "Decolonizing Drug Studies in an Era of Predatory Accumulation," *Third World Quarterly* (2018): 385–98; George Karandinos, Laurie Kain Hart, Fernando Montero Castrillo, Philippe Bourgois, "The Moral Economy of Violence in the US Inner City," *Current Anthropology* 55, no. 1 (2014); Philippe Bourgois, Laurie Kain Hart, George Karandinos, and Fernando Montero, "The Political and Emotional Economy of Violence in US Inner City Narcotics Markets," in *Ritual, Emotion, Violence: Studies on the Micro-Sociology of Randall Collins*, edited by Elliot Weininger, Annette Lareau, and Omar Lizardo, 46–77 (London: Routledge, 2019); Joseph Friedman, George Karandinos, Laurie Kain Hart, Fernando Montero Castrillo, Nicholas Graetz, Philippe Bourgois, "Structural Vulnerability to Narcotics-Driven Firearm Violence: An Ethnographic and Epidemiological Study of Philadelphia's Puerto Rican Inner-City," *PLoS One* (2019); Philippe Bourgois, Laurie Kain Hart, George Karandinos, and Fernando Montero, "Coming of Age in the Concrete Killing Fields of the US Inner City," in *Exotic No More: Anthropology for the Contemporary World*, 2nd ed., edited by Jeremy MacClancy, 19–41 (Chicago: University of Chicago Press, 2019); and Philippe Bourgois, Laurie Kain Hart, Fernando Montero Castrillo, George Karandinos, "From Primitive to Predatory Accumulation at the Retail Endpoint of the Global Narcotics Industry on US Inner City Streets," *Social Analysis* (under submission).

**REFERENCES**

Alexander, Michelle. 2010. *The New Jim Crow: Mass Incarceration in the Age of Color-blindness*. New York: New Press.

Appel, Hannah. 2019. *The Licit Life of Capitalism*. Durham, NC: Duke University Press.

Arias, Enrique Desmond. 2006. *Drugs and Democracy in Rio de Janeiro: Trafficking, Social Networks, and Public Security*. Chapel Hill: University of North Carolina Press.

Auyero, Javier, and María Fernanda Berti. 2015. *In Harm's Way: The Dynamics of Urban Violence*. Princeton, NJ: Princeton University Press.

Bender, William, and David Gambacorta. 2019. "Dozens of Philadelphia Police Were Reinstated after Top Brass Tried to Fire Them. Once-Secret Records Show How It Keeps Happening." *Philadelphia Inquirer*, September 12.

Bonilla, Frank, Ricardo Campos, Hunter College, and Centro de Estudios Puertorriqueños. 1986. *Industry and Idleness*. New York: Centro de Estudios Puertorriqueños.

Bourdieu, Pierre. 2000. *Pascalian Meditations*. Translated by Richard Nice. Stanford, CA: Stanford University Press.

Bourgois, Philippe. 2003. *In Search of Respect: Selling Crack in El Barrio*, 2nd ed. New York: Cambridge University Press.

Bourgois, Philippe. 2010. "Recognizing Invisible Violence: A 30-Year Ethnographic Retrospective." In *Global Health in Times of Violence*, edited by Barbara Rylko-Bauer, Paul Farmer, and Linda Whiteford, 17–40. Santa Fe, NM: School for Advanced Research Press.

Bourgois, Philippe. 2015. "Insecurity, the War on Drugs, and Crimes of the State: Symbolic Violence in the Americas." In *Violence at the Urban Margins*, edited by Javier Auyero, Philippe Bourgois, and Nancy Scheper-Hughes, 305–21. Oxford: University of Oxford Press.

Bourgois, Philippe. 2018. "Decolonizing Drug Studies in an Era of Predatory Accumulation." *Third World Quarterly* 39, no. 2 (February 13): 385–98. https://doi.org/10.1080/01436597.2017.1411187.

Bourgois, Philippe, and Laurie Kain Hart. 2011. "Commentary on Genberg et al. (2011): The Structural Vulnerability Imposed by Hypersegregated US Inner-City Neighborhoods—A Theoretical and Practical Challenge for Substance Abuse Research." *Addiction* 106, no. 11: 1975–77.

Bourgois, Philippe, and Laurie Kain Hart. 2016. "Pax Narcotica: Le marché de la drogue dans le ghetto Portoricain de Philadelphie." Translated by Simon Bourdieu. *L'Homme* 219–20: 31–62.

Bourgois, Philippe, Laurie Kain Hart, George Karandinos, and Fernando Montero. 2019. "Coming of Age in the Concrete Killing Fields of the US Inner City." In *Exotic No More: Anthropology for the Contemporary World*, 2nd ed., edited by Jeremy MacClancy, 19–41. Chicago: University of Chicago Press.

Caban, Pedro. 2002. "Puerto Rico: State Formation in a Colonial Context." *Caribbean Studies* 30, no. 2: 170–215.

Contreras, Randol. 2013. *Stickup Kids: Race, Drugs, Violence and the American Dream*. Berkeley: University of California Press.

Denvir, Daniel. 2013. "Why Is Eric Burke Still a Philly Cop?" *Philadelphia City Paper*, January 30. Accessed December 20, 2013. https://mycitypaper.com/cover/why-is-eric-burke-still-a-philly-cop/.

Denvir, Dan. 2014. "Why Philly Can't Breathe, Either." December 12, 2014. https://mycitypaper.com/cover/why-philly-cant-breathe-either/.

Dietz, James. 1982. "Puerto Rico in the 1970s and 1980s: Crisis of the Development Model." *Journal of Economic Issues* 16, no. 2: 497–506.

Durkheim, Émile. 1951. *Suicide: A Study in Sociology*. Translated by John Spaulding. New York: Free Press.

Elias, Norbert. 1978. *The Civilizing Process*. New York: Urizen.

Epps, Garrett. 2016. "The Legal Residue of American Empire." *Atlantic*, June 16.

Farmer, Paul. 2003. *Pathologies of Power: Health, Human Rights, and the New War on the Poor*. Berkeley: University of California Press.

Geneva Small Arms Survey. 2012. *Small Arms Survey 2012: Moving Targets*. Cambridge: Cambridge University Press.

Goldstein, Daniel M. 2004. *The Spectacular City: Violence and Performance in Urban Bolivia*. Durham, NC: Duke University Press.

Gottschalk, Marie. 2015. *Caught*. Princeton, NJ: Princeton University Press.

Granovetter, Mark S. "The Strength of Weak Ties." *American Journal of Sociology* 78, no. 6 (1973): 1360–80.

Green-Ceisler, Ellen. 2003. "Disciplinary System Report." PN-PA-0002. Philadelphia: Philadelphia Police Department, Integrity and Accountability Office.

Karandinos, George, Laurie Kain Hart, Fernando Montero Castrillo, and Philippe Bourgois. 2014. "The Moral Economy of Violence in the US Inner City." *Current Anthropology* 55, no. 1: 1–22.

Marin, Max, Ryan Briggs, and Nina Feldman. 2019. "The Misconduct Lawsuit That Unraveled Ex-Commissioner Richard Ross's Career Is One of Dozens in Recent Years." WHYY, August 23. https://whyy.org/articles/phillys-female-cops-sue-police-department-over-civil-rights-abuses-every-other-month-records-show/.

O'Donnell, Guillermo. 1993. "On the State, Democratization and Some Conceptual Problems: A Latin American View with Glances at Some Postcommunist Countries." *World Development* 21, no. 8: 1355–69.

Pennsylvania Crime Commission. 1974. *Report on Police Corruption and the Quality of Law Enforcement in Philadelphia.* Harrisburg: Pennsylvania Crime Commission.

Richards, Eugene. 1994. *Cocaine True, Cocaine Blue.* New York: Aperture.

Roebuck, Jeremy. 2017. "Seth Williams' Corruption Trial: The Case against the Philly DA Explained." *Philly.com,* June 20.

Rosenblum, Daniel, Fernando Montero Castrillo, Philippe Bourgois, et al. 2014. "Urban Segregation and the US Heroin Market: A Quantitative Model of Anthropological Hypotheses from an Inner-City Drug Market." *International Journal of Drug Policy* 25, no. 3: 543–55.

Ruderman, Wendy, and Barbara Laker. 2011. "For Some Cops, Getting Overtime Is No Work at All." *Philadelphia Daily News,* February 4.

Ruderman, Wendy, and Barbara Laker. 2015. *Busted: A Tale of Corruption and Betrayal in the City of Brotherly Love.* New York: HarperCollins.

Santory Jorge, Anayra, and Mareia Quintero Rivera, eds. 2018. *Antología del Pensamiento Crítico Puertorriqueño Contemporáneo.* Buenos Aires: CLASCO.

Scheper-Hughes, Nancy, and Philippe Bourgois. 2004. "Introduction: Making Sense of Violence." In *Violence in War and Peace: An Anthology,* edited by Nancy Scheper-Hughes and Philippe Bourgois, 1–27. Oxford: Blackwell.

Volk, Steve. 2011. "SPECIAL REPORT: The Top 10 Drug Corners 2011." Edited by Jonathan Valania and illustrated by Jay Bevenour. *Phawker,* August 23. https://web.archive.org/web/20201111234018/http://www.phawker.com/2011/08/23/special-report-the-top-10-drug-corners-2011/.

Wacquant, Loïc. 2010. "Class, Race and Hyperincarceration in Revanchist America." *Daedalus* 139, no. 3: 74–90. https://doi.org/10.1162/DAED_a_00024.

Williams Walsh, Mary. 2017a. "Hedge Fund Sues to Have Puerto Rico's Bankruptcy Case Thrown Out." *New York Times,* August 7.

Williams Walsh, Mary. 2017b. "Tiny Territory, Debt in Billions: Fears Spread to Virgin Islands." *New York Times,* June 26.

# 11 SHIFTING SOUTH

COCAINE'S HISTORICAL PRESENT AND THE CHANGING
POLITICS OF DRUG WAR, 1975–2015

Cocaine has been with us as a hemispheric drug for more than a century, but today it is mostly stuck in the public imagination as an illicit but popular "party" drug in the United States and the catalyst of our never-ending violent "drug war" with Colombia. These images are seriously obsolete. This essay tries to make sense of the emerging reality of cocaine's rapidly shifting historical present by discerning larger changes in the drug in terms of its "global commodity chains," not per se a novel approach to studying drugs. What's new, I contend, is cocaine's commodity chain's significant sustained "shift south," away from the US market, which is reshaping its larger continuing production and trafficking networks throughout the Andes, reorienting mainly to emerging markets and transiting poles like Brazil (Bagley 2012; Felbab-Brown and Newby 2015; Vargas 2017).[1] The Age of Colombian Cocaine, associated with the former, receding chain, may now be properly periodized as 1975–2005, along with that chain's particular politics, which sustained the hemispheric drug war. These "big" trends may help to contextualize other discussions in this volume about the "moral economies" (as well as the political economies) of cocaine and crack cocaine.

An exercise to clarify this commodity chain shift south has implications, both very local and global, among them its fallout for the politics of drugs. It is now commonplace to assert, for example, that the US drug war in Latin America is at a crisis or crossroads. After a half century of compliance by Latin American states with the US-led, UN-sanctioned global prohibition regime, and after decades of aggressive interdiction and eradication policies against drugs like cocaine, Latin American elites are now openly talking back about drugs. Examples abound: the 2008 Latin American Commission on Drugs and Democracy, the Colombian and Guatemalan-commissioned 2013 OAS report that prioritizes public health and violence-averting strategies on drug traffic, the legalization of cannabis in Uruguay and Jamaica's decriminalizing reforms, or the region's global lead in UNGASS 2016 in efforts to overhaul the UN drug system (OAS 2013; Youngers 2013). Part of this crisis may be discursive, hiding a stubborn reality of entrenched militarized drug war apparatus, in both the United States and Latin America. But part of this pushback, or "blowback" as termed elsewhere (Gootenberg 2012), is unprecedented. The temptation is to attribute this political sea change to the patent "failure" in halting drug violence and illicit drug flows from the Andes or across Mexico into the United States, after so many decades, lost and ruined lives, and billions of dollars in this drug war. But these changes are more complicated and paradoxical. Rather than a simple cost-benefit or public policy question—in which case drug wars on both ends would have ended decades ago—it may reflect the pivot south in the larger drug commodity chain, as well as related changing sovereignties of national states like Colombia on the cusp of these commodity shifts.[2]

This essay broaches these implications by providing the first synthetic overview of cocaine's shift south: the historical precedents when cocaine originally moved north in the twentieth century; the dramatic changes in the US cocaine consumption and politics since about 2000; the drug's discernible movements south into Brazilian and other global markets; the southern swerve of coca-producing regions across the Andean ridge itself, with Peru a reemergent center of illicit cocaine; and the diversity of governing responses of Andean states to cocaine's shifting chain. As a historian writing about a presentist shift, I must hedge here that parts of this analysis are largely informed speculations about trends—ones that can become rapidly outdated by the continuous changes in global cocaine trafficking and consumption.

## HISTORICAL COCAINE SHIFTS

Some brief context on cocaine's past commodity chains highlights these changes underway today. "Global commodity chains" is a concept culled from Wallersteinian world systems sociology that traces the economic, social, and political-cultural pathways of goods across geographic space and borders (Bellone 1990; Bair 2005). The past century of cocaine's history roughly falls into four periods and geographies of changing cocaine commodity chains from the eastern Andes—the original zone of manufacturing the modern illicit drug cocaine from native Andean coca leaf and the zone from which it has rarely strayed (Gootenberg 2007a, 2007b, 2008: chapter 3).

The first era, from the 1880s to the 1940s, saw the rise and decline of a legal commodity chain of cocaine and coca for global medicinal and commercial uses, mainly from eastern Peru. It relied on an Andean technology of "crude cocaine" (a form of *pasta básica de cocaína*, PBC), which peaked at ten tons of export around 1905. Modern Dutch and Japanese colonial-industrial chains in Southeast Asia helped displace Peruvian cocaine in the early 1900s, though both of these rivals to Andean cocaine lay ruined by the end of World War II. The second era, from the late 1940s to the mid-1970s, saw the construction of illicit cocaine networks, responding to the postwar completion of a US-led cocaine prohibition regime across the Andes. Small peasants, "chemists," and smugglers mobilized from the eastern Andes, in Peru and Bolivia in the 1950s–60s, trafficking cocaine north through bases in Chile and Cuba. Illicit networks shifted along Cold War milestones such as the Bolivian revolution (1952), the Cuban revolution (1959), Nixon's (1969/70) declaration of the drug war against marijuana and heroin, and the 1973 coup in Chile. These last events proved key in the formation of a professional hemispheric trafficker class, at first mainly Cuban exiles. By 1975 the Pinochet regime had propelled trafficking centers decisively north to Colombia and Colombians. During this formative process, the capacity for cocaine rose from less than half a ton at the close of its legal life in 1950 to about ten tons by 1975. Cocaine's illicit rebirth was the start of a longer arc I term "cocaine's march *north*" (Gootenberg 2012) as the drug moved from rare to plentiful and oriented nearer to northern trafficking routes, customers, and drug politics in the United States.

Thus began the Age of Colombian Cocaine (1975–2005), cocaine's third major historical epoch. Its commodity chain lucratively concentrated in Colombia in two increasingly conflictive processes. The first, from 1975 to 1985, saw the swift buildup of regional processing, mafias, and exporter organizations known as the Medellín, Cali, and other "cartels"—a misnomer for such competitive uber-capitalist groups. Still tapping flows of peasant PBC coca paste from Peru's Upper Huallaga Valley and lowland Bolivia, the vestige of prior chains, Colombians innovated the wholesale routing of cocaine largely across the Caribbean into south Florida into the upscale 1970s American coke boom they helped to spark. Cocaine multiplied to a hundred tons by 1980 and by 1990 to a thousand-ton capacity, all such numbers being educated guesswork. Cocaine became far cheaper and assessible to users. By the late 1980s, 25 million North Americans had used the drug, and authorities, following cocaine's glamour phase, focused the drug war on the panic around the spiral of racially and socially downscaled smokable "crack" cocaine.

The second phase of the Colombian commodity chain, from 1985 to 2005, was propelled by the Reagan–Bush era US-Andean war on drugs, escalated amid the mayhem in south Florida, urban crack scares, and "national security" concerns. The civil war sparked by cocaine rivalries and US extradition campaigns in Colombia, a concerted US crackdown on Caribbean smuggling routes, and the Andean Initiative militarization of Peruvian and Bolivian drug wars by the early 1990s led to important shifts—just not the ones intended. Major transit routes shifted: the rise of Cali interests over Escobar's target Medellín Cartel swiftly shifted cocaine routing northwest across war-torn Central America toward the multiplying cartels of northern Mexico, that is, the Juárez, Sinaloan, and Gulf groups. By the mid-1990s, 80 percent or more of cocaine flowed into the United States through these Mexican corridors, and drug lords, enriched and empowered by cocaine's extraordinary border profits, gained the upper hand against both Colombian middlemen and the Mexican state. This was the prelude to the sanguinary Mexican drug war of the 2000s, the ultimate expression of cocaine's longer northern march. Moreover, also in the 1990s, Colombian roles consolidated in novel ways: coca growing, finally squeezed in Bolivia and Peru by strong-arm regimes, quickly regrouped in rural Colombia, with thousands of farmers enlisted as cocaleros in zones such as southeast Putumayo. This vertical integration of coca-cocaine in one nation fueled waves of violence as paramilitaries, leftist guerrillas like the FARC, mafias, and officials fought over growing spoils. The war on Colombian cartels in the 1990s mainly fostered more efficient, elusive, decentralized exporter nodes—soon hundreds—who began diversifying the drug to nascent European and Brazilian markets (Gootenberg 2012; Kenney 2007; Bagley 2012). Yet all through this high drug-war era, the capacity for growing coca and fielding cocaine never actually fell, indeed peaking at about 1,400 tons by 2000. Traffickers simply planted and smuggled more drugs to beat rising risks of interdiction. Moreover, the US-style kingpin targeting and coca eradication strategies, for several reasons, inadvertently escalated the drug violence. Thus by 2000, the Colombian epicenter of cocaine's commodity chain led to the explicit political alliance with the United States—Plan Colombia, 2000–2005—to battle the drug and its impact on security.

The newest phase of the cocaine political-commodity chain—what I coin here "shifting south"—began around 2005 and continues to unfold.

In some places, such as Brazil and southwest Europe, its precedents reach into the 1990s. In the largest sense, this movement reverses the course of cocaine's previous half-century historical march north. Yet few have viewed cocaine's fragmented changes in such a wider, more complete, geopolitical lens. Worth noting from the outset is that totals of estimated world cocaine production are not changing much (according to the 2017 UN World Drug Report, 746–943 tons, depending on which coca conversion ratio used), at most a 10 percent drop from the 1998–2016 period, and the global number of yearly prevalence users has actually grown modestly to 18.3 million people (UNODC 2016: figure 22; 2017: 39–42). Now, since 2016–17, some estimates (given Colombia's post-2016 cocaine spike) run to a historic high of over two thousand tons of illicit drug capacity. What's changing instead, in a series of momentous shifts, is the political geography of cocaine.

## THE RETREATING US COCAINE EPICENTER

The United States is no longer the dynamic pole in global cocaine markets. For reasons that puzzle drug experts, long-entrenched cocaine consumption began to drop sharply after 2005, with a marked ratchet down in 2007–8. At its peak in the 1990s, cocaine, with a global worth of some $85 billion, represented over half ($60 billion in current dollars) of annual US expenditures on illicit drugs. The United States hosted half of the world's 14 million regular cocaine users, including millions of low-end crack cocaine users. In the half decade since 2006, total US consumption of cocaine fell by half to less than 140 tons, and to less than a quarter of all monies spent on drugs. A groundbreaking 2015 study (Caulkins et al. 2015) revealed that the number of "chronic users" who drive demand fell by some 27 percent between 2006 and 2010 to below 2 million (US Office of National Drug Control Policy [ONDCP] 2014; UNODC 2014: part E). This is one of the steepest drug use drops ever recorded. Federal border seizures of cocaine fell from 160 tons to twenty tons, though dispersing Colombian traffickers are still working to reroute drugs away from Mexico through new weak spots like Honduras, Venezuela, Haiti, the Dominican Republic, and Puerto Rico— as explored by Bobea and Veeser in this volume. Meanwhile, the pool of heavy cocaine users appears to be aging, and many fewer young people are initiated in the drug. The annual prevalence of twelfth graders even trying cocaine fell from over 6 percent in 1999 to 2.6 percent in 2013. Larger urban or demographic transformations are likely at play. But a supply factor probably lies behind all these declines, as street prices of cocaine rose consistently after

2006–8, for the first time in three decades of drug war—from an average of $94 a gram in late 2006 to $174 a gram by late 2009, along with significant cuts in street drug purity. To be sure, this is quite a lag for claims of policy victory, as pushing drug prices up out of reach of users was the dominant official rationale behind US supply interdiction policies since the mid-1970s, decades in which domestic cocaine prices steadily fell until 2007.

Unfortunately, with cutbacks in US drug monitoring programs (DAWN and ADAM, based on hospital and arrest sampling, and the intrinsic unreliability of general drug consumption surveys), we actually know very little about drug consumption trends since these 2010 markers. But signs do suggest a continuing downward trend of cocaine (along with the upward trends in cannabis, heroin, and synthetic opioids), at least through 2015 (UNODC 2016). For example, ADAM II (a program that drug tests booked arrestees) shows a significant urban retreat of cocaine through 2012, and aging user populations in eight of ten major sites, with crack declining in all save New York (ONDCP 2012: ADAM III; 2015: Data Supplement). We know that cocaine-related deaths fell between 2006 and 2013 by 34 percent, a clear public health gain, reaching a low in 2009–10, and cocaine treatment admissions dropped in half through 2014. A 2013 Community Epidemiology Working Group (CEWG) multivariable assessment of cocaine found indicators of the drug still falling in seven of nineteen zones of study, with four stable and eight areas with mixed results. But a 2014 drug use estimate suggests that while 4.5 million Americans still used cocaine once in the prior year, there were only 1.5 million regular "past month" users and only 354,000 monthly users of crack and 58,000 new crack initiates—a small fraction of those found even in the early 2000s, when some two-thirds of consumption was via crack.[3] Among US college students, only 0.9–1.0 percent tried cocaine on a monthly basis in 2013–14, indicating falls—with crack the sharpest—across all class lines.

The trend—cocaine's "tipping point," or more punningly what Beau Kilmer has called "Uncle Sam's Cocaine Nosedive," is starting to attract social scientific analysis, though explanations tend to be speculative and scattershot. Indeed, Kilmer, one of the original Rand team that rigorously filtered the cocaine decline out of the last full US National Drug Survey of 2010, has generated no less than a "dozen hypotheses," none definitive, for cocaine's dive (Kilmer 2016). On the supply side these range from Colombian coca eradication, precursor chemical shortages, Colombian or Central American interdiction, fragmenting trafficking organizations, or their diversification into non-drug illicit activities, and governmental cooperation, disruption, and violence at the US-Mexico border. On the demand side, the evidence looks vaguer: globalized demand driving up US prices, the aging of heavy use cohorts, user substitution by other drugs (though with little direct evidence), and even lost surplus incomes from the 2008 recession. John Bailey and Juan Carlos Garzón (Garzón and Bailey 2015), on the other hand, focus exclusively on trafficking issues and speculate about four possible contributing effects for supply reductions in the United States: a "balloon effect" (the geographic spread of illicit coca to safer cross-border havens), the "cockroach effect" (trafficker dispersion under repression), a butterfly effect (random residual global events), and a "short-sheet effect" (unintentional policy effects). It is probably a good thing that serious researchers admit we don't know why, unlike doubtful official claims that Plan Colombia or the larger drug war triumphed in places like Colombia (Mejía 2015). A broader frame of commodity chain shifts may address some of these data or politically loaded uncertainties.

As a historian, it bears caution that our drug menus are constantly shifting in US history (Courtwright 1995; Musto 1999), so no one can rule out some kind of future cocaine resurgence. Indeed, by 2016–17, press reports began circulating about a cocaine comeback, publicly linked in a March 2017 State Department report on the surge of Colombian cocaine produced in advance of the FARC peace treaty, and by 2018, to dramatic interceptions of cocaine heading to US markets. Two "troubling signs" are a rise in past-month prevalence from 1.5 to 1.9 million in 2015 (strongest in the Northeast) and a steep climb in cocaine-related deaths in 2015–16. However, a closer look at available data by the leading analysts, Kilmer and Midgette (2017), classifies these as "mixed messages": the robust majority of indicators do not yet point to a trend, although they warn that a rise in first-time users today could lead to more heavy users down the road (Carnevale Associates 2016; Miroff 2017). The spike in cocaine fatalities is likely due to mixed use with opioids, especially lethal fentanyl.

What might cocaine's slide spell for the governance of drugs within the United States? As a historian of the drug, I submit that cocaine (given its enormous markup profitability and high risk structures) was the most consequential drug driving and informing the US drug war since the early 1980s. Cocaine dominated illicit drug expenditures (a majority prior to 2000); the drug war's overseas projection to the Andes, the Caribbean, and Mexico; and the related vectors of violent conflict surrounding multiple layers of cocaine trafficking. The rapid racialization and bifurcation of cocaine markets and users in the 1980s (i.e., the US crack scare) led directly to the domestic drug war's transformation into the punitive racial sentencing and incarceration regime of the 1990s and beyond (Reinarman and Levine 2004; Alexander 2010). Even middle-class white users began by the 1980s to fear the powder drug's powerful allure. (The majority of drug arrests, however, predominantly poor Latinos and Black youth, have always been about cannabis, and racial profiling aside, documented cocaine use rates by African Americans is typically lower than among whites.) From cocaine's takeoff era to the mid-1990s, a large portion of Americans polled felt that drug trafficking—meaning Latin American cocaine cartels—was a direct threat to US security. Indeed, President Ronald Reagan in 1986 institutionalized those fears in National Security Directive 221, which broadly militarized and escalated all fronts of the drug war.

Now, as any casual observer of the culture knows, backed by survey after survey, the United States is fast becoming a "pot nation"—in my humble opinion, a big gain in public health, perennial alcohol abuse aside. The dramatic problem drugs today are cheap Mexican brown heroin, meth (now cycling down), and a dramatic wave of abused pharmaceutical opioids like Oxycontin and fentanyl, responsible for tens of thousands of annual overdose deaths in America's heartland. There is some drug-war irony in the post-2000 rise of pharmaceutical synthetics in the United States, since they first arose as "import substitution" from the hardening of borders against imported illicit drugs (though Mexican crime groups and Chinese chemical suppliers now turn to wholesaling counterfeits of crossover Big Pharma products). It deflates the foreign drug war rationale as illicit drugs become increasingly "homeland" drugs. With a slight lag, the politics of drugs are changing at home: the most recent DEA National Drug Threat Assessment (a national survey across US law enforcement) reveals a remarkable shift in the perception of cocaine: whereas in 2007–9 it was still considered the lead "drug threat" by more than 40 percent of respondents, by 2013–15 it quietly slipped to the 5–10 percent range, replaced by rising fears of heroin. Cannabis, despite its surge in the culture, is thankfully no longer deemed a policing threat.[4] Even drug racialization is softening: that the current heroin "epidemic" in the United States is perceived as predominantly "white" (in contrast to Nixon's demonizing late 1960s Black heroin "crime" scare) has sparked a rapid attitudinal revolution, fully articulated by President Obama's final drug czar Michael Botticelli. Heavy or hard drug users are no longer deemed hardened criminals but "victims" with an evidence-based "brain disease" that needs family-like compassion and "public health" and "safety" interventions. In mid-2016, William Brownfield, assistant

secretary of state for narcotics (a former envoy to Colombia) testified before Congress that "We must today manage a strategic transition from cocaine to heroin. We've made great progress on cocaine. U.S. consumption
is down more than 50 percent, but heroin is exploding" (US Congress 2016:
3, cited in Arter 2016). In an intriguing disconnect, most Americans remain
unaware of cocaine's disappearing act. Instead, the surprisingly vibrant
US drug reform debate now overwhelmingly focuses on decriminalizing
cannabis, the incarceration crisis, and humane harm reduction strategies
toward heroin addiction and overdose. It is too early to tell if these policy
trends will survive Donald Trump's presidency, but given its dominant
(Caucasians as victims) racial politics, some avenues of drug reform may
persist. Whatever, cocaine's shift is one invisible structural change underlying liberalized drug debates and may color drug politics outside US borders, as addressed below.

## BRAZIL AND GLOBALIZING CONSUMPTION

Beyond the United States, the second major changing element in cocaine's
global commodity chain is globalizing consumption. While the grand sum
of illicit drugs potentially produced for global markets remains fairly stable at 800–1,000 tons, it is now being dispersed and consumed far more
widely. Cocaine flows south are snaking across varied sites in South America, Europe, West Africa, and across the southern Pacific. Brazil is the case
meriting most attention, for two reasons. Brazil has the potential to both
surpass the United States as the major consumption culture for cocaine,
and it may likely serve, like Colombia before, as the world's central distribution point for the drug.

The UN has long identified Brazil as the world's second largest cocaine
consumer nation, a solid trend by 2000 if not before. However, aggregate
consumption statistics are basically incommensurable and inconsistent in
methods compared to the counterpart market in the United States. By 2010,
Brazil already reportedly consumed a sum total of ninety-two tons of cocaine, about 18 percent of world use. However, a recent Brazilian survey
put the number of casual users at more than 3.3 million, which may therefore surpass the 1.5 million monthly users identified in the United States
in 2013, sampling problems aside. Moreover, Brazil's cocaine "prevalence"
has been swiftly rising since 2010: from 0.07 to 1.2 percent in 2012 and to
a current UN estimate of 1.75 percent, which leads into longer-term heavy
use. This is the world's second highest rate and four times the global adult

average (Bradley and King 2012; "Consumo de cocaína no Brasil" 2015; UNODC 2015c: 53–54).[5] Likely an exaggeration, journalists now roundly cite Brazilian coke consumption at "a ton" a day, which would account for a third of known world supply. Just as anecdotal, by 2009 some 80 percent of Brazilian bank notes tested positive for cocaine residues, the world's third highest rate.

Adding to this sense of cocaine's ubiquity is the visibility and conflict surrounding the drug. Brazil may have as many as a million crack users in the "cracolândias" (or "cracklands") of Rio de Janeiro and São Paulo (see also Rui, this volume). Now accelerating as well in northeastern cities and favelas, crack is repeating the cycle of oversupply, low-market drug retailing, racialization, and public health and policing alarmism that swept the United States in the decade 1985–95. Brazil is surely the world's current crack capital, even if some epidemiologists balk at sensationalized numbers (low-balled at 370,000 in Brazil's state capitals alone) as well as familiar user social stereotypes (Miraglia 2016). Now, a fifth of all clients seeking drug treatment, usually middle class, are for cocaine. Cocaine is notoriously cheap and purer in Brazil relative to international standards, given its proximity to Andean source countries and Brazil's extensive, well-oiled trafficking networks. It is hard to extrapolate whether Brazil has already or soon will surpass the United States as cocaine's largest aggregate market, given the faulty data in both countries. The UN *World Drug Report* (2016) unfortunately contained no new hard data on either country, although estimating South America's users at 4.5 million, close in number to North America's 5 million (UNODC 2016: figure 50). It is also hard to guess whether Brazil's current recession and political crisis will detract from, or actually add to, cocaine's dynamism in Brazil.

There are structural reasons behind Brazil's ascendancy as the next pole in cocaine's history, although the history of cocaine in Brazil is still sketchy. First, the taste for cocaine (as in the United States) has a long and storied past: urban bohemian scenes of the early twentieth century, hedonist cocaine use in nightclubs in Brazilian cities and ports during the mid-century decades of incipient illicit cocaine from the Andes, and a steadily rising practice among the growing modern middle classes and partying nouveau riche since the mid-1970s explosion of cocaine production in Colombia, Peru, and Bolivia (Resende 2006; Gootenberg 2008: 270–72).

Second, Brazil shares the world's longest contiguous land border with the Andean nations, a thoroughly porous, Amazonian frontier with the three post-1980s cocaine producers of Colombia, Peru, and Bolivia. Governing this sort of border makes governing the US-Mexico border look easy. The redoubts of potential Colombian cocaine production (shifting from Meta-Guaviare toward Vaupés, Guainía, Vichada, and Amazonas) are adjacent to Brazilian frontiers, though former reports signal that half of Brazil's cocaine originates in Bolivia (Van Dunn 2016; Vargas 2017: 8). It is not simply geography but the active expansion of Brazilian drug smuggling personnel and networks into Colombia, Peru, and Bolivia. Fluvial towns like Corumbá along the Paraguay River border between Bolivia and Brazil (seen in Robert Gay, this volume), Leticia with Colombia, and now Tabatinga and Manaus farther downstream from Peru, are becoming bustling cocaine smuggling crossroads to coastal urban consumers, complemented by a new overland Interoceanic Highway. Peruvian Jair Ardela Michue built a distribution hub at Manaus, a city of now 2 million, awash with both cocaine and drug corruption (Garzón 2010: 60–82; Romero 2014; Gay 2015). The Amazonian FDN (Família do Norte) gang is today in open violent conflict for control of that trade with coastal prison-grown groups like the PCC. Amazon River traffic is beset by cocaine-driven piracy. This is not to mention drugs crossing west from neighboring Paraguay, a smugglers' paradise in the "wild west" Triple Frontier region, and a veritable "narco-state" sandwiched between Bolivia and Brazil. Among the world's heaviest cannabis exporters, eastern border cities like Ciudad de Este are now spawning cocaine hubs run by the principal Brazilian gangs (Lohmuller 2015; Garat 2016).

Third, cocaine appears as a drug with a special affinity for countries, like Brazil, with sharp indices of social inequality, where both the ultra-wealthy and the excluded hyper-poor play out segmented relational roles in cocaine culture and networks (the United States, UK, Russia, Nigeria, and Italy are to varying degrees similar cases). Inequalities, including Brazil's still silent racial ones, possibly make Brazil structurally prone to cocaine, and its submarket crack, though most of the media and political spotlight naturally falls on the role of Brazil's easily corruptible public officials, high and low. Cocaine binges filled the press during Rio's income-grossing upscale events like the World Cup and Olympics. Brazil's other parallel to the United States is its ample internal arms market and the association of cocaine with both a high incidence and visible incidents of drug violence, and relatedly, rising racial incarceration. Brazil now holds the world's fourth largest imprisoned population.

Fourth, Brazil suffered the misfortune of blowback geography from the past US war on Andean cocaine. Colombian cartels, after the 1980s crackdown on Caribbean smuggling to the United States, sought out new contraband routes. After the 1990s, rival traffickers fled the drug war–style "decapitation" of cartels by Colombian authorities, some to Venezuela but mostly to Brazil. "Local marketing" soon emerged as an alternative lucrative business strategy, particularly when Colombian organizations paid partners in coke shares rather than cash (LaSusa 2016; Vargas 2017). Crack first appeared in the late 1980s as dispersing Colombian traffickers dumped cheap or surplus cocaine in Brazil. In recent years, the vaunted Venezuelan exit has withered (a business climate unstable even for traffickers), tilting ever more Colombian cocaine traffic south, likely in continuing Colombian-Brazilian partnerships (Fischer et al. 2016; Garzón and Wilches 2016: 44–47; Grillo 2016: chapters 10–11). In this larger shift, Brazil also quickly consolidated as the key transshipment path of cocaine to southern Europe via Guinea-Bissau, Nigeria, Ghana, Benin, and other easily penetrable states now known as West Africa's "cocaine coast," where seizures first spiked in exactly the years of cocaine's 2006–7 shift down. From 2010 to 2015, some 58 percent of cocaine seized in Europe was shipped via Brazil (vs. 20 percent traced to Colombia); by 2016, as much as 80 percent of cocaine in Europe reportedly transited via Santos, Brazil's mega-port, which also routes drugs around Africa to China. More than half of West Africa's coke discoveries, where consumption has mushroomed, also originate in Brazil (UNODC 2007; Nicoll 2011), and the same is likely true in the growing role of the Algerian coast in transshipment to Europe (Ben Yahia and Farrah 2019). In 2014, 30 percent of Brazil's record seizures of cocaine (forty-two tons) were destined for re-export. Whether engineered directly by scattering Colombian traffickers (and now reputedly Nigerian mafias traversing transnationally in Brazil), this role continues to grow in tandem with Brazil's modern dominance in southern Atlantic container shipping lanes. That Brazil is Latin America's industrial giant, with massive chemical sectors, means that cocaine precursor processing inputs are amply available for increasing refining of imported PBC, unlike Colombia, where chemical shortages from controls are now severe.

Fifth, at some point in this spillover from the Andean drug bonanza and US pressures against Colombian drugs, major cocaine retailing and trafficker groups began to consolidate in Brazil (see Taniele Rui's chapter, this volume). This drug surplus was captured by the highly organized and disciplined criminal gangs that connect favelas and prison complexes (e.g., in the 1970s by Comando Vermelho, CV, of Rio, or later Primeiro Comando da Capital, PCC, of São Paulo). Before the 1990s, Brazil's cocaine was still a modest, informal, dispersed "ant trade" crisscrossing a vast interior, squirreled along, for example, on baggage on Brazilian bus lines (Gay 2016). The CV's decisive strategic turn to cocaine (away from less lucrative cannabis) to finance operations wholesale occurred in 1982. It fueled the rise of drug lords like the ill-fated Ué (Ernaldo Pinto de Medeiros), the public late-1980s cocaine cornucopia in Rio, and escalating gang rivalry and soaring murder rates, and by the early 2000s even ventures (involving megadealers like Fernandinho Beira-Mar) to leverage wholesale arms-for-coke deals with the FARC guerrillas ("Polícia investiga relacão de Beira-Mar" 2001; Miraglia 2016: 4–5). The PCC fields its own Paraguayan networks, and drug gang criminality pervades the state apparatus in Espirito Santo, the small coastal state just north of Rio. Indeed, the fact that Brazil, like the United States, is a major small-arms producing and dealing nation no doubt adds to the potential lethality of national cocaine gangs.

It is hard to predict the longer-term policy and political implications for Brazil as the emerging if not leading global cocaine pole. Everything is cloudy at the moment, given Brazil's radical change of regime and political and economic crisis. Even before this, the country has shown a remarkably mixed complex of punitive crackdowns and innovative strategies toward cocaine—from the vaunted police "pacification" programs (e.g., the 2008–12 occupations of gang-ruled favelas by heavily armed, specially trained police units) to modest public health and harm reduction experiments with decriminalized cracolândias in São Paulo, to shoot-down threats against Andean trafficker flights, to mounting drug intelligence and drug policy aid to Bolivia in the aftermath of DEA's 2008 withdrawal from that country. The Brazilian Supreme Court has even judged drug possession laws formally unconstitutional, with mixed results in actual policing practices. Brazil, with one of the world's largest penal populations, suffers an incarceration crisis analogous to the United States, fueled by mounting cocaine arrests and subhuman prison conditions. In part, this mix, or mess, of policies reflects Brazilian federalism and the power of localities and cities to toy with new policies (Miraglia 2016: 11–12). Even given ambivalent federal drug policies, Brazil officially assumed a progressive (human rights and civil society) stance during the 2016 UNGASS global drug reform agenda, if far from a leadership role like Colombia's. This was before Brazil's recent dramatic swing to the right in government.[6] Brazil clearly wants to keep coca cultivation outside its own Amazonian regions (where some cultivation is rumored along Peruvian borders and as Peruvian coca spreads farther east into lowlands along the new Interoceanic Highway to Brazil) and somehow plug drug inflows from Andean states. I would venture that, should Brazil ever develop a cohesive or comprehensive cocaine policy, progressive or repressive, it could supersede the US role in adjacent Andean states.

In addition to Brazil, cocaine finds dynamic markets in Argentina (where it sparks corruption scandals and drug-related violence, especially in provinces or suburban shantytowns with lower-end "paca" smokers). Like Brazil, the country has growing transshipment and global trafficking roles; indeed, from 2005 to 2014 it was cited about twice as often as Colombia in global seizure reports (2,101 times), including forty-five destinations worldwide. Littoral Uruguay (via Paraguay) saw a tenfold jump in cocaine seizures from 2006 to 2014 (nearly 2.5 tons in 2009), and in part implemented its cannabis legalization package in order to focus on the more dangerous trafficking network. African nations like Nigeria and South Africa have significantly expanding cocaine consumer cultures, a spinoff of transit to Europe, with some 1.5 million users. Middle Eastern transit, from Lebanon to Turkey into the Caucus, Iran, and Russia, is a new frontier for African intermediaries. Markets continue robust in Europe, where cocaine use doubled to 124 tons from 1998 to 2008 as a result of Colombian supply diversions, and the UN recently estimated a 30 percent rise in consumption from 2011 to 2016 alone (UNODC 2010, cited in Felbab-Brown and Newby 2015; UNODC 2015c: esp. table 5). Briefly put, expansion of cocaine supplies to Europe jump-started in the early 1990s, diverted through coasts like Galicia, Spain (Carretero 2018), pioneered by diversifying (and pressured in their own hemisphere) Colombians. Today, there are high per capita indices of yearly coke use (1.4– 1.8 percent of adults) in Spain, Italy, the UK (notably Scotland), and Italy, a few surpassing the slipping US rate (under 1.5 percent when last gauged in 2012). About 40 percent of cocaine still enters from the south via Spain, and the rest mainly via Rotterdam, Belgium, and Northern Ireland. In 2015, Europe recorded 87,000 cocaine seizures amounting to 69.4 tons, led by Spain (twenty-two tons), Belgium (seventeen tons), and France (eleven tons). According to the OEDT (European Observatory of Drugs and Addiction), cocaine has been consistently growing in purity (104 percent) and falling in price from 2006 to 2015, a clear sign of expanding supplies, and trace cocaine is routinely found across European water supplies (cited in Vargas 2017: 2). In recent years a new and dramatic crack phenomenon has appeared in France (Peltier 2019), related (as in the American mid-1980s) to a drug surplus, but also among addicts seeking new pleasures in the country's scaled-up, publicly funded heroin substitution programs.

In the Pacific, on the other hand, high-price frontiers are driving new southern cocaine supply bridges to Australia, New Zealand, and Southeast

Asia. Half of Australia's cocaine is Colombian in origin (according to federal drug seizures), and 40 percent is from Peru, but some is rerouted from the Pacific coast of Mexico. Wealthy enclaves like Hong Kong, Shanghai, and other burgeoning Chinese cities could represent the drug's future destinations, some via Brazil, but more likely concealed directly in shipping containers from Asian-oriented Pacific ports of Peru or Chile. Cocaine seizures in Asia tripled between 1998 and 2014, shooting up 40 percent in 2014–15 alone. Some cocaine is also converging toward Asian markets from East Africa, as big 2016 seizures in Sri Lanka and Djibouti (the tiny Horn of Africa republic) reveal (UNODC 2016, 2017; Vargas 2017: 4–5).

In sum, cocaine use is no longer just a US or Colombian problem, in part because of the past US pressures that scattered the drug's networks around the globe. This could make some governments more skeptical of US-style cocaine policies, and others more directly concerned. Moreover, if cocaine eventually roots its future consumption centers in Europe or Asia, there is nothing to ensure that cocaine will remain a natural monopoly of Andean production. For example, legal colonial coca cultivation swiftly spread to ecologically apt Southeast Asia and even West Africa from 1900 to the 1930s (Gootenberg 1999: chapters 6–7), and these areas would face less transit risk to Asian or European markets, especially from the US DEA.

### COCA ON THE MOVE

The production zones of cocaine from coca leaf are also concertedly on the move south. Peru has a possibility of becoming the new Colombia, though these drug data of course vary. In 2013, the UNODC anointed Peru the world's top producer again, with over 340 tons of cocaine capacity, and Peruvian drug authorities peg their national capacity as oscillating between 450 and 350 tons. The ONDCP (US drug czar's office) placed Peru above Colombia's "production potential" of cocaine in four of six years since 2010, when Peru first topped Colombia at 280 tons to 240 tons. Whatever the social costs, merits, and time lags of Plan Colombia, we now know that Colombian coca cultivation fell overall by 50 percent from 2007 to 2012, though with a dramatic 2014–15 rebound. Colombia's capacity to refine cocaine dropped from 700 tons in 2001 to 245 tons in 2013, a perceptible waning of the historic Colombia-US cocaine chain, as some "90–95%" of cocaine found in the United States originates from Colombia (cf. ONDCP 2015; UNODC 2015a). What the Colombian state and police have gotten good at over time— because coca eradication (much less its on–off aerial fumigation) against beleaguered peasants is not, specialists realize, an efficient or fast way to stop the drug—was drug intelligence and seizures at labs on the ground (Garzón and Bailey, 2015; Mejía 2015). After 2016, however, the downward trend became muddled and then was reversed by today's dramatic resurgence of Colombian cocaine (over 200,000 hectares of coca by 2018, and an all-time high national cocaine capacity of 1,500 tons). Wholesale drug busts rose throughout 2016–18. Cocaine's resurgence is tied in most analyses to unforeseen political repercussions of the now beleaguered 2016 FARC treaty, which had sought to politically address cocalero grievances and illicit production; instead, for complex reasons, it led to a tripling of coca from 2013–16 (Acosta 2019; see also Idler, this volume). Furthermore, as Colombian drug specialist Ricardo Vargas warns us, the now hundreds of surviving Colombian trafficking groups remain highly adaptive, and may well be the "silent participants" in many of the global trafficking realignments seen above (Vargas 2017). Importantly, most of Colombia's newest round of illicit cocaine is still concentrating south, in Putumayo, Nariño, and Caquetá departments, now exiting southward across laxly policed Ecuadorian borders, ports, and shorelines, or toward Brazilian frontiers.

Rising in exactly 2005–8, Peru's resilient cocaine now mainly flows out of the remote southeastern VRAEM valley system (Valley of the Apurímac, Ene, and Mantaro Rivers), with at least a hundred tons flowing directly to Brazil, the rest south to Argentina and export bound. Peruvian coca rebounded a full 44 percent from 2000 to 2014. By 2014, the VRAEM alone supplied a fifth of the world's cocaine.[7] Peruvian officials claim there are only 55,000 cocaleros in the Amazon, a low guess given coca's rapid dispersal in recent years to remote lowland forests near the Brazilian and Colombian borders. Yet little Peruvian cocaine reportedly reaches north to the United States; indeed, according to the DEA's high-tech "cocaine signature" program, 90 percent is still of Colombian origin and only 7 percent Peruvian (ONDCP 2013; Pérez 2014: 161; UNODC 2014, 2016: 38; Soberón 2016). The return of Peruvian cocaine thus combines a classic "balloon" and "cockroach" effect from the north: the displacement of coca cultivation from Colombia, with exports handled largely by dispersing or fragmenting Colombian, Brazilian, and Mexican syndicates. What amplifies the impact of Peruvian drug supply is that, unlike Colombia, where most cocaine is caught in-country (some 165 tons in 2013), a negligible share of Peru's ballooning cocaine is stopped in Peru, barely 1–2 percent of VRAEM outflows in one recent report (Balbierz 2015). Bolivia mostly avoids the balloon, in a static third place in Andean cocaine, at about 150 tons. This buffer to cocaine's arc south likely relates to its national "social control" coca policies of the Chapare and Yungas districts (unlike Beni or Santa Cruz, nearer Brazil), though Bolivia still suffers territorial incursions by Peruvian or others trafficking drugs southward.

Moreover, even within Colombia's and Peru's national space, the geography of coca planting is also moving south. At its former peak, around the year 2000, Colombian coca farmers, with some 160,000 hectares, were invading virtually every niche of Colombian territory, including virgin northern zones such as the Darien, the Caribbean Guajira peninsula, the borderlands with Venezuela, and national parks and minority preserves, geographically dispersed by spraying operations (ONDCP 2013; UNODC 2014; Mejía 2015). In 2013, following a decade of concerted drug warfare against peasants, Colombia had only 48–69,000 hectares left in coca. Some 80,000 family units remain in coca, but account for merely 2–3 percent of agrarian product. The 2014–15 spike back to and beyond 2001 levels (160–180,000 hectares) is attributed to the perverse politics of the FARC treaty in their southern strongholds, where peasants in places like Putumayo and Nariño massively replanted coca to stake treaty land claims. By April 2017, more than 50,000 Colombian cocaleros had signed treaty Article 4 contracts to eliminate coca on the approximately 100,000 hectares now slated for intensive alternative development ("Colombia's Coca Production Soars" 2017; Granados 2017). If this political solution to illicit coca works—an increasingly doubtful outcome under the Duque administration and the FARC regrouping of 2019—it might close the Colombian drug war and Colombia's long dominance in the trade. These southern departments (Nariño, Cauca, Putumayo, and Caquetá) now account for more than three-quarters of coca cultivation. These zones also adjoin porous Ecuadorian border flows of precursor chemicals, now severely contained in central Colombia, and the weak state of Ecuador is actively becoming an outward transiting hub, for the very first time at significant scale. This geography also reflects cocaine's commodity push south, to zones marketable through southern Pacific ports such as Buenaventura and Guayaquil into the southeastward streams of Brazilian trafficking.

Similarly, Peru's new geography of coca has swerved south from the northern Huallaga to the southern VRAEM, toward Brazil and/or transit to Argentina. Instead of a policy push, this internal shift is rarely visualized in terms of larger Andean cocaine commodity chains. During the 1970s–80s boom, the Upper Huallaga Valley (UHV), notably San Martín and the Tocache district, became the heartland of Peruvian cocaine, funneling its peasant-made PBC north to the emerging Colombian cartels. In its heyday, around 1990, the greater Huallaga had some 120,000 hectares in illicit coca, that is, two-thirds of all Andean coca. But by the early 1990s, Colombian middlemen began pulling back to pursue coca at home, where coca crops bypassed Peru's in 1997, a link finished off by Fujimori's brief but intense CIA-assisted air war on the residual PBC "air bridge" to Colombia. Soon, alternative Amazonian water routes began draining drugs toward Brazil, though today most Peruvian cocaine alights from hundreds of ad hoc jungle airstrips. The VRAEM, which mostly lies in lowland Ayacucho, had coca and many ripe preconditions of social and political marginality, but the zone only rose to global prominence in 2005–8 with Colombia's coca fall-off (Bedoya Garland 2003; Soberón 2016; Van Dunn 2016: 513–14). A long, tense stalemate ensued there between peasants, traffickers, guerrillas, Peruvian drug police, and the army, unable to jump-start US-sponsored eradication, just rearticulated in a new 2017 Peruvian plan (Comisión Nacional 2017). Reports also reveal a still unquantifiable but strong movement of traffickers and peasant coca crews from the UHV to the far lower Amazon directly along the Brazilian frontier: the tri-border "Trapecio Amazónica" region connecting Santa Rosa del Yavarí (Peru), Leticia (Colombia), and Tabatinga (Brazil), or directly across from Colombia's southern Putumayo coca region. Peruvian officials, however, like to showcase instead the so-called Miracle of San Martín, the steep post-2005 drop in northern Peru coca bush attributed to integrated programs of eradication and crop substitution by cacao, coffee, or palm oil (Ruda and Zavaleta 2009; Manrique López 2015). My hunch is that localized policies of grassroots development or integrated security had less impact than coca's larger snake south along the South American commodity chain.

## ANDEAN POLITICAL RESPONSES

One remarkable side of cocaine's shift south down along the Andean ridge is the novel diversity of political and policy responses that it has opened in the three Andean states since 2006. In stylized shorthand, elaborated at great depth elsewhere (Gootenberg 2017), these are: Bolivia's defecting nationalist-indigenist "coca sí, cocaína no" control strategy; Colombia's triumphal state-building quest for a sustainable "post–drug war" control (now in retreat); and Peru's passive politics of "cocaine denial," a paradoxical response for the world's emerging top exporter (Durand 2014; Grisaffi and Ledebur 2016).

FIGURE 11.1 Examples of legal coca-based products for sale in Bolivia, including liquor, candies, and tea.

Bolivia's is the best-known response (see Grisaffi, this volume); since 2006, it has charted its own course in drug policies over the strenuous objections of the United States. Evo Morales has expelled the DEA, taken on the UN's global ban on indigenous coca leaf, diversified Bolivia's drug control partners, and developed so-called social control institutions that make coca sindicatos, with modest legal "cato" plots, themselves police illicit cultivation. The policy is deeply rooted in Bolivia's socially and geographically central relationship to coca leaf (if not the eternal symbol of Aymara resistance often portrayed), a product used or accepted now by most sectors of Bolivian society (see figure 11.1). The leaf became seen as the antithesis to cocaine, widely associated with "neoliberal" capitalism and past dictatorial and anti-drug repression of the late twentieth century. Social control channels a now recognized history of pro-coca campesino mobilizations and organization. The strategy, by most accounts, is both legitimate and working to lower coca crops, though actually working against cocalero interests (Farthing and Ledebur 2015; UNODC 2015b). Bolivian cocaine, as already noted, has remained contained in the years of cocaine's southern shift, and the country remains relatively free of drug violence. A small and poor nation has achieved a remarkable degree of sovereignty governing drug policy.

Colombia's is the most surprising response: long the battleground state and central ally in the US war against Andean cocaine, since about 2010 (during the Santos regime), the Colombian state has started staking out novel alternative paths to drug repression. Colombia hosted the OAS summit and subsequent report of 2012 that called for enhanced public health and anti-violence strategies against drugs, was a key sponsor of the 2015–16 UNGASS campaign to reform the restrictive UN drug system, unilaterally suspended US-supported fumigation of coca fields in 2015, and was working to fulfill a peace accord with a much-reduced FARC. The treaty includes an array of specific social measures (e.g., the much-debated Article 4) to retire both the guerrillas and allied peasant cocaleros from the cocaine trade. The complexities behind Colombia's turnabout can only be speculated (Gootenberg 2017: 12–23): the perceived tough "triumph" against cocaine (now seen as premature claims), the mobilizing centrality of visible drug violence and subversion since 1980 in Colombian urban and political life, a marginal deep history of national coca leaf, the growing capacities and unprecedented territorial reach of the state, the active role of a rising set of technocrats and intellectuals espousing alternatives to the long era of US drug war influence and ideology (OAS 2013; Arías et al. 2014; Neuman and Romero 2015; Richani 2016). Colombian governing elites watched cocaine and drug violence in retreat after 2005, but were concerned with making that last. An integrated Colombian intellectual and political class was speaking in terms of "post-conflict," "post–drug war" governance, though now with growing uncertainties. The United States, with few real solutions to offer Colombia for durable drug peace, cannot lose its ties with its most strategic Andean state.

Peru, in contrast to both Bolivia and Colombia, is not achieving new policies or greater sovereignty around cocaine. It is mired in what I call "cocaine denial" (Gootenberg 2017: 24–34). There is no apparent drug crisis in Peru, despite the country's renewed place in cocaine export for the fourth time in the drug's history; there is little news, research, social mobilization, lobbies, politicians, open violence, narco-culture, or policy initiatives about drugs (Cotler 1999; Vizcarra 2015). Faraway cocaleros or drug destabilization lie outside the national consciousness of an increasingly centralized Lima politics and media culture. The country remains passive or evasive to US anti-drug attentions. There are many reasons to speculate about for Peru's peculiar stance of denial: a deeply segregated historical and racial geography that keeps both coca-using highland "Indians" and the Amazonian cocaine tropics off mental maps, acts of historical oblivion around Peru's actually profound historical ties to the drug, a lack of visible drug business empires, weak public drug institutions, or today's boom-time neoliberal veneration of the market that tacitly accepts the social roles of illicit, corrupt, informal, and export activities of many stripes. Peru is thus, in my analysis, vulnerable to both continuing expansion of the VRAEM drug trade as well as weakly positioned against outside pressures, should either gain force.

In all, instead of aligned cocaine politics, much less homogeneous "drug reform" strategies, the Andean nations (with Ecuador until recently aside) are driving in three diverse directions as cocaine's commodity chains shift decisively south. How these diverging Andean drug politics fit into cocaine's global "shift south" from its waning northern political axis remains an open question, one that may inform a post–UNGASS 2016 politics of the trade negotiated more and more at the regional level.

## CONCLUSIONS

Apart from seriously grappling with the micro-dynamics, in specific cocaine-producing hotspots, transit spaces, drug scenes, or forms and sites of violence, what are some governance implications of understanding cocaine's latest commodity chain conjuncture? The resurgence of Peruvian cocaine appears like a "dagger pointed south" into South America and beyond, to a more global trafficking and consuming world.[8] This suggests, above all, that US drug politics, under mounting pressures at home, could feasibly become structurally detached from the latest incarnation of the global cocaine commodity chain. Why indeed should US drug authorities pay heed to cocaine if its menace points elsewhere? Why should new isolationists expend funding and drug war strategies against a drug that no longer underwrites the US domestic drug crises (now focused around opioids)? For example, such de facto drug diplomatic neutrality has already been adopted vis-à-vis Paraguay, one of the genuine narco-states of the Americas, a major transit hub for cannabis and cocaine throughout South but not North America.[9] A similar example is US tolerance of the poppy boom in Afghanistan, which directly impinges on addiction in China, Russia, and Europe, but not "homeland" populations. Should the present trend continue of shrinking or stable cocaine use in the United States, globalizing usage, anti-drug war movements in the United States (still mostly about cannabis and racial incarceration), and a denouement to Colombia's long civil wars and drug wars (now doubtful in post-Santos 2018), the long US-led drug war against Andean cocaine will lose its dynamic in a strategic alliance of Colombia and US drug warriors. The DEA and the military, when they even voice the unfashionable term *drug war*, are repositioning themselves against perceived threats of Central America's disintegration by gangs and drug exports, and against the threat of Pacific Mexican poppy and pharmaceutical supplies in the raging US opioid epidemic. Cocaine looks like an obsolete target, the stuff of Netflix retrospectives like *Narcos*. Instead of direct US involvement, Colombia's seasoned drug warrior specialists may act as proxies to areas like Peru or Central America to mobilize or militarize anti-cocaine campaigns (Tickner 2014). Amid these changed conditions, US responses have suddenly become the hardest of all to predict in the unfolding age of Donald J. Trump. For example, despite alarmist pronouncements about renewing the drug war on multiple fronts, Trump's budgets at first slashed funds for coca eradication projects—just more frivolous "foreign aid"—which effectively leaves nations like Colombia and Peru to their own devices. The rising Pacific power for these nations, China, has no perceptible stake yet in suppressing faraway cocaine.

Moreover, this shifting global commodity chain, along with the shock to Latin American governing elites of the carnage of the Mexican drug war (2006 on), may undergird the visibly diversifying politics of drugs in Latin America. Some observers (Dudley 2014) now note that shifting cocaine trafficking routes and rising cocaine consumption nodes in Latin America itself have resulted in a complex new array of lower-level criminal groups, well beyond Brazil, that are exacerbating levels of violence even as the region remains relatively democratic and stable. Bear in mind that overarching drug policy proposals are unlikely to come any time soon from the international arena, after the 2016 UNGASS talks, pushed by key Latin American states, failed to make a dent in global prohibition, beyond new human rights checks in the system. As observers note, the formerly hard-line enforcer role of the United States at the UN is increasingly superseded by Russia and China (concerned with opiates or amphetamine abuse) and even by a string of actively conservative African states inundated by cocaine and other drugs. In effect, any continuing impetus to global drug reform will likely devolve to regional or national blocs (Felbab-Brown and Trinkunas 2015; Kilmer 2016).

In the Americas, it might logically fall to the Brazilians or Argentines to pick up the pieces and advance new types of policies to contain Andean cocaine. Both are large nations afflicted by domestic drug dilemmas or panics but conflicted on how to confront drugs (security, health, or social policy?). Yet, given the recent political and economic meltdowns of South America's big powers, any comprehensive or integrated approaches are unlikely soon. In the meantime, in this political vacuum, the newfound agency and autonomy of national drug politics responses by Bolivia and Colombia (and Peru's habitual passivity) may most shape the future politics of cocaine. Cocaine's saga continues, in its new south-shifting forms, the legacy of a long drug war and changing drug menus in the United States that have finally reversed cocaine's prior march north.

**NOTES**

This is a reformulated version of a paper first presented at the LASA 2016 panel "Cocaine's Products: From Growing to Transit" (New York, May 2016). I thank panel organizers Desmond Arias and Tom Grisaffi; Robert Gay (Connecticut College) and Cleia Noia (SSRC-DSD) for suggestions about Brazil; and Beau Kilmer (RAND Corporation) for key corrections, as well as later general feedback at "Governance in the Global Narcotics Trade" (George Mason University, February 2017) and the ADHS drug history conference (Utrecht, June 2017).

1 Ricardo Vargas's recent work (2017) reads very similar trends from a Colombian perspective: http://razonpublica.com/index.php/conflicto-drogas-y-paz-temas -30/10422-colombia-y-el-mercado-mundial-de-la-coca%C3%ADna.html.

2 I deliberately chose the term *shifting south* over generic *globalization* because it more accurately pinpoints the geographies of coca production, as well as the diversification of trafficking routes and consumption nodes through the Global South (Brazil–Africa, etc.). Clearly, it is also part of the drug's larger global expansion away from the Colombia-US route, dating in some areas to the mid-1990s.

3 US National Institute on Drug Abuse (2013); Substance Abuse and Mental Health Services Administration (2014), https://www.drugabuse.gov/related -topics/trends-statistics/overdose-death-rates.

4 US Drug Enforcement Administration (2014): chart 2, "Percentage of NDTS Respondents Reporting the Greatest Drug Threat: 2007–2015." Consult the ONDCP website for Obama-era "safety" and "health" discourses of NIDA's Washington consensus "disease paradigm" of drugs (wishful thinking as cocaine lacks credible drug treatment or a "vaccine").

5 A 2014 crack study found 1.8 percent prevalence in thirty-one capital cities (Bastos and Bertoni 2014). See also Park (2009), http://www.cnn.com/2009 /HEALTH/08/14/cocaine.traces.money/.

6 Brazil, Foreign Ministry, March 14, 2016, speech of Luiz Guilherme Mendes de Paiva (national secretary for drug policy), http://www.itamaraty.gov.br/en

/speeches-articles-and-interviews/other-high-ranking-officials-speeches
/13527.

7  UN figures show a 14 percent reduction in Peruvian coca crops to 49,900 hectares in 2014, largely in ongoing Huallaga eradication (Youngers 2015: 6).

8  Paraphrasing Kissinger's sarcasm about Allende's Chile, doubly ironic since the
1973 coup he abetted led into the Colombia Age of Cocaine.

9  In 2010, Paraguay was dropped from the executive list of "narcotics transit
or producing" countries, because "Paraguayan marijuana is trafficked to the
neighboring countries of Brazil, Argentina, Chile, and Uruguay, but not the
United States. Paraguay does remain a transit country for cocaine produced
in Bolivia, Peru, and Colombia. But again, while a small portion of the cocaine
from these countries that transits Paraguay may be destined for the U.S., the
vast majority is transported to Brazil, Europe, Africa and the Middle East" (US
Department of State 2016).

### REFERENCES

Acosta, Luisa María. 2019. "Resurgence of Coca in Putamayo Reflects Colombia's Failed Strategy." *InSight Crime*, July 12. Accessed September 6, 2019.
https://www.insightcrime.org/news/analysis/resurgence-coca-putumayo
-colombia-failed-strategy/.

Alexander, Michelle. 2010. *The New Jim Crow: Mass Incarceration in the Age of Color-
blindness.* New York: New Press.

Arías, María Alejandra, Adriana Camacho, Ana María Ibáñez, Daniel Mejía,
and Catherine Rodriguez. 2014. *Costos económicas y sociales del conflicto en
Colombia: Como construer un pos-conflicto sostenible.* Bogotá: Universidad de
Los Andes.

Arter, Melanie. 2016. "State Department Official: Cocaine Consumption Down
More Than 50 Percent, 'But Heroin Abuse Is Exploding.'" *CNSNews.com*,
June 16. Accessed October 21, 2018. https://www.cnsnews.com/news/article
/melanie-hunter/state-department-official-cocaine-consumption-down
-more-50-percent.

Bagley, Bruce. 2012. "Drug Trafficking and Organized Crime in the Americas:
Major Trends in the Twenty-First Century." Washington, DC: Woodrow
Wilson International Center for Scholars, Latin American Program.

Bair, Jennifer. 2005. "Global Capitalism and Commodity Chains: Looking Back,
Going Forward." *Competition and Change* 9, no. 2: 153–80.

Balbierz, Patrick. 2015. "Peru: The New King of Cocaine." *World Policy*, February 3.
Accessed October 21, 2018. http://worldpolicy.org/2015/02/03/peru-the-new
-king-of-cocaine/.

Bastos, Francisco Inácio, and Neilane Bertoni. 2014. "National Survey on the Use
of Crack: Who Are the Users of Crack and/or the Like in Brazil? How Many

Are in the State Capitals?" Rio de Janeiro: ICICT/FIOCRUZ. http://www.arca
.fiocruz.br/bitstream/icict/10019/2/UsoDeCrack.pdf.

Bedoya Garland, Eduardo. 2003. "Las estrategias productivas y del riesgo entre
los cocaleros del valle de los ríos Apurímac y Ene." In *Amazonía: Procesos de-
mográficos y ambientales*, edited by Carlos E. Aramburú and Eduardo Bedoya
Garland, 119–53. Lima: CIPA. Accessed November 1, 2018. http://www.cies
.org.pe/sites/default/files/files/otrasinvestigaciones/archivos/amazonia
-proceso-demograficos-y-ambientales.pdf.

Bellone, Amy. 1990. "The Cocaine Commodity Chain and Developmental Paths
in Peru and Bolivia." In *Latin America and the World Economy*, edited by
R. Korzeniewicz and W. C. Smith, chapter 2. Westport, CT: Westwood.

Ben Yahia, Jihane, and Raouf Farrah. 2019. "Has Algeria Joined Africa's New
'Cocaine Coast'?" *ISS Today*, January 28. https://issafrica.org/iss-today/has
-algeria-joined-africas-new-cocaine-coast.

Bradley, Theresa, and Ritchie King. 2012. "Brazil Now Consumes 18% of the
World's Cocaine." *Quartz*, September 23. Accessed September 28, 2018.
https://qz.com/5058/brazil-now-consumes-18-of-worlds-cocaine/.

Carnevale Associates. 2016. "Coca Cultivation Makes a Comeback in Colombia." Policy brief, August. Accessed October 21, 2018. http://www
.carnevaleassociates.com/our-work/policy-information-briefs.html/article
/2016/08/26/coca-cultivation-makes-a-comeback-in-colombia.

Carretero, Nacho. 2018. *Snow on the Atlantic: How Cocaine Came to Europe*. London:
Zed.

"Colombia's Coca Production Soars to Highest Level in Two Decades, US Says."
2017. *Guardian*, March 14. Accessed September 28, 2018. https://www
.theguardian.com/world/2017/mar/14/colombia-coca-cocaine-us-drugs.

Comisión Nacional para el Desarrollo y Vida Sin Drogas. 2017. *Estrategía Nacional
de Lucha Contra las Drogras, 2017–21*. Lima: Government of Peru.

"Consumo de cocaína no Brasil e 4 vezes maior que a média mundial." 2016.
*Veja.com*, June 26. Accessed October 21, 2018. https://veja.abril.com.br
/saude/consumo-de-cocaina-no-brasil-e-4-vezes-maior-que-a-media
-mundial/.

Cotler, Julio. 1999. *Drogas y políticas en el Perú: La conexión norteamericana*. Lima:
Instituto de Estudios Peruanos.

Caulkins, Jonathan, Beau Kilmer, Peter Reuter, and Greg Midgette. 2015. "Cocaine's Fall and Marijuana's Rise: Questions and Estimates Based on New
Estimates of Consumption and Expenditures in U.S. Drug Markets." *Addiction* 110, no. 5: 728–36. doi:!0.1111/add.12628.

Courtwright, David T. 1995. "The Rise and Fall of Cocaine in the United States."
In *Consuming Habits: Drugs in History and Anthropology*, edited by J. Goodman, P. Lovejoy, and A. Sherratt, 206–28. London: Routledge.

Dudley, Steven. 2014. "Criminal Evolution and Violence in Latin America and the
Caribbean." *InSight Crime*, June 26. Accessed October 21, 2018. https://www

.insightcrime.org/news/analysis/evolution-crime-violence-latin-america
-caribbean/.

Durand, Ursula. 2014. *The Political Empowerment of the Cocaleros of Bolivia and Peru*. London: Palgrave Macmillan.

Farthing, Linda C., and Kathryn Ledebur. 2015. *Habeas Coca: Bolivia's Community Coca Control*. New York: Open Society Foundations.

Felbab-Brown, Vanda, and Ann Newby. 2015. "How to Break Free of the Drugs-Conflict Nexus in Colombia." Washington, DC: Brookings Institution.

Felbab-Brown, Vanda, and Harold Trinkunas. 2015. "UNGASS 2016 in Comparative Perspective: Improving the Prospects for Success." *Foreign Policy at Brookings*. Accessed October 21, 2018. https://www.brookings.edu/wp-content/uploads/2016/06/FelbabBrown-TrinkunasUNGASS-2016-final-2.pdf.

Fischer, Benedikt et al. 2016. "'Crack': Global Epidemiology, Key Characteristics and Consequences of Use, and Existent Interventions—A Review." In *Blueprint for Regulation: Coca, Cocaine and Derivatives*. Oxford: Beckley Foundation.

Garat, Guillermo. 2016. "Paraguay: The Cannabis Breadbasket of the Southern Cone." Transnational Institute, Drug Policy Briefing no. 46, October.

Garzón, Juan Carlos. 2010. *Mafia and Co.: The Criminal Networks in Mexico, Brazil, and Colombia*. Washington, DC: Woodrow Wilson Center for International Scholars.

Garzón, Juan Carlos, and John Bailey, 2015. "Displacement Effects of Supply-Reduction Policies in Latin America: A Tipping Point in Cocaine Trafficking, 2006–2008." In *The Handbook of Drugs and Society*, edited by Henry H. Brownstein, 482–504. Malden, MA: Wiley-Blackwell.

Garzón, Juan Carlos, and Julián Wilches. 2016. "El mal negocio de prohibir la coca." *Nexos* 460: 44–47.

Gay, Robert. 2015. *Bruno: Conversations with a Brazilian Drug Dealer*. Durham, NC: Duke University Press.

Gay, Robert. 2016. "Bringing Drugs to Market: An Ethnography of Cocaine." Paper presented at the meeting of the Latin American Studies Association, New York, May 25–27.

Gootenberg, Paul, ed. 1999. *Cocaine: Global Histories*. London: Routledge.

Gootenberg, Paul. 2007a. "Cocaine in Chains: The Rise and Demise of a Global Commodity, 1860–1980." In *From Silver to Cocaine: Latin American Commodity Chains and the Building of the World Economy, 1500–2000*, edited by Steven Topik, Carlos Maruchal, and Zephyr Frank, 321–51. Durham, NC: Duke University Press.

Gootenberg, Paul. 2007b. "The Pre-'Colombian' Era of Drug Trafficking in the Americas: Cocaine, 1945–1973," *Americas* 64, no. 2: 133–76.

Gootenberg, Paul. 2008. *Andean Cocaine: The Making of a Global Drug*. Chapel Hill: University of North Carolina Press.

Gootenberg, Paul. 2012. "Cocaine's Long March North, 1900–2010." *Latin American Politics and Society* 54, no. 1: 159–80. Accessed September 28, 2018. https://www.cambridge.org/core/journals/latin-american-politics-and -society/article/cocaines-long-march-north-19002010/14F709FD31182C72F 8A4C3E71027BFBD.

Gootenberg, Paul. 2017. "Cocaine Histories and Diverging Drug War Politics in Bolivia, Colombia, and Peru." *A Contracorriente* 15, no. 1: 1–35.

Granados, Marcela Osorio. 2017. "La papa caliente de la sustitución." *El Espectador*, May 13.

Grillo, Ioan. 2016. *Caudillos del Crimen: De la Guerra Fría a las narcoguerras.* Mexico City: Grijalbo.

Grisaffi, Thomas, and Kathryn Ledebur. 2016. "Citizenship or Repression: Coca, Eradication, and Development in the Andes." *Stability: International Journal of Security and Development* 5, no. 1: 1–16.

Kenney, Michael. 2007. *From Pablo to Osama: Trafficking and Terrorist Networks, Government Bureaucracies, and Competitive Adaptation.* University Park: Pennsylvania State University Press.

Kilmer, Beau. 2016. "Uncle Sam's Cocaine Nosedive: A Brief Exploration of a Dozen Hypotheses." In *After the Drug Wars: Report of the LSE Expert Group on the Economics of Drug Policy.* London: LSE.

Kilmer, Beau, and Greg Midgette. 2017. "Mixed Messages: Is Cocaine Consumption in the U.S. Going Up or Down?" Washington, DC: Brookings Institution.

LaSusa, Mike. 2016. "Brazil Is Top Cocaine Transshipment Country for Europe, Africa, Asia." *InSight Crime*, June 24. Accessed October 21, 2018. https:// www.insightcrime.org/news/brief/brazil-is-top-cocaine-transshipment -country-for-europe-africa-asia/.

Lohmuller, Michael. 2015. "Brazilian Organized Crime and Corrupt Politicians: Drug Trafficking in Paraguay." *InSight Crime*, June 8. Accessed October 21, 2018. https://www.insightcrime.org/news/brief/raids-unveil-bolivia -paraguay-brazil-cocaine-network-coordinated-by-the-pcc/.

Manrique López, Hernán. 2015. "Las bases históricas del milagro de San Martín: Control territorial y estrategias estatales contra el narcotráfico y subversión (1980–91)." *Politiai* 6, no. 11: 33–51.

Mejía, Daniel. 2010. "Evaluating Plan Colombia." In *Innocent Bystanders: Developing Countries and the War on Drugs,* edited by Philip Keefer and N. Loayza. Washington, DC: World Bank.

Mejía, Daniel. 2015. "Plan Colombia: An Analysis of Effectiveness and Costs." Washington, DC: Brookings Institution.

Mendes de Paiva, Luiz Guilherme. 2016. "Remarks during the Special Segment of the Commission on Narcotics Drugs on the Preparation for the UNGASS—Vienna, March 14." Accessed September 28, 2018. http://www

.itamaraty.gov.br/en/speeches-articles-and-interviews/other-high-ranking
-officials-speeches/13527.

Miraglia, Paula. 2016. "Drugs and Drug Trafficking in Brazil: Trends and Policies." Washington, DC: Brookings Institution.

Miroff, Nick. 2017. "American Cocaine Use Is Way Up. Colombia's Coca Boom Might Be Why." *Washington Post*. March 4. Accessed October 21, 2018. https://www.washingtonpost.com/news/worldviews/wp/2017/03/04/colombias-coca-boom-is-showing-up-on-u-s-streets/?utm_term=.41c6b204f290.

Musto, David. 1999. *The American Disease: Origins of Narcotic Control*, 3rd ed. New York: Oxford University Press.

National Drug Intelligence Center. 2010. "Drug Availability in the United States." Washington, DC: US Department of Justice.

Neuman, William, and Simon Romero. 2015. "Latin American Allies Resist U.S. Strategy in Drug Fight." *New York Times*, May 16. Accessed October 21, 2018. https://www.nytimes.com/2015/05/16/world/americas/latin-america-and-us-split-in-drug-fight.html.

Nicoll, Alexander, ed. 2011. "West Africa's 'Cocaine Coast.'" *Strategic Comments* 17, no. 5.

OAS. 2013. *Report on the Drug Problem in the Americas.* Washington, DC: Organization of American States.

Park, Madison. 2009. "90 Percent of U.S. Bills Carry Traces of Cocaine" CNN, August 17. Accessed September 28, 2018. http://www.cnn.com/2009/HEALTH/08/14/cocaine.traces.money/.

Peltier, Elian. 2019. "Paris Dispatch: Crack Cocaine Turns a Corner of the City of Lights into a Hell." *New York Times*, August 18.

Pérez, Ana Lilia. 2014. *Mares de Cocaína: Las rutas náuticas del narcotráfico.* Mexico City: Grijalbo.

"Polícia investiga relação de Beira-Mar com as FARC." 2001. BBC *Brasil*, April 22. Accessed October 21, 2018. https://www.bbc.com/portuguese/noticias/2001/010422_beiramar2.shtml.

Reinarman, Craig, and Harry G. Levine. 2004. "Crack in the Rearview Mirror: Deconstructing Drug War Mythology." *Social Justice* 31: 182–99.

Resende, Beatriz. 2006. *Cocaína: Literatura e outros companheiros de ilusão.* Rio de Janeiro: Casa da Palavra.

Richani, Nazih. 2016. "Colombia Peace: The War System Yields to Peace." American University Center for Latin American and Latino Studies Blog, January 11. Accessed October 21, 2018. https://aulablog.net/2016/01/11/colombia-peace-the-war-system-yields-to-peace/.

Romero, Simon. 2014. "Drug Trade Transforms an Amazon Outpost." *New York Times*, December 11. Accessed October 21, 2018. https://www.nytimes.com/2014/12/11/world/drug-trade-transforms-an-amazon-outpost.html.

Ruda, Juan José, and Alfonso Zavaleta, eds. 2009. *El mapa del narcotráfico en el Perú.* Lima: IDEI.

Soberón, Ricardo. 2016. "VRAEM: Convergencia de un modelo de desarrollo neoliberal y uno legal." In *Blueprint for Regulation: Coca, Cocaine and Derivatives.*
Oxford: Beckley Foundation.

Substance Abuse and Mental Health Services Administration. 2014. "Prevalence
of Cocaine and Crack Use in the U.S. by Demographic Characteristic 2014."
Accessed September 28, 2018. https://www.drugabuse.gov/related-topics
/trends-statistics/overdose-death-rates.

Tickner, Arlene B. 2014. "Colombia, the United States, and Security by Proxy."
Washington, DC: Washington Office on Latin America.

UNODC. 2007. "Cocaine Trafficking in Western Africa: A Situation Report."
Vienna: United Nations Office on Drugs and Crime.

UNODC. 2010. *World Drug Report.* Vienna: United Nations Office on Drugs and
Crime.

UNODC. 2014. *World Drug Report.* Vienna: United Nations Office on Drugs and
Crime.

UNODC. 2015a. *Colombia: Coca Cultivation Survey 2014.* Vienna: United Nations
Office on Drugs and Crime.

UNODC. 2015b. *Estado Plurinacional de Bolivia: Monitoreo de Cultivos de Bolivia.*
Vienna: United Nations Office on Drugs and Crime.

UNODC. 2015c. *World Drug Report.* Vienna: United Nations Office on Drugs and
Crime.

UNODC. 2016. *World Drug Report.* Vienna: United Nations Office on Drugs and
Crime.

UNODC. 2017. *World Drug Report.* Vienna: United Nations Office on Drugs and
Crime.

US Congress, Senate Committee on Foreign Relations. 2016. *Our Evolving
Understanding and Response to Transnational Criminal Threats.* 114th Congress,
2nd Session, June 16.

US Department of State, US Embassy Asunción. 2016. "Drugs and Chemical
Control." In *Paraguay: International Narcotics Control Strategy Report,* vol. I. Accessed June 2016. https://py.usembassy.gov/wp-content/uploads/sites/274
/vol-1-English.pdf.

US Drug Enforcement Administration. 2014. "DEA Releases 2015 Drug Threat Assessment." Washington, DC: DEA Public Affairs. Accessed October 21, 2018.
https://www.dea.gov/press-releases/2015/11/04/dea-releases-2015-drug
-threat-assessment-heroin-and-painkiller-abuse.

US National Institute on Drug Abuse. 2013. "Home: Cocaine and Crack." NIDA,
Community Epidemiology Working Group.

US National Institute on Drug Abuse. 2018. "Overdose Death Rates." Accessed
September 28, 2018. https://www.drugabuse.gov/related-topics/trends
-statistics/overdose-death-rates.

US Office of National Drug Control Policy (ONDCP). 2012. *National Drug Control
Strategy* (Annual report), Data Supplement. Accessed September 28, 2018

https://obamawhitehouse.archives.gov/sites/default/files/ondcp/2012_ndcs
.pdf.

US Office of National Drug Control Policy (ONDCP). 2013. "Coca in the Andes."
Accessed September 28, 2018. https://obamawhitehouse.archives.gov
/ondcp/targeting-cocaine-at-the-source.

US Office of National Drug Control Policy (ONDCP). 2014. *What America's Users
Spend on Illegal Drugs, 2000–2010*. Santa Monica: RAND Corporation. Accessed September 28, 2018. https://obamawhitehouse.archives.gov/sites
/default/files/ondcp/policy-and-research/wausid_results_report.pdf.

US Office of National Drug Control Policy (ONDCP). 2015. *National Drug Control
Strategy* (Annual report), Data Supplement. Accessed September 28, 2018.
https://obamawhitehouse.archives.gov/sites/default/files/ondcp/policy
-and-research/2015_data_supplement_final.pdf.

US Office of National Drug Control Policy (ONDCP). 2016. *National Drug Control
Strategy* (Annual report), Data Supplement. Accessed September 28, 2018.
https://obamawhitehouse.archives.gov/sites/default/files/ondcp/policy
-and-research/2016_ndcs_data_supplement_20170110.pdf.

Van Dunn, Mirella. 2016. "Cocaine Flows and the State in Peru's Amazonian
Borderlands." *Journal of Latin American Studies* 48, no. 2: 509–35.

Vargas, Ricardo. 2017. "Colombia y el mercado mundial de la cocaine." *Razón
Pública*, July 23. Accessed September 28, 2018. http://razonpublica.com
/index.php/conflicto-drogas-y-paz-temas-30/10422-colombia-y-el
-mercado-mundial-de-la-coca%C3%ADna.html.

Vizcarra, Sofía. 2015. "¿Estamos en camino a un narco-estado?" *Noticias: Ciencias
sociales y comunicaciones*, April 28. Accessed October 21, 2018. https://
puntoedu.pucp.edu.pe/noticias/estamos-en-camino-a-un-narcoestado/.

Youngers, Coletta A. 2013. "The Drug Policy Reform Agenda in the Americas."
International Drug Policy Consortium briefing paper, August. Accessed
on October 21, 2018. https://www.wola.org/sites/default/files/Drug%20
Policy/IDPC-briefing-paper_Drug-policy-reform-in-Latin-America_V2
_ENGLISH.pdf.

Youngers, Coletta A. 2015. "Building on Progress in Bolivia." Washington, DC:
Washington Office on Latin America. Accessed October 21, 2018. https://
www.wola.org/2015/08/building-on-progress-in-bolivia/.

CONCLUSION

# CONCLUSION
# RESPONDING TO COCAINE'S MORAL ECONOMIES

I sit writing this conclusion in Putumayo, Colombia, a region that for many years has suffered the ill effects of poorly thought through counter-narcotics policies. The department is one of the centers of Colombia coca production, with nearly 20,000 hectares under cultivation (Yagoub 2017). The region has suffered extensive government actions against the coca growers, whose income has long funded the Fuerzas Armadas Revolucionarias de Colombia (FARC). In the 1990s and 2000s, this involved extensive and ultimately failed policies that have had serial deleterious effects on the environment and the human population, all the while having little long-term effect on coca growing or drug production (Rincón-Ruiz and Kallis 2013). Here in Putumayo the demobilization of the FARC has had limited consequences for the coca trade since dissident groups, formerly FARC—connected gangs, and other criminal groups have stepped into the breach to manage and regulate the trade in the region. Indeed, the FARC peace process has had the effect of expanding cocaine production and conflict over it. Why?

This volume offers a partial answer to this question by examining the underlying dynamics of the global cocaine trade. The contributors to this volume have offered a more holistic perspective on the contemporary cocaine trade than those developed elsewhere. Insights into interconnections at sites of production, transshipment, and consumption can not only inform us just why existing policies fail but also offer new pathways to address some of the challenges produced by the cocaine trade and responses to it. In the case of Putumayo and other centers of Colombian coca production such as the Nariño and Cauca departments and the Catatumbo region, the FARC and other illicit actors have long played an important role in the cocaine trade. These areas' participation, however, was driven not so much by the war as by the need of Colombian peasants to support themselves, their families, and their communities. The end of the FARC–government conflict upset relations as some FARC units demobilized and other actors, including FARC dissidents, criminals, and the Ejercito de Liberación Nacional (ELN) guerrilla group moved into former FARC-protected growing areas, generating conflict and increasing the volume of coca growing as the FARC could no longer play a coordinating role in regulating the supply. It did not, however, end the need for Colombian peasants to find more effective ways to earn income through their engagement in a global trade that provides them with disproportionate income as compared to, say, growing plantains, a local product grown for subsistence. In the end, the peace process upset the structure of the cocaine supply chain and some of the localized reciprocity associated with it, generating greater conflict but not limiting coca growing or local populations' dependence on it. Addressing violence in Colombia and the way the cocaine trade is inserted into it requires understanding the normative exchanges and the forms of protection that manage a trade that a significant portion of the Colombian population depends on for their livelihood.

The chapters of this book have shown that across the cocaine value chain different moral economies emerge in which the exchange relations promoted by the drug trade affect interpersonal relations and, as a result, social, political, and economic governance. This book has made three central arguments that have important implications for policy making. First, like any other commodity, cocaine is produced and brought to consumers through a supply chain where illicit laborers and capitalists add value to the product as it approaches consumers. Second, each of these steps in the value chain generates, within the space where it operates, particular systems of localized exchange that contribute to the formation of local moral economies. These moral economies create a framework of localized expectations around how value generated at a particular point in the supply chain will be allocated among those working at that point on the value chain and those who live in the locale. Third, these commodity chains, their attendant capital accumulation, and the moral economies they produce have important effects on social, political, and economic relations in the areas where these exchanges take place. This can lead to criminals as well as other social actors engaged in the trade playing key roles in policy decisions and engaging in social, political, and economic leadership. While we focus on these dynamics in the cocaine value chain, other illicit commodities can produce different social and political dynamics. All of this, then, has implications for efforts by state and social actors to respond to the drug trade. This conclusion will first examine our findings on value chains, the moral economies they generate, the effects this has on social and political relations, and, finally, discusses the implications of this for drug-related policy making.

## COMMODITY CHAINS AND MORAL ECONOMIES

The chapters in this book have shown that the cocaine trade operates in very different ways at different locations in the value chain. The nature of the cocaine trade at a production site, as Grisaffi and Zellers-León show in their chapters, differs markedly from the nature of the cocaine trade at a transshipment site, as shown by Le Cour Grandmaison and Gay, or a primary consumption site, as shown by Rui. The nature of the trade at particular sites has immense consequences for how populations interact with the trade and the ways that the trade affects local exchanges.

Cocaine production sites are located primarily in poor rural areas of the Andes Mountains. Here drug production is inserted into agricultural communities where many inhabitants struggle to meet basic economic needs. As Grisaffi has shown, local familial and pseudo-familial reciprocal relations are key to maintaining exchanges amid hostile law enforcement and government regulations: cousins collaborate to supply the chemicals for base paste processing and drug workers sell their cocaine to godfathers—among a plethora of other configurations. Zellers-León shows how this trade is inserted into contentious local debates about culture and the capitalist economy in rural Colombia, where some indigenous leaders see the drug trade as undermining their community, while others consider it an important source of income for survival and to enable the purchase of consumer goods. Cocaine production brings resources into rural Andean communities that support limited exchanges and patronage among and within extended kinship groups and communities.

Here the cocaine trade often emerges within preexisting communities and relies on trust, with tight social bonds around agriculture, which may or may not have previously involved noncommercial coca growing and consumption, to move forward. Indeed, the trade often builds on preexisting social patterns, including kinship groups, fictive kinship, friends, and community working jointly in the labor-intensive process of growing, harvesting, and processing coca and base paste. As cocaine dollars flow into the area, the trade changes these areas, provides for some basic needs, and, indeed, can create real tensions, but its impacts are also limited, narrow, and strongly contextualized within the wider preexisting social relations and debates that operate within those communities. These tight ties and the patronage relations associated with them remain essential to the cocaine trade in these areas and, as a result, where the trade is successful can reinforce these preexisting relationships through the growth of income associated with the drug trade, which can expand and reinforce these relations. From the perspective of some in these communities, these resources make the community and individuals bigger and better than ever. As Zellers-León shows in her chapter, those who acquire motorcycles are often thought of as "El Grande" or a big shot, or as Grisaffi shows in Bolivia's Chapare province, coca profits are invested into the local community in the form of fiestas and other public celebrations. Reliance on these tight-knit relationships and the ways the trade supports and reinforces these relationships is, perhaps, one of the reasons this particular phase of the cocaine value chain is less violent than others.

In the context of Scott's work on Southeast Asian peasants, this is an interesting outcome. For Scott, the encroachment of global capitalist markets upsets traditional patronage relations, leading to rebellion, and in Latin America there is ample evidence of the complications that the global capitalist economy produces for poor peasants and the ways that this contributes to rebellion—the Zapatista uprising is a case in point. The cocaine trade, however, is an illicit economy that, as a result of its illicitness, poor agricultural communities can at least partially control to support preexisting exchange relations and survival, even as global capitalist markets create immense challenges for these populations. These benefits are, of course, only partial, and these peasants can never wholly control the trade within their communities, leading to violence, disorder, and, as Zellers-León shows, intense debate about the trade. Still, lying outside the legal economy, the trade offers important opportunities to reinforce existing moral economies in these areas.

Transshipment, smuggling, and commercialization is the phase of the cocaine commodity chain where the most value is added. In comparison with retail sales and coca growing and the early stages of processing, this phase is quite complex and requires skills in chemistry, money laundering, and smuggling, including operating airplanes and submarines and building extended tunnels under international frontiers. The risk in moving drugs across international borders dramatically increases the value of the drug, and the groups and individuals that control the drug through this stage accrue the largest share of the income associated with the cocaine trade. These elevated incomes are often associated with increased illicit competition and violence. It is for this reason that Colombian and Mexican drug trafficking organizations (DTOs), which have dominated global transshipment and smuggling since the 1980s, have become so wealthy and so violent. The power of major Mexican DTOs is evidenced in Le Cour Grandmaison's chapter. That said, not all transshipment and smuggling locales accrue as much money or concentrate income in the same way. The chapters by Idler, Fontes, Rodgers, and Gay offer different perspectives on this critical phase of the cocaine trade, in which smaller-scale organizations still concentrate a great deal of income, but not to the same degree as major global trafficking organizations. Elsewhere, Rivke Jaffe shows the deep involvement of gangs involved in transshipment in politics and governance of many neighborhoods in Jamaica (Jaffe 2013: 736–40).

The insertion of significant resources from the global cocaine trade into a particular locale is disruptive to local social and political arrangements, but it can create others. Le Cour Grandmaison's chapter makes this point most clear by noting how the manna of cocaine trade–related resources transform local patronage relations by putting drug traffickers at the center of those exchanges, giving them power over state institutions, social relations, and licit economic exchange. The traffickers discussed in Fontes's chapter exercise similar power by employing large numbers of people and providing for the livelihood of towns on the trail of drugs up to Mexico. The traffickers in Brazil that Gay writes about operate in what they refer to as an "ant" trade, where many small traffickers carry cocaine from the border with Bolivia to the large cities of southeastern Brazil, where drugs are shipped via Africa to Europe and, increasingly, consumed locally. In his chapter on Nicaragua, Rodgers shows how capital accumulated from drug trade participation affects the real estate and other markets in a Managua shantytown. It is in these areas that capital becomes concentrated among a handful of central market actors who are connected to large-scale prison gangs that dominate portions of the region's penitentiary systems and many of the city's shantytowns.

These moral economies are, at heart, unstable. Transshipment and smuggling means moving drugs through highly regulated areas with a marked state presence. Intense capital accumulation generates more competition. These all contribute to a great deal of violence and repression, even as there are incentives for risk-inclined individuals to participate in the market. Thus, the moral economies in the sites at this phase of the value chain are driven by the need to generate protection for key actors in the trafficking structure. Thus, criminal organizations operate amid a code of silence, and they seek to enforce that silence among wider segments of society while at the same time seeking to negotiate accommodations with the state (Lessing 2018). Operating in this environment means using resources and often force to ensure compliance with the demands of criminal groups. This usually involves criminal organizations taking over existing patronage networks and setting up independent ones to ensure support for their activities. As a result, criminal groups have been known to take over state structures, contribute to political campaigns, and provide jobs to large numbers of people. At the same time, minimizing the role of the state in areas where the drug trade operates also involves maintaining enough order in those places that residents see little reason to approach state actors about local problems, turning, amid the threat of violence, to criminals instead.

Transshipment and smuggling occur very much in between places and outside the types of protective confines that support drug production. At a large scale there are no preexisting local reciprocal orders like those that support the trade in agricultural areas. In the most unstable and sensitive spaces, however, smuggling has to turn to tight networks to move drugs between larger-scale transportation networks. Idler, in her chapter on Colombia's frontiers, shows how key transactions across the border are managed by groups that operate specifically in that space and act as agents transferring the drugs between actors that predominantly operate on one side of the border or the other. In this sense, her work reflects and adds to Frederico Verese's (2011: 4) insights on transnational mafias, which shows that, at least in some cases, organized crime groups have a great deal of difficulty moving beyond their country of origin. Transporting drugs across borders requires a very specific set of relationships and knowledge and can draw, in some cases, on preexisting networks of reciprocity in very specific areas at the margins of state power.

Consumption sites have their own moral economies. As a site of retailing and of reaching out to communities of consumers who have only a marginal investment in the drug trade itself, there are relatively few bonds of trust other than some limited underlying norms that users may practice for their own self-protection, and tight bonds in some narrow social networks. Rather, retail drug dealing is an activity where those involved in the trade may find themselves least protected from the law. Under these circumstances the trade requires the ability to market and sell an illicit product under the almost constant observation of law enforcement. Individuals, families, and communities living around this stage of the trade seek to manage the complexity and danger of the highly competitive and often diffuse criminal activity around consumption, the negative externalities caused by drug consumption in a neighborhood, and the pressure generated by law enforcement efforts to police these areas. These conditions are detailed in the chapters written by Bourgois, Hart, Karandinos and Montero, Bobea and Veeser, and Rui.

These dynamics generate relatively little capital accumulation. Under these circumstances the trade requires the ability to market and sell an illicit product under the almost constant observation of law enforcement. Individuals, families, and communities living around this stage of the trade seek to manage the complexity and danger of the highly competitive and often diffuse criminal activity around consumption, the negative externalities caused by drug consumption in a neighborhood, and the pressure generated by law enforcement efforts to police these areas. These conditions are detailed in the chapters written by Bourgois, Hart, Karandinos and Montero, Bobea and Veeser, and Rui. Dealers rarely become wealthy or emerge from poverty (Levitt and Venkatesh 2000; also see Rodgers, this volume). What money the dealers make is often spent on consumer goods for themselves, or supporting their extended family, as Robert Gay has shown in his discussion of a drug gang in a Rio neighborhood engaged primarily in retail drug sales (Gay 2005). There is little money available to support a wider patronage network. Despite these real challenges, the evidence presented here points to some ways that drug consumption generates moral economies. Given intermittent state repression and the risks faced by both gangs and consumers, there is a general expectation of silence and wider efforts to undertake the trade in such a way that it does not attract police attention and, sometimes, keep local residents on their side. A part of this is an understanding that, as Bobea and Veeser show, a gang will maintain basic order, controlling thefts and assaults, for example, in order to make residents less reliant on police who might interfere with their illicit activities. Venkatesh (1997) points out the contributions that residents of poor Chicago neighborhoods believe gangs make to their communities, and also the close interpersonal ties that are the basis of exchange relations and mutual protection in gang-controlled areas. Rui's chapter offers examples of this dynamic, where gang and civic leaders worked together in Rio to provide a relatively safe locale for crack users to consume in a favela rather than wandering on public streets. In São Paulo, on the other hand, problematic drug users were driven from shantytowns where they might antagonize neighbors and attract police attention. The Bobea and Veeser chapter shows, on the other hand, the economic multiplier effect that the drug trade can have in poor areas, as the trade infuses the local economy with otherwise absent resources that enable people to maintain their homes and keep their businesses afloat. To the extent that the drug trade concentrates resources, many of those resources are distributed to police and politicians to buy their support. So, in the end, this element of the trade produces some limited exchanges that reinforce local norms, but in ways that are not as broad or extensive as in transshipment locales or as deep as in producing areas. This has implications for thinking about the drug trade and the politics that surrounds it.

### NEW APPROACHES TO GOVERNANCE AND CHANGE

In the introduction to this volume, Grisaffi and I argued that much of the existing writing on violence and the drug trade in Latin America owes a significant intellectual debt to neo-Weberian approaches to the state. In this context, many scholars and policy makers see criminal organizations as groups that challenge the state's monopoly on the legitimate use of violence (O'Donnell 1993; Caldeira and Holston 1999; Snyder and Durán-Martínez 2009; Ungar 2011; Lessing 2018). More recently, some scholars have adopted a post-Weberian framework in which criminal groups contest state power and governance dynamics through competition and collusion with the state (Kalyvas 2015; Willis 2015; Arias 2017; Durán-Martínez 2018). These Weberian approaches, of course, contribute a great deal to our understanding of the region's governance, but they are, in themselves, insufficient to explain the ways in which the drug trade affects governance. Rather, we argue that the Marxist and anarchist traditions, which the moral economy framework emerges from, also provide important insights to understand the drug trade's governance dynamics. This section will analyze, in turn, how our approach and the findings discussed in this volume build on Weberian, Marxist, and anarchist approaches to understand governance.

Weberian approaches define governance either as an exercise in state power or, more recently, a product of its contestation by illicit actors. The discussion of value chains and their attendant moral economies sheds critical light on how the nature of state and illicit governance changes at different places along the commodity chain. As the Le Cour Grandmaison and Fontes chapters make clear, a substantial amount of the drug trade's capital accumulation ends up controlled by organizations operating in transshipment centers. This marked capital accumulation creates conditions where armed actors can undertake substantial governance activities, either directly challenging the state or co-opting large-scale state institutions, often at the municipal level. The substantially lower levels of capital accumulation at production and consumption sites narrow the role of trafficking groups in the governance of these sites. In consumption locales, governance roles are, as shown in Rui's and Bobea and Veeser's chapters, and in Venkatesh's work on Chicago, concentrated in neighborhoods where gangs involved in the drug trade exercise some degree of power. Often these are places where localized wholesaling and final processing occur, but also, as Rui shows, in sites of open consumption. Critically though this power is exercised in the restricted geographic space of particular neighborhoods, usually as a tool for minimizing police repression, in the case of production sites, illicit governance operates across a broader spectrum of locales, but, as the Zellers-León chapter shows, these are generally close-knit exchange networks that often involve evading state repression rather than efforts to confront or control the state, as is the case in transshipment and consumption sites. Of course, under some circumstances drug production sites can become important sites of counter-state activity, as evidenced by the operations of the FARC in protecting coca fields in some parts of Colombia. This, however, emerges, as Idler's chapter makes clear, amid other more complex trafficking activities, including transshipment. Similarly, Le Cour Grandmaison's chapter on Mexico shows that prior to the entry of cocaine transshipment, heroin production in Michoacán led to governance dynamics not too distant from those Grisaffi found in Bolivia. Thus, while the cases in our volume reaffirm the utility of Weberian approaches, they also provide important context for understanding the way in which the drug trade affects governance in varied ways at different stages of production.

Marxist approaches to politics also provide important insights into governance. The drug economy, like any economic activity, transforms the locales where it operates by changing social relations and the wider environment. In production sites, the acquisition of resources provides support for patronage networks in Bolivia, not establishing a counter-state but as a means for supporting social relations in coca growing areas. Similarly, as Zellers-León shows, the drug trade gives indigenous peoples access to improved transportation options, shifting their perspective on social relations and changing their existing economic and social horizons. In transshipment locales, the infusion of resources shapes economic opportunity structures. In Michoacán the concentration of capital gave illicit actors the ability to control much of the licit economy and to use their control over the licit economy to further leverage their social control in the state. Similarly, Gay shows how transshipment activities in Brazil contributed to gang control over prisons and enabled armed actors to use this platform to command other aspects of the drug trade. Finally, at consumption sites, Rui provides evidence of how the nature of illicit markets in Rio and São Paulo produced contrasting dynamics that drove drug users to and from shantytowns and the city center. Bobea and Veeser show how the nature of drug market competition, and the resources associated with it, buoy up poor communities through the recent crisis in Puerto Rico. Elsewhere, Philippe Bourgois demonstrates how the resources obtained through the trade not only provide for survival needs but also for unattached young men to develop a sense of attachment and at times even respect (Bourgois 1995). At a global level, Roberto Saviano has argued that capital controlled by illicit actors has played a critical role in providing liquidity to global capital markets (Saviano 2015).

Illicit markets are also sites of social conflicts that mobilize actors and change how they think about the politics of the place where they live. Grisaffi's chapter on Bolivia illustrates how the illicit market has helped to create a coca growers' union that was, at the national level, critical to bringing Evo Morales to power. At the local level, the success of the coca growers' union and their movement has transformed the relationship between the coca growers and government officials, leading to the surprising dance between a police officer and a leader of the coca growers' union. Similarly, Zellers-León elucidates how the acquisition of motorcycles by those involved in the coca market led to intense debates within the Nasa about the nature of their community and how new contacts with the global (illicit) market have affected norms and practices within that community. Le Cour Grandmaison's chapter shows how the intense power exercised by the drug cartels, which were even able to take over large segments of the legal economy, led eventually to the establishment of local self-defense groups that had success in driving the cartel out of some areas. Elsewhere, Eduardo Moncada has shown how in Medellín, another city where drug trafficking organizations succeeded in taking control of much of the legitimate economy a generation ago, work by business organizations, capital disadvantaged by the drug trade, to help reestablish order in the city was critical in promoting political reforms that limited the control that criminal groups could exercise (Moncada 2016). In consumption locales, Bobea and Veeser demonstrate how the extension of puntos has changed the way the wealthy think about their own neighborhoods.

Finally, though, this volume also shows the self-regulatory elements of the moral economy that emerge from the concept's anarchist roots. Grisaffi's chapter makes clear how the illicit trade supports and maintains preexisting social relations in certain Bolivian communities. Gay's chapter shows the way that prison gangs have sought to regulate elements of the conflict that are part of drug markets. Similarly, Rui's chapter makes evident the self-regulatory functions of illicit structures in efforts to avoid police actions against the neighborhoods where the trade is based.

On the whole, this provides a very different perspective on the governance activity associated with illicit trade that is developed within a narrow Weberian framework. Here order emerges not just from the actions of state institutions and their organizational collaborators and competitors. In other words, economic and social structures are not epiphenomenal to state institutions and their competition with other groups. Rather, consistent with Marxist approaches to politics, the state and criminal power emerge from economic dynamics. These models suggest that stability and disorder come not just from institutional interactions but from the ways that economic and social dynamics interact with the state and with illicit organizations. And social structures often have self-regulating dynamics, in particular when operating outside the constraints of law, consistent with anarchist theories.

From a scholarly perspective, this means that we need to study the cocaine trade beyond the logics of violence and control so prominent in the dominant Weberian approaches. On one level this means taking seriously how the drug trade is bound up with identity and finding one's place in society, as Bourgois made clear in *In Search of Respect* (1995) and is similarly shown by Zellers-León's chapter in this book and Adam Baird's (2012) article on masculinity and gangs. Similarly, this should also emphasize the ways many elements of the drug trade are self-regulating, largely operating beyond state repression. Peter Leeson (2009), in his anarchist account of piracy, similarly shows how that illicit activity historically generated forms of internal dispute resolution, regulation, and property ownership

quite apart from formal state regulation. None of this means that the Weberian elements of control and competition are irrelevant, but, rather, that
they coexist in the context of other criminal dynamics best understood in
the context of other intellectual traditions.

This points to two critical insights for policy making. First, illicit economies can be as productive of order as they can be of disorder. Any response to illicit markets has to keep in mind the ways that efforts to
change those illicit markets can generate unintended consequences.
Understanding how illicit organizations are enmeshed with the economy
and society is critical to addressing the challenges posed by the drug trade.
Second, the structure of the value chain and its attendant moral economies
provides a framework for thinking about these interactions and developing
responses, both at particular sites on the value chain and across its length.
I will discuss these in the next section.

### Addressing Cocaine Value Chains amid Moral Economies

As Grisaffi and I wrote in the introduction to this volume, existing responses
to the drug trade are manifestly insufficient. Gootenberg's chapter made
clear that for fifty years the war on drugs has failed to control drug consumption and has visited extensive harm, largely on poor young people who live in
areas proximate to the centers of the trade and, in some contexts, has contributed to mass imprisonment. In the face of the toll of this conflict, the
modal response from reformers is to call for marijuana legalization, which is
positive but highly limited. Some more radical reformers call for a broader legalization, but this largely has not gained traction. Both of these approaches
appear to focus largely on efforts to either end drug consumption or, often
within a narrow band, to legalize that consumption. These approaches sidestep the processes through which much of the cocaine trade operates and
the problems faced by most of the individuals and communities affected
directly by the drug trade. Indeed, it largely ignores the lived experience of
the cocaine trade, offering inauthentic responses mainly focused on the interests and moral claims of political leaders in wealthy societies that have for
half a century offered failure and suffering, and, in more recent years, some
limited new consumption opportunities for the middle classes.

The main solutions offered today to the problem of the cocaine trade and
its violence are either greater repression or a change in the prohibitionist regime. The failure of repression as a solution is, at this point, manifest, and it
is rapidly losing support globally even as it remains entrenched in key places
in society and the state. The alternative approach is a revision of the prohibi-

tionist regime. While this approach has rapidly gained support over the last decade, to date most of the debate has focused on the legalization of marijuana and, perhaps, the partial decriminalization of small amounts of other drugs. Neither approach really addresses the dynamics that support and maintain the drug trade. Both of these approaches, however, fail to address what draws people along the cocaine value chain into the trade in the first place, leading to both ineffective and pernicious responses from the state but, also, reinforcing the worst effects of the trade in these communities.

Part of the reason that these approaches are unlikely to succeed is revealed by value chains and their attendant moral economies. The global capitalist economy incorporates large portions of the world's population, including the inhabitants of rural Putumayo, small-town Michoacán, or inner-city Rio, San Juan, or New York, in ways that disadvantage them and extract from them the value of their own labor and the wealth of the land they live on. Suffering in the global capitalist economy its national instances, the inhabitants of these areas look to each other and for new opportunities to survive and enrich themselves. Exploited by the licit economy, some inhabitants turn to the illegal to support themselves and the communities and networks that they have depended on. These dynamics of exchange and mutual support, along with demand from consumers, lie at the heart of the resilience of the global cocaine trade in the face of a fifty-year-old war on drugs. Disrupting the drug trade only leads to new players and, as Gootenberg shows in his chapter, shifts to new places because supportive dynamics remain in the locales where the trade has operated and already exist in other places where the trade is more limited. Legalizing cocaine is perhaps one piece of an effective policy to address the drug trade, but without addressing the ways marginalized spaces are excluded by the global economy through participation in the cocaine trade, legalization will only cause people to look for resources through other illicit markets such as extortion, as occurred in Jamaica after that country's participation in the global cocaine trade decreased dramatically in the early 2000s. So how can we more effectively approach the cocaine trade?

Moral economies provide a framework to think through effective solutions to the problems generated by cocaine value chains. The food riots that Thompson wrote about and the peasant revolts discussed by Scott emerge distinctly from the perceived injustices of an expanding capitalist economy that disrupts what some see as morally grounded exchange relations within a given community. The drug trade, too, is a response to these disruptions. Addressing the pernicious effects of the drug trade involves taking seriously the ways the capitalist economy undermines the dignity and sense of justice among some of the communities most exploited by that economy. The moral economy approach offers solutions.

Key to any solution to addressing the moral framework in which the cocaine trade emerges is scholars and policy makers taking seriously bottom-up efforts to address the drug trade, its attendant violence, and the wider development concerns that draw so many into the drug trade. As Arturo Escobar (1995) has pointed out in the Colombian context, effective and equitable development requires that key decisions be made by the inhabitants of regions rather than the state, private enterprise, or international institutions. Thus, while providing jobs or greater resources to a region, these will not necessarily make much difference to involvement in the drug trade unless the inhabitants of the region are effectively engaged in the process of managing that development and ensuring that benefits flow into supporting communities in that area. This goes beyond fair trade coffee or ecotourism as ways to more effectively integrate peripheral areas into global markets; rather, it focuses on genuinely participatory development strategies oriented around not just encouraging capital to concentrate in a region but doing so in ways that are driven by local interests and where there is some equity in the distribution of those resources.

For some time, efforts to address the challenges posed by the drug trade have been largely focused on individuals and, through them, the community in aggregate. In drug production areas, this means an emphasis on crop substitution, fair trade, and ecotourism programs that seek to provide individuals with economic opportunity. Similarly, at transshipment and consumption sites, governments have invested in education and job opportunity programs to increase labor market participation. While these steps are positive, they provide for individuals who compete with each other locally rather than creating resilient communities. Certainly, governments should make a special effort to invest specifically in communities. At the same time, it is important that whatever policies are under consideration, communities should lead in decision making. Community-driven development agendas will go much further in building robust support for local reciprocity and building a tighter fabric for the future of the community than top-down efforts focused on imagining what communities need.

A critical element of this process is redistribution. Resources must flow from the centers of national and global capitalism to these peripheries, even if those peripheries are located in the heart of the some of the world's wealthiest and largest cities. In an era of rising inequality and concentration of global wealth, addressing the challenges of the global drug trade, if we are in fact serious about doing so, involves reorienting the direction of capital and resource flows—that is to say, putting more money in the hands of communities on the margins of the global economy and empowering those same communities to determine their own future. As we can see with Bolivia's coca control policy (Grisaffi, Farthing, and Lebedur 2017), shifting legitimate funds into these communities and giving local populations control over those resources will enable local actors to use these funds to reinforce local reciprocity networks without having to depend on the illicit actors to supply them with resources.

Of course, this type of shift has to occur with oversight and support. In Colombia, royalty payments to municipalities that produce certain natural resources frequently become a tool of corrupt politicians and a target of criminals and guerrillas (Eaton 2006). As a result, this shift in resources has to be accompanied by efforts to ensure that funds are spent for legitimate ends, and it also means that security is provided to enable communities to freely decide how to spend these resources, rather than having criminals pressure local organizations to spend money on contracts that benefit criminal organizations, as occurred with participatory budgeting in Medellín (Abello Colak and Guarneros-Meza 2014; Arias 2017). Beyond providing security for effective decisions and addressing corruption, such efforts also require an investment in supporting communities and their efforts to develop their own development agendas and plans.

Both Marxist and anarchist conceptions of moral economies focus on perceptions of justice and equity among the economically marginalized. The global economy, as it is currently structured, works for just a few of us, with billions seeking to support themselves on a pittance. The poor and working class in marginal and peripheral areas are willing to engage in the drug trade despite its risks because, as we show here, of the ways that the trade supports them, their families, their friendship and kinship networks, as well as their broader communities. The drug trade is resilient because of the ways that it supports wider groups, and to some degree reconciles injustices. It can be hard for those of us who live and work in the seats of privilege to perceive how the drug trade could support a vision of justice; our failure, as often as not, is one of not fully being able to imagine how difficult life is for the poor and how complex their struggles to survive in the advanced capitalist economy can be.

None of this should be taken, however, as a normative judgment on the trade or participation in the trade, but as a reflection of the empirical contexts reflected in this book. The drug trade is resilient because of the ways that it supports peoples and communities even as it also visits hardships on those same populations and places. Addressing the sense of injustice that helps drive people to the trade is critical to helping to reduce some of the desire on the part of the marginalized to engage in what many perceive to be victimless crimes that only enhance their ability to survive. An effort to ensure justice for these communities on their own terms is essential to addressing the problems generated by the cocaine supply chain.

This involves supporting locally driven development projects, more rewarding and better-paying jobs, and justice for the excluded. A key piece of addressing not just drug commodity chains but also a host of other global tensions is redistributing resources from the world's wealthiest and most privileged populations to the billions suffering from economic marginalization and exclusion. These are all big projects that will not come to fruition in the short term. The next section will focus on how policy makers and others concerned about the pernicious effects of the drug trade and the repression of it can address a variety of challenges along drug supply chains.

### Policy Responses

How can government agencies and other actors seek to use value chains and their underlying moral economies to ameliorate the most pernicious effects of the cocaine trade and its repression? Key to these efforts is to understand the different phases of the cocaine trade and how each of these phases generates a particular moral economy and tensions within it. Effective responses to the trade, then, depend on understanding and addressing the nuances of those tensions to help to control the most dangerous elements of the value chain. This section focuses on how to develop policy frameworks that minimize the negative effects of the drug trade by considering both how to respond effectively to violent actors operating in these spaces and by reflecting on how to address wider concerns that make participation in the trade compelling.

One of the central concepts that this volume has put forward is that the drug trade is much more deeply implicated in existing social and economic systems than scholars and policy makers typically acknowledge. Certainly, many acknowledge that the drug trade addresses important economic needs for some populations at the margins of legal economies. Far fewer acknowledge the underlying reciprocities that surround the wider drug economy and the ways that this illicit business penetrates and builds upon preexisting norms and exchanges among an array of disadvantaged communities along the whole value chain to advance the interests of its various participants. This has significant implications for how governments and other agencies seek to craft policies to respond to the drug trade, both in terms of upsetting the orders generated by the drug trade, which can lead to conflict and impoverishment, and in actually producing less contraband-dependent outcomes that more effectively meet the needs of populations that participate in the market. Understanding this can push scholars and policy makers to respond to the problems of the drug trade as people experience them.

Responding to cocaine at sites of production is a particularly challenging activity because of the location of coca production with regard to centers of government power and the ways that the trade becomes inserted into tight local networks of reciprocity. The evidence presented here, though, points to fault lines that can emerge even in tightly knit communities. Not everyone is always of like mind, and the drug trade can exacerbate local tensions dividing communities. Understanding these fault lines is essential to effectively responding to the drug trade in these areas. In responding to the cocaine trade, however, it is also important to understand the ways that the trade funds survival, consumption, and reciprocity networks in these communities. Seeking to directly remove the trade or, alternately, replace cocaine with a much less lucrative agricultural product will likely fail to actually control the cocaine trade, and perhaps will even encourage coca growers to align with rebels, as has occurred in Colombia. Responding to the coca trade at the sites of production requires understanding the particular ways that populations in these areas have been poorly integrated into global capitalist markets and the ways that the capitalist market has undermined local regulatory and reciprocal structures in ways not unlike those identified by Scott and Thompson in other eras and places. Responses, thus, should consider not just ways to improve insertion into capitalist markets, by aiding local development initiatives, transferring knowledge, and investing in infrastructure, among other things, but also how to support and reinforce local networks of reciprocity.

Responding to the problems of transshipment sites is complicated. As the principal sites of capital accumulation and illicit expertise, these areas generate powerful criminal organizations that can challenge or compromise the state. Critically, the resources associated with the drug trade in these areas are so significant that large numbers of state officials may have an interest in perpetuating and protecting the trade. This poses immense challenges to developing effective responses. As noted earlier, though, these conditions often promote social reactions to drug trafficker power, frequently by legal capital, whose profits the drug trade impinges on as it concentrates illicit capital in particular locales. This was clearly the case in some of the reaction by business sectors that have helped rebuild Medellín (Moncada 2016) and organized a paramilitary response to the drug trade in Michoacán, as outlined in Le Cour Grandmaison's chapter. So at least one of the keys to addressing the challenges posed by illicit capital in transshipment sites is understanding the social and economic fault lines created by the accumulation of illicit capital. This, of course, is not easy, since many legitimate capitalists invest in the drug trade and provide it with support until they see their legal businesses compromised, and there are many poor who see the drug trade as a way to provide for themselves and even advance socially. It is also critical to note that all transshipment is not the same, and some locales have more limited illicit capital accumulation. These sites and other areas directly disadvantaged by the cocaine trade, such as places where drug income makes it more difficult to export legal products, are important sites for understanding the emergence of effective local anti-drug trade coalitions. Understanding these dynamics offers another set of sites that can support productive interventions that can build support for limiting the more pernicious effects of the trade.

Policy responses in consumption sites are again quite different from those in production and transshipment sites. Here the wealth of middle- and upper-class consumers feeds the value chain, making efforts at other sites worthwhile. At the same time, much of the trade is undertaken by less well-off individuals living in those consumption sites, who are often just as poorly integrated into global capitalist markets as their counterparts in production and transshipment sites. In these locales, authorities can seek to discourage consumption and address addiction as strategies to reduce demand. To the extent that governments continue to pursue prohibitionist policies, such policies should be undertaken with equity across classes. The poor should not lose years of their lives to prison while the middle classes and the wealthy pour money into the cocaine trade with some impunity. Incarceration policies should be more humane and should governments consider and address how long-term imprisonment of working-age adults affects household survival as well as the education and development of children and adolescents in affected households (Bagley and Rosen 2015). Similarly, governments and other actors should focus on how to reduce the deleterious effects of drug consumption by, for example, seeking to limit the crime, abuse, and disease that drug users are subject to by dealing in an illegal market. Governments also need to address the deleterious effects of mass and concentrated consumption. Drug dealers and distribution networks are also an important target of policies to address the challenges posed by the drug trade. Here governments should focus on how to control the violence associated with the trade and decreasing the urgency that some feel to join gangs. This involves providing meaningful opportunities for people to advance economically outside the drug trade, but also coordinated state actions against violent offenders (Arias and Ungar 2009). It also involves ameliorating some of the most negative effects of the trade itself. This can involve a partial, regulated legalization, which is likely essential to controlling the broad violence associated with the cocaine trade.

Until now legalization debates have focused on producing a highly circumscribed market for marijuana in a few places. While these are positive developments for a variety of different types of cannabis users, these changes are likely to make little difference for the major issues associated with the drug trade in Latin America: criminal organizations, illicit market violence, and addiction. Dealing with these issues would require a much broader legalization effort that would focus on drugs that are widely seen as objectionable. Legalizing cocaine is not likely to take place in the near future and is far from a solution to the complex problems that people face along its complex value chain. The legalization of cocaine would be at best a single action that would have to be part of a broader policy that looked at the various relationships that support and are supported by cocaine along the length of the commodity chain. Indeed, disrupting the value chains with legalization could lead to more violence as criminal groups turn to new markets such as extortion to meet their social obligations and advance their economic projects. Even if existing criminal groups leave illicit markets, this shift would open spaces for new illicit groups, likely leading to conflict. To the extent that such a policy would be successful, it would have to account for the complex exchange relationships and moral economies that compose the value chain.

## CONCLUSION

The introduction to this volume recounts the story of Sebastián, a human guarantor of cocaine shipments from Peru to Bolivia. This story, like many others recounted in this volume, illustrates how the cocaine trade builds economies and relationships around it as individuals operating in the illicit penumbra of the global economy seek to earn, survive, and realize their economic and social aspirations, often under very difficult circumstances.

In Sebastián's story, service businesses are built up around an illicit airfield in rural Bolivia, and individuals are paid significant sums of money to be present in a place to guarantee the validity of the contract. Successful market participants may retire from this occasionally dangerous work to build homes, take care of family, and invest in new businesses.

The chapters we have presented here and this conclusion have sought to move beyond the narrow reading of exchange relationships that underlies much of contemporary drug policy. This vignette makes these complexities clear. On the one hand, we have sought to contextualize the underlying moral economies of the drug trade along its complex value chain, showing that both normative and economic desires drive and make the trade resilient. The cocaine trade does not exist the way it does just because a small number of malefactors make money. Rather, the drug trade has broad tolerance if not active support in many communities around the Americas because it supports critical exchanges and the survival of households in those communities despite the violence associated with the trade. To respond to the drug trade's negative effects, it is important that policy makers across the region understand more fully why so many people engage in and tolerate the trade. It is not just because there is money to be made or because they are afraid, but because the trade supports individuals, families, and communities in ways the global capitalist economy fails to do. Rather than telling people they should not deal in drugs, governments and other drivers of policy should consider more deeply why people have turned to the illicit trade in the first place.

This book suggests that taking drugs seriously means that we need to focus more centrally on the economic and moral exchanges around it. This means moving beyond understanding drugs in the Manichaean framework of the war on drugs and the ludic consumption culture of the middle and upper classes. Understanding moral economies requires us is to move beyond understand the drug trade in decisions made by political leaders in the US. Rather, a nuanced analysis requires us to acknowledge that there are multiple different and competing moralities that exist along the cocaine value chain. The economic policies advanced by the leaders of dominant global economies do not meet the needs of the majority of the world's population; indeed, as wealth becomes more concentrated, the portions of the working and middle classes of some of the world's leading global economies have turned to radical right-wing ideas to demand that their governments redress the failure of their economies to meet their families' economic needs. The situation of deprivation is much more dramatic along Latin America's cocaine value chain. Understanding the interests and needs of other peoples is essential to understanding the drug trade.

Latin American leaders often seek to sidestep these same moral questions when they blame the cocaine trade on drug consumption habits in the United States. While certainly this is true, Gootenberg points out that this dynamic is changing as consumption shifts south. More importantly, though, Latin American countries are not violent and their populations do not engage in illicit economic activities because of drug consumers in the United States and Western Europe alone. They do so largely because of the complex and often exclusionary political and economic systems of their own countries. The region has its own long history of violence and illegality that preceded the emergence of the modern cocaine trade in the late 1970s. To address the challenges of violence and crime in Latin America, leaders in the region need to consider how their own political and economic regimes produce and reinforce not just the drug trade but a host of other forms of violence.

In the end, far too much of this discussion has gone on among political leaders, bureaucrats, and scholars working near the seats of power, be it in New York, Washington, or London. To the extent that normative concerns are heard, they are those of politicians and bureaucrats seeking to advance regulations and well-connected populations, principally at consumption sites. In all of this we know far too little about the moral universe of the poor who survive in and around these trades. This book has drawn attention to those economies and the value chains they are built around. Critical to addressing these challenges of the drug trade is incorporating the voices of those who live and work in proximity to the trade in discussions of the trade and the various responses to it.

This volume has sought to provide a new way of thinking about the interconnections that operate in the cocaine trade. Whereas most studies have focused on how the trade operates in particular contexts, this volume has systematically examined the ways the cocaine trade operates in different places. We have shown that localized forms of exchange define the nature of how the trade operates in these locales. All of this points to particular strategies to ameliorate the challenges posed by the trade in different locales.

**NOTE**

The research reported here was funded in part by the Minerva Research Initiative (OUSD[R&E]) and the Army Research Office/Army Research Laboratory via grant #W911-NF-17-1-0569 to George Mason University. Any errors and opinions are not those of the Department of Defense and are attributable solely to the author(s).

**REFERENCES**

Abello Colak, Alexandra, and Valeria Guarneros-Meza. 2014. "The Role of Criminal Actors in Local Governance." *Urban Studies* 51, no. 15: 3268–89.

Arias, Enrique Desmond. 2017. *Criminal Enterprises and Governance in Latin America and the Caribbean.* New York: Cambridge University Press.

Arias, Enrique Desmond, and Mark Ungar. 2009. "Community Policing and Latin America's Citizen Security Crisis." *Comparative Politics* 41, no. 4: 409–29.

Bagley, Bruce M. and Jonathan D. Rosen. 2015. "Analytical Conclusions: The Search for Alternative Drug Policies in the Americas." In *Drug Trafficking, Organized Crime, and Violence in the Americas Today,* ed. Bruce M. Bagley and Jonathan D. Rosen. Gainesville: University Press of Florida.

Baird, Adam. 2012. "The Violent Gang and the Construction of Masculinity amongst Socially Excluded Young Men." *Safer Communities* 11, no. 4: 179–90.

Bourgois, Philippe. 1995. *In Search of Respect: Selling Crack in El Barrio.* New York: Cambridge University Press.

Caldeira, Teresa P. R., and James Holston. 1999. "Democracy and Violence in Brazil." *Comparative Studies in Society and History* 41, no. 4: 691–729.

Denyer Willis, Graham. 2015. *The Killing Consensus: Police, Organized Crime, and the Regulation of Life and Death in Brazil.* Berkeley: University of California Press.

Durán-Martínez, Angélica. 2018. *The Politics of Drug Violence: Criminals, Cops and Politicians in Colombia.* New York: Oxford University Press.

Eaton, Kent. 2006. "The Downside of Decentralization: Armed Clientelism in Colombia." *Security Studies* 15, no. 4: 533–63.

Escobar, Arturo. 1995. *Encountering Development: The Making and the Unmaking of the Third World.* Princeton, NJ: Princeton University Press.

Gay, Robert J. 2005. *Lucia: Testimonies of a Brazilian Drug Dealer's Woman.* Philadelphia: Temple University Press.

Grisaffi, Thomas, Linda Farthing, and Kathryn Ledebur. 2017. "Integrated Development with Coca in the Plurinational State of Bolivia: Shifting the Focus from Eradication to Poverty Alleviation." *Bulletin on Narcotics* 61, no. 1: 131–57.

Jaffe, Rivke. 2013. "The Hybrid State: Crime and Citizenship in Urban Jamaica." *American Ethnologist* 40, no. 4: 734–48.

Kalyvas, Stathis N. 2015. "How Civil Wars Help Explain Organized Crime—And How They Do Not." *Journal of Conflict Resolution* 79, no. 1: 1517–40.

Lessing, Benjamin. 2018. *Making Peace in Drug Wars: Crackdowns and Cartels in Latin America*. New York: Cambridge University Press.

Leeson, Peter. 2009. *The Invisible Hook: The Hidden Economics of Pirates*. Princeton, NJ: Princeton University Press.

Levitt, Steven D., and Sudhir Alladi Venkatesh. 2000. "An Economic Analysis of a Drug-Selling Gang's Finances." *Quarterly Journal of Economics* 115, no. 3: 755–89.

Moncada, Eduardo. 2016. *Cities, Business, and the Politics of Urban Violence*. Stanford, CA: Stanford University Press.

O'Donnell, Guillermo. 1993. "On the State, Democratization, and Some Conceptual Problems: A Latin American View with Glances at Some Postcommunist Countries." *World Development* 21, no. 8: 1355–69.

Rincón-Ruiz, Alexander, and Giorgios Kallis. 2013. "Caught in the Middle, Colombia's War on Drugs and Its Effects on Forest and People." *Geoforum* 46: 60–78.

Saviano, Roberto. 2015. *Zero, Zero, Zero: Look at Cocaine and All You See Is Powder. Look through Cocaine and You See the World*. New York: Penguin.

Snyder, Richard, and Angélica Durán-Martínez. 2009. "Does Illegality Breed Violence? Drug Trafficking and State Sponsored Protection Rackets." *Crime, Law, and Social Change* 52, no. 3: 253–73.

Ungar, Mark. 2011. *Policing Democracy: Overcoming Obstacles to Citizens Security in Latin America*. Washington, DC: Woodrow Wilson Center.

Varese, Federico. 2011. *Mafias on the Move: How Organized Crime Conquers New Territories*. Princeton, NJ: Princeton University Press.

Venkatesh, Sudhir Alladi. 1997. "The Social Organization of Street Gang Activity in an Urban Ghetto." *American Journal of Sociology* 103, no. 1: 82–111.

Yagoub, Mimi. 2017. "Which Regions of Colombia Are Playing the Biggest Role in the Coca Boom." *InSight Crime*, March 23. https://www.insightcrime.org/news/analysis/which-regions-colombia-biggest-role-coca-boom/.

# CONTRIBUTORS

**ENRIQUE DESMOND ARIAS** is Marxe Chair of Western Hemisphere Affairs and Professor at Baruch College and the Graduate Center, City University of New York. His research focuses on security and politics in Latin America and the Caribbean. He is the author of *Criminal Enterprises and Governance in Latin America and the Caribbean*, *Drugs and Democracy in Rio de Janeiro*, and is co-editor of *Violent Democracies in Latin America* (Duke University Press). In addition to his scholarship, he has served as a consultant to the Ford Foundation, the United Nations Development Programme, the United Nations Office on Drugs and Crime, and the United Nations Human Settlement Programme (UNHabitat). As part of his work with these last two organizations, Arias was the principal author of the United Nations' *Introductory Handbook on Policing Urban Space*.

**LILIAN BOBEA** is an Assistant Professor of Criminal Justice at Fitchburg State University and a Mandate Holder at the UN Working Group on mercenaries and private security. She is a Fulbright, Hubert H. Humphrey, Woodrow Wilson/LAP, and DSD/SSRC fellow. She is the author of the books *Violencia y Seguridad Democrática en República Dominicana* (2011), *Soldados y Ciudadanos en el Caribe* (2002), and *Entre el Crimen y el Castigo: Seguridad Ciudadana y Control Democrático en América Latina y el Caribe* (2003), and is co-author of *La Seguridad en el Caribe: Reformas y Cooperación Regional* (2009), *Seguridad Ciudadana en las Américas* (2007), and *Changes in Cuban Society since the Nineties* (2005). She is also author of numerous academic articles, and book chapters.

**PHILIPPE BOURGOIS** (PhD, Anthropology) is a cultural and medical anthropologist who has conducted fieldwork in Central America (Costa Rica, Panama, Nicaragua, El Salvador, and Belize) and in the urban United States (East Harlem in New York, San Francisco, North Philadelphia, and Los Angeles). In Central America his research addresses the political mobilization of ethnicity, immigration, labor relations, and the relationship between intimate violence and political/structural violence. In the United States he focuses on the political economy of US inner-city apartheid and the carceral and psychiatric management of poverty and unemployment. As a "public anthropologist," he tries to bring critical political-economic social science theory to bear on urgent social problems and advance a theoretical understanding of the interface between social inequality and power and how it manifests in individual experiences of social suffering. Currently, Bourgois is publishing on incarceration, substance abuse, violence, homelessness, mental illness, and HIV prevention. With Laurie Hart (UCLA), George Karandinos (Harvard), and Fernando Montero (Columbia), he is co-authoring a book entitled *Cornered*, based on almost a dozen years of collaborative participant-observation fieldwork in a violently policed, segregated Puerto Rican neighborhood dominated by open-air narcotics markets, currently dealing in heroin/fentanyl, in North Philadelphia.

**ANTHONY W. FONTES**, geographer and ethnographer, writes and teaches about violence, migration and forced displacement, transnational illicit economies, mass incarceration, and the politics of security in the Americas. His research has been funded by the Open Society Foundations, the Andrew Mellon Foundation, and the H. F. Guggenheim Foundation. His first book, *Mortal Doubt: Transnational Gangs and Social Order in Guatemala City* (2018), winner of the 2018 William LeoGrande Award, explores cycles of violence and migration in the making of extreme peacetime insecurity in Central America's Northern Triangle. His ethnographic fieldwork trespasses the blurred boundaries between the underworld, the state, and law-abiding society, scaling between the intimate and the global to illuminate how transnational forces impact the personal and the everyday. His current book project, *The Walls Close In: Borders, Prisons, and the American Dream*, delves into the global rise of revanchist anti-immigrant politics through the lens of the "Central American Migration Crisis" that began in 2014. Combining multisited transnational ethnography and discourse analysis, this project explores how the infrastructures and politics of immigration and imprisonment entwine in the twenty-first century.

**ROBERT GAY** is a Professor of Sociology at Connecticut College. He has spent the past thirty-five years conducting fieldwork in the favelas of Rio de Janeiro. He has written three books. His first, *Popular Organization and Democracy in Rio de Janeiro: A Tale of Two Favelas* (1994), examines ways in which neighborhood associations challenged long-standing, elitist ways of doing politics. His second, *Lucia: Testimonies of a Brazilian Drug Dealer's Woman* (2005), tells the story of a woman who became intimately involved in drug gang life during the 1990s. His third book, *Bruno: Conversations with a Brazilian Drug Dealer* (Duke University Press, 2015), is based on extensive interviews with a former leader of the Comando Vermelho, Brazil's oldest and arguably most powerful organized crime faction.

**PAUL GOOTENBERG**, SUNY Distinguished Professor of History and Sociology at Stony Brook University (New York), and Chair of History, is a commodity studies specialist and global drug historian. He trained as a Latin Americanist at the University of Chicago and Oxford. His drug-related works include *Andean Cocaine: The Making of a Global Drug* (2008), *Cocaine: Global Histories* (1999), and, with Liliana M. Dávalos, *The Origins of Cocaine: Peasant Colonization and Failed Development in the Amazon Andes* (2018). From 2011 to 2014 he chaired the Drugs, Security and Democracy fellowship (DSD) of the Social Science Research Council, a research program supported by the Open Society Foundations. Gootenberg is now General Editor of the forthcoming *Oxford Handbook of Drug History* and President-Elect of the Alcohol and Drugs History Society (ADHS).

**ROMAIN LE COUR GRANDMAISON** received his PhD in Political Science from the Sorbonne University (Paris-1). His dissertation, titled "Violent Intermediaries. Drug Cartels, Autodefensas, and the State: From Political Brokerage to Patronage Wars in Michoacán, Mexico," focused on the role of brokers within dynamics of violence in Mexico. Since 2013, he has conducted more than three years of fieldwork in Mexico. In 2019, he coedited with Professor Jacobo Grajales the book *The State, After All: Building Authority Amidst Violence* [L'État malgré tout: Produire l'autorité dans la violence].

**THOMAS GRISAFFI** is Associate Professor in the Department of Geography at the University of Reading. Trained as an anthropologist, Grisaffi works on topics including coca and cocaine production and its global commodity chain, indigenous social movements in the Andes, alternative development in drug crop producing zones, and democracy. His book with Duke University Press, titled *Coca Yes, Cocaine No: How Bolivia's Coca Growers Reshaped Democracy* (2019), is an ethnography of the Movement toward Socialism (MAS) as it transformed from an agricultural union, criminalized as a result of US-led drug war policies, into Bolivia's ruling party. Grisaffi is the principal investigator on a project titled "Drug Crops and Development in the Andes: Regional Applicability of Innovative Drug Crop Control Policy," which is supported by the Global Challenges Research Fund and a co-investigator on the European Research Council–funded project, "Anthropologies of Extorsion."

**LAURIE KAIN HART** is Professor of Anthropology and Global Studies and Director of the Center for European and Russian Studies at the University of California at Los Angeles. Her research focuses on the long-term effects on persons and communities of ethnopolitical conflict, civil war, state-engineered population displacements, migration, borders, nationalism, racism, globalization, and ethnospatial segregation. As a former architect, she is particularly interested in the impact of spatial, architectural, and geopolitical forces on social inequality and marginalization, and the links between macro-social and political forces and individual subjectivity. Regionally, she specializes in Greece, the broader Mediterranean area, and the urban US, with special emphasis on the intimate experience of the structural violence of inner-city segregation. She is currently working on a co-authored book, provisionally called *Cornered* (under contract), analyzing the carceral and psychiatric management of US urban poverty and segregation in Philadelphia.

**ANNETTE IDLER** is the Director of Studies at the Changing Character of War Centre, Senior Research Fellow at Pembroke College, and is at the Department of Politics and International Relations, all University of Oxford. She is also Visiting Scholar at Harvard University's Weatherhead Center for International Affairs. Dr. Idler's work focuses on the interface of conflict, security, and transnational organized crime. She has conducted extensive fieldwork in and on crisis-affected regions of Venezuela, Colombia, Ecuador, Myanmar, and Somalia. Dr. Idler is the author of *Borderland Battles: Violence, Crime, and Governance at the Edges of Colombia's War* (2019), published in Spanish (2021), and coeditor of *Transforming the War on Drugs: Warriors, Victims, and Vulnerable Regions* (forthcoming in 2021). Her work has appeared in journals such as *World Politics, Third World Quarterly*, and the *Journal of Global Security Studies*.

**GEORGE KARANDINOS** is a medical student and PhD candidate in Anthropology at Harvard University. He is co-authoring a book entitled *Cornered*, drawing on four years of resident ethnographic research on a heroin- and cocaine-selling corner in Philadelphia.

**FERNANDO MONTERO** (Mellon Postdoctoral Fellow, Society of Fellows, Columbia University) is an anthropologist specializing in security regimes and the war on drugs in the Americas. His current book project examines the everyday life of military occupation in the Afro-indigenous Moskitia region of Central America (Nicaragua/Honduras). Centering on the sexual and romantic affairs between Miskitu women and Nicaraguan and Honduran soldiers in recently occupied Miskitu coastal villages, the book interrogates Central American security regimes, not only in relation to the history of war and extractivism in Afro-indigenous regions, but also vis-à-vis Afro-indigenous kinship and gender norms, property forms and economic practices, and overlapping jurisdictions of regional governance. This project builds on Montero's earlier field research on policing and mass incarceration in the segregated Puerto Rican neighborhood of North Philadelphia.

**DENNIS RODGERS** is Research Professor of Anthropology and Sociology at the Graduate Institute of International and Development Studies, Geneva (Switzerland), and the PI of the ERC Advanced Grant–funded project "Gangs, Gangsters, and Ganglands: Towards a Global Comparative Ethnography" (GANGS). His research focuses on issues relating to the dynamics of conflict and violence in cities in Latin America (Nicaragua, Argentina) and South Asia (India). Much of his work involves the longitudinal study of youth gangs in Nicaragua, but he also works on the political economy of development, the politics of socio-spatial segregation, participatory governance processes, the historiography of urban theory, and the epistemology of development knowledge.

**TANIELE RUI** is Professor of Anthropology at University of Campinas, Brazil. Her areas of interest include drug policies and their connection with poverty, urban vulnerability, and precarious life. During the last decade (2009–19) she conducted fieldwork research with homeless, crack users, and dealers in São Paulo and Rio de Janeiro. Her book *Nas tramas do crack: Etnografia da abjeção* received Honorable Mention from the Society for Latin American and Caribbean Anthropology (SLACA Book Prize, 2015). Email: tanieler@unicamp.br.

**CYRUS VEESER** is Professor of History at Bentley University in Waltham, Massachusetts. He is the author of *A World Safe for Capitalism* (2002) and *Great Leaps Forward* (2009). He has been a Fulbright, NEH, and Charles Warren Center fellow. His current work, *Origins of American Internationalism: How Depression and War Launched the American Century*, is forthcoming. His next project examines the US government's understanding of Che Guevara's revolutionary strategy of *foquismo*, in particular the implications of its premise that Latin American peasants were ripe for "spontaneous" rebellion.

**AUTUMN ZELLERS-LEÓN** graduated from Temple University with her PhD in Anthropology in 2018. Her research examines the impact of the drug trade on indigenous communities in Colombia. Her work is based on over three years of fieldwork in the country's southwestern region and focuses on how economic changes in indigenous territories are perceived through moral notions of youth and adulthood. Through her work she aims to show both how indigenous communities grapple with the political and economic challenges of the drug trade, and how drug policy has limited the fulfillment of multicultural rights for indigenous people. She teaches as an adjunct professor in the Philadelphia area with a focus on Latin America, drug policy, and racial justice.

# INDEX

*Page numbers followed by f indicate figures; page numbers followed by t indicate tables.*

Chile, 289

China: cocaine consumption in, 308

*cifra negra*, 186n18

*cistenero* (gas smuggler), 64n8

citizenship rights, 13, 88, 90n22

Ciudad de Este, 297

Clawson, Patrick, 23

clientelism, 56, 119, 124, 166–68, 182–83, 185n2, 322. *See also* patronage

Coalcomán, 173–74

coca and coca cultivation, 80f; acreage of, 34, 49, 52, 74, 302, 303, 304, 317; aerial fumigations, 77, 97, 301, 306; availability of, 101; in borderlands, 74; cocaine compared with, 41; in Colombia, 20, 71, 301–2; crop substitution options, 86, 105, 304, 330, 333; cultivation of, 18, 21, 41; demand for, 290, 291; dependency on, 34n3; drying coca, 53f; eradication programs, 44, 49, 61, 70, 287, 290, 292, 304; government support of, 44; legalization of, 22, 63, 64n5; price fluctuations, 45–46, 48–50, 52, 304; ritual and medicinal uses of, 101; social and economic opportunities generated by, 29; state government, 22; substitutes for, 49; traditional uses of, 99; VRAEM (Apurímac, Ene and Mantaro River Valley), 1, 2, 7f, 18, 22f, 302–3

cocaine: accessibility of, 289–90; addictions, 152, 293; aging user populations, 291–92, 293; capacity of, 289, 290; commercial use of, 289; counter-narcotics operations, 170; decline of, 292, 295; history of, 288–89; legalization of, 329, 335; markets for, 143, 194, 210, 262, 290, 293, 295; opioids, 8, 264, 293, 294; political geography of, 287, 288, 291–92, 295, 298–302, 309n2; precursor chemicals, 34n4, 47, 50, 53, 63n2, 74, 122, 135n4, 170, 292, 319; pricing of, 18, 127, 143, 153, 241, 242, 264, 291–92; production sites for, 5, 41, 51, 54, 63n2, 81–82, 319; quality of, 296, 300; racialization of cocaine markets, 293–94; seizures of, 291, 293, 298, 300–301; supply reductions in the United States, 292, 293;

surveys on, 292, 293; trace evidence of, 296, 300. *See also* consumption spaces for drugs; crack cocaine; smuggling; transshipment sites; *individual country headings (e.g., Colombia)*

cocaine commodity chains, 6 (map), 27t; of Age of Colombian Cocaine (1975–2005), 289; Andean border regions, 72, 290; brokers, 79–81, 80f, 82, 132–33; brokers in, 29, 79–81, 80f; cocaine consumption, 291, 294–95; Colombian coca farmers in, 28; continuity in, 70, 71, 289–91; drug production in Colombia, 96; drug use, fluctuations in, 291; Dutch disease, 19; financieros in, 83–84; geographic shifts in, 33, 287, 288, 295, 298–302, 309n2; globalizing consumption, 295–96; legal commodity chains (1880s–1940s), 289; lifeworld produced by, 18–19; noneconomic bonds in, 220; nonstate groups involved in, 79–81; price fluctuations, 291–92; social connections along, 220; southward shift of, 287, 288, 295, 298–302, 309n2; stakeholders in, 219–20; state authority, 14, 84–85. *See also* borders and border crossings; corners; gangs; puntos; smuggling; transshipment sites

cocaine hydrochloride (crystallized cocaine), 1, 47

cocaine production: agricultural unions on, 57; cocaine alkaloid extraction, 50; costs of, 12, 50, 63n2, 289; gasoline in, 47, 50, 53–54, 62, 63n3, 74, 75f, 145; labor for, 18, 48, 50–51, 54; networks of drug traffickers, 80; PBC *(pasta básica de cocaína)*, 289, 298, 303, 304; precursor chemicals, 34n4, 47, 50, 53, 63n2, 74, 122, 170, 292, 319; reciprocity in, 51–52, 54; sites for, 5, 41, 51, 54, 63n2, 81–82, 319; sugar production compared with, 5–6. *See also* paste production

cocaine signature program (DEA), 302

cocaine trafficking: in Barrio Luis Fanor Hernández (Managua, Nicaragua), 193–94; Caribbean network for, 194;

Guatemalan government involvement in, 141, 143; illicit cocaine networks (late 1940s), 289; intermediaries in, 300; Middle East routes, 300; in the Pacific, 300–301; paramilitaries involvement in, 73; Puerto Rico to United States, 213; rivalries in, 143; southward movement of, 287–89, 295, 302, 309n2; trajectory of, 289, 300; Upper Huallaga Valley (UHV), 289, 303, 304; VRAEM (Apurímac, Ene, and Mantaro River Valley), 302–3; water transport, 23, 24, 55f, 80, 136n13, 304

coca leaf, 7f; chewing of, 41, 42, 43, 44, 100–101; consumption of, 28, 42, 43–44; labor, 20, 28, 50–51, 61; legal uses of, 44, 63, 305f; markets for, 28–29, 34n5, 47, 51–53; purchase of, 51, 52f; stomping method, 50–51, 63n3; symbolism of, 305; traditional uses of, 42, 49, 51, 99, 305

"Coca si, cocaína no" (Bolivia), 45, 100, 304

"Coca yes—cocaine no" (Bolivia), 45, 100, 304

Cochabamba Tropics. *See* Chapare, Bolivia

*cocinas* (kitchens), 82

cockroach effect, 293, 302

coke. *See* crack cocaine

Colombia: Age of Colombian Cocaine (1975–2005), 289–90; alternate paths to drug repression, 306, 330; anti-drug initiatives, 301–2, 303, 304, 306, 308, 330; AUC (Autodefensas Unidas de Colombia), 73; border areas of, 72, 296–97, 322; Brazilian drug smuggling networks, 297; cartels, 18, 170, 297–98; coca cultivation in, 18, 20–22, 34n5, 42, 48, 71, 290, 301–4; cocaine production in, 70, 73, 297, 301–2; drug policies in, 76; drug supply chain to Puerto Rico, 215–16; DTOs (drug trafficking organizations), 321; FARC (Fuerzas Armadas Revolucionarias de Colombia), 29, 70–71, 73, 74, 76, 80, 81, 88; Indigenous communities in, 98–99, 101, 103; Law 30 (1986), 98; as narco-democracy, 96; Norte del Valle Cartel (Colombia), 196; paramilitary groups in, 73–74, 96; Plan Colombia, 76, 98, 290,

293, 301; post-drug war, 304; Rastrojos, 70, 80; revenue from coca and cocaine trade, 48; royalty payments to municipalities/incentive payments, 330–31; second phase of Colombian commodity chain (1985–2005), 290; suspension of coca field fumigations, 306; trafficking to Europe, 300; United States relations with, 76, 96, 170, 290, 293, 306, 308. *See also* individual FARC (Fuerzas Armadas Revolucionarias de Colombia)

Colombian commodity chain (second phase: 1985–2005), 290

comandos (*facções*), 233

Comando Vermelho (Red Command, CV). *See* CV (Comando Vermelho)

Comité de Orden y Disciplina (COD), 155

Community Epidemiology Working Group (CEWG), 292

compadrazgo (godparenthood, fictive kinship), 52, 53, 54–55, 56, 64n6, 169

Complexo do Alemão (favela): military occupation of, 243

consumer culture: allure of drug dealing, 150–53; conspicuous consumption of drug dealers, 195–96, 199, 201, 202–3, 221, 234; cultural loss, 29, 94–95, 103–5, 112–13; motorcycles, 29, 94–95, 108–12, 151, 152, 320, 326; predatory accumulation, 279, 281–82

consumption spaces for drugs: control of, 171, 242, 243–44, 245, 256, 266–67, 268; moral economies of, 322–23; policy responses at, 334; territory of, 210, 215–16, 233, 242, 243–45, 291–92, 295; visibility of, 216, 232, 236, 239–40, 242, 243, 261, 263. *See also* corners; puntos

container shipping lanes, 298

corners: competition for, 278; earnings, 262; hand-to-hand retail sales at, 258, 264, 266; police interference, 265–66; rentals of, 259, 268, 274; resident ethnographic research of, 254, 259, 261–63; risks, 265–66; rivalries for, 278; supply chain for, 257, 261, 267, 268; territorial control of, 32, 262–63, 265; visibility, 261

conspicuous consumption by, 195–96, 199, 201, 221, 234; entrepreneurship, 23, 31, 202–3, 216–17, 227, 271; exchange rates, 129–30; imprisonment of, 30, 132, 133, 213; infrastructural conspicuous consumption, 202–3; intangible benefits of embodied capital, 200–203; intimidation by, 223, 225, 229; investments by, 31, 131, 199–200, 219, 321, 335; police interference, 265–66; politicians relations with, 219; recruitment of, 150–52, 153, 213–14, 224; self-regulation by, 209, 219–20; territorial interests of, 171, 224–27, 226–27, 243–46; violence, 32, 196–97, 204, 239, 248n15. *See also* corners; gangs; puntos

Drug Threat Assessment (DEA), 294

drug trade. *See* gangs; Indigenous communities; neighborhoods; transshipment sites; violence

drug trafficking: border crossings, 23, 70, 74–75, 126–27, 136nn13–14; child support, 158–59; collaborators in, 97, 194–95; corruption, 97, 129, 131–32; drug supply, 126; economic opportunities, 142; human guarantees in, 1–2; impact of, 69; military involvement in, 126; post-natural disaster reconstruction aiding, 205n2; prison guards as collaborators, 158; production compared with, 97; professionalization of, 171, 196–97, 289; profits of, 127, 129–30, 142, 190, 195, 197; security threat of, 294; suppliers, 127; and the survival of women, 158–59; trafficking routes, 6 (map); as *trafico de formigas*, 127; transactions in US dollars, 129–30; violence, 143, 144

drug users: addicted populations, 199, 226, 237, 335; aging population, 292, 293; census of, 245, 294; displacements of, 238–39, 243–46; drug dealers as, 152, 158, 196; harassment of, 243–44; imprisonment of, 32; income for, 244; living conditions of, 244; medical and welfare services for, 244; pacification processes, 244, 245; as petty criminals,

244; physical condition of, 258; police, 244; public assistance for, 244–45, 299; racial stereotypes, 293–94, 295, 296; relocations of, 235, 239, 243–44, 247n3; social stereotypes, 296; state repression of, 244, 245

DTOs (drug trafficking organizations): authority of, 31; in Guatemala, 30, 140, 141; hegemonic power of, 30; leaders of, 175; local political authority challenged by, 30–31; relations with local government, 31; relations with local population, 31; state government relations with, 30–31; weakness of the state, 14. *See also* CV (Comando Vermelho); Templarios

Dubner, Stephen, 190

Ecuador, 74, 302, 303

Edelman, Marc, 9

Eduardo (assistant to Robert Gay), 120, 121f

education, 144; community support for, 223–24; dropout rate, 145, 151, 223, 275; generation gap in, 104; government investment in, 330; impact of imprisonment on, 334; indigenous youth education program, 104; school attendance and involvement in drug trafficking, 151, 266; as social capital, 50, 192; teachers, 104–5, 226–28

El Carmen (Guatemala), 142, 143

El Carmen bridge, 144f

El Chamale (Juan Ortiz), 145–47, 149

El Chayo (Nazario Moreno Gonzalez), 172

elections in Mexico, 24

El Galito (Guatemala), 149–54, 149f

Elias, Norbert, 282

el Indio Viejo (narco), 194–96; arrests of, 197–98; authority of, 196; Barrio Luis Fanor Hernández gang attack on, 196; cartelito of, 196; imprisonment of, 197; institutionalization of drug business, 197; monopolization of narcotics trade in Nicaragua, 197; Norte del Valle Cartel (Colombia) links with, 196; relations with, 201–2. *See also* Cartelito of Barrio Luis Fanor Hernández

El Mas Loco (Nazario Moreno Gonzalez), 172

embodied capital, 191, 192, 200–204

Emilio (motorcycle owner), 108

employment: in agriculture, 177–78, 186n24; of homeless and addicted populations, 226; impact of imprisonment on, 334; job opportunity programs, 330; legal employment, 31, 199–200, 204, 271; in making crack cocaine, 194; offered by narcotraffickers, 146–48, 254; training for, 24–25

entrepreneurship, 23, 31, 202–3, 216–17

eradication programs, 44, 49, 61, 70, 287, 290, 301, 304

Escobar, Arturo, 329

Escobar, Pablo, 96, 290

Espirito Santo, Brazil, 299

Estação de Luz train station (São Paulo, Brazil), 233, 238

Europe, 1, 290–91, 298, 300

Evangelical Christianity, 106, 210, 212

Evelio, Maroc (student), 105–6, 110

everyday violence, 270

*expendios*, 194, 195

exploitation: negative asymmetric reciprocity (Lomnitz), 183

extortion rackets, 173–74, 175–78, 180–81, 185n11, 186n21

*facções* (comandos), 233, 241–42

families: cartels' support of, 25, 150–52; coca cultivation, 28, 34n3; cocaine trafficking networks, 140–41, 194; compadrazgo (godparenthood), 52, 53, 54–55, 56, 64n6; of drug dealers, 2, 144, 150–52, 212, 213, 223; financial dependence, 54; household incomes, 102–3, 106, 263; housing for, 211–12; impact of imprisonment on, 334; involvement in drug trafficking, 144, 150–53; reciprocity in, 54; social mobility of, 50, 104, 106; survival strategies, 25, 33, 150–54; victims of gang violence, 152

FARC (Fuerzas Armadas Revolucionarias de Colombia): as arbiters, 29, 88; coca-growing areas controlled by, 80, 81; cocaine trafficking, 80, 290; CV (Comando Vermelho), 299; election of, 326; funding of, 73, 317; impact on cocaine market, 290; peace treaty, 70–71, 302, 303, 306, 317; relations with local communities, 81–82; reorganization of, 303; Treaty (2016), 74, 302, 303, 306; violence, 290

farmers: changing roles of, 97; coca fumigation, 49, 77; in cocaine commodity chain, 52; as consumers, 94–95; cultivated acreage in Colombia, 303; as drug consumers, 94–95; on drug trade, 43; economic mobility of, 15, 48–50, 51, 77, 97, 104; financieros, 82–83; government relations with, 45, 49, 57–58, 59, 77, 326; mutual aid as characteristic, 51; police relations, 58–59; rebels aligned with, 333; revenue from cocaine, 34n6, 50; stereotypes of, 96–97

favelas of Rio de Janeiro, 118, 123, 233, 241–42, 243, 244–45

FDN (Família do Norte), 297

FELC-N (anti-narcotics police force), 61

Feltran, Gabriel, 237, 238

fentanyl, 8, 264, 293, 294

Field, Les, 98

fieldwork, ethnographic: with coca farmers, 41–42; drug users' daily routines, 244; interaction with drug bosses (bichote), 254; resident ethnographic research, 254, 259, 261–63

financieros, 82–85, 88–89

firearms, 145, 161n4, 267, 268, 273, 274; arms-for-coke deals, 299; firearm deaths, 268, 276–77, 281; ownership in the United States, 279, 281; purchases by young men, 279–81; smuggling, 279, 299; violence, 268, 273–74, 276–77, 280–81

focus groups, 104–5, 214–15, 220–21, 224–25

*Folha de São Paulo*, 235–36

Fontes, Anthony, vii (map), 30, 321, 324

food riots, 8–9, 329

former drug dealers, 193, 198–203, 213–14, 217, 271

heroin substitution programs, 300
Hirata, Daniel, 233
Hobbs, Joseph J., 98
Holston, James, 87, 237
homeless population, 212, 226, 238
homicides, 121, 135n2, 236–37, 279–80
Hong Kong, 301
honor, concepts of, 30
household incomes, 102–3, 106, 263
housing: barriadas, 211, 212, 216, 224,
    226; drug dealers, 196; for drug users,
    243–45; homeless population, 212, 226,
    238; intimidation of tenants, 204–5; for
    low-income families, 211–12; rental pay-
    ments, 204; social segregation, 211–12;
    of women, 204–5, 219
human capital formation, 25
human guarantees: for drug deals, 1–2
human rights defender (interviewee),
    79–80
hustlers, 258, 264, 266
hyper-incarcerations, 151–52, 263, 264, 266
hypermasculinity, 33, 267

Idler, Annette, vii (map), 28–29, 46, 321, 322
illicit cocaine networks (late 1940s),
    289–90
impossible reciprocity (Geffray), 183
incarceration policies, 32–33, 238, 240,
    268–70, 271, 273–75, 294, 299, 334
Indigenous communities, 326; coca as
    sacred plant in, 99; coca leaf use, 42;
    contact with illegal armed groups, 95;
    drug use in, 98–99, 105, 106; in global
    commodity chain, 95; global consumer
    culture, 94, 102, 108–9, 111; guerrillas
    and, 103; impact of drug crop economy
    on, 102; indigenous farmers in, 94–95;
    leadership in, 95–96, 102–4, 106, 108–9,
    111; negative stereotypes of, 111–12; qual-
    ity of life, 95, 99, 103, 112, 113; relations
    with state authorities, 87–88, 90n22,
    102–3; traditional values, 99, 103.
    See also farmers; unions
inmates: cartel's protection of, 151–52;
    incarceration as life-saving, 275–76;

interpersonal violence, 269–70, 281;
    interviews with, 274–76; recidivism,
    281; reintegration into legal labor mar-
    ket, 271, 281; self-protection, 269–71,
    281; social capital of, 281; survival of,
    270–71
intangible benefits: usefulness of, 204
interview participants/informants on:
    appointment of the *jefe*, 175; bichote's
    courage, 267; border areas as start-
    ing points of trafficking routes, 74; on
    cartel patronage, 150–52; on chronic
    incarceration, 273–75; coca cultivation,
    41–42; coca eradication, 77; cocaine
    production, 81–82; crack sales in Rio's
    slums, 241; desire for upward mobility,
    268; drug dealers, 32; drug market
    leadership, 218; establishing cocaine
    workshops, 54, 81–82; ex-combatants
    couple, 81–82; fieldworkers interaction
    with, 254, 255–56, 259, 263; firsthand
    knowledge of murder victims, 218–19;
    focus groups, 104–5, 214–15, 220–21,
    224–25; gangs, 133, 173–74, 213–14; on
    the golden age of the drug trade, 213–14;
    household income of, 230n13; impact
    of drug trade on young people, 217; in-
    formal violence as means of protection,
    222; the intangible benefits of drug
    dealing, 201–2; interview methods,
    218–19, 230n13; involvement in drug
    trafficking, 29–30, 125–26; on level of
    violence surrounding drug business,
    218–19; massacres to establish domina-
    tion, 214, 217; on multiplier effect of
    drug revenue, 219; non-state players'
    relations with communities, 81–82; po-
    lice relations, 217–18; prison conditions,
    58, 132–33, 273–75; professionalization
    of drug market, 216–17, 218; punish-
    ments administered by cartel members,
    174; punishments administered by
    community members, 222; puntos,
    213, 215–16; recruitment of dealers,
    213–14; researchers' interactions with,
    32, 41–42, 45, 267, 273–75, 283; social

hazards of drug crop cultivation, 104–5; social mobility, 108; the state as threat to livelihoods, 85–86; state government as threat to villagers, 85–86; supply chain steps, 79–80; survival in prisons, 270–71, 281; Templarios' extortion racket, 173–74, 177–78, 180; transportation of drugs, 1–2, 139–40

Jacarezinho, 243
Jaffe, Rivke, 321
Jaimito (interviewee, Puerto Rico), 216, 217
Jamaica, 185n5, 288, 321, 329
*jefe de plaza* (local boss): control of elections, 179; extortion racket led by, 175–76; relations with local governments, 178, 179; as shadow mayor, 179–80
Jogador, Orlando (Orlando da Conceição), 133
Johnson, Simon, 192
Jonas (indigenous youth activist), 94
*joseadores* (hustlers), 258, 264, 266
Juanga (El Gallito resident), 30, 150–54, 152, 158
Juarez Cartel, 170, 290
"just-in-time" delivery services, 202–3

Kalyvas, Stathis, 13, 14
Karandinos, George, 10–11, 31
Katz, Cindy, 94
Kensington (aka North Philadelphia): familial relationships, 277; firearm deaths in, 273–74, 276–77, 276f; narcotics market in, 258–59, 262–63; police confrontations, 255–59; street language, 255, 257, 258, 261, 267; visibility of narcotics market, 263; white customer base, 258, 263. *See also* bichote; Leo (drug dealer, Tito's brother); Tito (caseworker);
Kilmer, Beau, 292, 293
kinship networks: baby boy nicknames, 276, 279; brothers in, 32, 267; cocaine trade, 319; coca sales networks, 52–53; compadrazgo (godparenthood), 52, 53, 54–55, 56, 64n6; drug trade, 22, 32, 53; in paste production, 28, 51–52, 54, 63n2;

support networks, 22, 26, 144, 146–47, 150–53, 271, 329
Knights Templar (Caballeros Templarios). *See* Templarios
Koch, Insa, 9, 58, 222

La Familia Michocana (The Michoacán Family), 165, 170, 172
*langosta blanca* (cocaine), 194
La Shadow (female trafficker), 159
Las Monjas, 226
Latin American Commission on Drugs and Democracy, 288
La Tuta (Servando Goméz Martínez), 172
La Unidad Móvil de Patrullaje Rural (Rural Mobile Patrol Unit), 48
Law 30 of 1986 (Colombia), 98
Lázaro Cárdenas, 170
Le Cour Grandmaison, Romain, vii (map), 30, 319, 321, 324, 326
Lee, Rensselaer, 23
legal commodity chain of cocaine and coca (1880s–1940s): PBC (*pasta básica de cocaína*), 289, 298, 303, 304
legal employment, 31, 145–46, 199–200, 204, 271
Leo (drug dealer, Tito's brother), 32, 267, 273–75, 283
Lessing, Benjamin, 248n12
Leticia (Colombia), 297, 304
Levitt, Steven, 190
lime production, 176, 177, 186n24
Llorens Torres in Santurce (public housing), 211
local boss (*jefe de plaza*): control of elections, 179; extortion racket led by, 175–76; relations with local governments, 178, 179; as shadow mayor, 179–80
Lomnitz, Claudio, 183
Lopez Bonilla, Mauricio, 141
lost boys generation, 221
loyalty, 51, 222–23, 226
Lucas (cocaine supplier for Raffy), 261, 267, 268
Lucia (interviewee of Robert Gay), 121f, 125
lumber production, 176

Núcleo Interdisciplinar de Açao Para a
    Cidadania (Interdisciplinary Nucleus of
    Action and Citizenship; UFRJ), 244–45
Nuervo Progresista party, 209

OAS report (2013), 288
OAS summit, 306
Obama, Barack, 294
objectified capital, 192–93
Ochoa, Fabio, 170
OEDT (European Observatory of Drugs
    and Addiction), 300
O Estado de São Paulo, 236
Oikonomakis, Leonidas, 63n1
oil industry, 77
Olympics (summer 2016), 241, 243, 245,
    247n2, 297
Omaira (teacher), 104–5
ONDCP (US drug czar's office), 301
Operation Blast Furnace, 48–49
Operation Coronado, 170
Operation Millennium, 170
opioids, 8, 264, 293, 294
opium, 8, 33, 142–43
Orlando da Conceição (Orlando Jogador),
    133
Ortiz, Juan (El Chamale), 145–47, 149
OSF (Open Society Foundations), 245
oxycontin, 294

paca smoking, 300
Pacific: cocaine trafficking in the, 300–301
pacification programs, 244, 245, 299
Pac-Man (drug dealer), 198
Painter, James, 47, 48
Panama Red (bichote), 259, 260–61,
    267–68
Paraguay, 297, 299, 307, 310n9
paramilitary groups, 73–74, 80, 96, 141,
    165, 170, 234, 333
Parque Victoria (barriada), 216
Partido Revolucionaria Institucional (PRI),
    24, 178, 181
paste production, 27t; costs of, 18, 51,
    63n2, 74, 79–80; financieros, 82–85,
    88–89; market value of, 1, 63n2, 79–80,

85–86; police interventions in, 85–86;
    reciprocity in production of, 28, 51–52,
    54, 63n2; sales of, 47–48, 54–55, 85; sites
    of, 12, 43, 61, 63n2, 63n3, 289; smuggling
    of, 33, 85–86, 132
patronage, 24, 26, 27t, 30, 166, 172, 259,
    267, 319, 320
Pavón prison, 132–33, 142, 151, 154–58, 155f,
    161n9
Pavo Real (Peacock), 155
Paz y Paz, Claudia, 141
PBC (pasta básica de cocaína), 289, 298, 303,
    304
PCC (Primeiro Comando da Capital):
    Carandiru Massacre (1992), 237–38,
    248n7; community relations, 238–39; on
    crack use, 238–39; CV (Comando Ver-
    melho) relations with, 242; enforcement
    by, 233, 246; FDN (Família do Norte),
    297; Paraguayan networks, 299; power
    of, 235, 238; rules of, 238; social control
    by, 239–40
peasants, 8, 9, 11–12, 55, 99, 303
Pedro (interviewee San Juan), 216, 220
Pellegrini, Alessandra, 98
penitentiaries, 238, 248n12
Peru: Andean Initiative, 290; Brazilian
    drug smuggling networks, 296–97; Cali
    cartels, 23, 24, 73, 85, 289, 290; coca
    cultivation in, 18, 20, 33, 42–43, 73,
    302, 304; cocaine denial in, 304, 306–7;
    cocaine manufacture, 289, 301; cocaine
    trafficking, 289–90, 301–2, 304; coca
    paste from, 63n2, 289; eradication plan
    (Comisión Nacional 2017), 304; legal
    commodity chain of cocaine and coca
    (1880s-1940s), 289; United States ties
    with, 306; Upper Huallaga Valley, 289,
    303–4; village in, 22f; VRAEM (Apurí-
    mac, Ene and Mantaro River Valley), 1,
    2, 7f, 18, 22f, 302–3
Philadelphia: corruption in, 260; court
    systems, 257–59, 263–65, 268–69, 275;
    Muslims (Philadelphia prison gang),
    271; narcotics units in, 258–59; police
    corruption, 260–61; shootings in Phila-

delphia neighborhood, 276f; street dealing in, 32; unemployment in, 263–64. *See also* Raffy (bichote)

Philadelphia, Puerto Rican neighborhoods in: familial relationships, 277; firearm deaths, 273–74, 276–77, 276f; narcotics market in, 258–59, 262–63; police confrontations, 255–59; street language, 255, 257, 258, 261, 267, 268; unemployment in, 263–64. *See also* bichotes; Tito (caseworker)

Picard, Elizabeth, 182

pichicateros (drug workers), 47–48, 50

Piketty, Thomas, 193

Pinochet regime (Chile), 289

*pisa-cocas*, 50–51, 54

Plan Colombia, 76, 98, 290, 293, 301

Plan Consolidation (Colombia), 76

Plan Patriota (Colombia), 76

police: accountability, 259–60; agricultural unions of Chapare relations with, 57–58; bichotes' provocations, 255–58, 260–61; bribery of, 26, 31, 200; collusion with traffickers, 97; corruption of, 97, 129, 131–32, 141, 150, 217, 219, 260; in drug trade, 141, 217, 219, 227, 260–61; incursions of, 217–18, 244, 245; influence on communities, 223; involvement in drug market, 55–56, 129, 131, 219; narcotics units, 61, 259–60; neighborhood deployments, 26, 31, 153, 217–18, 223, 243; pacification programs, 243, 244, 245, 299; racial profiling used by, 264; response to visibility of drug users, 243, 247n3; sexual harassment by, 260; suppression of local political activism, 59; tensions with gang leaders, 255–57; unions, 260; violence, 32–33, 217–18, 219, 256–58

precursor chemicals, 34n4, 47, 50, 53, 63n2, 74, 122, 135n4, 170, 292, 319

PRI (Partido Revolucionaria Institucional), 24, 178, 179, 181

price and production controls, 127, 176–77

Primeiro Comando da Capital (First Command of the Capital, PCC), 26, 233

prison guards, 158, 214, 269, 270

prisons: in Brazil, 38, 240, 299; businesses in, 155, 157; Carandiru Massacre (1992), 237–38, 248n7; cash flow into/prison economy, 157; cellphones in, 157, 161n10; CV (Comando Vermelho) presence in, 122, 132–33, 136n10, 248n12; detection devices, 157, 158; drug market in, 150, 157–59, 238, 246; gang control in, 30, 122, 132–33, 134, 214, 233, 271; gendered nature of visitation, 158, 159; governance, 154–55, 158–59; government raid on, 155–56; Ilha Grande prison, 122; incarceration policies, 32–33, 238, 240, 268–70, 271, 273–75, 294, 299, 334; interpersonal violence, 269–70, 279–81; mass incarceration policy in São Paulo, Brazil, 238, 240; overcrowding, 134, 136n20, 156–57, 159, 161n9, 238, 240, 269, 281; penitentiaries, 238, 248n12; population statistics, 156f; privileges in, 132, 136n16, 155; protection models in, 214; racial violence in, 269–70, 271; recruitment for criminal organizations, 31; security technologies, 157, 158; segregation of criminal factions in, 133; self-respect, 270, 281; state investments in, 157, 159; survival in, 270–71, 281; visitors to, 157–59, 278–79; women as smugglers into, 158, 159; young prisoners, 32, 268, 273–75, 283

pro-coca campesino mobilizations, 305

prostitution, 238

protection tax (*derecho piso*), 176

public housing projects, 211–12, 216, 225–26, 230n4

Puente Blanco, Catano: community activism, 223

Puerto Rican neighborhoods in the US: cocaine wholesale markets in, 262; drug corners in, 262–63, 265; fieldwork in, 254, 262–63

Puerto Ricans: imprisonment of, 268–70; legal labor force participation, 272; poverty of, 272; relations with African Americans, 270

Puerto Rican youth: ambition of, 273–74, 276; baby boy nicknames of, 276, 279; exclusion from legal labor market, 282–83; firearms, 267, 268, 273, 274, 277, 279; friendships among, 276–79; in the global narcotics industry, 272; incarceration of, 273–75; murders of, 275–76; social networks, 276–81; vulnerability of, 269–70, 275–76

Puerto Rico, vii (map); arms smuggling, 279; Colombian drugs in, 216; domestic economy, 272–73; in drug commodity chain, 31, 210, 215–16, 230n3, 262, 291; government attacks on punto leadership, 215; homicides in, 279–80; migrations to the United States, 272–73; as transshipment point, 31, 210, 230n3; United States hegemony in, 272–73

puntos: changing nature of, 217–18; community ties, 213, 216, 224; discipline within, 214, 215, 217, 220; in drug supply chain, 215–16; informal violence as means of protection, 222; instrumental violence of, 222–23; internal struggles, 214–15; job opportunities, 213–14, 216; leadership of, 214, 215, 216–17; mediation between, 213, 222; organization of, 212, 214–15, 216; state policing of, 215; territories of, 213, 216, 217; violence in, 219–20, 221; visibility of, 216; young men in, 213–14

*púsheres*, 194, 195, 196, 198–99

Putumayo, Colombia, 20, 77, 88, 290, 302, 304, 328

Quiroga, Jorge, 49

racial profiling, 96–97, 100, 263–64, 293–94, 297, 308

Raffy (bichote): challenges to leadership of, 258, 259–60, 261; charisma of, 255, 256–57; control of the block, 258, 259, 260–61; fieldworkers interactions with, 254–61; imprisonment of, 259, 267, 268; Lucas (cocaine supplier for), 261; Panama Red (bichote), 259, 260–61, 267–68; police confrontations, 255–57, 260–61; relationship with neighbors, 259, 267; researchers' relations with, 254, 259; sales point of, 258, 259, 260–61; as source of employment, 254; visibility of, 261

Ramon Antonini (residentiale), 213–14

Rastrojos, 70, 80

Ray (teacher, San Juan), 226–28

Reagan administration, 48–49, 290, 294

real estate investments, 199–200, 204, 219

reciprocity, 10–11, 43, 211, 226, 319; as boundaries of community, 51; clientelism, 56, 124, 166–68, 182–83, 185n2, 322; in cocaine supply chain networks, 78–81; coca sales, 52–53; compadrazgo (godparenthood), 52, 53, 54–55, 56, 64n6; establishing cocaine workshops, 5, 81–82; expectations of, 30; mutual obligation, 10–11, 51, 52, 53, 54–55, 56, 64n6; in paste production, 28, 51–52, 54, 63n2; sponsorship for communal events, 42–43, 56, 61, 124, 146; trust relationships, 26, 29, 78–82, 84

recuperate (use of term), 111

Redes de Maré (NGO), 244

researchers: in favela of Vigidal, 118; first encounters with, 118; first encounters with cocaine, 118; informants for, 117–18; relations with drug dealers, 22, 150–52, 213, 218, 219, 220, 259, 271; risks to, 117

*resguardos* (reservations), 100

*residenciales públicos*, 211–12, 213

residents: assimilation of homeless and addicted populations, 226; conflict among, 216; on drug dealers' influence, 223; fieldworkers' relations with, 263; involvement in drug trade, 216, 219; on occurrences of violence, 218–19, 220–22; police, tensions with, 256–58; reciprocal relationships of, 226; relations with police, 218–19, 223–25; responses to violence, 221–22, 226; silence of, 120, 152, 323; surveys of drug-related violence, 218–19

sponsorship for communal events, 42–43, 56, 61, 146

sporting events, 241, 243, 245, 247n2, 297

Steinberg, Michael, 98

Suchiate River, 143, 144f

sugar production, 5, 15, 145

symbolic violence (Bourdieu), 266

synthetic opioids, 292

Tabatinga (Brazil), 297, 304

taxi drivers, 2, 55

TC (Terceiro Comando), 123, 133, 134

TCP (Terceiro Comando Puro), 233, 243, 244

teachers, 104–5

Tecun Uman, 142

Teixeira, Alessandra, 236–37

Templarios: agricultural sector controlled by, 176–77; Apatzingán as cartel capital, 189; armed mobilization against, 183–84, 185n11, 187n34; Autodefensas de Michoacán, 30–31, 165–66, 170–71, 185n11; clientelism of, 183; collective armed uprising against, 187n34; conflict against, 170–71, 185n11; extortion system of, 175–78, 180–81, 185n11, 186n21; formation of, 170, 171, 172; influence of, 173; political influence of, 178–80; sanctions for disobedience, 182–83; social controls of, 173–74; street patrols, 174

Téofilo (indigenous legal scholar), 110

Terceiro Comando Puro (Pure Third Command; TCP). See TCP (Terceiro Comando Puro)

Thompson, E. P., 8–9, 11, 72, 99, 329, 333

Tierra Caliente region, 170, 172–73, 176, 185n11, 186n21

tiradores, 215–16

Tito (drug dealer caseworker): ambition of, 32, 255–56, 267, 268; bichote, relations with, 254, 258, 267–68; corner of, 268, 273; incarceration of, 268–70, 271; Leo (drug dealer, Tito's brother), 32, 267, 273–75, 283; as mediator, 255–56; response to police harassment, 255–56, 258

Tocache district, Peru, 303

tortilla-making business, 176, 191, 201–3

trafficking routes, 6 (map), 7

trafico de formigas (ant traffic), 127, 136n15

tramitadores (paper processors), 143, 145–47

transshipment sites, 27t; Brazil as, 122; cartelization process in, 171; cocaine storage at, 122; commodity chain, 20; criminal organizations at, 333; DTOs (drug trafficking organizations), 321; illicit capital at, 333; Michoacán, Mexico, 171; Puerto Rico as, 31, 210, 230n3; southward shift of cocaine commodity chains, 287–88, 295, 298–302, 309n2; state presence in, 23–24; transportation networks, 23–24; wealth accumulation in, 320–21. See also borders and border crossings

Trompas (Guatemalan drug dealer), 30, 139, 142, 148

Trump, Donald, 295, 308

trust relationships, 29, 71, 78–82, 84, 213

Uchoa, Marcos, 235

Uê (Ernaldo Pinto de Medeiros), 133, 299

UHV (Upper Huallaga Valley), 289, 303–4

UMOPAR (Rural Mobile Patrol Unit), 48–49, 57–58

UNGASS (2016), 288, 299, 306, 307, 308

unions: arbitration by, 43, 59–60; authority of, 43, 45–46, 56–57, 59, 61; in Bolivia, 22, 326; in Chapare, 43, 57–58, 61; coca growers' relations with, 28, 64n5; on cocaine production, 57, 64n10; control of coca sales, 64n5; land control by, 45, 59, 60; MAS (Movimiento al Socialismo), 44, 49, 57, 63n1; mediation in drug industry, 59–60; meetings of, 45, 46f, 59; political activism of, 49, 50, 61; relations with government agencies, 22, 28, 42, 46, 57–58; suppression of organized criminal activity, 60–61

United Nations: cocaine consumption in Brazil, 295–96; drug system, 288; global ban on indigenous coca leaf, 305; on the legal coca market, 64n4; Single

visitors to prisons, 157–59, 278–79

VRAEM (Apurímac, Ene and Mantaro River Valley), 1, 2, 7f, 18, 22f, 302–3

Wallerstein, Immanuel, 288

water transport of drugs, 23, 24, 55f, 80, 136n13

weapons, 267, 268, 273, 274, 277, 279–81

Weber, Max, 12, 14, 323, 327

Weingast, Barry R., 192

West Africa: drug trafficking routes in, 298

white factory. *See* cocaine production

Williams, Raymond, 99

Williams, Seth, 260

Wiwi (hustler), 257–58, 277

women: childcare, 105; as community leaders, 223–24; drug market roles of, 51, 52f, 57, 85–86, 139–40, 151–53, 158–60, 198; employment, 104–5, 149, 159; guarded by gang members, 214; housing, 204–5, 219; intimidation by gangs, 173–74; involvement in community activism, 223–24; as landowners, 51; mothers of drug dealers, 213; motorcycles, 108; on occurrences of violence, 221; on police and elected officials' complicity in drug trade, 219; as prison drug smugglers, 158, 159–60; as prison visitors, 158, 159; single-parent households, 104–5, 213; violence against, 152, 159, 204–5

young men: access to weapons, 273, 274, 276; allure of money/addiction to money, 274–75, 282; ambitions of, 32, 255–56, 258, 267, 268, 273, 282; baby boy nicknames of, 276, 279; cartel enforcers, 174; in cocaine production, 50–51; delinquency, 105, 109–10, 139; desire for mobility, 274–75; gang affiliations, 213–14; hypermasculinity, 33, 267; incarceration of, 32, 268, 273–75, 283; informal violence as means of protection, 222; as punto employees, 213; recruitment of, 30, 151, 213–14, 218; self-respect, 326, 327; vigilantism, 222; violence, 234, 264

young people: alienation of, 221–22; ambitions of, 32, 256, 258, 268, 282; community support for, 144, 223–24; on consumer culture, 29, 94, 109–10; desire for upward mobility, 2, 33, 218, 282; on drug use, 1, 105, 224, 264, 266, 291; gang membership in prison, 214; on illicit crops, 104–5; impact of drug production on community, 104; leadership of, 94, 95, 110; motorcycle ownership, 29, 108–9; police violence toward, 257–58; recruitment of, 213–14, 218, 224; as risk-takers, 1, 2, 218–19; spaces for, 224; unemployment, 2, 264; US crack consumption statistics on, 292; young women in drug culture, 257–58

Zapatista uprising, 320

Zellers-León, Autumn, vii (map), 29, 319, 320, 325, 326

zero-tolerance policies, 215

Zetas (paramilitary cartel), 141, 165, 170

Zone 3 (Guatemala City), 148–49, 148–51, 149f

Zone 6 (Guatemala City), 139